The Kennedy World in Medallic Art

John F. Kennedy and His Family
in Medals, Coins, Tokens, and Other Collectibles

William R. Rice

Whitman Publishing, LLC
PUBLISHING SINCE 1934
Whitman.com

The Kennedy World in Medallic Art
John F. Kennedy and His Family in Medals, Coins, Tokens, and Other Collectibles

ISBN: 0794842364
Printed in the United States of America
© 2014 Whitman Publishing, LLC

Correspondence regarding this book may be mailed to Whitman Publishing, Attn: Coins and Collectors, 3101 Clairmont Road, Suite G, Atlanta, GA 30329; or emailed to info@Whitman.com (subject line: Kennedy World).

Disclaimer: No warranty or representation of any kind is made concerning the accuracy or completeness of the information presented, its use in purchases or sales, or any other use. Much information in this book has never been published in a single volume before, and in the future corrections, amplifications, and additions may be made.

If you enjoy *The Kennedy World in Medallic Art*, you will also enjoy *America's Money, America's Story* (Doty), *History of the United States Mint and Its Coinage* (Lange), *Numismatic Art in America* (Vermeule), *100 Greatest American Medals and Tokens* (Bowers and Sundman), *Pictures From a Distant Country: Seeing America Through Old Paper Money* (Doty), *Abraham Lincoln: The Image of His Greatness* (Reed), *Milestone Coins: A Pageant of the World's Most Significant and Popular Money* (Bressett), and other books by Whitman Publishing. Whitman is a leading publisher in the antiques and collectibles and American history fields. For a catalog of related books, hobby supplies, and storage and display products, please visit Whitman Publishing online at www.Whitman.com.

Content

Foreword

Gerald J. Steinberg

On November 22, 1963, the world's population of Americans abruptly reached a standstill at 1:07 p.m. Dallas time.

For a period of three days, our personal lives simply ceased to exist. Children and adults spent their waking hours glued to their television sets, watching over and over the assassination photos of our beloved president, the wanton slaying of the suspected killer, and the funeral cortege and procession.

If 250 million Americans suffered such a severe and devastating shock, it was only appropriate that the nations of the world suffered from the same type of disbelief. They, in turn, produced the greatest output of memorials ever seen before or since.

Schools, libraries, stadiums, parks, museums, coins, medallions, busts, porcelain ware, literature—and the list goes on and on—named in honor of John Fitzgerald Kennedy.

One phase of this memorial outpouring that has been somewhat unique and quite extensive is the medallic art portraying many facets of his short—but fascinating—term of office and lifetime of experiences. In the mid-1960s, two books dealing strictly with this subject were rushed into publication without a thorough compilation of the myriad number of numismatic, exonumatic, and metallic items on the market.

This 21st-century publication approaches the approximately complete and historically accurate field. William Rice has spent many years immersed in accumulating even the slightest details regarding each and every item portrayed in this remarkable publication. Our historians will remain deeply indebted to Rice for his gigantic addition to the field of John F. Kennedy medallic art and related historical memorabilia.

Gerald J. Steinberg
Boynton Beach, Florida

A successful dentist for many years, Dr. Gerald Steinberg has exhibited his extensive collection of Kennedy stamps at major philatelic shows around the United States. His collection of Kennedy material now encompasses over half a million various items. In the early-1970s, Dr. Steinberg attempted to open a Kennedy Museum in Washington, D.C., but found the business could not sustain itself, and the project was unfortunately abandoned. Today, Dr. Steinberg spends his retirement teaching elementary school students geography lessons using postage stamps; he also visits VA hospitals, helping to rehabilitate wounded soldiers by providing stamps for projects to exercise their hands so that they might return to a healthy life.

Preface

If each of us takes a moment to shut out the noise of our daily lives and, in that cherished quiet time, reflect on another human being that has changed our life in some manner—be it financial, educational, or spiritual—we may then realize that that person has become part of our own being. Such was my motivation to write this book.

It was the era of letter writing when I began researching Kennedy medallic art. If you wanted to obtain information or acquire a medal from some distant country, it took a week or two for the mail to get overseas and two or three weeks for a return answer with a price; then, a week or two for funds to be received and another three weeks to receive the medal. The "old timers" will agree that building a collection and keeping up with medal releases back in those days was real work. Most medals obtained from outside the United States took up to two months to obtain. Any records of cherished additions to your collection were written with a ballpoint pen or typed on a Royal manual typewriter—which you could count on to never go off line.

There were also obstacles within the United States in the days prior to the computer age. If a new medal was cast by an artist in Connecticut, it may be months or perhaps more than a year before it was public knowledge. Collectors eagerly awaited the next issues of *Antique Trader*, *Coin World*, and *Numismatic News*, not realizing at the time that information was already two to three weeks old—if not older.

Looking back to that time, all that effort does not seem possible in today's age of instant gratification, communication, and electronic payments.

In June 1963, I had been invited to join the crowd that would welcome President Kennedy to the Naval Ordinance Test Station at China Lake, California. At the time, my father was the chief master-at-arms, but I was sadly unable to attend because of Air Force duties in northern California. Since I missed the event, the man I most respected in the world—my father—gave me a bronze medal bearing President Kennedy's image and commemorating his visit. The moment that the medal was placed in my hand, the die had been cast for the long road ahead. Three years later, when I first saw a copy of Ed Rochette's book, *The Medallic Portraits of John F. Kennedy*—which cataloged many of the items I had been collecting—I remember thinking that it was a validation, that collecting Kennedy medallic art was a worthy hobby, revealing a wealth of world history and knowledge.

My belief in its educational and cultural value was rewarded when my public display at the 1968 California Exposition in Sacramento, "The Many Faces of John F. Kennedy in Medallic Art," was enthusiastically received by thousands of attendees and won several exposition honors. I stood there, watching parents bend down and try to explain to their children the ideals and respect that President Kennedy brought to America. I could see that many people were relieved to talk about how they felt, and, in a strange way, I thought that the display must be therapeutic for some of the attendees. I was moved by the facial expressions and quiet visitors passing the display, as if they were taken back five years to a day of great loss and pain but were pleased that someone was publicly honoring the memory of John F. Kennedy. Adding to the emotional impact of this showing was the death of the president's brother Robert F. Kennedy just three months earlier in Los Angeles.

Many of the thoughts and illustrations for this book were first put down on paper by me more than 45 years ago. In August 2010, I had a meeting in Boston with Whitman Publishing, where the original manuscript for the book you are now reading was first viewed. Since that time, many necessary and positive changes have occurred thanks to those at Whitman who have worked tirelessly to make this book a success.

This volume will encompass most previously-known medallic art items cataloged by Rochette and Aubrey Mayhew. The new, unrecorded material covers a time span of 48 years—from 1966 to the present—as well as items unknown during that earlier period.

I must admit that there are many omissions. This volume is not complete and could not possibly be, as new items are both discovered and created to honor the many accomplishments of President Kennedy and his years of public service. As I myself have done in the past, I would ask that collectors in the future correct, add to, and expand upon the information contained in this volume. This way, the hobby and its history stay alive and accurate.

The John F. Kennedy Presidential Library and Museum in Boston continues daily to catalog and preserve thousands of items and documents so that the public may take advantage of the educational and research opportunities contained therein. I would urge anyone who has not visited the Kennedy Library to spend a morning or afternoon in a place that represents a time of greatness in America.

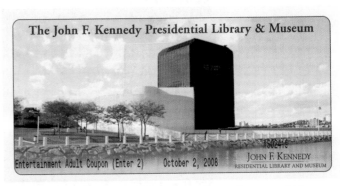

Ticket to the John F. Kennedy Presidential Library and Museum.

I ask the reader of this volume to look into the photographs and see within them the spirit of that time—Kennedy's time. Just as we save a piece of jewelry or a letter from a loved one, so must I write this book, not only for myself and others who remember the men from Boston, but for the future young souls who might hear their call from the past. It was, and will always be, a time when we as Americans and citizens of the world each felt that we all had worth, substance, and mattered to our fellow man. Remembering and holding on to what was good is the glue that binds us all together. I have found when holding a Kennedy medal in my hand that it opens a door to the past history of society—a past of which I am an active part. An attempt at understanding the past gives us all the opportunity to hope for a more peaceful future.

Please take a moment of reflection for this family who carried the light ahead of us so we would not walk our path forward in the dark.

Give their memory a salute, for we shall never see their like again.

Credits and Acknowledgments

Forgive my grief for one removed,
Thy creature, whom I found so fair.
I trust he lives in thee, and there
I find him worthier to be loved.

—Alfred, Lord Tennyson

This book is dedicated to Penn Jones
Jr., American hero, patriot, and friend.

A Tribute to the Pioneers

Edward C. Rochette.

It is true that past history should be the building blocks of the future, and in that context I would like to pay tribute and say thank you to the following pioneers in the field of Kennedy medallic art. These authors and researchers provided the way for me and many others to appreciate the love and respect paid to the memory of President Kennedy through the worldwide craftsmanship of Kennedy medallic art. It is for this reason that I so titled this book.

First, my deep gratitude and admiration for Edward Rochette, author of *The Medallic Portraits of John F. Kennedy* in 1966, the first book on Kennedy medallic art. Without the contribution and help of Ed and his lovely wife, Maryanne, this volume would not have been possible.

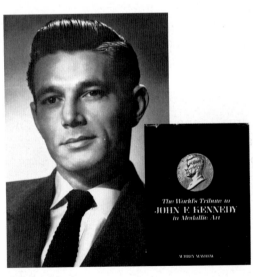

Aubrey Mayhew.

Warm thanks and remembrance to Dr. Gerald Steinberg and his gracious wife, Phyllis. Dr. Steinberg's knowledge as a collector and researcher and his contribution to the field of JFK memorabilia has been of the highest caliber. I deeply appreciate his contribution to this book.

In 1966, Aubrey Mayhew generated great interest worldwide with his publication *The World's Tribute to John F. Kennedy in Medallic Art*. Aubrey assisted me with several hours of research and contributed knowledge of Kennedy medals. Now, even though he is no longer with us, I thank him for his efforts and time.

Joseph A. Garduno.

I would like to give a special thanks to Joseph A. Garduno, who created a museum for President Kennedy in Glendora, California, back in 1966. His book, *Museum for a President,* caught my attention back then and, although the museum was only active for 10 years, our correspondence during that time was very enjoyable.

Five years after the passing of President Kennedy, Alex J. Goldman published a 144-page work on memorials created around the world in honor of the 35th president—from Australia to Austria, from the top of Mount Kennedy in Canada to Brazil in South America. Alex's book, *John Fitzgerald Kennedy: The World Remembers,* has an abundance of photos of monuments and buildings renamed after the fallen president. Additionally, there is a small section illustrating a few international postage stamps and medals.

Dan Brody.

I cannot leave this page without giving mention and a heartfelt thank you to Dan Brody of Long Beach, California. Back in the 1970s, Dan rented a small building in downtown Long Beach and welcomed school classes and the general public to view his large Kennedy memorabilia collection. His collection consisted of extensive medallic art and Kennedy historical items. He invited me and my family to visit his museum, and we spent two delightful days viewing the collection and learning about his efforts to preserve John F. Kennedy's memory.

Knowing that time is not a person's best friend and that the passage of these men and women is just on the horizon—as is my own—I am honored to be able to thank these pioneers of this exciting, educational, and rewarding endeavor and say, yes, my friends, the torch is still burning brightly, and "the dream shall live on."

Harvey Goldberg

Harvey Goldberg.

I am honored to acknowledge a friend and associate, Harvey Goldberg, who resides with his wife Joyce in Clark, New Jersey.

Many years ago, a mutual friend of ours by the name of Bonnie Gardner, founder and president of the Torchbearers Club in Lakewood, California, had invited me to attend the Southern California Democratic Convention in Los Angeles. I was asked to speak to the club on the subject of John F. Kennedy's memory and the possibility of a Kennedy library and political education center in the Sierras above Sacramento. At that time I was not aware that Bonnie Gardner and Harvey, who lived on opposite sides of the United States, knew each other and were closely involved in collecting memorabilia of the Kennedy legacy.

More than 35 years after that event, Harvey and I became acquainted quite by accident and, since that time, have become very good friends. He has my deepest appreciation for his counsel and help in making this book a reality.

Harvey began collecting Kennedy campaign memorabilia back in 1964, when he had the privilege of attending the Democratic National Convention in Atlantic City, New Jersey. He was present when Robert Kennedy spoke to the delegates and received a 22-minute standing ovation from the convention floor, a truly historic moment in political-convention history. Shortly after, he joined the American Political Items Collectors and later helped build a special-interest chapter of the group: KPIC—the Kennedy Political Items Collectors—of which he is now the director.

Several times a year, Harvey publishes a multi-page color photo newsletter, *Hyannisporter*, for Kennedy political-item collectors. Harvey has published eight different catalogs of memorabilia related to John, Robert, and Edward Kennedy, most recently a full-color trilogy completed in 2011. These three books document more than 6,000 campaign-related items. Harvey's personal collection consists mainly of campaign items, ribbons, badges, and posters. He believes that the detailed stories and history behind the items are what is really important. "When I add an item to my collection, I seek out the Who, What, Where, and Why, and in taking that approach, I realize great satisfaction and the true joy of collecting."

Harvey is a retired educator, having taught senior high-school industrial arts for more than 35 years in northern New Jersey. Working from home, he continues to write articles and edit material for a number of hobby-related publications and newsletters.

 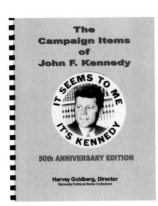 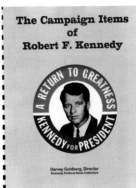 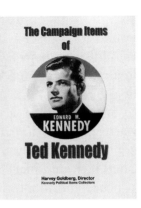

Contributors

Thank you to the following for contributing their time and memories to this loving endeavor:

Alfred Trafford
Boston Historical Society
Bruce Jacobs
Claire Garrard
Claire M. Burke
David Lewis
Dick Johnson
Don Hymer
Emily Watlington
Frances E. Smith
George Huber
Hai Yan
Heather L. Jones
Iris Burns
Jacob Lederman
Jean Small
Jean Tatge
Jeff Morin
Jeff Shevlin
Jim Wagner
Joel Benjamin
Joe Levine
Joel Reznick
John Allen
John F. Kennedy Museum
John F. Kennedy Presidential
Library and Museum
John Hutt
Joseph J. Hovish
Kathryn Dodge
Kenneth Bressett

Ken Potter
Leon D. Humiston
Lester Stark
Linda Eade
Marilyn V. Rice
Maryrose Grossman
Matthew Burns
Mike Dunham
Mike Spinnler
National Rifle Association
New York City Municipal Art Society
Patricia M. Rice
Paul Firth
Pedro Villarrubia
Randy Thern
Ray Herz
Richard Goodman
Richard Hartzog
Robert Booth
Sheree Firth
Stacey Chandler
Stephen Plotkin
Steve Allen
Steve Medley
Vicki Hymer
Victor Melendy
Vincent Zike
Wayne Lensing
William A. Smith
Yosemite National Park Library

Introduction

Collecting memories of the past is a worldwide human pursuit. A hug and a last photo taken at the airfield as a husband and father boards the aircraft bound for a place with an unpronounceable name. A lock of hair saved from a child's first haircut. A medal for a sacrifice given at the Battle of the Bulge, in a rice paddy on a freezing morning in Korea, in the red clay of Khe Sanh, or a heroic action in the desert heat of the Middle East. A family cross, a rosary, perhaps a scarf given in a last fleeting moment to keep a loved one warm on their journey. These precious items link and bind us to the time gone by so quickly from our lives. They are stored away in some little cherished box, or a place as private as the human heart, where a loved one can be at peace and touch those who are missed.

Medals are tangible items that can represent many facets of the human experience. They can honor an individual's accomplishments, show sacrifice for duty to God and country, or provide recognition of work performed in service to those who need a helping hand. They can show great artistic accomplishments in the fields of education and entertainment, and—in the case of this volume—they can honor and remember a leader of the free world who was taken long before his time and before his work here on Earth was finished.

America and its 35th president grew up together in the early sixties—and what a time we had. Those of us who lived and worked through those 1,000 days will never forget how excited and puzzled the unknown made us as the countdown for Alan Shepard and *Freedom* 7 began and we took the first step toward U.S. space exploration. Nor will we forget the press conferences we looked forward to, because everyone from coast to coast wanted to hear what President Kennedy had to say and the way he would say it. He would laugh and the country would laugh with him. He was making friends and improving relations with the nations of the world that loved freedom and making those that didn't listen to a free people and a democracy on the move. He frightened some who feared his power, but even with this knowledge, and at overwhelming risk to himself, he stood up before us all with the greatest of courage. Together, we moved ahead as a truly United States of America.

President Kennedy was not without faults, but he was a man who would never compound one mistake with another. He would learn from first-year administration errors. He was determined to have meaningful legislation clear Congress so that all Americans could live more productive and rewarding lives, both for this generation and for generations yet unborn.

Although the last 18 years of his life were spent in great physical pain from ailments little discussed during his lifetime, he was able to inspire courage and bring hope to those who listened to his message. He possessed that rare ability to transcend himself and envision a world that, even now, most people cannot comprehend. Throughout his public service, John F. Kennedy always respected the citizens of the Republic, and it was this openness and honesty, along with sound programs, that won him the trust and respect of the American people.

Abraham Lincoln once said, "If you would win a man to your cause, first convince him that you are his true friend." I strongly feel John F. Kennedy must have been a student of many of Lincoln's thoughts and ideas, for this awareness and understanding was a dominant part of his personal and public life. Like Lincoln before him, John F. Kennedy believed in the U.S. Constitution and all the wisdom contained therein.

Sometime after the darkest week in American history, the world dried its eyes and went back to work, even though a part of our spirit was missing from our personal and collective lives. For those of us who witnessed that day when the earth but for a short time stopped, the question that will never leave our minds is what would have been the future of America had President Kennedy been allowed to stay with us for a while longer?

Monuments sprang into existence around the world: from a ferry in New York to a forest in Israel; a plaza in Ireland to a Red Cross government center in Hong Kong; a youth center and garden in Copenhagen to a mountain in Alaska; an airport in the United States, a main artery in Paris, and a large memorial in Berlin. Avenues, freeways, turnpikes, streets, and roads that traverse the world to new and exciting places carry his name.

After a time of great loss and mourning, John's brother Robert was to pick up the torch and carry on the tradition so profoundly marked out by his brothers before him. As time passed, Robert was to march to his own drumbeat. Disturbed greatly by the current direction of the country and leadership, he was to set a new course to sail. Bobby was like a tree that loved the wind, bending and changing direction when reason and logic deemed it to be the right thing to do—not for himself, but rather for the America he loved. He never lost sight of his roots and the lessons learned through the many challenges he overcame throughout his life. (I had the privilege of greeting him and shaking his hand when he arrived at the Stockton, California, airfield just days prior to his passing. I remember thinking at the time how much energy, effort, and courage it took on his part to "fight the good fight" when, instead, he could have been enjoying himself at home or on vacation somewhere.) Just as Robert F. Kennedy was in the process of winning the prize he so desired, recharting the course of America, in an instant he, too, was gone.

Tragedy has created many times for reflection in the Kennedy family, but it has never stopped their dedication to the ideals and goals of the American Dream and their belief that politics can be, in Robert's words, "an honorable profession" if men of honor and courage will make it so. Edward M. Kennedy devoted his life to the U.S. Senate and will be remembered and respected as the "Lion of the Senate" from this time forward. Edward's accomplishments have enriched and will continue to enrich the lives of citizens for many years to come. He will be remembered as one of the truly great statesmen of American government and history.

With varied occupations, younger members of the Kennedy family have picked up the torch and are keeping the spirit alive, thus honoring those who served years before their birth. The appointment of President Kennedy's daughter, Caroline, as U.S. ambassador to Japan has been welcomed in diplomatic circles around the world.

President Kennedy himself was a collector and his personal collection of scrimshaw tells us of his interest in history's valor and tragedy. He took genuine pleasure in presenting medals and recognition to those individuals who had made a contribution toward the betterment of mankind. One of his first acts as president was to reinstate the rank and earned medals of Republican ex-president General Dwight D. Eisenhower. His last official act before going to Dallas, Texas, was to sign a bill authorizing a medal to be struck for the Garment Workers' Union.

America and the world laughed with them and we cried for them. Now history has moved on, our vision is slightly blurred, and our memory has faded. However, the many items and photos within this book are reminders of a time in the history of America when its people were young and we were able, if but for a short time, to see the vision of America our forefathers dreamed of, to believe it was within reach and that our own efforts would make it so.

How To Use This Book

John F. Kennedy Medallic Art and Related Historical Items Catalog Numbering System

Years ago, when *The Medallic Portraits of John F. Kennedy* was first formulated by Ed Rochette, the question arose concerning a catalog numbering system that could be easy for collectors to use and would stand the test of time. Rochette investigated this issue, giving it a great deal of thought, so that the final result would be a workable, clear, and concise Kennedy-item catalog system.

In Rochette's original volume, the total items cataloged were approximately 558. With 173 original designs available, Rochette's work included many varieties of these designs in various metals. This volume you now hold in your hands contains more than 1,500 variations of countless originals from all over the world, with a catalog describing an additional 1,200 items.

I have found the Rochette system to be superior to all other catalog systems, including those of the Franklin Mint and Aubrey Mayhew, and many others produced over the years.

With his permission, I have expanded the Rochette system to include my own additions of new categories and spin-off varieties to this time-proven Kennedy medallic-art catalog system. The Kennedy challenge coin (KCC) listing is one example of those additions.

The benefits of this flexible system will be appreciated for years to come. Items that have no known issue date are designated K-63A, which explains why that grouping is so numerous. As an item issue date is found through future research, it can be removed from the K-63A category and put into the year category in which it belongs. I encourage collectors to conduct research in this endeavor and provide corrections when discovered and documented.

There are countless examples of Kennedy medallic art and this volume does not contain every item ever produced in this category. However, appendix A contains a more thorough catalog of Kennedy items with additional descriptions of each item.

The following is an explanation of the Rochette-Rice Kennedy Catalog System:

K-60-1: K = Kennedy; 60 = year issued; 1 = first item cataloged

K-63-9: K = Kennedy; 63 = year issued, item issued prior to assassination; 9 = ninth item cataloged

K-63A-1: K = Kennedy; 63A = year issued, item issued after assassination and when item issue date is unknown; 1 = first item cataloged

RK-1-2003: RK = Robert Kennedy; 1 = first item cataloged; 2003 = year issued (if known)

KCC-1: KCC = Kennedy challenge coin; 1 = first challenge coin cataloged

CCC-4: CCC = commemorative coin cover; 4 = fourth commemorative coin cover cataloged

Kennedy Family History

For I can assure you that we love our country; not for what
it was, though it has always been great; not for what it is,
though of this we are deeply proud; but for what it someday
can, and, through the efforts of us all, someday will be.

—*John F. Kennedy, February 13, 1961*

The Kennedy Family

John F. Kennedy with his father and maternal grandfather, John F. Fitzgerald, in 1946.

The Fitzgeralds

John Frances Fitzgerald

John Frances "Honey Fitz" Fitzgerald, the maternal grandfather of John F. Kennedy, was the son of Irish immigrants. He was elected to Boston's Common Council in 1891 at the age of 28, and became a member of the Massachusetts State Senate only one year later. After serving in the U.S. House of Representatives from 1895 to 1901, Fitzgerald was elected mayor of Boston. He served two non-con-secutive terms in this role, from 1906 to 1908 and from 1910 to 1914. Politics was his calling and Honey Fitz had the gift of the gab. He was a showman and he was well liked by his constituents.

Following a new trend to have "Old Home Week," a time when inhabitants of a city, past and present, come together in celebration, Fitzgerald, in his role as mayor of Boston, decided to promote a "Welcome Back to Boston" Old Home Week from July 28 to August 3, 1907. With the slogan "A bigger, better, busier Boston," Fitzgerald convinced both the Massachusetts legislature and multiple businesses to invest millions of dollars for improvements to the city—an investment which paid off when new port traffic arrived from Europe. Tokens were struck for this event and today they are extremely rare.

In 1946, Honey Fitz helped his grandson John plan his congressional campaign strategy. After Kennedy's victory, his grandfather predicted that "Jack" would one day occupy the White House as the president of the United States. Although he passed away in 1950, 11 years before this would become a reality, President Kennedy renamed the presidential yacht the *Honey Fitz* in honor of his grandfather.

Rose Fitzgerald Kennedy, circa 1939.

K-00-1: The reverse shows Faneuil Hall in Boston.

Hon. John F. Fitzgerald, Mayor of Boston.

Postcard depicting John F. Fitzgerald.

phine Fitzgerald and the mother of John F. Kennedy.

In September 1908, Rose and her younger sister Agnes entered a convent boarding school called Blumenthal, close to the German border in Holland, which they would attend for one year. In a letter Rose wrote to her mother the following month, she explained that she was working toward becoming a Child of Mary, the highest honor a child of the Sacred Heart can receive. Eight months later, in April 1909, a letter arrived in Boston from 18-year-old Rose saying, "I received my medal for the Child of Mary today and as I told you before, this is the highest honor and blessing a Sacred Heart girl can get and one which we all strive for."

Rose was first introduced to politics as a child due to her father's involvement in local government, and she rubbed elbows with many famous political figures, including President William McKinley. As the mother of politicians, Rose hosted many "Kennedy teas" that were sponsored by the Democratic Party. During John F. Kennedy's presidential campaign, Rose worked tirelessly, attending meetings and speaking with voters about her son and his policies.

Rose Fitzgerald Kennedy

Born on July 22, 1890, Rose Elizabeth Fitzgerald was the eldest child of John F. and Mary Jose-

K-00-2: Child of Mary medal. The inscription on the obverse reads SHOW THYSELF TO BE A MOTHER in Latin.

K-72-14

K-2009-14A

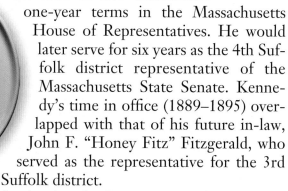

K-00-5

his mother and sisters. He later launched his career with the purchase of three saloons and entered into the whiskey-importing business.

In 1884, Kennedy began the first of five consecutive one-year terms in the Massachusetts House of Representatives. He would later serve for six years as the 4th Suffolk district representative of the Massachusetts State Senate. Kennedy's time in office (1889–1895) overlapped with that of his future in-law, John F. "Honey Fitz" Fitzgerald, who served as the representative for the 3rd Suffolk district.

After leaving the Senate, Kennedy continued his political career in a variety of offices, including as elections commissioner and as fire commissioner. He would later serve as an inspiration to his politically inclined grandsons, John, Robert, and Edward Kennedy.

Joseph Patrick Kennedy

Joseph Patrick Kennedy, father of John F. Kennedy, grew up in Boston. He received a B.A. from Harvard University in 1912 and, shortly thereafter, began his career in finance as the assistant state-bank examiner for Massachusetts.

The Fitzgerald and Kennedy families would often summer together at Old Orchard Beach in Maine. It was here that Joseph Kennedy and Rose Fitzgerald first met in their youth. After Kennedy's graduation from college, their courtship became serious. They were married on October 7, 1914. The newlyweds traveled from Boston for a two-week honeymoon at the Greenbrier Resort located in White Sulphur Springs, West Virginia.

A strong woman and a dedicated philanthropist, Rose Fitzgerald Kennedy passed away at the age of 104 in 1995.

The Kennedys

Patrick Joseph Kennedy

Known as P.J., Patrick Joseph Kennedy was born in 1858 to Irish Catholic immigrants. Losing his father at an early age, Kennedy left school at 14 to work on the Boston docks in order to support

Family resemblance: John F. Kennedy (left) and his father, Joseph (right).

In the early 1930s, Kennedy entered into politics by investing his then-considerable wealth and influence into Franklin Delano Roosevelt's first and second presidential campaigns. He was appointed chair of the Securities and Exchange Commission, then chair of the U.S. Maritime Commission; later, in 1937, Roosevelt named him the U.S. ambassador to Great Britain.

After leaving politics, Kennedy convinced his son John to run for office in 1946.

K-71-39

K-00-3: This brass key tag, naming the resort where the Kennedys honeymooned, is very rare.

K-2009-14

2

JFK's Early Life

John F. Kennedy with his dog at Hyannisport, Massachusetts, in 1925.

Childhood

John Fitzgerald Kennedy was born in Brookline, Massachusetts, on May 29, 1917. Named after his maternal grandfather, John "Honey Fitz" Fitzgerald, Kennedy lived with his family in Brookline for ten years until moving to New York in 1927.

Although he was often ill, Kennedy was an active child, and competition was enthusiastically encouraged by his parents. He enjoyed sailing, swimming, and football, a sport he played at school throughout his youth. While Kennedy was thought by his peers and teachers to be a keen and intelligent child, he was not always a motivated student, excelling only in his favorite subjects, history and English. He was very involved in extracurricular activities, including a stint as the business manager of the school yearbook during his time at the Choate School in Connecticut.

Kennedy had a financially privileged childhood. The family spent summers at their home in Hyannisport, Massachusetts, and often

K-00-4: On May 29, 1918, John Fitzgerald Kennedy's first birthday party was held. *The Encyclopedia of Silver Marks, Hallmarks and Makers' Marks* illustrates that the Q7 mark officially dates this medal 1918, one year after the birth of the 35th president. It is unknown who had this medal made for this special occasion, but my research shows that it was designed by Swedish silversmith C. G. Hallberg, an outstanding artist who produced special orders for Tiffany's of New York.

It is my belief that this medal was commissioned by Joseph P. Kennedy Sr. from Tiffany's, where he was a banker at the time.

For the Collector and Historian

Memorabilia relating to John F. Kennedy's early life is seen in the marketplace from time to time. In the February 2013 auction of the estate of David Powers, lot 4 included five small "snapshots of JFK as a teenager with family and friends while fishing and on horseback," plus an 8-by-10–inch photographic reprint of the Kennedys "lounging on the porch." These six photographs sold for $450.

spent the holiday season at a second vacation home in Palm Beach, Florida. However, Kennedy's father, Joseph—a fiercely proud and independent businessman—instilled within his children this same independence and drive to be successful in their own right.

K-00-6: 1931 Swim Club medal awarded to John F. Kennedy.

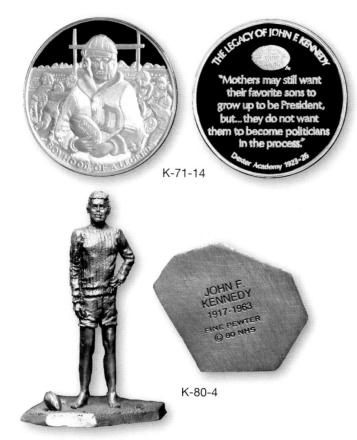

K-71-14

K-80-4

The First Boy Scout to Become the President of the United States of America

Front cover of *John F. Kennedy: The New Frontiersman* by Charles P. Graves.

Lord Baden-Powell started the Scouting idea in England in 1907. The Boy Scouts of America came into being on February 8, 1910, when William D. Boyce, an American publisher, and Daniel Carter Beard, an illustrator and author, brought the program to the United States. Reverend Otis Tiffany Barnes, pastor of the Reformed Church of Bronxville, New York, launched Bronxville Troop One on June 30, 1916. Meetings were held in a barn adjacent to the Reformed church. The barn was rebuilt into a cabin in 1919. By then, Troop One had grown to more than 75 boys, and the decision was made to split the original Troop One and form a second troop—Troop Two.

In 1929, a skinny 12-year-old boy named John Kennedy joined Raven Patrol in Troop Two. He worked hard every day of his Scouting years (1929–1931). He started out as a Tenderfoot, graduated to Second Class, advanced to First Class—earning his merit badges along the way—and finished his Scouting years with the rank of Star Scout. Little else is known about the president's Scouting years in Bronxville as records were destroyed by fire, floods, and time. However, he remained active in Scouting for most of his adult life. Kennedy was district vice chairman of the Boston Council from 1946 to 1955, an executive board member for four years, vice president for one year, a National Council representative for two years, and national honorary president in 1961.

Kennedy was elected to the presidency of the United States the same year that the Boy Scouts of America celebrated their 50th anniversary. As a leader of the Scouts' Minuteman Council, he said, "For more than 50 years, Scouting has played an important part in the lives of the Boy Scouts of this nation. It has helped to mold character, to

Given to President Kennedy by the Boy Scouts of America. The trophy reads 1962 #1 VIP.

form friendships, to provide a worthwhile outlet for the natural energies of growing boys, and to train these boys to become good citizens of the future. In a very real sense, the principles learned and practiced as Boy Scouts add to the strength of America and her ideals."

It should be noted that in 1929, Troop One was to board a ship and attend a jamboree in Birkenhead, England. As the steamship *Samaria* was preparing to leave the pier in New York, some 70 youth and leaders of the Communist Young Pioneers marched on the pier with banners reading "DOWN WITH BOY SCOUTS—UP WITH YOUNG PIONEERS." A brawl broke out, sending the Scouts on to England; the Communists were arrested. If young John F. Kennedy was not in the American send-off crowd, he was certainly made aware of what had happened

The flag of Troop Two.

when the news was received back at the cabin meeting of Troop Two in Bronxville. We can probably assume that this was the first encounter that Kennedy had with Communist ideology.

K-60-28

K-63A-325

University Life

In 1936, John F. Kennedy began his collegiate career at Harvard where his older brother, Joe, was already in attendance. While not as ambitious as Joe—who had told his family as a child that he would be the first Catholic president of the United States—Kennedy was actively engaged in sports and academic groups while at Harvard.

When his father was appointed ambassador to Great Britain in 1937, Kennedy's interest in politics and world affairs increased. Two years later, he toured Europe in preparation for his senior thesis. He returned to London not long before the outbreak of World War II.

Back at Harvard and motivated by the outbreak of war, Kennedy's senior thesis addressed Germany's recent accumulation of power and Great Britain's failure to prevent World War II. It was published in 1940 under the title *Why England Slept*, and was the first of two books written by Kennedy during his lifetime. He graduated from Harvard with a degree in international affairs that same year.

K-71-31

3

Military Service

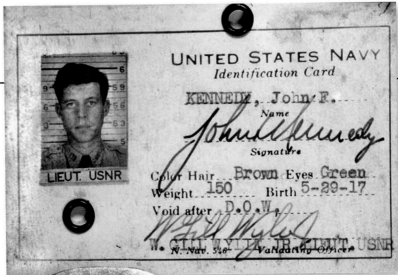

Lieutenant Kennedy's
Navy ID and dogtag.

Patrol Torpedo Boats and John F. Kennedy

After joining the U.S. Navy in September, 1941, Lieutenant John F. Kennedy's first command was motor torpedo boat *PT-101*, whose command he assumed in December 1942. This assignment was at Melville, Rhode Island, and lasted until February 23, 1943.

In his biography of Kennedy's brother Robert, Evan Thomas writes that at this time (February 1943), John F. Kennedy sent his mother, Rose, a gift of a silver PT-boat tie clip and asked her to turn it into a pin for herself.

Sixty days later, Kennedy arrived on Rendova Island, part of the Solomon Island chain, and took command of *PT-109*, then attached to Squadron Two. (It is interesting to note that when young JFK joined the Boy Scouts of America back in 1929, he was assigned to Troop Two.) While on patrol in the dark early morning of August 2, 1943, *PT-109* was rammed and cut in half by the Japanese destroyer *Amagiri*. Kennedy made multiple trips through shark-infested waters to assist the wounded men under his command.

Kennedy on *PT-109* in 1943.

Returning to the United States due to illness, he later spent a short time as an instructor at a PT-boat training program in Miami, Florida.

Memories of brotherhood and courage must have filled his mind and heart on January 20, 1961, as, from the presidential reviewing stand, he watched a full-scale replica of *PT-109* with old shipmates aboard moving slowly along the inaugural parade route for the 35th president of the United States, John Fitzgerald Kennedy.

Kennedy and the crew of *PT-109* in 1943.

Military veterans boarding a replica float of *PT-109* to participate in the inauguration parade on January 20, 1961.

Kennedy and his surviving crew members were rescued after island scouts Biuku Gasa and Eroni Kumana discovered them. Kennedy asked the two to deliver a note to the nearest coast watcher but Gasa refused, fearing the Japanese who might search them. Instead, he suggested that Kennedy scratch a message on a green coconut as it would go unnoticed. Five nights later, on August 7, the remaining crew was picked up by *PT-157*.

For his courageous acts during this ordeal, Lt. Kennedy was awarded the Navy and Marine Corps Medal and the Purple Heart. After spending 24 days under medical care, he was reassigned to command *PT-59*, where he remained from September 1, 1943, through November 18, 1943.

Additional military medals awarded to Kennedy were the American Defense Service Medal, the American Campaign Medal, the Asiatic-Pacific Campaign Medal (with three stars), the World War II Victory Medal, and the Navy Good Conduct Medal.

Pers-E24-EPC:mew
19 June 1961

LIEUTENANT JOHN FITZGERALD KENNEDY, U. S. NAVAL RESERVE, RETIRED, 116071/1109
TRANSCRIPT OF NAVAL SERVICE

29 May 1917	Born in Brookline, Massachusetts
8 Oct 1941	Ensign, U. S. Naval Reserve
1 Oct 1942	Lieutenant (junior grade) for temporary service
1 Oct 1943	Lieutenant for temporary service
1 Mar 1945	Placed on Retired List of the U. S. Naval Reserve in the rank of Lieutenant

SHIPS AND STATIONS	FROM	TO
Office of the Chief of Naval Operations, Navy Department, Washington, D. C.	Oct 41	Jan 42
Commandant, Sixth Naval District	Jan 42	Jul 42
U. S. Naval Reserve Midshipmen's School Northwestern University, Chicago, Illinois	Jul 42	Sep 42
Motor Torpedo Boat Squadrons Training Center, Newport, Rhode Island	Sep 42	Dec 42
Motor Torpedo Boat Squadron FOUR	Dec 42	Feb 43
Ass't Supervisor of Shipbuilding, Jacksonville, Florida (CFO Motor Torpedo Boat Squadron FOURTEEN)	Feb 43	Feb 43
Motor Torpedo Boat Squadron TWO	Feb 43	Dec 43
Motor Torpedo Boat Squadrons Training Center, Newport, Rhode Island	Dec 43	Mar 44
Subchaser Training Center, Miami, Florida	Mar 44	May 44
U. S. Naval Hospital, Chelsea, Massachusetts	May 44	Mar 45

MEDALS AND AWARDS

Navy and Marine Corps Medal
American Defense Service Medal
American Campaign Medal
Asiatic-Pacific Campaign Medal
World War II Victory Medal

A document saved by Evelyn Lincoln, President Kennedy's personal secretary. It lists the particulars of Kennedy's military service and the medals for which he was eligible.

K-00-8: Navy Good Conduct Medal.

K-00-9: Navy and Marine Corps Medal.

Ted Robinson and the Cane Photo

This famous "Cane Photo" was taken by Ted Robinson, who was a member of the crew that rescued Lt. Kennedy and his fellow survivors in the Solomon Islands. Mr. Robinson shared memories with me in his Sacramento, California, home several years ago. He informed me that days after the rescue, he and Kennedy took turns taking photographs of each other leaning on the cane. Ted Robinson has spent many years lecturing at schools and other public events about his experiences with the future U.S. president. The cane is now in the Smithsonian.

John F. Kennedy, leaning on the now-famous cane.

Ted Robinson examines the photograph he took of Kennedy leaning on his cane.

K-00-11:
World War II
Victory
Medal.

K-00-10: Purple Heart.

K-00-12:
Asiatic-Pacific
Campaign
Medal.

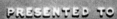

K-00-13: American
Defense Service Medal.

K-00-14: American
Campaign Medal.

PRESENTED TO

SEN. JOHN F. KENNEDY

COMBAT VETERAN, PATRIOT,
CONGRESSMAN AND SENATOR
ONE WHO TYPIFIES THE HIGHEST
IDEALS, A LEADER WHO IS
STANDING ON THE THRESHOLD
OF THE FUTURE OF THE
UNITED STATES OF AMERICA
AND THE WORLD.

101st INFANTRY

VETERANS ASSOCIATION
1958

Given to Senator John F. Kennedy in 1958.

Letters Between Biuku Gasa and President Kennedy

February 6, 1961.

Dear Sir,

In my reverence and sense of your greatness I write to you. It is not fit that I should write to you but in my joy I send this letter. One of our ministers, Reverend E. C. Leadley, came and asked me, "Who rescued Mr. Kennedy?" And I replied, "I did."

This is my joy that you are now President of the United States of America. It was not in my strength that I and my friends were able to rescue you in the time of war, but in the strength of God we were able to help you. The name of God be praised that I am well and in my joy I send this loving letter to you, my friend in Christ. It is good and I say "Thank You" that your farewell words to me were those printed on the dime, "In God We Trust." God is our Hiding Place and our Saviour in the time of trouble and calm.

I am your friend,
Biuku Gasa

Biuku Gasa.

The coconut carried by Biuku Gasa.

President Kennedy writes at his desk in the Oval Office.

K-2008-16

K-63A-193

March 11, 1961.

Dear Biuku:

Reverend E. C. Leadley has recently sent me your very kind message, and I can't tell you how delighted I was to know that you are well and prospering in your home so many thousands of miles away from Washington.

Like you, I am eternally grateful for the act of Divine Providence which brought me and my companions together with you and your friends who so valorously effected our rescue during time of war. Needless to say, I am deeply moved by your expressions and I hope that the new responsibilities which are mine may be exercised for the benefit of my own countrymen and the welfare of all of our brothers in Christ.

You will always have a special place in my mind and my heart, and I wish you and your people continued prosperity and good health.

Sincerely,

John F. Kennedy

K-63A-321

K-63A-326

K-71-43

KCC-79. *See chapter 19.*

K-73-3A

KCC-82. *See chapter 19.*

Pre-Presidency

K-71-25

K-71-23

Congressional Career

After his impressive military career, John F. Kennedy's father convinced him to run for Congress. With his election to the 11th congressional district of Massachusetts in 1946, Kennedy's political career was born. He served three terms in this position. During his tenure, Kennedy worked on a variety of issues, including public housing, social security, and foreign policy.

Aided by the support of his family—his brother Robert managed the campaign—Kennedy was elected to the U.S. Senate in 1952, defeating Republican incumbent Henry Cabot Lodge II. While senator, Kennedy was nominated for the vice presidency, but he finished second to a senator from Tennessee. This defeat did not mar his political career, and in 1958 he was re-elected to a second term as senator.

For the Collector and Historian

Written by John F. Kennedy during his time as a senator, *Profiles in Courage* is the second of Kennedy's published works. Two copies inscribed by JFK were auctioned in 2013; they sold for $2,701 and $9,250.

Not surprisingly, items from the 1960 presidential campaign are some of the most sought after Kennedy memorabilia, and they range in price from under $20 to more than $10,000. Campaign items available for purchase include tie clasps, "Kennedy for President" buttons and pins, brochures, and campaign fliers. In 2013, a presidential campaign poster signed by JFK sold for $1,256, and a signed red, white, and blue "Win with Kennedy" campaign hat was auctioned for $8,400. At the auction of the estate of David Powers, a set of 15 campaign buttons and tabs sold for $500.

Senator Kennedy was known as a senator of the people; he crusaded for civil rights, foreign aid for underdeveloped nations, and labor reform. He took particular interest in expanding industry in Massachusetts to combat unemployment.

Profiles in Courage

Plagued by osteoporosis of the lower back, which was aggravated by his time in the military, Kennedy underwent multiple bouts of back surgery in the 1950s.

In recovery in 1956 and away from the U.S. Senate, he wrote *Profiles in Courage*, an account of eight American politicians who risked their careers for their ideological values. These politicians included John Quincy Adams, who left the Federalist Party due to his support of the Louisiana Purchase and Thomas Jefferson's Embargo Act, and Lucius Lamar, who made continued efforts during Reconstruction to mend the rift between the North and the South. Lamar was

also in opposition to the 1878 Bland-Allison Act, which required the U.S. Treasury to buy a specific amount of silver and use it to mint silver dollars.

Written with extensive contributions from Kennedy's friend and advisor Theodore Sorensen, *Profiles in Courage* was awarded the Pulitzer Prize for Biography in 1957.

An educational poster printed by Perfect Learning.

K-76-29: Profiles in Courage silver cameo collection. For the set, see chapter 20.

K-61-10C

K-71-32

K-2009-6

1960 Presidential Campaign

John F. Kennedy announced his presidential candidacy in January 1960. With Lyndon B. Johnson as his running mate, Kennedy accepted the Democratic nomination on July 13, declaring in his acceptance speech, "we stand today on the edge of a New Frontier."

Kennedy's campaigning skills, bolstered with the help of his family and, in particular, his brothers Robert and Edward, outmatched those of Richard Nixon. The Republican candidate had made a mistake by promising to campaign in all 50 states, while Kennedy concentrated on the swing states and those with a large number of electoral votes.

As the first Catholic presidential nominee, Kennedy had to contend with questions regarding the influence of his faith upon presidential policy. Some voters worried that the Pope would gain a stronghold in U.S. politics if Kennedy were to enter office. On September 12,

A photograph taken by the author at Westgate Ball Park in San Diego, California, during the 1960 presidential campaign. Richard Nixon stands with his wife, Pat.

Advertisement in *Coin World*, October 27, 1960.

1960, he stated, "I am not the Catholic candidate for president. I am the Democratic Party candidate for president who also happens to be a Catholic. I do not speak for my church on public matters, and the church does not speak for me."

Kennedy and then–Vice President Nixon appeared together in the first televised U.S. presidential debates. Nixon had campaigned mere hours before the first debate and therefore appeared tense and exhausted. Kennedy, who

had rested beforehand, was relaxed and eloquent. An estimated 70 million viewers watched the first debate. These debates helped Kennedy to pull ahead in the polls—albeit only marginally.

In one of the closest U.S. presidential campaigns in history, John F. Kennedy defeated Richard Nixon to become, at the age of 43, the youngest man and first Catholic to be elected president of the United States.

K-60-2

K-71-35

K-60-2B

K-2007-10

K-71-18

K-2009-3

K-71-21

K-63A-289

A Question of Coins

Richard M. Nixon

Nixon Declines Coin Comment

Republican Candidate Vice President Richard M. Nixon declined Coin World's invitation to comment on commemorative coinage with thanks.

"Our problem is that he receives a great many inquiries similar to yours, and the press of his schedule does not permit him the time which would be required in order to do an adequate job on each one," Herbert G. Klein, special assistant to the vice president wrote.

"The vice president has asked me to express his appreciation for your recent letter in which you so cordially made available to him an opportunity to prepare a statement for publication in response to your inquiry," the assistant said.

The vice president extends his very best wishes, Klein relayed.

Senator Kennedy To Study Commemorative Coin Issue

"The question of commemorative coins is one which I have not yet carefully considered," U. S. Senator John F. Kennedy told Coin World in a communication from the Kennedy-for-president headquarters in Washington.

Kennedy discussed commemorative coinage to this degree in response to an inquiry from Coin World.

"I appreciate your bringing it to my attention and you may be sure I shall keep your views in mind," the presidential aspirant said.

(Editor D. Wayne Johnson, of Coin World, quizzed both Kennedy and Vice President Richard M. Nixon as to their stand on commemorative coins as a method of preserving history. The vice president has not yet replied.)

Senator Kennedy apologized to

Senator John F. Kennedy

Editor Johnson for a delay in responding to the inquiry. He blamed his busy campaign schedule.

Coin World, 1960.

Presidency

We dare not forget today we are the heirs of that first revolution. Let the word go forth from this time and place, to friend and foe alike, that the torch has been passed to a new generation of Americans—born in this century, tempered by war, disciplined by a hard and bitter peace, proud of our ancient heritage, and unwilling to witness or permit the slow undoing of those human rights to which this nation has always been committed.

—John F. Kennedy, January 20, 1961

Inauguration

The Inaugural Committee
requests the honor of your presence
to attend and participate in the Inauguration of

John Fitzgerald Kennedy
as President of the United States of America
and

Lyndon Baines Johnson
as Vice President of the United States of America
on Friday the twentieth of January
one thousand nine hundred and sixty one
in the City of Washington

Edward H. Foley
Chairman

Invitation to the inauguration of John F. Kennedy and Lyndon B. Johnson, January 20, 1961.

For the Collector and Historian

Some of the most highly sought-after presidential medals are those associated with campaigns and inaugurations. There is a vast number of Kennedy inauguration and campaign-related medals that were produced in large quantities and are relatively inexpensive. One of the most famous Kennedy medals—Gilroy Roberts's inaugural medal—is available to those on a smaller budget, running between $30 and $60.

Anything with a provenance closely connected to the president will attract more attention from collectors; for example, the bronze Roberts inaugural medal presented to David Powers by President Kennedy, encapsulated in Lucite with an inscribed

Presidential Inaugural Address

On Friday, January 20, 1961, John F. Kennedy was sworn in as president of the United States in front of a crowd of thousands. After reciting the oath of office, President Kennedy delivered one of the most famous inaugural addresses in the history of the presidency.

Written by Kennedy and his speech writer Ted Sorensen, this famous address covers a wide range of issues, including the relationship between the United States and the Soviet Union, the rich and the poor, and duty to one's country and to mankind. The following is an excerpt from President Kennedy's inaugural address.

In your hands, my fellow citizens, more than mine, will rest the final success or failure of our course. Since this country was founded, each generation of Americans has been summoned to give testimony to its national loyalty. The graves of young Americans who answered the call to service surround the globe.

Now the trumpet summons us again; not as a call to bear arms, though arms we need; not as a call to battle, though embattled we are; but a call to bear the burden of a long twilight struggle, year in and year out, "rejoicing in hope, patient in tribulation"—a struggle against the common enemies of man: tyranny, poverty, disease, and war itself.

Can we forge against these enemies a grand and global alliance, North and South, East and West, that can assure a more fruitful life for all mankind? Will you join in that historic effort?

In the long history of the world, only a few generations have been granted the role of defending freedom in its hour of maximum danger. I do not shrink from this responsibility—I welcome it. I do not believe that any of us would exchange places with any other people or any other generation. The energy, the faith, the devotion which we bring to this endeavor will light our country and all who serve it, and the glow from that fire can truly light the world.

And so, my fellow Americans: ask not what your country can do for you—ask what you can do for your country.

My fellow citizens of the world: ask not what America will do for you, but what together we can do for the freedom of man.

Finally, whether you are citizens of America or citizens of the world, ask of us here the same high standards of strength and sacrifice which we ask of you. With a good conscience our only sure reward, with history the final judge of our deeds, let us go forth to lead the land we love, asking His blessing and His help, but knowing that here on earth God's work must truly be our own.

K-61-3B

K-61-4

K-61-18: Designed by Costantino Affer, Italy.

K-61-39: Worn by members of Kennedy's presidential staff.

K-61-19D: Inaugural marching medal presented to JFK in 1961 on his 44th birthday.

K-61-44

K-61-20C: Designed by E. Monti, Italy.

K-61-45

K-61-29

K-61-60: White House Service Medal.

K-71-13

K-88-8

K-71-44

K-2007-5A

K-72-9A

K-2008-6

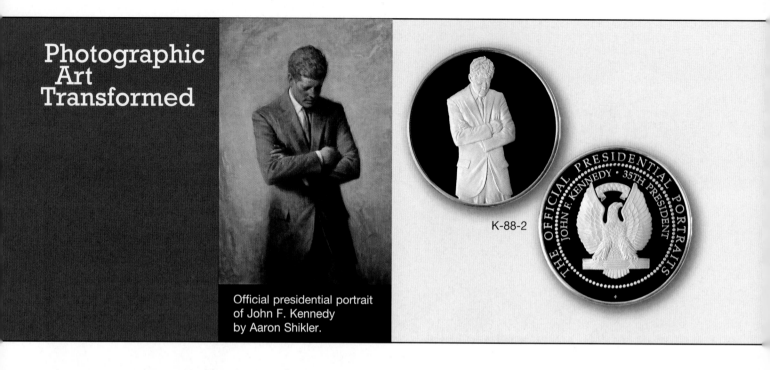

Photographic Art Transformed

Official presidential portrait of John F. Kennedy by Aaron Shikler.

K-88-2

Official Presidential Medal

Presentation of the inaugural medal to President Kennedy by co-chairmen Edward H. Foley and Bruce Sundlun of the Inaugural Committee, January 27, 1961.

Born in Philadelphia in 1905, Gilroy Roberts grew up under the influence of his father, a professional sculptor. Roberts possessed his father's gift and became an assistant sculptor and engraver at the U.S. Mint in 1936. In 1947, Chief Engraver John R. Sinnock passed away, leaving behind the unfinished design for the Benjamin Franklin half dollar. Roberts was appointed the ninth chief engraver and sculptor by President Harry Truman and it was he who finished the design for the Franklin half dollar in his new professional capacity.

Roberts also fashioned many national medals, including the official U.S. Mint presidential medals for presidents Truman, Eisenhower, Kennedy, and Johnson.

Kennedy's inaugural medal was designed by Gilroy Roberts (obverse) and Frank Gasparro (reverse); together, they also designed the Kennedy half dollar after the president's assassination. Roberts met with President Kennedy in the White House in 1961 to work on his portrait for the presidential medal, a portrait that he later used as inspiration for the obverse of the Kennedy half dollar.

K-61-7

President Pleased As He Okays Design

President John Fitzgerald Kennedy's official presidential medal, to be struck at the Philadelphia Mint, will be ready for over-the-counter sale there in two weeks.

Gilroy Roberts, chief engraver of the United States Mint, said on April 24 from his Philadelphia office that work was 80 per cent completed on the traditional medal for the nation's 35th chief executive.

Roberts' work on the Kennedy medal marks the fourth time he has designed for a presidential Mint series. He said he had the privilege of taking the medal drawing to President Kennedy's office recently for his inspection.

"He was pleased, and all those in the office seemed to be pleased," the chief engraver said.

Roberts designed the obverse of the medal; his assistant, Frank Gasparro, executed the reverse.

Coin World readers will not want to miss the first of a series, "How Our Coins Are Made" by Gilroy Roberts, chief engraver of the United States Mint, adopted from an illustrated talk he gave at the American Numismatic Society recently. Engraver Roberts is currently editing the material for technical correctness.

The same engraving team of Roberts-Gasparro worked on the first presidential medal for Dwight D. Eisenhower. Roberts' artistry appears on the second Eisenhower medal and a medal for Harry S. Truman.

Former President Eisenhower was not a medal enthusiast, Roberts said recently in New York at a speech he gave at the American Numismatic Society.

"The president (Eisenhower) had been photographed and his pictures were painted so many times . . ." Roberts theorized, "that (he) was not interested in medals."

"In fact," the engraver told A.N.S. listeners, "they (the Eisenhower administration) wanted to use an inaugural medal that was issued by the Inaugural Committee which is a different thing,
(Continued on Page 3)

Coin World, 1961.

6

Presidential Crises

Cuban stamps depicting what Cubans call *La Victoria de Girón*—the victory at Giron Beach.

Bay of Pigs, April 1961

The invasion of Cuba was conceived in March 1960 at the encouragement of U.S. Senator Prescott Bush and with President Eisenhower's approval. The oversight of the plan was given to its "Action Officer," Vice President Richard Nixon, in collaboration with the Central Intelligence Agency (CIA), headed by Allen Dulles. Plans were made to send 1,500 well-trained Cuban exiles (Brigade 2506) to execute a secret amphibious landing on the Cuban shore of *Bahía De Cochinos*, the Bay of Pigs.

The plan was called Operation Zapata. In June 2011, I was told by a participant in the operation that all preparations were completed and ready to execute by the end of September 1960 but, for an unknown reason, they were held back for seven months until after John F. Kennedy was elected president.

A little more than 60 days after his inauguration, on April 17, 1961, President Kennedy, immersed in moving his new administration forward, regrettably gave the go-ahead for Operation Zapata. In the August 10, 1965, issue of *Look* magazine, Theodore Sorensen recalls that Allen Dulles had visited the Oval Office and asserted, "I stood right here at Ike's desk. . . and told him I was certain our Guatemalan operation would succeed." (The operation of June 1954 that restored a non-Communist government to Guatemala.) "And Mr. President,

For the Collector and Historian

Historians often name the Bay of Pigs and the Cuban Missile Crisis the two most politically important events of the Kennedy administration. As special assistant to President Kennedy, David Powers was present during these tense and trying times.

Powers's personal file on the Bay of Pigs, containing a handwritten account of the event, index cards, and information on Operation Zapata, sold for $1,400 in February 2013. Even more extraordinary was the sale of the pen used by JFK at the signing of the "Interdiction of the Delivery of Offensive Weapons to Cuba," a proclamation prohibiting the sale and delivery of weapons to the country; it sold at the 2013 auction for $24,000.

the prospects for this plan are even better than they were for that one."

The failure, two days earlier, of an air strike by old B-26s from Nicaragua to disable Fidel Castro's planes gave notice to the Cubans that an invasion was coming. The CIA had also informed a public relations firm representing the exiles' political front about the invasion. When the invasion force of 1,400 men was overwhelmed by 20,000 members of the Cuban army, Kennedy issued a stand down. The CIA objected, asking for another air strike, but it would not have had any chance of success without complete U.S. military involvement. This President Kennedy was not prepared to give.

There are those today who believe that CIA assurances were given to Brigade 2506 that, should the plan fail, President Kennedy would send in the U.S. military. However, Kennedy held true to the U.S. principles of nonintervention and stuck to his agreement with the CIA and joint chiefs concerning the original plan of limited non-military support. He trusted and believed what his advisors had stated the plan encompassed, not realizing that other interests were being served.

Had Kennedy ordered the military to invade Cuba there would have been worldwide repercussions. The United States might have spent years fighting with guerilla forces in the mountains of Cuba while Castro gained support and sympathy from other Latin American countries and Russia mobilized more troops in Berlin.

President Kennedy went on national television and, while informing the American public of the failed operation, took upon himself the full responsibility for the entire situation. This was a display of character that would continue throughout his presidency.

Shortly after the Bay of Pigs, Kennedy flew to Camp David and conferred with former president Dwight D. Eisenhower, and later in New York with former president Herbert Hoover and General Douglas MacArthur. Later that year, Kennedy and his wife, Jacqueline, met publicly with members of Brigade 2506 in Miami, Florida.

K-61-37

K-61-54

K-61-55

K-61-56

K-71-33

K-86-5

Cuban Missile Crisis, October 1962

At daybreak on the morning of October 15, 1962, a U.S. Air Force pilot took off in a Lockheed WU-2 high-altitude aircraft attached to the 4028th Strategic Reconnaissance Weather Squadron headquartered at Laughlin Air Force Base in Texas. Later that day, when the CIA was asked to examine film taken during the flight, they found what looked like SS-4 Soviet-made medium-range ballistic-missile sites under construction at San Cristobal, Cuba.

President Kennedy was immediately notified and returned to the White House in a hurry from a trip to Chicago, with the excuse of having a slight respiratory infection. Awaiting him was the possibility of World War III and 13 days of unknown terror for the entire world.

The president called an emergency TV press conference on October 22, 1962, and informed the nation of the impending missile crisis. He stated that the world had been brought to the "abyss of destruction."

Five days later, on October 27, Major Rudolf Anderson Jr., an Eagle Scout and father of three, climbed into the cockpit of a U2-C aircraft, serial number 56-6676, stationed at McCoy Air Force Base in Orlando, Florida. During this high-altitude mission, he was shot down by a Soviet S-75 Dvina surface-to-air missile over Banes, Cuba. On October 31, the secretary of the United Nations announced to the world that Major Anderson was dead. Major Anderson was the only casualty of the Cuban crisis.

Shortly after, by order of President Kennedy, and authorized by Title 10, Section 8742 of the U.S. code, Major Anderson was posthumously awarded the first Air Force Cross, as well as the Distinguished Service Medal, the Purple Heart, and the Cheney Award. The body of Major Rudolf Anderson Jr. was interred at Woodlawn Memorial Park in Greenville, South Carolina.

Several medals have been struck for this historic 13-day event, which has also been commemorated with television specials and a motion picture, *Thirteen Days*, starring Kevin Costner. The Thirteen Days limited-edition medal (K-2000-6) was presented at the opening-night premiere of the film on January 12, 2001.

K-2008-18

K-71-15

K-63A-267

K-83-4

K-63A-290

K-2000-6

K-63A-331

7

Presidential Visits

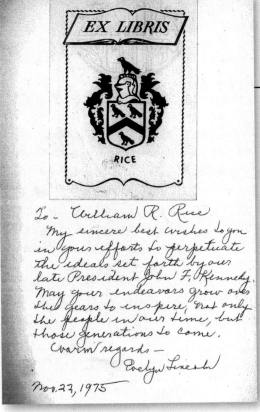

Inscription to the author from Evelyn Lincoln.

President Kennedy Visits Yosemite National Park, August 17 and 18, 1962

In November 1975 President Kennedy's personal secretary, Evelyn Lincoln, recollected the president's visit to Yosemite National Park on August 17 and 18, 1962.

The president was overwhelmed with the beauty of Yosemite from the moment our flight arrived and landed at the heliport on the valley floor. John Preston, the park supervisor, was there to greet the president and I could tell they both immediately enjoyed each other's company.

The president really enjoyed meeting park visitors and employees as he toured throughout the valley floor up to the Tunnel View. The presidential party spent the night at the beautiful Ahwahnee Hotel. He was able to see Glacier Point from the window of his second floor room, and

For the Collector and Historian

Collect what you like and the value will follow. There is intrinsic worth in the hidden facts and new historical information that can be discovered with each item of Kennedy memorabilia.

One of the most prolific items in this category is the PT-boat tie clip, given to the young blind boy who had a memorable meeting with President Kennedy in 1963. Many varieties of this tie clip were made, and one can be purchased for as little $12.50. However, a PT-boat tie clip presented to a recipient by President Kennedy himself will, of course, have a higher price; one given to Eugene L. Dawson by the president sold for $2,230 in 2013.

later that night he watched the traditional Glacier Point Firefall from the outside balcony.

Later the next day when we had a moment alone, the president asked me to make a note for a future appointment and return vacation visit to Yosemite. At no other time in all our travels worldwide did he ever ask me something of that nature, which told me how much he valued his positive Yosemite experience.

Early to rise the next morning, the president had a breakfast that consisted of fresh orange juice, two four-minute eggs, crisp bacon, and a cup of Sanka coffee.

California governor Pat Brown, Congressman Harold Bizz Johnson, Congressman Sisk, and Secretary Udall flew into the park for an early-morning meeting with the president. Lin-

In a brief ceremony on the Ahwahnee lawn, park superintendent John Preston presented President Kennedy with an honorary park-ranger badge plaque.

coln recalls, "Within a few hours [of the meeting] we lifted off in the helicopter. We were now off to a dedication of San Luis Dam in Los Banos. I could feel that the president was slightly disappointed that more time could not have been spent in that beautiful place. I know that if he had lived beyond Dallas, the president would have returned again to Yosemite."

The Chamizal Dispute, January 14, 1963

The Chamizal dispute was a border conflict between the United States and Mexico regarding 600 acres of land on the U.S.–Mexico border between El Paso, Texas, and Ciudad Juárez, Chihuahua.

The Mexican-American War, fought from 1846 to 1848, concluded with the Treaty of Guadalupe Hildalgo, which stated that the official border between the two nations would be marked by the middle of the Rio Grande. Due to natural causes, between 1852 and 1868, the river shifted south, and approximately 600 acres of land became U.S. territory. Known as *El Chamizal*, this land was incorporated as part of El Paso. However, both Mexico and the United States claimed ownership. Mexico claimed that the boundary between the two nations was fixed and, therefore, the land was rightfully theirs. The United States maintained that due to the natural and gradual erosion of the river and its surrounding land, El Chamizal was U.S. property.

While many attempts to arbitrate between the two nations were made by various panels, neither country could agree on a peaceful and equitable solution. However, in 1963, President Kennedy met with President López Mateos of Mexico and brokered a solution to the ongoing problem. The agreement awarded 366 acres of the land to Mex-

President Kennedy at China Lake,
June 1963.

ico and the two nations would share the burden of rechanneling the river in order to prevent further U.S.–Mexico boundary disagreements.

The Chamizal National Memorial, established in 1974 in El Paso, is a museum dedicated to the efforts of diplomacy between the two nations and their leaders.

On the Chamizal Settlement, President Kennedy remarked that "the solution of this controversy will serve as a notable example to the world at large and will contribute to world peace by again demonstrating that all differences among nations, regardless of how complicated they may be, can be resolved through friendly negotiations."

K-63-5A

China Lake Visit, June 7, 1963

Located in the Indian Wells Valley in the Mojave Desert of California is a 1,000-square-mile area known as NOTS (Naval Ordnance Test Station). The valley is hemmed in by the Sierra Nevada to the west and the Slate and Panamint ranges to the east.

The U.S. Navy had called it Classified Project I-63, and it was not until one week before the event that the public was informed that on June 7, 1963, NOTS at China Lake would be hosting a visit by the president of the United States, John F.

Kennedy. Accompanying the commander-in-chief would be Secretary of Defense Robert McNamara, Secretary of the Navy Fred Korth, Chief of Naval Operations Admiral George Anderson, California governor Edmund G. Brown, and California senator Clair Engle. NOTS chief master-at-arms for the visit was Senior Master Chief Donald Masterman Smith, U.S.N.

All residents of the Ridgecrest–China Lake area were asked not to make any long-distance telephone calls on June 7, between the hours of 9:00 a.m. and 4:00 p.m., as extra phones were being installed to accommodate the 250 members of the visiting press. Public schools in the area, with a combined elementary and high school enrollment of 3,400 students, were allowed to start their summer vacation one day early in preparation for the important event.

At 10:55 a.m., the station commander, Captain Charles Blenman Jr., welcomed President Kennedy to the area. Moments later the official party was seated in the reviewing stand for a 50-minute aerial demonstration of the U.S. Navy's finest airpower. After an inspection of the base facilities and lunch at Captain Blenman's home, the president departed for Los Angeles at 2:30 p.m.

A medallic tribute to President Kennedy's visit and commemoration of the 20th anniversary of NOTS was offered for public sale on August 17, 1963. The head of the graphic arts branch technical information department of China Lake, Charles B. Nardone, designed the obverse from composite photographs of President Kennedy. The reverse design was the skilled work of Lynn Nowels, head of the presentation art and design section of the graphic arts branch.

The Los Angeles Stamp and Stationery Company was commissioned to strike the China Lake Kennedy medal and, well educated in the token- and medal-manufacturing field, they set to work using a toggle press that had been in operation since 1891. The original striking consisted of 6,500 pieces in brass alloy. Six medals of this first group were gold plated for presentation to President Kennedy and other dignitaries.

Some time later, the U.S. Navy ordered an additional 1,500 medals struck as the demand for them began to grow. A separate request by the Indian Wells Valley chapter of the Navy League and the NOTS Maturango Museum for 1,000 more medals brought about a third striking. Visitors were able to purchase a medal upon visiting the museum. The price was $1 each.

The death of the president created a new demand for this already popular keepsake, and the final striking of 1,000 medals was completed in the first few months of 1964.

Little Blind Boy "Sees" Mr. President

The *Bakersfield Californian*, June 7, 1963

SAN DIEGO (AP)–A blind boy stood by the helicopter waiting for President Kennedy. The boy was Joey Renzi, age 11 and it was a letter in braille that Joey wrote to Kennedy which attracted the President's attention. In it, Joey told how he wanted to shake the President's hand because "it wouldn't do me any good to stand on the roadside while all the other kids were watching."

'Sees' President

The boy, born prematurely, has been blind virtually all his life.

Doctors say an over-rich oxygen mixture in an incubator caused hemorrhages which destroyed his sight.

But he can see a great deal with his hands, as he did Thursday when, in his mind's own bright pictures, he saw the president.

K-63-3: Obverse, large letters.

K-63-3A: Obverse, small letters.

K-63-3: Reverse.

All Joey heard was a big car stop, he felt a large hand reach for his and another touched his shoulder.

Tells of Meeting

He told afterwards what was said:

"He said he enjoyed seeing me, and I told him what an honor it was to meet him, and he gave me a tie clasp, and I gave him my letter. And he said, "I hope you can come to the White House and visit me sometime.""

The tie clasp was a gold miniature PT boat with the word "Kennedy" on it. The boy's letter told the President "I will treasure this experience all my life."

K-63-21A

What He 'Saw'

What could Joey's hands tell him about the President?

"He's kind of tall," said Joey. "He's real neat looking. He has kind of like an English—no, I guess it's a New England accent. And he has a strong grip. A real strong grip for a big, important man like the president."

After their brief talk, the president climbed into the waiting helicopter, the engine roared and dust flew.

"Goodbye, Mr. Kennedy," Joey shouted into the windblast. "Goodbye, sir!"

"Can he see me?" he asked. "Did he wave back?" "Yes," Joey was told, "he waved." Joey listened until the helicopter was out of sight.

"This has been the best day in my life—ever," he said.

Tie Bars, Clasps, and Pins, 1960 to Date

K-60-15: Variety 1, gold color.

K-60-15B: Variety 1, silver color.

K-60-21: Variety 3, silver color.

K-60-21A: Variety 3, silver color, tac.

K-63A-323: Variety 4, gold color.

K-63A-324: Variety 5, gold color.

K-79-5: Variety 6, gold color.

K-63A-22: Variety 7, gold color.

K-60-30: Variety 8, gold color.

President Kennedy at Whiskeytown, September 28, 1963

President Kennedy dedicates the Whiskeytown Dam, September 28, 1963.

In September 1963, President Kennedy was invited to speak at the dedication of the Whiskeytown Dam. The following are excerpts from his address.

I appreciate the chance to be here in Whiskeytown and to say a few words in this distinguished community. I was reminded, when I read my itinerary, of a poem by Stephen Vincent Benet called "American Names," and he started it off:

I have fallen in love with American names,

The sharp names that never get fat,

The snakeskin-titles of mining-claims,

The plumed war-bonnet of Medicine Hat,

Tucson and Deadwood and Lost Mule Flat.

Then he goes on to talk about some famous American names, not Whiskeytown, but I think he could add it to the roster, because the name of this community tells a good deal about the early beginnings of this state and country.

I have come across the United States in the last five days, starting at Milford, Pennsylvania, which was the home of Gifford Pinchot, who was, with Theodore Roosevelt, the first great conservationist in this country. Imagine how small their country was, how few the people, and yet how dangerous it was in the early part of this century. How great was that danger, that this great natural inheritance of ours, given to us by nature, given to us by God, would be wiped away; the forests ruined, the streams destroyed, wasted for the people, water going to the sea unused. And because of the

39

dedicated work of men actually who did not come from this part of the country, who came from the East—Pinchot, Theodore Roosevelt, and later Franklin Roosevelt—this great national effort was made to realize our resources, to make them useful. And all of you who are here today in the state of California are here because of the wise decisions that were made by those who came before, and the wise decisions that you are making now.

When you support the effort which Governor Brown described—to set aside funds for a bond issue for recreation—it may not come before you immediately, but it will make it possible for your children to live better. This country is changing. We had a 58-hour week, a 48-hour week, a 40-hour week. As machines take more and more of the jobs of men, we are going to find the work week reduced, and we

are going to find people wondering what they should do. I want to make it possible, and you do—make it possible for them to see green grass, to travel throughout this great, rich country of ours, not just in other parts of the world, but here in the United States, where I have seen parts of this country which are second to none, to any in the world, and where too many people east of the Mississippi are unaware of what golden resources we have in our own United States.

Every time we make a determination to set aside a seashore for the use of future generations, every time we build these great projects, we develop the water resources, we set aside recreational areas, we can be sure they are going to be used. Three hundred and fifty million Americans will live in this country of ours in the short space of less than 40 years, where

President Kennedy views the beauty of Whiskeytown Lake.

now there are 180 million. What will they do? What kind of a country will they find? How much recreation will be possible for them? I think if we make the right decisions now they will be as grateful to us as we were and are to Gifford Pinchot and Theodore Roosevelt for the things they did 45 and 50 years ago.

I wonder how many people realize in the eastern United States, where I come from, what a great national asset we have. This is not just California. This is one country, 50 separate states but one country. And people move very freely from east to west and west to east. I won-

der how many people here today were born in the state of California. Would they hold up their hands? And how many were not born in California? It shows that what we are doing— we are a mobile, moving country. Our national assets belong to all of us. Children who were born in the East will grow up in the West, and those born in the West will grow up in the East. And we will find by concentrating our energies on our national resources, on conserving them, but not merely conserving and saving them, but by developing and improving them, the United States will be richer and stronger.

John F. Kennedy Commemorative Whiskeytown Gold Coins

President John F. Kennedy dedicated Whiskeytown Dam September 28th, 1963. This was his last visit to California before his assassination November 22, 1963. The people of Shasta County donated funds for the construction of an unusual memorial to the memory of his visit. The memorial is at the dam itself and consists of a steel frame 15 feet long and 7½ feet high, mounted on a 2-foot rock base. The steel frame has six marbelized cement plaques sculptured by Roberto Ciabani, recently from Italy, and now residing in Medford, Oregon. Each plaque depicts a different interest of the late President, such as the Peace Corps, Civil Rights, Conservation, Defense of Liberty. The largest plaque is a picture of the President as he addressed the crowd at the dedication. Inscribed on the plaque are the words: "President John F. Kennedy, dedicated Whiskeytown Dam, September 28th, 1963. In memorium ... Assassinated November 22nd, 1963 ... He was his own profile in courage." In between the plaques there are open spaces so that the viewer can see the beauty of Whiskeytown Lake in the background.

John F. Kennedy Commemorative Whiskeytown Gold Coins

President John F. Kennedy dedicated Whiskeytown Dam September 28th, 1963. This was his last visit to California before his assassination November 22, 1963. The people of Shasta County donated funds for the construction of an unusual memorial to the memory of his visit. The memorial is at the dam itself and consists of a steel frame 15 feet long and 7½ feet high, mounted on a 2-foot rock base. The steel frame has six marbelized cement plaques sculptured by Roberto Ciabani, recently from Italy, and now residing in Medford, Oregon. Each plaque depicts a different interest of the late President, such as the Peace Corps, Civil Rights, Conservation, Defense of Liberty. The largest plaque is a picture of the President as he addressed the crowd at the dedication. Inscribed on the plaque are the words: "President John F. Kennedy, dedicated Whiskeytown Dam, September 28th, 1963. In memorium ... Assassinated November 22nd, 1963 ... He was his own profile in courage." In between the plaques there are open spaces so that the viewer can see the beauty of Whiskeytown Lake in the background.

THE BROTHERS . . .

Robert F. Kennedy Commemorative Whiskeytown Gold Coins

"Some men dream the dream that was, and ask, 'Why?'. I dream the dream that never was and ask, 'Why not'?"

Senator Robert F. Kennedy was assassinated June 4, 1968 in Los Angeles, California while campaigning for the Presidency of the United States. He was the second member of his family to run for the Presidency in a decade, and the second to die at the hands of an assassin. His public career spanned 16 years. He was among the youngest Attorney Generals, at the age of 35, in the history of the United States. In 1964 he became the Senator from the state of New York in an easily won election. In earlier years he had served as chief counsel for the Senate Rackets Committee. He lies buried beside his brother in Arlington National Cemetary.

Brochure from the Redding Chamber of Commerce in California detailing the John and Robert F. Kennedy Whiskeytown commemoratives.

We can fulfill our responsibilities to ourselves and those who depend upon us.

I am proud to be here. I am proud to be associated with those who are contributing to this country, who are making it better, not merely right now, today, but who are looking to the long future of those who come after us. I congratulate you on what you have done. Thank you.

K-63-25

K-68-1A

K-65-5A

K-68-2A

Other Presidential Visits

K-61-13: Illinois.

K-71-16: The Vatican.

K-71-24: Vienna, Austria.

K-62-6

K-88-12: Vienna, Austria.

K-88-11: France.

43

K-88-13: West Germany.

K-2008-4: Berlin, Germany.

K-88-14: Berlin, Germany.

K-2008-15: Berlin, Germany.

8

Presidential Law-Making

The Peace Corps

Senator Hubert Humphrey,
Vice President Lyndon B. Johnson,
and President John F. Kennedy,
February 7, 1961.

Brainchild of Hubert Humphrey, the Peace Corps was ushered into being by President Kennedy. The Corps was authorized by an act of Congress passed on September 22, 1961.

The following is an excerpt from *A Man For All People: A Pictorial Biography of Hubert H. Humphrey* by Ralph G. Martin, discussing Humphrey's friendship with John F. Kennedy.

> I worked hard for Kennedy in that 1960 campaign. I did not hold grudges in politics, and I worked hard and loyally supported President Kennedy during his presidency.
>
> He picked up my Peace Corps idea and helped put it into law. I appreciated that because the big thing in gov-

For the Collector and Historian

A little-collected and little-known category of Kennedy memorabilia is White House supplies—the letter openers, ink stamps, seals, and writing utensils used by John F. Kennedy during his administration.

In 2013, two pens used by the president to sign important bills into law were auctioned. The first was the pen used by JFK to sign the 1961 Peace Corps Act. An Esterbrook fountain pen, this extraordinary piece has "The President—The White House" written on its side. It sold for $17,400.

The second, again an Esterbrook fountain pen, still retains some ink on the nib. It was used by JFK to sign the Maternal and Child Health Bill into effect. Matted and framed, it was accompanied by a photo of Kennedy with his sister Eunice at the bill's signing on October 24, 1963. This pen sold for $14,400.

ernment is to make something happen and it might have taken a lot longer without his presidential push.

He had my support in the Senate and he knew it, and called on it often. He had my friendship and he knew that also.

He was a man of special grace and a special style. I cried when he died. His death was a personal loss to me. Like others, I wept. I miss him.

K-78-1

Executive Order 10924: Establishment and Administration of the Peace Corps in the Department of State

By virtue of the authority vested in me by the Mutual Security Act of 1954, 68 Stat. 832, as amended (22 U.S.C. 1750 et seq.), and as President of the United States, it is hereby ordered as follows:

SECTION 1. Establishment of the Peace Corps. The Secretary of State shall establish an agency in the Department of State which shall be known as the Peace Corps. The Peace Corps shall be headed by a Director.

SEC. 2. Functions of the Peace Corps.

(a) The Peace Corps shall be responsible for the training and service abroad of men and women of the United States in new programs of assistance to nations and areas of the world, and in conjunction with or in support of existing economic assistance programs of the United States and of the United Nations and other international organizations.

(b) The Secretary of State shall delegate, or cause to be delegated, to the Director of the Peace Corps such of the functions under the Mutual Security Act of 1954, as amended, vested in the President and delegated to the Secretary, or vested in the Secretary, as the Secretary shall deem necessary for the accomplishment of the purposes of the Peace Corps.

SEC. 3. Financing of the Peace Corps. The Secretary of State shall provide for the financing of the Peace Corps with funds available to the Secretary for the performance of functions under the Mutual Security Act of 1954, as amended.

SEC. 4. Relation to Executive Order No. 10893. This order shall not be deemed to supersede or derogate from any provision of Executive Order No. 10893 of November 8, 1960, as amended, and any delegation made by or pursuant to this order shall, unless otherwise specifically provided therein, be deemed to be in addition to any delegation made by or pursuant to that order.

John F. Kennedy

The White House

March 1, 1961

K-70-3

K-2004-5. *See chapter 17.*

K-71-38

K-63A-10F

K-71-50

K-63A-276

Executive Order 10977: Establishing the Armed Forces Expeditionary Medal

By virtue of the authority vested in me as President of the United States and as Commander in Chief of the Armed Forces of the United States, it is hereby ordered as follows:

SECTION 1. There is hereby established the Armed Forces Expeditionary Medal, with ribbons and appurtenances, for award to personnel of the Armed Forces of the United States who after July 1, 1958:

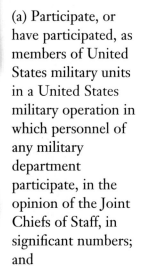

Armed Forces Expeditionary Medal.

(a) Participate, or have participated, as members of United States military units in a United States military operation in which personnel of any military department participate, in the opinion of the Joint Chiefs of Staff, in significant numbers; and

(b) Encounter, incident to such participation, foreign armed opposition, or are otherwise placed, or have been placed, in such position that, in the opinion of the Joint Chiefs of Staff, hostile action by foreign armed forces was imminent even though it did not materialize.

SEC. 2. The medal, with ribbons and appurtenances, shall be of appropriate design approved by the Secretary of Defense and shall be awarded by the Secretary of the military department directly concerned, and by the Secretary of Transportation with respect to the United States Coast Guard, under uniform regulations to be issued by the Secretary of Defense.

SEC. 3. The medal shall be awarded only for operations for which no other United States campaign medal is approved. For operations in which personnel of only one military department participate, the medal shall be awarded only if there is no other suitable award available to that department. No more than one medal shall be awarded to any one person, but for each succeeding operation justifying such award a suitable device may be awarded to be worn on the medal or ribbon as prescribed by appropriate regulations.

SEC. 4. The medal may be awarded posthumously and, when so awarded, may be presented to such representative of the deceased as may be deemed appropriate by the Secretary of the department concerned.

John F. Kennedy

The White House
April 4, 1961

Executive Order 11016: Authorizing Award of the Purple Heart

July 27, 1962

Memorandum for

The Secretary of the Air Force

This matter has been discussed here -- also a new Executive Order re Purple Heart was issued.

The problems to be studied include:

(1)   Should a Purple Heart be given to all U.S. prisoners who can prove injury during captivity?

(2)   Should Purple Heart be restricted to wounds by enemy fire?

(3)   Should Purple Heart be restricted to military personnel?

(4)   How would we improve present standards and criteria for this award? Do we need a change? Do we need clarification, etc?

Sir, we would appreciate receiving the USAF views concerning this matter.

GODFREY T. McHUGH
Brigadier General, USAF
Air Force Aide to the President

Atts

K-00-10

Memorandum for the secretary of the Air Force.

WHEREAS General George Washington, at Newburg-on-the-Hudson, on August 7, 1782, during the War of the Revolution, issued an Order establishing the Honorary Badge of Distinction, otherwise known as the Badge of Military Merit or Decoration of the Purple Heart; and

WHEREAS the award of that decoration ceased with the closing of the War of the Revolution and was revived on February 22, 1932, out of respect to the memory and military achievements of General George Washington, by War Department General Orders No. 3:

NOW, THEREFORE, by virtue of the authority vested in me as President of the United States and as Commander in Chief of the armed forces of the United States, it is ordered as follows:

SECTION 1. The Secretary of a military department, or the Secretary of Transportation with regard to the Coast Guard when not operating as a service in the Navy, shall, in the name of the President of the United States, award the Purple Heart, with suitable ribbons and appurtenances, to any member of an armed force under the jurisdiction of that department and any civilian national of the United States who, while serving under competent authority in any capacity with an armed force of that department, has been, or may hereafter be, wounded—

(a) in any action against an enemy of the United States;

(b) in any action with an opposing armed force of a foreign country in which the armed forces of the United States are or have been engaged;

(c) while serving with friendly foreign forces engaged in an armed conflict against an opposing armed force in which the United States is not a belligerent party;

(d) as the result of an act of any such enemy or opposing armed force;

(e) as the result of an act of any hostile foreign force;

SEC. 2. The Secretary of a military department, or the Secretary of Transportation, shall, in the name of the President of the United States, award the Purple Heart, with suitable ribbons and appurtenances, posthumously, to any person covered by, and under the circumstances described in, paragraph 1 who, after April 5, 1917, has been, or may hereafter be, killed, or who has died or may hereafter die after being wounded.

SEC. 3. A wound for which the award is made must have required treatment by a medical officer.

SEC. 4. The Purple Heart shall be forwarded to the next of kin of any person entitled to the posthumous award, without respect to whether a previous award has been made to such person, except that if the award results from service before December 7, 1941, the Purple Heart shall be forwarded to such next of kin upon his application therefore to the Secretary of the department concerned.

SEC. 5. Except as authorized in paragraph 4, not more than one Purple Heart shall be awarded to any person, but for each subsequent award a Gold Star, or other suitable device, shall be awarded to be worn with the Purple Heart as prescribed by appropriate regulations to be issued by the Secretary of the department concerned.

SEC. 6. When authorized by the Secretary of the department concerned, the award of the Purple Heart may be made by subordinate military commanders, or such other appropriate officers as the Secretary concerned may designate.

SEC. 7. The Secretary of the department concerned may prescribe such regulations as he considers appropriate to carry out this order. The regulations of the Secretaries of the departments with respect to the award of the Purple Heart shall, so far as practicable, be uniform, and those of the military departments shall be subject to the approval of the Secretary of Defense.

SEC. 8. This order supersedes Executive Order No. 10409 of November 12, 1952, entitled "Award of the Purple Heart to Persons Serving with the Navy, Marine Corps, or Coast Guard of the United States". However, existing regulations prescribed pursuant to that order, together with regulations prescribed under the authority of General Orders No. 3, War Department, February 22, 1932, shall, so far as they are not inconsistent with this order, remain in effect until modified or revoked by regulations prescribed by the Secretary of the department concerned under this order.

John F. Kennedy
The White House
April 25, 1962

Executive Order 11046: Authorizing Award of the Bronze Star Medal

By virtue of the authority vested in me as President of the United States and as Commander in Chief of the armed forces of the United States, it is hereby ordered as follows:

SECTION 1. The Bronze Star Medal, with accompanying ribbons and appurtenances, which was first established by Executive Order No. 9419 of February 4, 1944, may be awarded by the Secretary of a military department or the Secretary of Transportation with regard to the Coast Guard when not operating as a service in the Navy, or by such military commanders, or other appropriate officers as the Secretary concerned may designate, to any

Bronze Star Medal.

person who, while serving in any capacity in or with the Army, Navy, Marine Corps, Air Force, or Coast Guard of the United States, after December 6, 1941, distinguishes, or has distinguished, himself by heroic or meritorious achievement or service, not involving participation in aerial flight—

(a) while engaged in an action against an enemy of the United States;

(b) while engaged in military operations involving conflict with an opposing foreign force; or

(c) while serving with friendly foreign forces engaged in an armed conflict against an opposing armed force in which the United States is not a belligerent party.

SEC. 2. The Bronze Star Medal and appurtenances thereto shall be of appropriate design approved by the Secretary of Defense, and shall be awarded under such regulations as the Secretary concerned may prescribe. Such regulations shall, so far as practicable, be uniform, and those of the military departments shall be subject to the approval of the Secretary of Defense.

SEC. 3. No more than one Bronze Star Medal shall be awarded to any one person, but for each succeeding heroic or meritorious achievement or service justifying such an award a suitable device may be awarded to be worn with the medal as prescribed by appropriate regulations.

SEC. 4. The Bronze Star Medal or device may be awarded posthumously and, when so awarded, may be presented to such representative of the deceased as may be deemed appropriate by the Secretary of the department concerned.

SEC. 5. This order shall supersede Executive Order No. 9419 of February 4, 1944, entitled "Bronze Star Medal." However, existing regulations prescribed under that order shall, so far as they are not inconsistent with this order, remain in effect until modified or revoked by regulations prescribed under this order by the Secretary of the department concerned.

John F. Kennedy

The White House
August 24, 1962

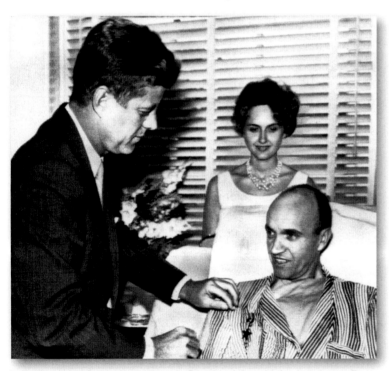

President Kennedy pins a Bronze Star Medal on Major Lawrence R. Bailey Jr., recently released after being held prisoner by Communist forces in Laos. The ceremony takes place at Walter Reed Army Hospital where Bailey is recuperating on August 28, 1962. Bailey's daughter Barbara looks on.

Executive Order 11085: The Presidential Medal of Freedom

By virtue of the authority vested in me as President of the United States, it is hereby ordered as follows:

SECTION 1. Prior orders. The numbered sections of Executive Order No. 9586 of July 6, 1945, as amended by Executive Order No. 10336 of April 3, 1952, are hereby amended to read as follows:

"SECTION 1. Medal established. The Medal of Freedom is hereby re-established as the Presidential Medal of Freedom, with accompanying ribbons and appurtenances. The Presidential Medal of Freedom, hereinafter referred to as the Medal, shall be in two degrees.

"SEC. 2. Award of the Medal.

(a) The Medal may be awarded by the President as provided in this order to any person who has made an especially meritorious contribution to (1) the security or national interests of the United States, or (2) world peace, or (3) cultural or other significant public or private endeavors.

"(b) The President may select for award of the Medal any person nominated by the Board referred to in Section 3(a) of this Order, any person otherwise recommended to the President for award of the

Presidential Medal of Freedom. Pictured is the actual medal posthumously awarded to John F. Kennedy. It is on display at the John F. Kennedy Presidential Library and Museum.

Medal, or any person selected by the President upon his own initiative.

"(c) The principal announcement of awards of the Medal shall normally be made annually, on or about July 4 of each year; but such awards may be made at other times, as the President may deem appropriate.

"(d) Subject to the provisions of this Order, the Medal may be awarded posthumously.

"SEC. 3. Distinguished Civilian Service Awards Board.

(a) The Distinguished Civilian Service Awards Board, established by Executive Order No. 10717 of June 27, 1957, hereinafter referred to as the Board, is hereby expanded, for the purpose of carrying out the objectives of this Order, to include five additional members appointed by the President from outside the Executive Branch of the Government. The terms of service of the members of the Board appointed under this paragraph shall be five years, except that the first five members so appointed shall have terms of service expiring on the 31st day of July 1964, 1965, 1966, 1967, and 1968, respectively. Any person appointed to fill a vacancy occurring prior to the expiration of the term for which his predecessor was appointed shall serve for the remainder of such term.

"(b) A chairman of the Board shall be designated by the President from time to time from among the membership of the Board appointed from the Executive Branch.

"(c) For purposes of recommending to the President persons to receive the President's Award for Distinguished Federal Civilian Service, and to carry out the other purposes of Executive Order No. 10717, only the members of the Board from the Executive Branch will sit. The names of persons so recommended will be submitted to the President without reference to the other members of the Board.

"SEC 4 . Functions of the Board.

    (a) Any individual or group may make recommendations to the Board with respect to the award of the Medal, and the Board shall consider such recommendations.

    "(b) With due regard for the provisions of Section 2 of this Order, the Board shall screen such recommendations and, on the basis of such recommendations or upon its own motion, shall from time to time submit to the President nominations of individuals for award of the Medal, in appropriate degrees.

"SEC. 5. Expenses. Necessary administrative expenses of the Board incurred in connection with the recommendation of persons to receive the Presidential Medal of Freedom, including expenses of travel of members of the Board appointed under Section 3 (a) of this Order, during the fiscal year 1963, may be paid from the appropriation provided under the heading 'Special Projects' in the Executive Office Appropriation Act, 1963, 76 Stat. 315, and during subsequent fiscal years, to the extent permitted by law, from any corresponding or like appropriation made available for such fiscal years. Such payments shall be without regard to the provisions of section 3681 of the Revised Statutes and section 9 of the Act of March 4, 1909, 35 Stat. 1027 (31 U.S.C. 672 and 673). Members of the Board appointed under Section 3(a) of this Order shall serve without compensation.

    "SEC. 6. Design of the Medal. The Army Institute of Heraldry shall prepare for the approval of the President a design of the Medal in each of its degrees."

SEC. 2. Other existing orders.

    (a) Section 4 of Executive Order No. 10717, establishing the terms of service of the members of the Distinguished Civilian Service Awards Board, is hereby amended to read "The members of the Board shall serve at the pleasure of the President", and the other sections of that Order are amended conformably to this Order.

    (b) Except as otherwise specifically provided in this Order, existing arrangements for conferring medals and honors shall continue in effect.

John F. Kennedy
The White House
February 22, 1963

The Forgotten Kennedy Medal

On October 16, 1963, President Kennedy sat at his desk in the Oval Office and signed public law 88-143. Beginning as Senate Bill S-743, public law 88-143 was introduced by California senators Thomas H. Kuchel and Clair Engle. It passed the Senate on June 26, 1963, and was later passed by the House of Representatives on October 7 of that same year.

Public law 88-143 authorized the U.S. Mint at Philadelphia to strike a unique, limited national medal honoring the 250th anniversary of the birth of the historic pioneer Padre Junipero Serra.

This tribute medal was the first national medal to honor the life of a Catholic priest. Junipero Serra was born in Majorca, Spain, on November 24, 1713. In 1769, at the age of 56, he started the first California settlements.

It is ironic that on November 24, 1963, President Kennedy's body lay in state in the Capitol building not far from the statue of Padre Junipero Serra chosen as the model for the medal.

The honor of creating the design was assigned to U.S. Mint artist Frank Gasparro, who was to also design the reverse of the Kennedy half dollar shortly thereafter.

Five medals were struck in gold and were presented to President Johnson, Pope Paul VI, Generalissimo Franco, Serra International, and a California museum.

Only 9,000 of the .900 fine silver medals were struck, of which 3,000 were distributed to Rome and to Catholic missions throughout California. The medals were struck from March to December 31, 1964, at which time the authorization expired.

President Kennedy's passing made the Junipero Serra medal a historic dual reminder, a memento of both a saint and a martyred U.S. president.

The President's Farewell to Medallic Art

One of the first and also the last laws signed by John F. Kennedy was related to medallic art.

In his newly elected office only 62 days, the president signed his third legislative bill: public law 87-3. This law restored the military rank of general—with all due medals—to his predecessor, the 34th president of the United States, Dwight D. Eisenhower.

Just two days prior to his scheduled trip to Dallas, Texas, on November 22, 1963, Kennedy signed his last bill, public law 88-185, which authorized the striking of medals to commemorate the founding of the first Union Health Center in America, established by the International Ladies' Garment Workers' Union. The medal was struck by the U.S. Mint in Philadelphia, Pennsylvania, and presented by Kennedy's successor, Lyndon B. Johnson, at a ceremony honoring the health center's 50th anniversary in 1964.

K-64-34

K-63-23

9

Presidential Gifts and Awards

Presidential Presentations

The President Chooses His Medals

President Kennedy took 400 inaugural medals, designed by Ralph J. Menconi (K-61-8), and an unknown quantity of presidential medals, designed by Paul Manship (K-61-1), to his first summit meeting in Europe.

William T. Louth, president of the Medallic Art Company in New York City, where both medals were struck, told *Coin World* that the State Department ordered 1,000 of the newly released inaugural medal. The president planned to distribute 400 of these medals bearing his portrait to officials on his European trip to Paris, London, and Vienna, according to a State Department official.

According to Louth, an officer in the chief of protocol office picked up 400 medals on May 29 (the president's birthday) from Medallic Art's plant at 325 East 45th Street in New York City for the summit trip to Europe.

Kennedy had used the 2-3/4 inch inaugural medals as gifts on an earlier trip he made to Canada. "The presidential party was stimulated by the warm reception of the medals in Canada," said Louth. "The State Department approached us to manufacture a miniature of the inaugural medal."

Louth explained that his firm was about to strike a similar medal for Presidential Art Medals of Dayton, Ohio, bearing a portrait of Kennedy on a medal 1-1/4 inches in size. This medal was designed by Ralph J. Menconi, and it launched the Presidential Art Medals series of presidential medals. Because of the success of this series, Menconi was named "The Sculptor of Presidents."

A sample of this presidential medal was sent to the State Department as soon as the first strikes were made. This resulted in the order of 1,000 medals for President Kennedy's use in Europe.

For the Collector and Historian

One of the rarest presidential tokens and medals is the JFK Appreciation Medal, given as a gift to dignitaries during his European trip. These medals appear in larger rare-coin and token auctions from time to time and are eagerly sought by enthusiasts. In 2013, one sold for $1,000. But those on a budget can build a very nice collection of Kennedy medals and tokens, in an attractive variety of sizes, shapes, and compositions, for less than $100.

Special cards were printed to accompany each medal with the inscription "Compliments, John F. Kennedy, President of the United States."

The vice president of Presidential Art Medals, Max Humbert, said he was "overwhelmed by the announcement of President Kennedy's intended use of their medal." He further stated, "Collectors have accepted our medal also, as the platinum version of the medal sold out in one day."

K-61-8: Presidential medal designed by Ralph J. Menconi; bronze.

K-61-1: Inaugural medal designed by Paul Manship.

K-61-8A: Presidential medal designed by Ralph J. Menconi; silver.

K-61-8C: Presidential Art Medals process set.

K-73-27

Awards and Medals Presented by President Kennedy, 1961–1963

On March 23, 1961, President Kennedy presents the Young American Medal for Bravery to Shirley O'Neill of San Francisco, California, and Donald McGregor of Brunswick, Georgia.

Kennedy presents the NASA Distinguished Service Medal to Astronaut Commander Alan Shepard on May 8, 1961.

During the presentation of the NASA Distinguished Service Medal to Alan Shepard, Kennedy dropped the medal on the wooden platform. This cartoon, from a 1961 issue of *Coin World*, satirizes the event.

On April 19, 1961, Kennedy presents the National Geographic Society's Gold Medal to Jacques Cousteau.

Kennedy awards the Medal of Bravery to Loretta Agnes Jaronik as part of the Justice Department's Young American Medals program. Jaronik, an 18-year-old woman from Indiana, was commended for rescuing a young boy in a fire on May 7, 1963. Also present at the ceremony were Robert F. Kennedy, Senator Birch Bayh from Indiana, J. Edgar Hoover, and Senator Margaret Chase Smith from Maine.

K-61-38: John F. Kennedy Appreciation Gift to Supporters medal.

K-62-1: U.S. Mint Appreciation medal, presented by Kennedy during a trip to Europe.

Awards and Medals Presented by President Kennedy for the Year 1961

Medal of Freedom: awarded to Paul Henri Spaak, secretary general of NATO; February 21, 1961.

Young American Medal for Bravery: awarded to Shirley O'Neill and Donald McGregor; March 23, 1961.

National Geographic Society gold medal: awarded to Jacques Yves Cousteau; April 19, 1961.

NASA Distinguished Service Medal: awarded to astronaut Alan B. Shepard; May 8, 1961.

Collier Trophy: awarded to USN Admiral William F. Raborn Jr.; June 15, 1961.

Distinguished Service Medal: awarded to USAF Chief of Staff General Thomas D. White; June 28, 1961.

Distinguished Service Medal with gold star: awarded to USN Admiral Arleigh A. Burke; July 26, 1961.

President's Cup Regatta Trophy: awarded to Chuck Thompson and Boat Miss Detroit; August 9, 1961.

National Security Medal: awarded to Allen Welsh Dulles; November 28, 1961.

Clifford B. Harmon International Trophy: awarded to pilots Joseph A. Walker, A. Scott Crossfield, and Robert M. White; November 28, 1961.

continued on next page

Albert Parvin Foundation Award: awarded to Secretary General of United Nations Dag Hammarskjöld; November 28, 1961

Rockefeller Public Service Award: awarded to Dr. Robert H. Felix, assistant surgeon general; Livingston T. Merchant, ambassador to Canada; Dr. Thomas B. Nolan, director, geological survey; Deputy Director Elmer B. Staats, Bureau of Budget; Colin F. Stam, Bureau of Internal Revenue; November 29, 1961.

Enrico Fermi Award: awarded to R. Hans Bethe, professor of physics, Cornell University; December 1, 1961.

Kennedy presents the Congressional Gold Medal to Robert Frost.

Presentation of the Congressional Gold Medal to Robert Frost, White House FishRoom, March 26, 1962

President Kennedy: Well, gentlemen, it's a great honor for me, speaking on behalf of the Congress and the people of the United States, to present this much deserved and rather rare action—award—to Mr. Robert Frost.

I suppose in a sense he is disappointed that this was not a more controversial decision by the Congress, but instead was a unanimous one. We are proud of you, Mr. Frost—

Robert Frost: Both parties.

President Kennedy: What? Both parties. [*laughter*] In fact, the only thing, really, that we have been able to agree on since you were here, in a long time.

But I think we are proud of Mr. Frost and his interpretations of what we feel is the best of America, and, therefore, I present this award

to our very good friend. Would you say a word here?

Robert Frost: Of course this is sort of the height of my life, you know, and on a wave of poetry, isn't it? And that ought to be enough to say.

This has been going on for some time, so that as somebody said, the obverse of it could be one party and the reverse the other—and the verse mine. And there it is. Doing my age justice. And, oh dear, how grateful I am to you personally. That is going to be in the book I am handing you—ever since you wrote the *Profiles*, that is where it began.

And right down to him making an office of the Fine Arts, right in the White House where you can keep track of them.

There's the book. [*Frost hands Kennedy a book of his poetry*] I have written that in there. You can't read it—my writing. Just one suggestion to put into it, you know, that you call it the Office of the Fine Arts and leave the word "cultural" off it? Just for me. And I hope it may last long before it becomes too much of a department.

A voice: Mr. President, you have said Robert Frost. Would you mind naming his whole name?

President Kennedy: Well, that's all we ever call him, isn't it?

Robert Frost: Yes, my whole name is Robert Lee Frost.

President Kennedy: Robert Lee Frost. [*laughter*]

Robert Frost: In a speech, whenever I incautiously say the Civil War, I always say "The Civil War—between the States," and make it all right with the South, and the "Lee" does the rest. That is a great, great thing. And you think so as well.

Presentation of the Congressional Gold Medal to Bob Hope, White House Rose Garden, September 11, 1963

President Kennedy: Bob, the garden is filled with some of your old friends from the Congress. We are glad to see them here. 97 members of Congress sponsored this legislation—97 Senators—and I think the overwhelming support it was given in the Congress and in the country, Bob, shows the great affection that all of us hold for you and, most especially, the great appreciation we have for you for so many years going so many places to entertain the sons, daughters, brothers, and sisters of Americans who were very far from home.

So, in passing this bill, in making this medal—and it is one of the really rarest acts of the Con-

Bob Hope accepting the Congressional Gold Medal.

gress. I think, since the end of the second war, this has been done on only 10 or 11 occasions—Dr. Salk, Billy Mitchell, Justice Brandeis. It has been one of the rarest honors given to Americans, and it is a great pleasure for me on behalf of the Congress to present this to you. We have a splendid picture of you. I hope everyone will have a chance to look at it. I present it to you on behalf of the people of the United States.

Bob Hope: Thank you very much, Mr. President. That is very nice. I suggested to Senator Symington I should have had a nose job, but he said "there would have been less gold." I actually don't like to tell jokes about a thing like this because it is one of the nicest things that has ever happened to me, and I feel very humble—although I think I have the strength of character to fight it—and I am thrilled that you invited all the senators and congressmen up here with us. For a while it looked like a congressional investigation, but I really appreciate this very much.

And this is sort of an anticlimax to some great thrills that I have had touring the world, and I want to thank the Defense Department, and especially Stuart Symington who started all our Christmas trips and has been more or less a den mother to all of us all these years. But I do appreciate it and I want to thank the president for inviting my family, I enjoyed meeting them, and this will mean a lot to my kids. It won't explain why I wasn't in the service, but at least it will point out which side I was on. Thank you very, very much. I think it is deductible.

President Kennedy: You might read the other side, Bob. I will read it. It says: "Presented to Bob Hope by President Kennedy in recognition of his having rendered outstanding service to the cause of democracies throughout the world. By the Act of Congress, June 8, 1962."

Bob Hope: That is very nice and I want to say I also played in the South Pacific while the president was there, and he was a very gay, carefree young man at that time. Of course, all he had to worry about then was the enemy. But it is thrilling to note that 20 years later, he is still on government rations. Which way is the golf course?

President Kennedy: You go right out there.

Bob Hope: Thank you very much.

Gifts and Awards Presented to President Kennedy, 1961-1963

President Garnett D. Horner of the White House Correspondents' Association presents silver lanterns to President Kennedy on February 25, 1961.

The mayor of West Berlin presents a replica of the Freedom Bell in Berlin to Kennedy on March 13, 1961.

The ambassador of Ireland presents the Kennedy coat of arms to Kennedy on March 17, 1961.

Photograph of King Bhumibol of Thailand decorated with medals of honor. A gift to Kennedy in 1963.

Photograph of President Miguel Ydigoras Fuentes of Guatemala decorated with medals of honor. A gift to Kennedy in 1961.

A gift to Kennedy from the people of New Ross, Ireland, on his trip to that country in June 1963.

K-60-29: A gift to Kennedy from Prince Rainier of Monaco, husband of film star Grace Kelly.

K-61-46: Simón Bolívar medal, presented to Kennedy in Venezuela.

K-61-31: Notre Dame Laetare gold medal, presented to Kennedy on November 22, 1961. This image is from the summer 1961 issue of *Notre Dame*.

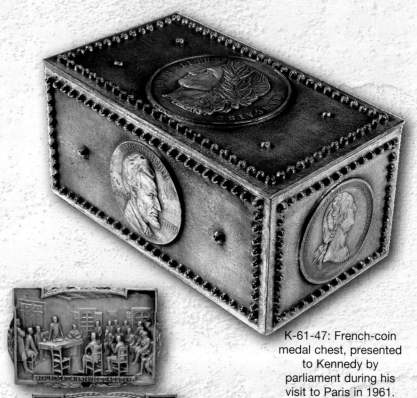

K-61-47: French-coin medal chest, presented to Kennedy by parliament during his visit to Paris in 1961.

K-61-48: José Gervasio Artigas medal, given to Kennedy from Uruguay.

K-61-33: Awarded to Kennedy from the Radio and Television Executives Society for his televised press conferences.

K-61-49:
100th Anniversary of Italian Unification medal, presented to Kennedy from Italy.

K-61-57: Knight Grand Cross of the
Equestrian Order of the Holy Sepulchre
of Jerusalem. Presented to Kennedy by
His Beatitude Benedictos of Jerusalem.

K-61-52: Presented to Kennedy
during his visit to Columbia in 1961.

K-61-53: A gift to Kennedy from
La Société Arthus-Bertrand in Paris, France.

K-62-9: Mexico City medal of honor, given to Kennedy
during his presidential visit on June 29, 1962.

K-62-12: Presented to Kennedy by Prime Minister David Ben-Gurion of
Israel, honoring the 10th anniversary of the death of Chaim Weizmann.

The President and the National Rifle Association

In 1961, John F. Kennedy was awarded lifetime membership in the National Rifle Association of America (NRA) by its executive vice president, Franklin L. Orth.

Founded in 1871, the NRA places significant emphasis on the Second Amendment to the United States Constitution, which protects the right of individuals to keep and bear arms. The NRA patterns itself as America's longest-standing civil rights organization and is an influential political group. It promotes firearm safety, marksmanship, and self-defense training.

In a letter of reply to NRA executive Orth, Kennedy accepts his membership, praising the role that the Association fills in the national defense effort.

Colt presentation New Frontier revolvers, a gift to President Kennedy.

Kennedy visits a gun factory in 1963.

NATIONAL RIFLE ASSOCIATION OF AMERICA
INCORPORATED 1871
1600 RHODE ISLAND AVENUE
WASHINGTON 6, D.C.

OFFICE OF THE
EXECUTIVE VICE PRESIDENT

March 7, 1961

The Honorable John F. Kennedy
President of the United States
The White House
Washington, D. C.

Dear Mr. President:

In a recent address you referred to the need of a nation of Minutemen. In the category of "bearing arms" the Minuteman heritage is preserved today in its basic form by the members of the National Rifle Association of America. Throughout its long history of almost a hundred years, this Association has been dedicated to the promotion of the social welfare and public safety, law and order, and the national defense; and to the education and training of citizens of good repute in the safe and efficient handling of small arms. Through our 400,000 individual members, 10,000 chartered clubs and close affiliation with the Armed Forces, we encourage rifle and pistol shooting and conduct competitive contests to further these objectives.

Our endeavors involve individual participation in an art which historically bears the burdens of defense in times of crisis. Traditionally, Americans have been renowned in their skill with firearms in conflicts past. Now, through competitive shooting and the hunting sports, we are increasing the knowledge of young Americans in these important skills through our dynamic program. This is a tremendous asset in our arsenal of democracy and represents a strength of citizenship in being.

In the spirit of the Minutemen of 1776, and to your leadership of today in calling for a nation of Minutemen, "citizens who are not only prepared to take up arms but citizens who regard the preservation of freedom as a basic purpose of their daily life," we pledge our unstinting efforts.

We would be highly honored if you would accept a Life Membership in the National Rifle Association of America in support of our endeavors to contribute to this concept.

Cordially yours,

Franklin L. Orth
Executive Vice President

Letter to President Kennedy from Franklin L. Orth of the NRA.

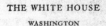

THE WHITE HOUSE

WASHINGTON

March 20, 1961

Dear Mr. Orth:

On the occasion of Patriots Day, I wish to offer my congratulations and best wishes to the National Rifle Association of America which over the past years has done credit to our country by the outstanding achievements of its members in the art of shooting.

Through competitive matches and sports in coordination with the National Board for the Promotion of Rifle Practice, the Association fills an important role in our national defense effort, and fosters in an active and meaningful fashion the spirit of the Minutemen.

I am pleased to accept Life Membership in the National Rifle Association and extend to your organization every good wish for continued success.

Sincerely,

Mr. Franklin L. Orth
Executive Vice President
National Rifle Association
of America
1600 Rhode Island Avenue
Washington 6, D. C.

President Kennedy's reply
to Franklin L. Orth.

10

Satirical and Critical Pieces

Anti-Kennedy Sentiment

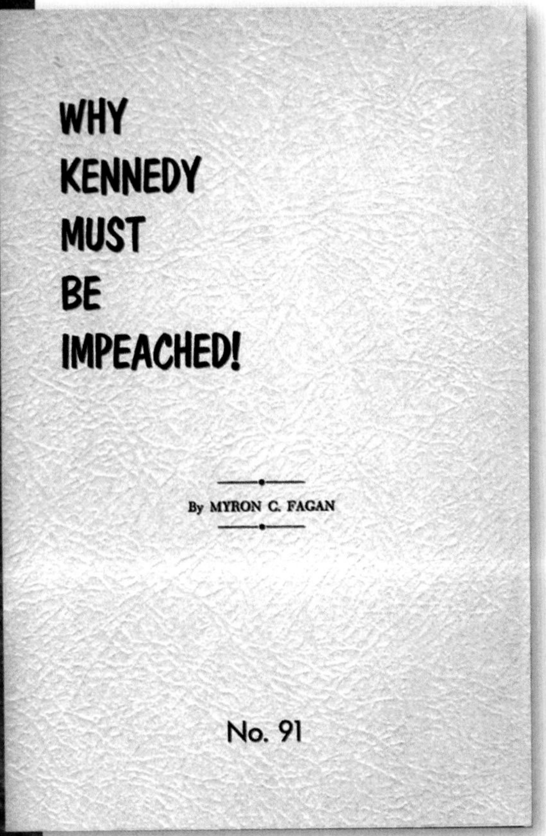

**WHY
KENNEDY
MUST
BE
IMPEACHED!**

By MYRON C. FAGAN

No. 91

Published by the Cinema Educational Guild in 1962.

The detractors of the Kennedy administration in the 1950s and early 1960s were mainly Southerners and Republicans. There was great anxiety felt by those in power who feared losing control over a way of life that had been in place for hundreds of years. For the most part, this control resided in two separate areas: those attempting to keep minorities in their place and stem the tide of the advancing Civil Rights movement, and the larger power structure with a controlling economic force that reached beyond the borders of the United States and into the global arena.

While the first group exercised their misguided views at the street level, the other and more powerful group wielded this power to change governments and affect the lives of millions around the world. It operated in secrecy, with clandestine meetings on a golf course in Vir-

For the Collector and Historian

While anti-Kennedy medals and memorabilia are certainly not as popular as those in support of JFK, there is a niche market for collectors interested in this unique part of Kennedy history.

A 6-1/2-by-3-1/2–inch negative campaign card, printed by the Christian Nationalist Crusade for the 1960 presidential campaign, sold at auction in 2013 for $132. On one side, the card reads "Stop Kennedy. Why?" The opposing side lists seven reasons not to vote for him.

Satire of President Kennedy's welfare bill.

ginia or in a box seat at a racetrack in California. This influential group looked beyond national issues and focused instead on the global economy. President Kennedy had spoken of this group during an address to the American Newspaper Publishers Association in April 1961, and had a thorough understanding of the problems it caused and its disregard for the U.S. Constitution.

Formed in earlier presidential administrations, a third and more dangerous element existed that worked in the shadows. Under the cloak of national security, this element had obtained an annual budget that could not be officially audited by the American public; it was kept that way with the help of compromised elected officials. Members of this group went wherever they wanted, did what they wanted, and over time became a separate and invisible branch of the U.S. government.

A shopkeeper posts a sign in his store window prohibiting John F. and Robert F. Kennedy from entering.

After the failure of the Bay of Pigs and the subsequent high-level firings by the Kennedy administration, President Kennedy had publicly discussed his desire to reassign the power and duties of this organization to other U.S. security agencies. This set off alarms within all branches of the military-industrial security circles and more fuel was added to the anti-Kennedy bonfire.

Many theories implicating other anti-Kennedy factions have been presented over the years—from Nikita Khrushchev's involvement to Fidel Castro's revenge over an earlier failed assassination attempt devised by the Central Intelligence Agency. Countless theories and many later claims, well heralded by the national media, proved to be diversions and not to have any substance in fact.

To this day the anti-Kennedy movement is alive and well. It seems that not a month goes by without a new allegation of misconduct or scandal attempting to drive another tabloid nail into the Kennedy coffins. However, the devotion and service of the Kennedy family to the Constitution and republic of the United States has weathered the test of time. Nevertheless, as President Kennedy himself said, "Friends come and go. . . but a good enemy lasts forever."

K-S-5

K-S-6

Robert Bashlow's Catholic States of America Medal

This 32 mm satirical anti–John F. Kennedy medal was struck in London, England, by the John Pinches Company and was the design of the famous—and infamous—entrepreneur and numismatic coin dealer Robert Bashlow. The medal, produced and sold by the Robert Bashlow Company, located at 14 Washington Place in New York City, was supposedly a practical joke. It is dated 1963. The implication meant by the medal was that by the end of 1963, the Catholic Church would be poised to take over the entire American political scene.

Bashlow had many varied interests that he personally financed. He published books, not only on numismatics but also on human sexuality, Vietnam-era draft dodging, and music. Bashlow was a close friend of numismatic icon Walter Breen, who also wrote many books on coin history.

Years later, Bashlow was evicted from his Riverside Drive apartment in New York City for failure to pay his rent on time and fighting with his landlord. At the time of his eviction by marshals, many of his personal items disappeared.

The *New York Times* reported that in July 1979, Robert Bashlow was one of two Americans who perished in a fire at the Hotel Corona de Aragón in Zaragoza, Spain, when a pastry machine exploded in the kitchen of the hotel. A total of 80 souls died in the ensuing fire or from injuries sustained therein.

The Bashlow John F. Kennedy medal was produced in the following amounts with a plain, smooth edge:

K-S-2: 32 mm, bronze with a mintage of 1,200 pieces.

K-S-2A: 32 mm, silver with a mintage of 75 pieces.

K-S-2B: 32 mm, gold, .916 fine, with a mintage of 3 pieces.

It is reported that one K-S-2B is housed in the Smithsonian Institution in Washington, D.C.

K-S-2

The *Amarillo Globe-News*, April 5, 1999

DALLAS (AP)–Spray paint–wielding vandals caused thousands of dollars worth of damage over the weekend to the John F. Kennedy Memorial.

The black-and-red graffiti on the interior walls of the downtown memorial might have been done by a hate group because of the painted images, including a swastika, said Officer Leroy Quigg of the Dallas police gang unit.

Police believe the vandalism occurred late Friday night or Saturday morning. Cleanup should be completed in a few days, officials at the nearby Sixth Floor Museum said.

The monument attracts about 500,000 visitors annually. It also was vandalized in 1997.

The memorial, built in 1970, consists of 50-foot-high white concrete walls that surround a square black marble slab bearing the name of the president, who was assassinated nearby in 1963. It is owned by the city and Dallas County, with the county responsible for providing security.

John Nagel, a staff member at the nearby Conspiracy Museum, said he noticed the spray paint Saturday afternoon while leading a tour group.

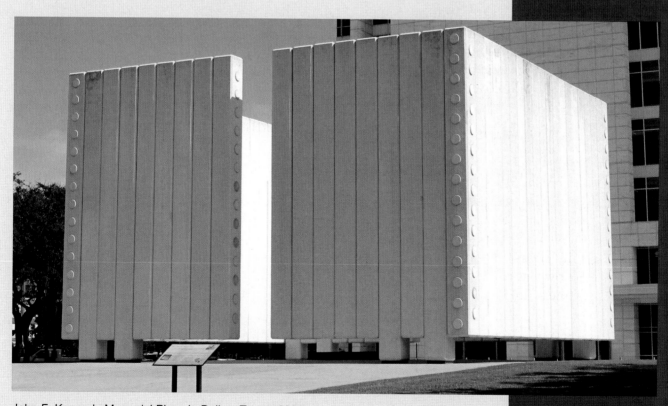

John F. Kennedy Memorial Plaza in Dallas, Texas, 2009.

11

JFK, Jacqueline Kennedy, and Their Children

A likeness of Jacqueline Kennedy Onassis by Hai Yan.

First Lady

Jacqueline Lee Bouvier was born in Southampton, New York, in July 1929. Throughout her childhood, "Jackie," as she was known by friends and, later, the media, was involved in a variety of extracurricular activities, from equestrianism to ballet to learning foreign languages.

For the Collector and Historian

While many Kennedy collectors focus on the president, there is no shortage of coins, tokens, medals, and other memorabilia relating to his wife, Jacqueline, and their two children, Caroline and John Jr.

A patron of the arts during her tenure at the White House, Jackie Kennedy is perhaps today more widely known as a fashion icon. While fashions change, her personal style continues to be emulated by designers around the world. A gold-gilt metal cross brooch and a gold-gilt metal bead necklace, from the estate of Jackie Kennedy, sold for $32,124 in 2013. That same year, a stunning black velvet two-piece outfit worn by Jackie was sold at auction for $39,600.

Personal correspondence can be a sensitive subject for collectors and dealers. In May 2014, a trove of letters written by Jackie to the Reverend Joseph Leonard before and during her marriage to JFK, and after his assassination, were withdrawn from a planned auction. The Dublin, Ireland, Catholic church that owned the letters announced that "Representatives of All Hallows College and the Vincentian Fathers are now exploring with members of Mrs. Kennedy's family how best to preserve and curate this archive for the future."

After his unexpected death in 1999, collectors became more interested in John Jr. memorabilia than ever before. A collector purchased a baby shirt belonging to John Jr. for $660 in 2013. A birthday card for his father, signed by two-year-old John Jr., was also sold at auction for $17,000 in 2013.

She attended Vassar College, where she studied literature, history, art, and foreign languages, and spent her junior year studying abroad in Paris, France. It was during this year away that Jackie began to cultivate her passion for knowledge and culture, a passion which would later materialize in her role as First Lady.

Starting in 1951, she worked for the *Washington Times-Herald*, interviewing her future husband's presidential rival Richard Nixon for her column. It was during this time that she met John F. Kennedy and the two were married in September 1953.

Jackie was a driving force behind her husband's 1960 presidential campaign. She often accompanied him as he traveled throughout the country and was well liked by the voters they encountered. However, during the campaign, she learned that she was pregnant with their second child and was instructed by her doctors to remain at home. This did not stop Jackie: from her house she answered campaign letters, gave interviews, and wrote a weekly column which was distributed nationwide.

As First Lady, Jacqueline Kennedy worked to restore the interior of the White House, which she felt lacked historical significance. She also initiated the publication of the first White House guidebook and called for a congressional bill awarding possession of the White House furnishings to the Smithsonian Institution. Jackie firmly believed that the White House should be a beacon of American history and culture.

She took an interest in the preservation of historic architecture. Following the assassination of her husband, Jackie initiated the creation of the John F. Kennedy Presidential Library and Museum, choosing renowned architect I.M. Pei to design the building. In New York City, she led a campaign to renovate Grand Central Station, and during her time in the White House she sought to stop the destruction of historic buildings in Lafayette Square.

In 1968, Jackie married Greek shipping magnate Aristotle Onassis. They were married until his death in 1975. A devoted mother, wife, and preserver of cultural heritage, Jacqueline Kennedy Onassis died on May 19, 1994. She was laid to rest beside her first husband, President Kennedy, in Arlington National Cemetery.

View of the restored Red Room in the White House, May 8, 1962.

K-71-49

K-61-57A: Dame Grand Cross of the Equestrian Order of the Holy Sepulchre of Jerusalem. Presented to Jacqueline Kennedy by His Beatitude Benedictos of Jerusalem.

K-84-5

K-61-58: A gift from the First Lady of Columbia.

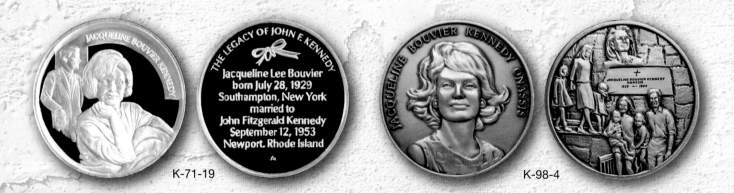

K-71-19

K-98-4

K-2001-3. *See chapter 17.*

K-2002-3. *See chapter 17.*

K-2009-15: Unique Italian cameo of
Jacqueline Kennedy carved from a
sardonyx shell from the Bahamas.
Created by Paolo Scognamiglio for
this publication.

K-2002-4. *See chapter 17.*

K-63A-7F

K-2009-14K

K-63A-265

New York City Municipal Art Society Jacqueline Kennedy Onassis Annual Award Medal

This medal, originally called the President's Medal, was renamed for Jacqueline Kennedy Onassis after her death in 1994 in honor of her tireless efforts to preserve and protect New York's great architecture.

The current and past presidents of the Municipal Art Society choose each year's recipient. The medal is given to an individual who, by his or her work and deeds, has made an outstanding contribution to the city of New York.

The sculptor was Daniel Chester French. Each medal is solid bronze and measures 102 mm.

K-94-4 obverse: The original seal of the New York City Municipal Art Society, established in 1893.

K-94-4 reverse: This medal was struck for the author and engraved for this book.

Jackie O Silver Round

Five years after the death of her husband John F. Kennedy, and just a few short months after the murder of Robert F. Kennedy, Jacqueline Kennedy, fearing for the safety of herself and her children, married Aristotle Onassis. Jacqueline left the United States with her children and took up residence on the Greek island of Skorpios. Onassis's 25-year-old son Alexander, a flight instructor who introduced John F. Kennedy Jr. to flying, was mysteriously killed on January 22, 1973, in a private-plane crash. (John F. Kennedy Jr. also died in a mysterious plane crash, in 1999.)

It is rumored that shortly after investigating his son's death, Onassis hired investigators to look into the assassinations of John and Robert F. Kennedy. He was about to make an important announcement in 1975 on the findings when clandestine photographs of Jacqueline privately sunbathing surfaced in the German press. The source of the 14 photographs was reported to be paparazzi on an offshore boat using telephoto lenses on their cameras. Another story later surfaced that Italian paparazzo Sittimio Garritano, posing as a gardener, took the pictures.

The grace and dignity of Jacqueline Kennedy well overshadowed the revealing photographs shown in publications around the world, including *Hustler* magazine. However, the incident may have shown Aristotle Onassis that, where a photograph could be taken on his private island, a rifle scope could have the same view. The findings of Onassis's investigations were never made public. He passed away that same year, never revealing any information concerning the deaths of John, Robert, and Alexander.

An advertisement in the August 1975 issue of *Hustler* magazine promoted this so-called coin as a pure silver, limited serial-numbered edition of only 500. Promoted by Leisure Time Products, the "coin" came with a certificate of authenticity stating it was manufactured and struck by the Pacific Mint in 1975.

K-75-9

play courage and idealism within the political arena. The award is named for her father's Pulitzer Prize–winning book.

Caroline Kennedy was appointed ambassador to Japan by President Barack Obama in 2013.

K-2009-14M

The Kennedy Children

Caroline Bouvier Kennedy

Born in 1957, Caroline Kennedy was only three years old when her father took the presidential oath of office. As a child at the White House, Caroline was the recipient of multiple gifts of state, including a puppy from Nikita Khrushchev and a pony from Lyndon Johnson. However, Caroline was remarkably unspoiled and was known to be a well-rounded and often shy child.

Following the assassination of President Kennedy, Jacqueline moved her children to an apartment on Fifth Avenue in New York City. Caroline received her Bachelor of Arts from Radcliffe College in 1980, and, while working at the Metropolitan Museum of Art, she met her future husband, exhibit designer Edwin Schlossberg. In 1988 she followed in the footsteps of her uncles, Robert and Edward, and received her law degree. She is a member of both the New York and Washington, D.C., bar associations.

In 1989, along with other members of her family, Caroline created the Profile in Courage award, which recognizes public officials who dis-

John Fitzgerald Kennedy Jr.

Strands of Love figurine: Jacqueline with son John Jr.

K-71-29

K-99-2

K-88-17

K-99-3. *See chapter 17.*

K-2009-14L

John F. Kennedy Jr. was born only 17 days after his father was elected to the presidency. One of the most iconic images of John Jr. was taken at President Kennedy's funeral procession, during which the young boy saluted his father's casket as it passed by.

John Jr. graduated from Brown University in 1983 with a Bachelor of Arts degree in history. While he spent some time working at the Center for Democratic Policy, he was unsure whether he wanted to pursue a career in the "family business" of politics. Instead, John Jr. had a passion for acting, and performed on the stage during his time at Brown. He later performed in New York City.

After receiving his law degree from the New York University School of Law in 1989, John Jr.

served as a prosecutor in the Manhattan district attorney's office. Six years later, he founded *George*, a political and lifestyle monthly magazine.

John Jr. received his pilot's license in 1998, an act which distressed his sister, Caroline, who thought it a risky endeavor. On July 16, 1999, John Jr. flew both his wife, Carolyn Bessette-Kennedy, and her sister Lauren to a wedding in Martha's Vineyard, Massachusetts. The plane failed to arrive as scheduled at Martha's Vineyard Airport, and days later the bodies of John Jr. and his passengers were found.

The ashes of John F. Kennedy Jr. were scattered from the Navy destroyer USS *Briscoe* on July 22, 1999.

Patrick Bouvier Kennedy: The President Says Goodbye to His Son

In August 1963, Patrick Kennedy, the second son of John and Jacqueline Kennedy, was born prematurely. Due to an affliction of the lungs, he lived only two days after his birth.

Upon being told that his son had passed away, the president was heard to say, "He put up quite a fight. He was a beautiful baby." With his wife miles away in recuperation, the president of the United States of America went upstairs alone to the hospital room where he had slept the night before, sat on the bed, and cried.

Baby Patrick's funeral and internment took place at Holyhood Cemetery, close to the home where his father had been born. At the service, the president removed a gold Saint Christopher's medal from around his neck—a gift from his wife at their wedding—and with God's and parents' love, he placed the medal inside his son's casket and said goodbye.

Following President Kennedy's assassination, Patrick Kennedy was reinterred on December 3, 1963, alongside his father at Arlington National Cemetery.

The St. Christopher's medal pictured here is not the medal placed in Patrick's casket. It is similar to the medal that was worn by President Kennedy's first son, John Fitzgerald Kennedy Jr.

The Kennedy Rocker

With the exception of the axe used by the first U.S. president, George Washington, when he chopped down the cherry tree, the title of the most outstanding piece of presidential memorabilia must belong to the famous Kennedy rocking chair, made by the P&P Chair Company of Ashboro, North Carolina, and upholstered for the White House by Larry Arata.

John F. Kennedy was only six years old when Arata began work at the Shaw Furniture Company in Boston, Massachusetts. Seven years later the strain of the Great Depression resulted in the closure of the oldest furniture company in America. However, Arata wisely decided to continue doing the work he loved best. In 1930, he opened a small upholstery shop on Cape Cod with his brother Louis.

Building a reputation for quality, Arata's efforts were rewarded when his work was noticed by Jacqueline Kennedy in 1961. He soon found himself Washington-bound with a job as the first resident upholsterer in the history of the White House.

The president's physician, Janet Travell, suggested that the president's existing rocking chair, which he had possessed since his Senate days, needed strengthening. This brought Arata to an examination of the chair and the discovery that it did not properly fit the chief executive. Drawing on his years of experience, Arata set out to construct a new, better-quality rocking

The Kennedy Rocker.

The inscription reads, "To William and Patricia Rice. As the world was inspired by our beloved President Kennedy so may your inspirations always rise like a fountain. Larry and Norma Arata, April 1975."

chair. The result was a piece of furniture constructed with health, longevity, and beauty in mind. Little did Arata know that the product of his labor would become one of the lasting symbols of the 35th president's New Frontier.

The rocker, constructed from North Carolina oak, weighs 43 pounds. It has been balanced and designed to fit both men and women, regardless of weight or height. The steam-bent curved back posts sweep inward, providing the maximum back support possible.

The honey-white custom upholstered cushions were made using the highest-quality rubber and the chair has a medium-brown fruitwood finish. Later improvements to the style were made, including a custom headrest, a felt-covered writing board, and a foot stool for added comfort.

President Kennedy's successor, Lyndon B. Johnson, had an identical rocker made by Arata; the color of his upholstery was chocolate brown. The chair in the photos is the chair made by Arata for this author.

Arata married Norma Zandrino on February 20, 1963, while both were working for President Kennedy. They resided in McLean, Virginia, where they customized chairs up until Arata's passing in September 1979.

Larry, Norma, and I corresponded several times during the early 1970s and what a pure pleasure it was to have known this wonderful and caring couple. Norma ended our last conversation years ago with a quote by Will Rogers that was a favorite of Larry's: "It is great to be great, but it is greater to be human."

K-71-40

This Kennedy Rocker was presented to President Kennedy by the commander of carrier division one and the crew of the USS *Kitty Hawk* during the president's visit to San Diego, California, on June 6, 1963. This chair is on display at the John F. Kennedy Library and Museum in Boston, Massachusetts.

12

The Assassination

Assassination of John F. Kennedy

On November 21, 1963, President Kennedy and his wife arrived in Texas to tour the state with Governor John B. Connally Jr. and Senator Ralph Yarborough. The following day, on November 22, 1963, Kennedy was assassinated while driving through Dallas amongst crowds that had gathered to cheer the president's arrival. Taken to Parkland Hospital, he was pronounced dead that afternoon.

Only hours later, police arrested Lee Harvey Oswald for the murder of J.D. Tippit, a Dallas police officer. Oswald was subsequently charged with the assassination of the president, although he claimed that he had not shot either Kennedy or Tippit.

President Kennedy and his wife, Jacqueline, on November 22, 1963, in Dallas, Texas. Minutes later, Kennedy was assassinated.

For the Collector and Historian

The holy grail of the Kennedy collectors' world is an item directly related to the assassination of John F. Kennedy. Avid collectors seek out memorabilia from that tragic day in Dallas and will often pay thousands of dollars for it. However, there are many medals memorializing his assassination, and these are readily available in the marketplace for much lower prices.

Perhaps one of the most expensive Kennedy-related items ever sold is the white 1963 Lincoln Continental used to convey JFK, Jackie Kennedy, and Texas governor John Connally to Carswell Air Force Base on the morning of the assassination. Designated "Limo One," this was the last vehicle to safely carry the president before his death in Dallas mere hours later. It sold for $318,000 in 2013.

Less extravagant—yet still significant—was the original Dallas police-department badge worn by Officer James M. Chaney during the 1963 motorcade in which Kennedy was assassinated. Chaney was on a police motorcycle 15 feet behind the president when JFK was shot. This remarkable item sold for $3,503 in 2014.

On November 24, 1963, while handcuffed to Detective James Leavelle, Oswald was fatally shot by Jack Ruby, a Dallas nightclub owner.

The Warren Commission, an investigative task force created by President Lyndon B. Johnson, sought to uncover the mystery surrounding Kennedy's assassination. While the Warren Commission stated that Oswald had acted alone, it was unable to convincingly explain the murder. A later investigation in 1979 explored the possibility of a second gunman.

The Commission presented its report to President Johnson in September 1964. The report was published that year; 142,918 copies of the 888-page document were sold. The Commission's hearings were also published in 26 volumes. 4,000 sets were printed, and the majority of sets were sold to libraries for in-house research. A reported 2,316 sets were destroyed.

In volume five of the 26-volume set, Jack Ruby is recorded as saying to Chief Justice Warren,

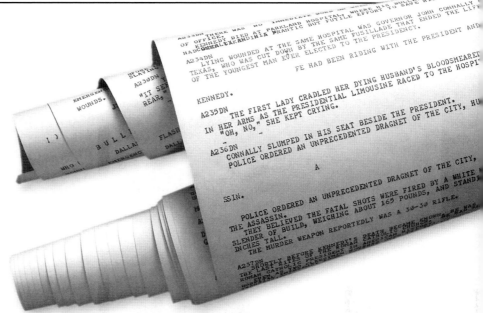

Army Corps of Engineers teletype dated November 22, 1963—the day of President Kennedy's assassination.

"Get me out of Dallas and I will tell you things that will shock the world. A whole new form of government is going to take over the country and I will not live to see you again."

One of the most notorious crimes of the 20th century, the true story behind the assassination of John F. Kennedy remains a mystery.

K-71-45

K-70-6

K-65-13

K-2014-2

K-2008-9

K-2009-1

K-63A-329

Assassination Scene Medal

In November 1964, there was quite a bit of confusion at the Karlsruhe State Mint in Germany over which Kennedy assassination medal should be struck for delivery to American customers. Distributor Deutsche Numismatik in Frankfurt-Main had to clarify the situation through a Nebraska Numismatics bulletin.

The firm explained:

> Number of trial pieces struck were three of the small size, 13 grams and 30 millimeters in silver, and three of the large size, 70 grams and 60 millimeters in silver. Dies of the small size are to be destroyed. The large size with the Oswald reverse is now being struck for export only. This large size is from the same dies as the three large size trial strikes, so that it was impossible to tell the copies sold to Americans and others outside Germany from the trial impressions.
>
> All medals with DALLAS 1963 now bear the inscription (on obverse), DALLAS MCMLXII. The 1963 imprint was on an old die used erroneously by the Karlsruhe Mint.
>
> Several pieces with the imprint XX DUK 986 were also erroneously struck and sold; thereafter the misprint was noted. Actually, this XX DUK 986 is only for the large golden 20 ducats, for which the size 60 millimeters is the same.
>
> The large 60 millimeter silver dies with the Oswald reverse are now being used for export production. The entire number of silver medals has been limited to 10,000 pieces.

The medals could be purchased directly from Deutsche Numismatik for $12.50 plus $1.00 postage. At the time, officials at the distributing firm noted that some customers received the erroneous medals with the 1963 date and others received the correct MCMLXIII date; because of this, a certain amount of confusion resulted.

Examples of these medals were struck by the Karlsruhe Mint in Germany. Reeded-edge varieties were struck in Italy and additional sizes in gold and silver were struck by Numismatica Venezolana, the Italcambio affiliate for South America.

K-63A-76: U.S-only reverse.

K-63A-77: Europe-only reverse.

K-63A-77G: Little is known about the Cusus ut Memoria Vivat reverse, which was struck sometime before the end of 1966.

A Day in Dallas

Wanted For Treason

This handbill was passed out in Dallas, Texas, by agitators along the parade route while the president's motorcade passed by on November 22, 1963. Following Kennedy's assassination, the Warren Commission sent U.S. Secret Service agents to track down the author and printer of the handbill. Working from late November 1963 to May 1964, the agents found that Robert G. Klause had printed the flyer and that Robert Alan Surrey had ordered it.

When Robert Alan Surrey testified before the Commission on June 16, 1964, he took the Fifth on all questions concerning the leaflet. His testimony can be found in volume five of the report by the Warren Commission on the hearings and testimony regarding the Kennedy assassination.

Surrey was an associate of retired U.S. Army general Edwin A. Walker. In April 1961, President Kennedy ordered Secretary of Defense Robert McNamara to investigate stories that Walker, an active-duty Army general, was trying to indoctrinate his troops in the ways of the John Birch Society. The Society, which was headquartered in Dallas, preached that multiple presidents and government officials, including John F. Kennedy, were controlled by Communists. Although no evidence was found against General Walker, he was reassigned to Hawaii. He instead chose to resign, with President Kennedy accepting his resignation. Shortly after, General Walker returned to civilian life and local politics in the state of Texas. Whether Walker had any involvement with this handbill remains unknown.

WANTED

FOR

TREASON

THIS MAN is wanted for treasonous activities against the United States:

1. Betraying the Constitution (which he swore to uphold):
   He is turning the sovereignty of the U.S. over to the communist controlled United Nations.
   He is betraying our friends (Cuba, Katanga, Portugal) and befriending our enemies (Russia, Yugoslavia, Poland).

2. He has been WRONG on innumerable issues affecting the security of the U.S. (United Nations-Berlin wall-Missle removal-Cuba-Wheat deals-Test Ban Treaty, etc.)

3. He has been lax in enforcing Communist Registration laws.

4. He has given support and encouragement to the Communist inspired racial riots.

5. He has illegally invaded a sovereign State with federal troops.

6. He has consistantly appointed Anti-Christians to Federal office: Upholds the Supreme Court in its Anti-Christian rulings.
   Aliens and known Communists abound in Federal offices.

7. He has been caught in fantastic LIES to the American people (including personal ones like his previous marraige and divorce).

Welcome Mr. Kennedy to Dallas

Also seen on the day of Kennedy's assassination was an anti-Kennedy flyer printed that morning in the *Dallas Morning News.* This flyer, authored by a group calling themselves the American Fact-Finding Committee, strongly criticized Kennedy for possessing what they believed to be Communist affiliations and sympathies.

14—Section 1   The Dallas Morning News   Friday, November 22, 1963

WELCOME MR. KENNEDY
TO DALLAS...

. . . A CITY so disgraced by a recent Liberal smear attempt that its citizens have just elected two more Conservative Americans to public office.

. . . A CITY that is an economic "boom town," not because of Federal handouts, but through conservative economic and business practices.

. . . A CITY that will continue to grow and prosper despite efforts by you and your administration to penalize it for its non-conformity to "New Frontierism."

. . . A CITY that rejected your philosophy and policies in 1960 and will do so again in 1964—even more emphatically than before.

MR. KENNEDY, despite contentions on the part of your administration, the State Department, the Mayor of Dallas, the Dallas City Council, and members of your party, we free-thinking and America-thinking citizens of Dallas still have, through a Constitution largely ignored by you, the right to address our grievances, to question you, to disagree with you, and to criticize you.

In asserting this constitutional right, we wish to ask you publicly the following questions—indeed, questions of paramount importance and interest to all free peoples everywhere—which we trust you will answer . . . in public, without sophistry. These questions are:

WHY is Latin America turning either anti-American or Communistic, or both, despite increased U. S. foreign aid, State Department policy, and your own Ivy-Tower pronouncements?

WHY do you say we have built a "wall of freedom" around Cuba when there is no freedom in Cuba today? Because of your policy, thousands of Cubans have been imprisoned, are starving and being persecuted—with thousands already murdered and thousands more awaiting execution and, in addition, the entire population of almost 7,000,000 Cubans are living in slavery.

WHY have you approved the sale of wheat and corn to our enemies when you know the Communist soldiers "travel on their stomachs" just as ours do? Communist soldiers are daily wounding and/or killing American soldiers in South Viet Nam.

WHY did you host, salute and entertain Tito — Moscow's Trojan Horse — just a short time after our sworn enemy, Khrushchev, embraced the Yugoslav dictator as a great hero and leader of Communism?

WHY have you urged greater aid, comfort, recognition, and understanding for Yugoslavia, Poland, Hungary, and other Communist countries, while turning your back on the pleas of Hungarian, East German, Cuban and other anti-Communist freedom fighters?

WHY did Cambodia kick the U.S. out of its country after we poured nearly 400 Million Dollars of aid into its ultra-leftist government?

WHY has Gus Hall, head of the U.S. Communist Party praised almost every one of your policies and announced that the party will endorse and support your re-election in 1964?

WHY have you banned the showing at U.S. military bases of the film "Operation Abolition"—the movie by the House Committee on Un-American Activities exposing Communism in America?

WHY have you ordered or permitted your brother Bobby, the Attorney General, to go soft on Communists, fellow-travelers, and ultra-leftists in America, while permitting him to persecute loyal Americans who criticize you, your administration, and your leadership?

WHY are you in favor of the U.S. continuing to give economic aid to Argentina, in spite of that fact that Argentina has just seized almost 400 Million Dollars of American private property?

WHY has the Foreign Policy of the United States degenerated to the point that the C.I.A. is arranging coups and having staunch Anti-Communist Allies of the U.S. bloodily exterminated.

WHY have you scrapped the Monroe Doctrine in favor of the "Spirit of Moscow"?

MR. KENNEDY, as citizens of these United States of America, we DEMAND answers to these questions, and we want them NOW.

THE AMERICAN FACT-FINDING COMMITTEE
"An unaffiliated and non-partisan group of citizens who wish truth"

BERNARD WEISSMAN,
Chairman

P.O. Box 1792 — Dallas 21, Texas

Celebrating Kennedy

Never before has man had such capacity to control his own environment, to end thirst and hunger, to conquer poverty and disease, to banish illiteracy and massive human misery. We have the power to make this the best generation of mankind in the history of the world—or make it the last.

—*John F. Kennedy, September 20, 1963*

13

Mourning and Remembering the President

The Loss of a Great Man

A John F. Kennedy shrine in Dallas, Texas, in 1973.

Following his assassination, the body of President Kennedy was returned to the White House on November 23, 1963. Pallbearers brought the mahogany casket to the East Room, where it was draped with black crepe. Kennedy's body remained in the East Room for 24 hours, where it was attended by family members, friends, and government officials.

On Sunday, November 24, Kennedy's casket was carried by a horse-drawn caisson along Pennsylvania Avenue amidst a mourning crowd of thousands. Ken-

For the Collector and Historian

Presidential memorial medals and tokens are among the most commonly seen pieces that commemorate John F. Kennedy. These can easily be found in the secondary market in coin-shop inventories, in online auction venues like eBay, and at coin and collectibles shows. Many of the more common pieces, such as aluminum and brass gas-station tokens, can be located, with some searching, for less than a dollar. Flea markets, antique shops and malls, yard sales, and similar venues can bear fruit for the patient collector.

Among the most sought-after memorial items are those relating directly to JFK's funeral. In 2013, a set of seven signatures of Kennedy's pallbearers sold for $1,560. Five vintage color photographs of the funeral procession also sold that year for $900.

John F. Kennedy memorial in Hyannis, Massachusetts, 2005.

A young girl places flowers in front of a John F. Kennedy memorial bust.

nedy's body would lie in state at the Capitol Rotunda. Here, Jacqueline Kennedy and her daughter Caroline knelt beside the casket that held their beloved husband and father. Following eulogies given by Chief Justice Earl Warren and other government officials, the Rotunda was opened to the public. Hundreds of thousands waited in line for up to ten hours to pay their respects to the slain president. The Rotunda stayed open all night to accommodate the multitudes who flocked for one last glimpse of their president.

The following day, more than one million people stood along the route of the funeral procession, which ended at Arlington National Cemetery. Millions more were transfixed by the coverage on television. President Lyndon B. Johnson, sworn in following Kennedy's assassination, marched in the funeral procession alongside his wife and two daughters. He had been advised against doing so, due to the potential risk of a second assassination, but felt that it was

something he must do. When he moved into the Oval Office the following day, Johnson found a letter from Jacqueline Kennedy, thanking him for his participation.

Following the burial services at Arlington, Jacqueline Kennedy lit an eternal flame to shine continuously over her husband's grave. President Johnson declared November 25, 1963, a national day of mourning. The country came to a standstill as it grieved for the loss of its great leader.

K-64-44

K-73-4A

K-65-22: Uniface.

K-74-11A

K-67-17: Uniface.

K-74-12: Uniface.

K-71-57A

K-81-2

K-98-1

K-2007-2

K-98-3

K-2008-7

K-2006-3

K-2008-8

K-2007-1

K-2009-2

K-2009-4

K-2009-14C

K-2009-8

K-2009-16

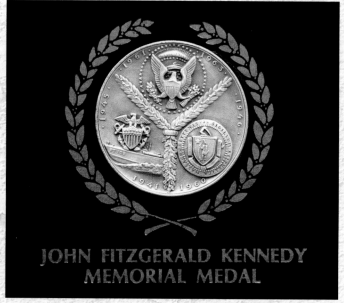

K-63A-1A: Designed by Ralph J. Menconi.

K-63A-6

K-63A-138

K-63A-25A

K-63A-178

K-63A-52

K-63A-212: Uniface.

K-63A-119

K-63A-214: Type one, uniface.

K-63A-215: Type two, uniface.

K-63A-263

K-63A-216: By Gerald Steinberg.

K-63A-327

K-63A-217: By Gerald Steinberg.

K-63A-332

K-63A-259: Uniface.

Remembering Serial Number 2V56

Figurine of Black Jack.

Many years ago, newsman Walter Cronkite produced a two-record LP set, *Sounds of the Sixties*, in remembrance of a 10-year period in American history unlike any other before. Within the multitude of events, speeches, and sounds recorded on this album, one sound hardly noticed or remembered is that of Serial Number 2V56's hooves, recorded on November 25, 1963.

He was named Black Jack and he had the spirit of the great horses throughout history. After that march on the day of John F. Kennedy's funeral, he was embraced by every person who cast their eyes upon him. With Arthur Carlson holding the reins, Black Jack walked into history alongside the likes of Sea Biscuit, Man o' War, and Secretariat. Many who witnessed this procession had the thought that the spirit of the New Frontier and its leader, John Fitzgerald Kennedy, was somehow within the soul of that magnificent animal.

As the caisson moved past the crowd of those saying goodbye to their beloved president, Black Jack danced and tossed his head, as if he was trying to resist going to that day's final destination—Arlington Cemetery. Black Jack had served in hundreds of funerals, but his actions on this day almost suggested that he knew this funeral was different and that after today the world would never be the same—for man or beast.

Black Jack lived 13 more years after the day that the world stopped to honor the 35th president. Army Serial Number 2V56 passed away the year that America celebrated its 200th birthday, but not before taking three U.S. presidents and General Douglas McArthur to their respective final resting places.

The last of the quartermaster-issued horses, Black Jack had earned his apples, hay, and birthday cakes throughout the years of his life, with upwards of 1,000 funerals on his resume. He was buried on February 9, 1976, in Summerall Field at Fort Myer, Virginia. More than 400 people attended his funeral.

K-71-46

Chase Commemorative Society John F. Kennedy Memorial Medal

Almost four years after the assassination of the 35th president, the Chase Commemorative Society (CCS) issued a John F. Kennedy silver medal honoring his memory. This medal was the 11th in a series honoring great men, which include George Washington, Thomas Edison, and Winston Churchill. It was the first medal of the Society's second series. One medal was struck for each member; CCS membership was locked in and not to exceed 1,934. The cost of each membership was $16.90.

The medal's sculptor was Rolf Beck and it was minted in 1967. It is 39 mm, with a reeded edge containing a serial number.

K-67-12

Convention Memorials

K-64-32A

K-64-33

K-64-45

K-63A-225

K-68-47A

K-68-47

K-63A-234: Uniface.

Conception of "What Could Have Been"

By David Lewis

There was magic in the air and President Kennedy was in office. I was 22 and full of ideas and hope for change. I remember him flying over our blue-collar home, always three helicopters for security, and I felt so proud. Local tradesmen talked about working at the Kennedy Compound in Hyannis Port, Massachusetts, and meeting him or Jackie and the kids. People were always talking about the Kennedys—and you didn't say anything bad about them in front of my mother!

Then an assassin's bullet took it all away. For three days, there was no television other than that concerning President Kennedy's death and funeral; the radio played a constant dirge. The country fell silent and mourned.

As the years rolled by, we watched John-John grow into an extraordinary young man who just happened to look like a Greek god. Echoes of past hopes and dreams began to reappear. I waited for him to make his political move. Then that terrible plane crash again took it all away.

After the accident, I sketched a scene of the president and little John-John in an intimate father-and-son moment. I showed it to a friend of mine who was friendly with Senator Ted Kennedy. I suggested a bronze statue for the Kennedy Memorial. He took two copies—one for Caroline and one for the senator. Six weeks passed; then I heard that they thought that it was a good idea, but Caroline had said that "to depict John Jr. as a little boy would detract from his memory." The senator suggested he be depicted as an adult.

My first reaction was that the president had never known his son as an adult. Then the possibilities flooded in—creative, spiritual, mystical. It made so much sense.

My next sketch was the president and John Jr. walking together. The president was barefoot with his pants rolled up and shirt tails out, walking on the beach with his arm on his son's shoulder. John Jr. was in Bermuda shorts and a t-shirt, his head turned toward his dad, their eyes not quite meeting. Another six weeks passed; but Caroline thought it was too intimate a moment. The senator suggested they both be looking at the water. "What Could Have Been" was conceived.

A prominent businessman was interested in the project and got me on the agenda of the monthly meeting at the Chamber of Commerce. Forty-five minutes after my pitch, I received a phone call. The Chamber was very enthusiastic, wanted to be involved, and would do the fundraising.

We approached the Kennedy Memorial Committee to see about placing the life-size statue there. We were turned down. The chairman's father had worked with Jackie, designing the memorial, and there could be no changes.

After many meetings with business and civic committees, it was decided with a unanimous vote of the town council to install the sculpture at the intersection of South Street and Ocean Street, overlooking the inner harbor.

Town council meetings are held on Thursday nights and are covered by the local press. The following morning, the Associated Press had picked up the story and a picture of my sketch. By that afternoon, three Boston TV stations interviewed me, and by Monday morning, I was on *The Today Show*.

The story and sketch of the President walking on the beach with his grown son set off vibrations which went around the world and can still be felt today. The overwhelming majority of people embraced the spirituality and mystical ideas that the image evokes. The next two weeks were a whirlwind; reporters from across the country, Europe, and Asia called for interviews. The Sunday edition of the *New York Times* featured an article on the image and its message.

The *Cape Cod Times* had a negative response. I found out later that they only printed negative letters to the editor. They were told to be controversial to sell more papers. The editorial called the sketch "tacky and odd."

Caroline, still grieving for her brother, came back to the Cape and a friend told her about the controversy. Everybody had an opinion. It was the subject of conversation everywhere. Not wanting her family to be hurt even more, she told us to "put the project in abeyance." My friend and I agreed that the family's feelings came first. It was the death knell for the statue. Caroline and the senator asked the John F. Kennedy Museum to put the bronze maquette on permanent display. It is still there.

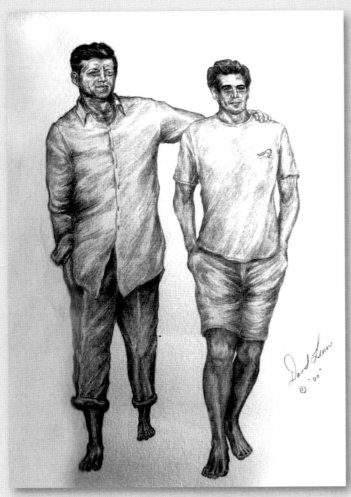

David Lewis's sketch of "What Could Have Been."

The bronze maquette of "What Could Have Been," on display at the John F. Kennedy Presidential Library and Museum.

John F. Kennedy Sports Memorial Amateur Athletic Union Medal

Type One: K-64-31

This is a beautiful issue completed in 1964 as a fundraiser for the Amateur Athletic Union (AAU). It is made of solid cast bronze and is 5-1/2 inches in diameter with a fine sculpted head of a young John F. Kennedy facing right. It is interesting to note that this first issue has coin alignment, unlike the second issue of 1968, which has medal alignment.

Reverse

Obverse

Type Two: K-68-3, Olympic Issue

The first issue of this medallion was restricted to 25,000 pieces, and was distributed exclusively through American Airlines for the benefit of amateur sports in the United States. The obverse shows the Olympic rings and the date 1968. The reverse was changed and the lettering FIRST ISSUE was placed upside down on the center ring. A hole on the reverse allows for a wall mount.

Obverse

Reverse

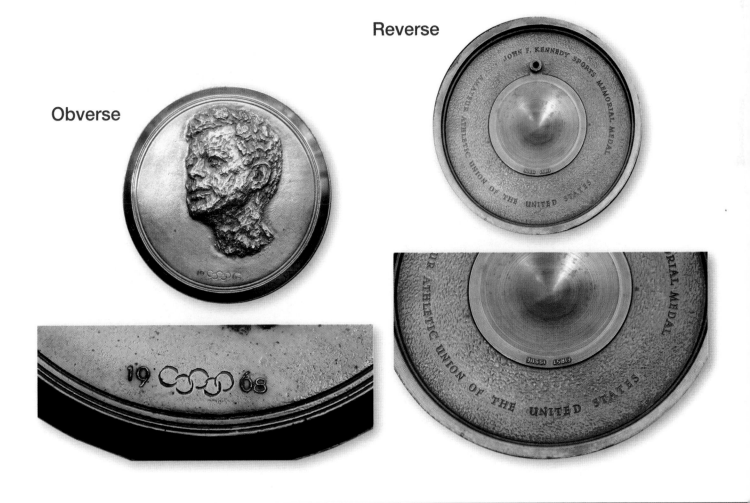

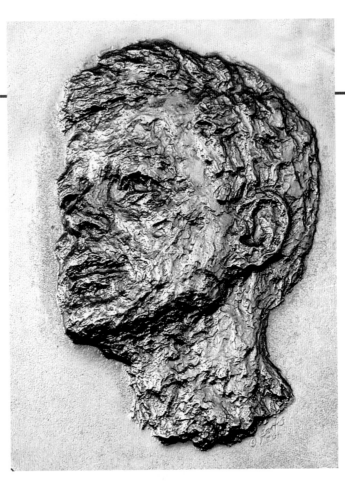

Type Three: K-68-3A

This variety is considered a second issue and was given as a gift of appreciation for a contribution of $10.00 or more to the International Amateur Sports Development Fund or AAU. The AAU emblem replaced the Olympic rings on the obverse and the words FIRST ISSUE were removed from the pad on the reverse. The sculpted bust of John F. Kennedy is identical on all three varieties of this medal and all other features remain equal.

Obverse

Reverse

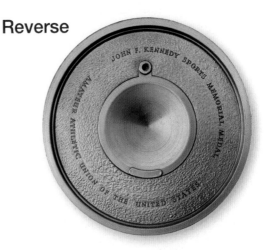

Namiot "Labor of Honor" Medal

Presents Unique Medal To Mrs. J. F. Kennedy

An aged, Russian-born engraver of Brooklyn, N. Y., has completed what he terms a "labor of honor"—a medal commemorating the late President John F. Kennedy — and has s e n t the unique result of his work to the President's widow.

"It was not designed so that copies could be made," he said. "It was only for Jackie and for Caroline and John-John, so they will know what kind of man their father was when they grow up."

Charles Namiot, 76, began his apprenticeship as an engraver at the age of nine, in Kiev, Russia and became an engraver of religious icons before coming to this country at the age of 16.

He had made portrait medals of other public figures, including Franklin D. Roosevelt, Herbert Hoover and New York City's colorful former mayor, James J. Walker.

The Roosevelt medallion is on exhibit at the Hyde Park, N. Y., Museum. Two other of Namiot's medals, portraying Lenin a n d S t a l i n, are said to be in the permanent collection of the Museum of Fine Arts in Moscow.

Namiot's Kennedy medal features a portrait of the 35th President facing left, with the legend: "In Memoriam, 1917-1963, A Profile in Courage," on the obverse.

For the reverse legend, he has selected the quotation: "By creativity, self-discipline and justice, man can endure."

Namiot chose this quotation, he said, because he feels "it typifies the man."

Coin World.

K-63A-15

John and Robert F. Kennedy Memorials

K-68-9

K-68-70

K-68-46

K-68-63

K-77-4: Uniface.

K-63A-224

K-68-63A

K-63A-268

14

The Kennedy Half Dollar and Related Coins

Public Law 88-256, 88th Congress, H.R. 9413

AN ACT

To provide for the coinage of 50-cent pieces bearing the likeness of John Fitzgerald Kennedy.

Be it enacted by the Senate and House of Representatives of the United States of America in Con-

For the Collector and Historian

More than a half-century later, the Kennedy half dollar not only survives but thrives, due to numerous reinvigorating circumstances. In 1992, after many years of the mostly unexciting clad circulation strikes and Proofs, the U.S. Mint reintroduced silver Proof sets containing 90 percent silver examples of the Kennedy half dollar. This reminded old-time collectors of the beautiful 90 percent silver coins with which the series made its debut in 1964, and introduced a new generation of collectors to the enticements of the series.

The 1998-S Matte Finish silver issue, included in special commemorative sets with the Robert F. Kennedy silver dollars, was a popular and extremely attractive issue.

The 1964 Specimen, Special Strike, or Special Mint Set (SMS) Kennedy halves are the rarest of all the 1964 SMS coins and it is estimated that perhaps only a dozen exist. The circumstances surrounding their production are also unexplained. Among the most mysterious modern coinage issues, the little-known 1964 SMS coins set a world record in 2013 when the finest known PCGS-certified five-piece set changed hands for $151,200.

Nonetheless, collecting the Kennedy half series and its many varieties is a venture that can be started out quite modestly. Given the vast amount of so-called "junk" or common-date circulated 90 percent silver that washes around the numismatic marketplace, one can even occasionally find doubled-die obverse 1964 Kennedy halves and repunched-mintmark 1964-D Kennedy halves in such hoards.

Both NGC and PCGS have Kennedy half dollar registry sets that allow a collector to focus on broad or narrow collections, as one desires. For example, some collectors choose to focus only on the 90 percent silver and 40 percent silver Kennedy halves struck for circulation in 1964 and 1965–1970, respectively. Others limit themselves only to Proof coins.

gress assembled. That in lieu of the coinage of the 50-cent piece known as the Franklin half dollar, there shall be coined a silver 50-cent piece which shall bear on one side the likeness of the late president of the United States, John Fitzgerald Kennedy, and on the other side an appropriate design to be prescribed by the Secretary of the Treasury.

Approved December 30, 1963.

Legislative History

House Report No. 1038 (Commission on Banking and Currency)

Congressional Record, Vol. 109 (1963):

December 17: Considered and passed House.

December 18: Considered and passed Senate.

The Creation of the Kennedy Half Dollar

Gilroy Roberts.

Reminiscences
By Gilroy Roberts

Shortly after the tragedy of President Kennedy's death on November 22, 1963, Miss Eva Adams, the director of the Mint, telephoned me here at the Philadelphia Mint and explained that serious consideration was being given to placing President Kennedy's portrait on a new-design U.S. silver coin and that the quarter dollar, half dollar, or the one dollar were under discussion. For the design, they were weighing the merits of either a front view or a profile for the obverse, and the possibility of using the Seal of the President of the United States for the reverse. From the standpoint of good composition and elegance of design, the profile is much superior to any other view for the presentation of a portrait in bas-relief on a circular medal or coin. This is almost a universally held opinion among designers and artists and it was strongly recommended here that a profile be used.

A day or so later, about November 27, Miss Adams called again and informed me that the half dollar had been chosen for the new design; Mrs. Kennedy did not want to replace Washington's portrait on the quarter dollar. Also it had been decided to use the profile portrait that appears on our Mint List Medal for President Kennedy and the presidential seal that had been used on the reverse of this and other Mint medals.

Since the Franklin half dollar had not been issued for the statutory 25-year period, new legislative authority would be required. However, we were to begin immediately because they wanted to start striking the new half dollar in January 1964—only about four weeks away. This seemed almost an impossibility, but the fact that we had large models on hand for both sides made the problem less insurmountable.

There was still a great amount of work to be done; all stops were out. Frank Gasparro tackled the reverse and the obverse became my problem.

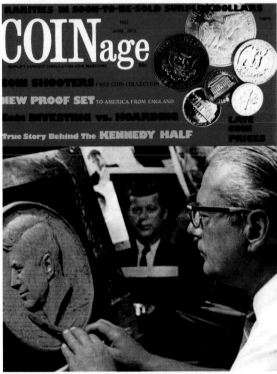

June 1972 front cover of *COINage* featuring Gilroy Roberts and the Kennedy half dollar.

Starting back with the original plastilene model of President Kennedy's portrait, which he had approved, the coat was deleted, and the periphery was changed to bring the head nearer center and to decrease the size of the circle in relation to the portrait. The background was reshaped to provide the required depressed field necessary for proper coinage, and the inscription and date required by law were established.

On December 10, White House press releases were issued by President Johnson stating the reasons and the steps required to establish the new coin.

Work on the processing to the die stage continued. An intermediate reduction was made, approximately five inches in diameter, drastically reducing the relief, and from this intermediate, preliminary trial dies with further reduction in relief were made. On December 13, trial strikes were produced and these were immediately delivered to Miss Adams in Washington.

The following week, Miss Adams requested my presence in Washington to discuss the new half dollar with her and with other U.S. Treasury department officials.

Both sides of the trial strikes received very favorable comment; however, Secretary of the Treasury Dillon wished to have Mrs. Kennedy's opinion and wanted me to accompany him at that time. On December 17, we met Mrs. Kennedy and Attorney General Robert Kennedy. Mrs. Kennedy was favorably impressed with the design on both sides of the coin but

Secretary of the Treasury C. Douglas Dillon with John F. Kennedy in 1961.

felt it would be an improvement if the part in the hair was less pronounced and more accents were added. They also had in mind a design showing a full figure or half figure of the late President. There was simply not enough time to create new designs and medals, get approvals, and have the new coin in production by January 1964. I strongly advocated the simplicity and directness of a profile portrait as being the best possible arrangement for a handsome, outstanding coin whose beauty would endure—and there could be no doubt as to the identity of the subject.

Mrs. Kennedy's suggestions were carried out on the intermediate size and another trial die was made for the obverse. New trial strikes were prepared. Secretary of the Treasury Dillon wanted to see this second trial piece and on December 27, I flew to West Palm Beach where the secretary and Mrs. Dillon inspected the strikes. They both felt that Mrs. Kennedy's wishes had been complied with and, in their opinion, the coin was very handsome. It was decided to proceed with tooling up for production. The congressional act authorizing the Kennedy half dollar was approved on December 30, 1963.

Time was fast running out and if we did not have working dies for Proof half dollars, the coiner would be unable to start Proof coin production. This meant that up until the time dies were available, some 30 or 50 employees would be without work. Extreme pressure was exerted to push this program through and by January 2, 1964, Kennedy half dollar Proof dies were delivered and our tremendous Proof coin production could get started. Some minor problems still had to be ironed out for regular production, but by January 30, 1964, Denver had started production of regular half dollar coinage using the new design. Sometime during the following week, the Philadelphia Mint started striking regular half dollar coinage.

On February 11, 1964, Assistant Secretary of the Treasury Robert Wallace, Director of the Mint Eva Adams, Assistant Director of the Mint Fred Tate, Superintendent of the Mint Michael Sura, and other U.S. Treasury and Mint officials held ceremonies concurrently at the Denver and Philadelphia Mints to commemorate the striking of the new U.S. half dollar bearing the late president's portrait, issued by a sorrowing nation as a fitting and enduring memorial honoring our former president, John F. Kennedy.

On March 5, 1964, an initial delivery of some 26 million new Kennedy half dollars was made to the Federal Reserve banks for eventual issue to the local banks and to the people of our country.

K-64-1I: The original design of the obverse of the Kennedy half dollar.

K-64-10: A gift to the author
from Gilroy Roberts.

Reminiscences
By Frank Gasparro

Shortly after President Kennedy's death, plans were being made to create a lasting and significant memorial to his memory. After careful consideration and various suggestions made throughout the nation, the final decision was made by Congress to make a coin with the late president's portrait on the obverse and an appropriate design on the reverse.

The Mint received word from the Bureau that President Kennedy's portrait on the obverse of the U.S. Mint Presidential Inaugural List Medal, executed by Gilroy Roberts, and the presidential seal on the reverse of the same medal, designed by me, were to be used for the coin. This same presidential seal, incorporated in this medal, was personally selected by the late president to be used for the reverse of the 1961 inaugural medal.

Time was limited, but as we at the Mint had on hand the Kennedy medal patterns, it was possible to proceed with haste with this coin. However, the models in plaster form had to be considerably lowered in relief and the basins, or backgrounds, of these plasters had to have the correct curvature and heights for coinage striking. The obverse and reverse lettering and borders necessary for coinage had to be exe-

Ad for Kennedy half dollar holders.

cuted and balanced for correct composition in relation to the center motifs.

While waiting for the final decision from Congress as to the denomination approved for coinage, I made three rough patterns incorporating the quarter, half dollar, and dollar lettering. On November 28, 1963, we received official word at the Mint from Director Eva Adams to prepare our models for the Kennedy half dollar and we began our work the same day. On December 12, we completed our trial dies. At 9:00 a.m. on December 13, we struck our first trial pieces. (Of course, mechanical difficulties in the way of production had to be worked out in days to come.) The same day, I boarded a jet plane for Washington, D.C., to deliver the coins to Miss Adams, who in turn submitted them via Secretary of the Treasury Dillon to the White House and President Johnson.

As to my experience with this reverse, I was fortunate to have my design accepted by Mrs. John F. Kennedy, the White House, and the Treasury Bureau.

Errors on coins are keenly sought by coin enthusiasts and I had to make a very careful check of the heraldic symbols on the presidential seal. The American eagle in this seal must hold 13 arrows in the right claw and 13 leaves with 13 olives in the branch in the left claw. The eagle's head is turned to the left, facing the olive branch. Thirteen small stars are arranged behind the eagle's head. The shield in the center covers the eagle's breast and has seven vertical stripes. Finally, 50 stars encircle the center motif as in the official presidential seal.

This seal was the culmination of many experiences with the study and execution of the American eagle in medallic work. The manner I used in designing the composition of the reverse was pre-planned. I deliberately sunk the eagle into the background so that the circle of 50 stars around the eagle and the border lettering appeared to radiate from the center motif. The E PLURIBUS UNUM was greatly enlarged in comparison to the official presidential seal so that it could be easily read by the naked eye.

Before the coin was acceptable, we had to make numerous steel reductions from model to coin size. Finally, coinage production was begun at 11:00 a.m. on February 11, 1964, amidst great excitement at the Philadelphia Mint and the Denver Mint.

I had the good fortune to be with Miss Eva Adams, Assistant Secretary of the Treasury Wallace, Superintendent Sura of the Philadelphia Mint, other dignitaries, TV cameras, newsreel photographers, and newspaper cameramen. Miss Adams gave the signal for the Philadelphia Mint and the Denver Mint (by telephone) to proceed with the coinage production of the Kennedy half dollar on a 24-hour basis.

K-64-1: The final design of the Kennedy half dollar.

A Gift from Gilroy Roberts to Kenneth Bressett's Son

Like millions of Americans I vividly remember the day of the Kennedy assassination. I was deeply moved by the death of this great statesman. It was fitting that our president should be remembered forever via the beautiful coin that was immediately authorized and quickly placed into circulation. Even now, 50-plus years later, his coins are popular icons throughout the world, reminding generations of the greatness and legacy of John F. Kennedy. The tradition of honoring important heroes with portrait coins began more than 2,200 years ago in ancient Rome. Examples of these still exist today. People 2,000 years from now will similarly remember this great American president.

Kenneth Bressett
Senior Editor, A Guide Book of United States Coins

Kennedy Half Dollar Memorabilia

The Kennedy Half Dollar That Traveled Through Time

A Kennedy half dollar features prominently in *The Twilight Zone* episode "Profile in Silver." Harvard history professor Joseph Fitzgerald travels back in time to try to observe the death of his ancestor, President John F. Kennedy. He cannot resist the temptation to intervene, and manages to thwart the assassination, earning the president's gratitude. Later, a Secret Service agent finds a 1964 Kennedy half dollar the professor dropped, compelling Fitzgerald to reveal the truth—including late news he has received that Kennedy's salvation caused a rip in the fabric of time, putting the world on a path to global war and destruction. John F. Kennedy bravely volunteers to go back in time and allow his own assas-sination. Instead, Fitzgerald sends him into the future and takes his place in the fateful Dallas motorcade.

K-63A-233: Replica of the Kennedy half dollar.

1965 Kennedy Half Dollar

TREASURY DEPARTMENT

[To the right of this press release is The Department of the Treasury seal]

WASHINGTON, D.C.

December 28, 1965

FOR RELEASE: P.M. NEWSPAPERS
WEDNESDAY, DECEMBER 29, 1965

FIRST STRIKING OF HALF DOLLARS FROM NEW
COINAGE MATERIAL AT U.S. MINT AT DENVER ON THURSDAY

Production of the new half dollar, authorized by the Coinage Act of 1965, will start on Thursday, December 30, at 10:00 a.m. at the Denver Mint.

The new half dollar will continue to bear the Kennedy design approved by the Congress two years ago. Coin designs are retained for 25 years unless the Congress directs an earlier change.

The new half dollar will contain 40 percent silver compared to the traditional 90 percent silver half dollars. However, in appearance the new coin will be nearly identical to the old half dollar as it will have outer layers of 80 percent silver. The core will be 21 percent silver -- lowering total silver content to 40 percent.

All of the new half dollars will bear the date 1965 until the shortage of this denomination has been overcome. Some 390 million 90 percent silver Kennedy half dollars made during 1964 and 1965 all bear the date 1964.

The new half dollars will be placed in circulation early next year. They will be shipped to the Federal Reserve Banks and branch banks and will be used by them in their regular weekly coin shipments to supplement the supply of circulating half dollars, through the medium of commercial banks, throughout the country.

(MORE)

F-319

- 2 -

This was the procedure followed in issuing the first of the three new coins -- the 25-cent piece -- authorized by the Coinage Act of 1965. Production of the new quarter, which has cupronickel faces bonded to a core of pure copper, began August 23, 1965 and circulation began November, 1965. In the past two months, over 400 million of the new quarters have been placed in circulation. The Philadelphia Mint has begun minting of the new, non-silver dime -- also with cupronickel faces clad on a core of pure copper. Circulation of this coin is also expected to begin early in the new year.

The new dimes, quarters and half dollars are three layers "clad" coins because this construction permits duplication in a non-silver coin, or a coin with low silver content, of the electrical properties of coins of 90 percent silver. This allows the new coins and the old; 90 percent silver coins, to be used interchangeably in coin operated devices.

The switch to coins of lower silver content, or none, was made necessary by a growing world silver shortage.

The silver coinage will continue to circulate, side by side with the new coinage.

The Coinage Act of 1965, which became law on July 23, 1965, made no change in the penny, the nickel or the silver dollar. There are no plans at present for minting of silver dollars.

Like the Kennedy half dollars dated 1964, those dated 1965 will not bear a mintmark. The Coinage Act of 1965 specifies that no mintmarks will be authorized until five years from the date of initial issuance.

oOo

Press release from the U.S. Department of the Treasury.

"Assassin's Challenge" Coin

I call this the "Assassin's Challenge" coin. I do not know of any reason why the average golfer would want to shoot for a hole in the head of John F. Kennedy. Perhaps the number four on the tail feathers of the presidential seal represents the group of shooters present in Dallas on November 22, 1963.

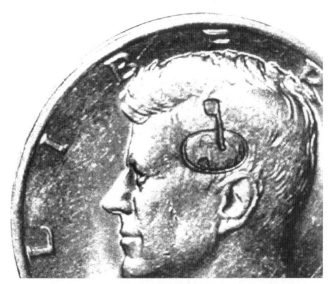

K-63A-319

Kennedy Half Dollar 50th-Anniversary Sets

Uncirculated Coin Set

This set contains two Uncirculated Kennedy half dollars, one from the U.S. Mint at Denver and one from the Philadelphia Mint. Each coin in this set and in the Kennedy half dollar Silver Coin Collection has the original design from the obverse of the 1964 Kennedy half dollar.

Gold Proof Coin

Struck at the U.S. Mint's facility in West Point, this coin contains three-quarters of a troy ounce of .9999 fine, 24-karat gold. Inscriptions on the obverse include the dual years 1964–2014. The encapsulated coin is packaged in a custom-design brown mahogany hardwood presentation case with a removable coin well. A certificate of authenticity, signed by U.S. Mint Deputy Director Richard A. Peterson, accompanies each coin.

Other Half Dollar Items

K-64-1N: Counterfeit strike.

K-64-11B

K-64-11: Embossed Kennedy half dollar; obverse.

K-64-11: Obverse.

K-64-11: Reverse.

K-64-58

K-75-12

SOUVENIR HALF DOLLAR

P E A C E
1917

L O V E
1963

John Fitzgerald Kennedy

★ ★ 1968 ★ ★

69#

This wooden script was issued by
Jack W. Gladfelter, Seven Valleys, Pa.
as a unique souvenir in honor of our
Thirty-Fifth President of the
United States of America.
JOHN FITZGERALD KENNEDY

K-68-57

K-76-31: Metal stamp.

J.F.K.
HALF DOLLAR
Mini Bar

STERLING

K-73-19

K-86-7: Commemorating the 100th anniversary of the
dedication of the Statue of Liberty.

K-2001-5: Kennedy half dollar pictured on reverse.

K-88-21: Commemorating the 50th anniversary
of the Racine Numismatic Society.

K-2008-17: Grabener coin press medal stamped over the
1991-D Kennedy half dollar. The reverse was struck by
Daniel Carr, owner of the Moonlight Mint.

K-96-2

K-2012-5

K-2013-6

K-63A-145A

K-63A-240

K-63A-336

Presidential Series Dollar Coin

On March 10, 2014, the Citizens Coinage Advisory Committee (CCAC) began its review of the proposed designs for the six Presidential dollar coins to be released in 2015 and 2016. These coins commemorate the 33rd through 38th presidents, including John F. Kennedy, Lyndon B. Johnson, and Richard M. Nixon.

In the March 31, 2014, issue of *Coin World*, Bill McAllister discussed the CCAC's process of deliberation in regards to these presidential portraits.

> [The panel] was less than thrilled by the images the Mint's artists had created for the presidents whose dollar coins will be issued in 2015 and 2016. The eight committee members present at the March 10 session at U.S. Mint headquarters in Washington, D.C., were so split over the proposed presidential images that they could not initially muster enough votes to formally endorse any of the images proposed for Richard M. Nixon or Gerald R. Ford.

While the panel eventually endorsed a profile of Nixon highlighting his prominent nose and a straightforward image of Johnson, the question of John F. Kennedy was, as McAllister notes, far more controversial.

> Five images were submitted. The panel found one too youthful, looking like Robert F. Kennedy, the president's brother [see Design 4],

and said another makes him look too fat [see Design 2]. Panel members finally threw their support to a design showing a somewhat downcast president after being reminded that the image is patterned after the official Kennedy portrait by Aaron Shikler in the White House [see Design 1].

Heidi Wastweet, a member of the CCAC panel, was touched by the image and asserted that the images on the presidential coins do not always have to be heroic.

The Commission of Fine Arts (CFA) was next to review the five proposed designs. Unlike the CCAC, the CFA was unable to endorse the image of Kennedy in a downward pose (Design 1) as the gathered panel believed that it places excessive emphasis on the top of his head and would not translate into a successful sculptural design. The CFA found the second design, of Kennedy facing right, the most suitable; however, they also concluded that the likeness was unsatisfactory.

The recommendations of both the CFA and the CCAC were submitted to the U.S. Treasury secretary, Jacob J. Lew, who took their proposals under consideration.

John F. Kennedy's Presidential Series dollar coin joins two other commemorative dollar coins, celebrating his sister Eunice Shriver and his brother Robert (see appendix C).

Design 1.

Design 2.

Design 3.

Design 4.

Design 5.

15

Celebrating His Achievements

JFK's Achievements

While he was only in office for a little more than 1,000 days, John F. Kennedy's life and achievements continue to be celebrated throughout the United States to this day. Across the country exists a multitude of monuments in his likeness and institutions bearing his name. Kennedy spent his life in dedicated service to the country he loved, as both a military officer and a politician. He was a champion of the Civil Rights movement, and fought to end poverty, lower unemployment, and expand the country's horizons through U.S.-manned space travel. He encouraged the United States—and the world—to think bigger, work harder, and adhere to strong morals and ideals.

For the Collector and Historian

While he was president, John F. Kennedy's achievements were as numerous as they were varied. He was a proponent of the Civil Rights movement; he championed U.S. space exploration; he and his wife celebrated the arts by welcoming national and international writers, musicians, and artists to the White House. Medals, tokens, and other items commemorating JFK's achievements and passions are frequently found in the marketplace and can be quite affordable.

The rarer of these items will cost the avid collector a little more. In the 2013 estate sale of David Powers, many pieces in his collection fell into this vast category. Photographs of JFK watching the take-off of the experimental *Mercury* spacecraft sold for $1,110; a resolution signed by President Lyndon B. Johnson renaming the National Cultural Center the John F. Kennedy Center for the Performing Arts was purchased for $18,000; and a 1964 small-scale replica of the bust of John F. Kennedy which appeared at the dedication for the opening of the Center for the Performing Arts was auctioned for $2,750.

K-67-3A

K-67-8

K-69-6B

K-69-18

K-71-20

K-82-8

K-71-4: Type one.

K-71-4A: Type two.

K-74-4

K-74-13

K-79-2

K-80-2

K-96-1

K-2008-5

K-2008-19

K-2009-7

K-2013-11: Type one.

K-2013-12: Type two.

K-63A-7D

K-63A-16: Uniface.

K-63A-78D

John F. Kennedy International Airport

The New York International Airport, commonly called Idlewild, was renamed John F. Kennedy International Airport in 1963, one month after the assassination of President Kennedy. The airport received the new International Air Transport Association airport code of KIA, short for Kennedy International Airport. However, as the U.S. death toll in Vietnam became a serious and emotional issue for Americans (K.I.A., short for Killed in Action, was used in news reports of U.S. casualties during the war), the airport code was changed in 1968 to JFK. Since, the airport has become widely referred to by that abbreviation.

between the United States and Israel. Those recognized are presented with the John F. Kennedy Peace Award. It was designed by Joseph Kiselewski in 1964 and struck by the Medallic Art Company. The medal's reverse is inscribed with the recipient's name.

The medal was selected by the International Art Medal Federation (FIDEM) for presentation as an outstanding example of American medallic art at the International Exposition of Contemporary Medals in 1966. The medal is 76 mm and it was struck in bronze, sterling silver, and 14k gold.

The bronze striking (K-63A-166) was limited to 26 pieces, the sterling-silver striking (K-63A-166a) was limited to six pieces, and the 14k gold striking (K-63A-166b) to 11 examples. The edge of all medals is hallmarked MEDALLIC ART CO. N.Y.

K-77-1

K-63A-166: Bronze striking.

Other Awards

Awards Named for John F. Kennedy

The John F. Kennedy Peace Award

The Jewish National Fund of America annually recognizes one or more persons who have distinguished themselves in service to peace and democracy, and have promoted friendship

K-64-5

K-64-48

K-72-11

K-93-3

Years of Lightning focuses on John F. Kennedy's public life and his time in office. Among his achievements featured are the drafting of the Civil Rights Act of 1964 (written before his death with his brother Robert), the creation of the Peace Corps, the resolution of the Cuban Missile Crisis, and the Space Race.

K-72-13

K-72-13A: Reverse.

Years of Lightning, Day of Drums

A 90-minute documentary, *Years of Lightning, Day of Drums* was a memorial tribute celebrating the political life of President John F. Kennedy. Narrated by Gregory Peck, it was completed in 1964 and was released in theaters in 1966. The film was written and directed by Bruce Herschensohn and was produced by the U.S. Information Agency. It was not originally intended for public consumption but a special act of Congress allowed it to be shown in theaters.

K-72-13B: Reverse.

K-72-13C: Reverse.

16

Anniversary Memorabilia

John F. Kennedy's 50th Birthday

Paris Mint

KENNEDY

50th Anniversary Medal

(Illustration Actual Size)

Sculptured by Auguste de Jager

Only 200 Struck - 50 in each metal. Reverse die will be destroyed upon completion of striking.

Reverse Inscription: "50th Anniversary 29 Mai 1967. His memory belongs to all mankind."

Serially numbered. 688mm.

Bronze $10.00 — Silver-plated Bronze $11.50
Gold Plated Bronze $14.00 — Silver $59.50

Complete set **$92.25**

To be struck in November. Advance orders now being accepted. All offered subject to prior sale.

Nebraska Numismatics, Inc.

P. O. Box 1022   Omaha, Nebraska 68101

Medals from the Karlsruhe, Bavarian and Austrian State Mints, Nimmis Mundi, Spink & Sons, Ltd., and A. E. Lorioli Fratelli. Representatives for Aureus Magnus, John Pinches Ltd. and Monnaie de Paris.

Dealer Inquiries Invited.

Advertisement in *Coin World* for the Paris Mint's medal celebrating Kennedy's 50th birthday.

The history of this medal is confusing at best. On August 27, 1967, a press release from the Paris Mint stated that the medal was sculpted by Auguste de Jager, was 68 mm in size, and would be minted in November 1967.

Original Strikes

K-67-1: Bronze; dated 1967 on rim; serial numbers 1 through 50

K-67-1A: Gold-plated bronze; dated 1967 on rim; serial numbers 1 through 50

K-67-1B: .950 silver; dated 1967 on rim; serial numbers 1 through 50

For the Collector and Historian

Anniversary items are quite popular among collectors and non-collectors. An anniversary medal can serve as a snapshot in time, a keepsake of an event or a person near and dear to the buyer. For one collector, a single personally significant anniversary item might possess a higher value, both monetarily and sentimentally, than an entire set of mass-produced coins or medals that have no personal connection.

Medals commemorating the inauguration and assassination of John F. Kennedy are prolific, particularly since the 50th anniversary (in 2011) of his oath of office. These items can range in price from less than $20 to more than $1,000, depending on their condition and rarity. Sources include coin and collectibles conventions, hobby and antique shops, and online auction venues. Specialists in presidential medals and memorabilia often release mail-bid lists and price sheets for Kennedy-related (and other) items in their inventories.

K-67-1C: Silver-plated bronze; dated 1967 on rim; serial numbers 1 through 50

Unfortunately, the 50 bronze and 50 silver-plated bronze medals were lost en route to Frankfurt, Germany, from Paris, France, in a railroad derailment and fire.

In a letter dated February 21, 1968, the chief of commercial services at the Paris Mint told Ben Wall, president of Nebraska Numismatics, that the Mint would commence striking replacement medals for the 50 bronze and 50 silver-plated bronze medals. Medal numbers 21 through 44 of the .950 silver and gold-plated bronze must have also been lost as those medals were also restruck. In total, 148 medals with the date 1967 were lost. Only 52 medals dated 1967 survive.

Replacement Strikes

K-67-1D: Bronze; dated 1968 on rim; serial numbers 1 through 50

K-67-1E: Gold-plated bronze; dated 1968 on rim; serial numbers 21 through 44

K-67-1F: .950 silver; dated 1968 on rim; serial numbers 21 through 44

K-67-1G: Silver-plated bronze; dated 1968 on rim; serial numbers 1 through 50

Following the restriking of the replacement medals, the reverse die was destroyed.

The following information was made known in the trade papers:

The first 1967 .950 silver medal was donated to the John F. Kennedy Presidential Library and Museum by Jacqueline Kennedy.

The first 1967 gold-plated bronze medal was presented to Ed Rochette.

The first 1968 silver-plated bronze medal was presented to the American Numismatic Association.

K-67-1

The first 1968 bronze medal was presented to the Token and Medal Society.

The Inauguration of John F. Kennedy
25th Anniversary

K-86-3

50th Anniversary

K-2010-6. *See chapter 17.*

K-2011-3A

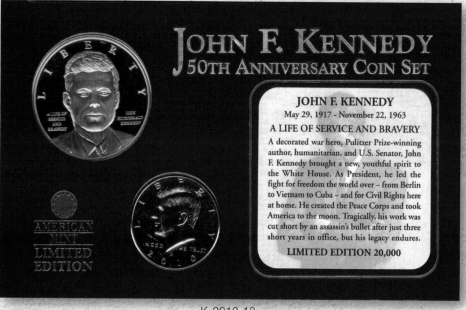

K-2010-13

K-2011-1

The Assassination of John F. Kennedy

10th Anniversary

25th Anniversary

October 25, 1973

Dear Friend:

It was a dozen years ago that I first met President John F. Kennedy. I was Chief Sculptor-Engraver of the United States then, and we got together to discuss his official medallic portrait.

Then, right after his assassination, I was given the most heartbreaking assignment of my life — creating the Kennedy portrait for the U.S. half-dollar.

Now, on the 10th anniversary of his passing, I've sculptured a new and very personal tribute to President Kennedy. The John F. Kennedy Memorial Medal.

John Kennedy, of course, was a strong man and a very human one. I've tried to capture those qualities in this new medal. The portrait on the obverse is intended to show him as a man whose handsome face reflects the tremendous responsibilities of leadership. As a contrast, I've chosen to depict him on the reverse at a moment of relaxed contemplation — a time when he was free to dream of our country's future.

It's my sincere hope that this medal will come to mean as much to you as it does to me.

Sincerely,

Gilroy Roberts

GR:tl

Letter from Gilroy Roberts that accompanied his 10th-anniversary memorial medal.

K-88-1

K-73-9

K-88-7

50th Anniversary
Keith Clark "Taps" Medal

It was a moment in world history that defied human comprehension.

A hush fell as Army bugler Sergeant Keith Clark stood at attention on a slope by the Custis-Lee Mansion—where President Kennedy had once stood looking toward the city of Washington, D.C., and said, "I could stay here forever."

The place was Arlington National Cemetery and the year was 1963. The day would always be remembered by those who were within earshot of what was about to come.

Having sounded "Taps" in front of President Kennedy just 14 days earlier for a Veterans Day ceremony, Sergeant Clark was well aware that this Monday, November 25, was a very different day. This was the day that President Kennedy was laid to rest.

He had left the world his legacy and now his final tribute was waiting.

Sergeant Clark raised his bugle and broke the silence of the world with 23 perfect notes, leaving one broken note to be remembered for the sorrow and tears of all who love liberty and freedom. Many felt that God had reached down from heaven and touched that note of remembrance for the soul of John Fitzgerald Kennedy.

According to retired Air Force bugler and historian Jari Villanueva, Sergeant Clark would often think of the Bible verse from Saint Paul's first letter to the Corinthians: "In a moment, twinkling of an eye . . . the trumpet shall sound and the dead shall be raised incorruptible, and we shall be changed."

This excellent medal pays tribute to the 50th anniversary of the "Taps" sounded by Sergeant Keith Clark and the funeral of the 35th president of the United States of America.

KCC-85

Bicentennial of American Independence

K-73-18

K-76-13: By Karen Worth.

K-76-22

K-75-8: By Gilroy Roberts.

K-76-23B

K-76-12

K-76-24

K-76-26

K-87-1: Isle of Man. *See chapter 17.*

ISLE OF MAN

JOHN F. KENNEDY   RONALD REAGAN

DWIGHT D. EISENHOWER   THOMAS JEFFERSON

FRANKLIN D. ROOSEVELT   BENJAMIN FRANKLIN

THEODORE ROOSEVELT   GEORGE WASHINGTON

                                    JAMES MONROE

ULYSSES GRANT   ABRAHAM LINCOLN

BICENTENARY
OF
AMERICA'S CONSTITUTION
1787 – 1987

Plaque commemorating America's Bicentennial, Isle of Man.

K-89-2

K-92-1A: Type one.

K-92-1: Type two.

Bicentennial of the First Presidential Election

K-89-6

17

Worldwide Coins and International Memorabilia

Worldwide Coins

John F. Kennedy Legal-Tender Euro

Located in the northeast of Italy is the Sovereign Republic of San Marino. Only 24 square miles in area, it is known as the oldest constitutional republic in the world. San Marino has the smallest population of all the members of the Council of Europe. It is a thriving community; they have no national debt, a budget surplus, and the lowest unemployment rate in Europe. San Marino also has the highest life expectancy for males in the world. The Republic's motto is Libertas (Freedom). A large amount of revenue is derived from the sale of collector postage stamps and coins.

A tribute to honor President Kennedy in the form of a legal-tender 2-euro coin dated 2013 was planned and advertised by San Marino. Hundreds of advance orders were made via the Web site eBay. Coin dealers were surprised by the escalating prices offered and thought that the U.S. coin market would be very accommodating for profit.

For the Collector and Historian

An extremely popular and well-represented category of Kennedy collectibles is that of international coins and other memorabilia. A beautiful and artistic medallic example of fine craftsmanship can be purchased from Beijing for less than $5. On the flip side, a JFK medal from Europe might cost more than $100. Bargains are out there in the marketplace. For example, Portugal and Belgium, among other European nations, have produced large Kennedy art medals that can be purchased for less than $50 by the average collector.

"World coins" (those issued outside the United States) are a very popular segment of the hobby, with their own periodical publications, regularly scheduled coin shows, and dedicated dealers. Many coin dealers who specialize in world coins (and therefore can be good sources for Kennedy collectors) belong to the American Numismatic Association (www.money.org) and/or the International Association of Professional Numismatists (www.iapn-coins.org). These organizations maintain lists of their dealer members on their Web sites.

Even though the theme of the coin was popular, and could relate to European history, the European Central Bank cancelled the coin's release, reporting that the theme was not related to San Marino. Despite the many eBay advance sales, official press releases, and public illustrations of the coin, the country was forced by the bank to issue an entirely different 2-euro coin honoring someone else.

After San Marino's efforts to honor the memory of John F. Kennedy on a legal-tender 2-euro coin were overruled by the European Central Bank, a new commemorative 5-euro collector's coin emerged. After a meeting of the Eco-Finance Council on January 31, 2000, the Council stated that "euro collector coins should be different from coins intended for circulation." A regulation was enacted that euro collector coins cannot have a face value equal to the following eight denominations: 1-, 2-, 5-, 10-, 20-, and 50-cent coins and 1- and 2-euro coins. This regulation allowed for the creation of the 5-euro John F. Kennedy 50th Anniversary Ich Bin Berliner tribute coin, of which 8,000 were struck. The coin's designers were Antonella Napolione and Claudia Momoni. The "R" denotes the mint in Italy where the coins were struck.

K-2013-1: The legal-tender 2-euro coin that was never struck.

K-2013-2: The commemorative 5-euro collector's coin.

Africa

Chad

K-70-15

K-2000-1

K-2000-2A

Liberia

K-93-9C

K-2000-12

K-99-3. *See chapter 11.*

K-2000-15

K-2001-1

K-2003-3

K-2001-3. *See chapter 11.*

K-2003-10

K-2002-3. *See chapter 11.*

K-2004-5. *See chapter 8.*

K-2002-4. *See chapter 11.*

K-2006-2

K-2008-12

Australia/Oceania

Micronesia

K-2004-4

K-2010-6. *See chapter 16.*

Republic of Guinea

K-69-7

Niue

K-93-6

Asia

Mongolia

K-2007-6

K-93-7

Europe

Malta

K-93-8

K-2004-1

K-94-2

The Middle East

United Arab Emirates

Palau

K-2007-9

K-64-2

West Samoa

K-2003-7

Memorial Architecture

The Kennedy Center in Copenhagen, Denmark.

Copenhagen City Hall, March 11th, 1976.

FORMANDEN

Mr. William R. Rice,

Dear Mr. Rice,

Answering your letter of February 6th about some information concerning the "Kennedy Center" in Copenhagen, I can inform you that Copenhagen Municipality operates a child and youth center called the "Kennedy Center", located in Nøjsomhedsvej in the Østerbro district of Copenhagen.

The name for the center was chosen in order to commemmorate President Kennedy and his work. At the inauguration ceremony this was expressed by the Social Welfare Mayor of Copenhagen, Mr. Børge H. Jensen, in the following words:

"We have desired to name this child and youth center after the late President Kennedy to honor him, and his work for the relaxation of international tension, for better understanding between nations, for freedom, tolerance and humanity. The attitudes underlying his work, and which we will remember with respect and gratitude, can be characterized by my giving quotations from three different speeches which he delivered as President:

"Let us never negotiate out of fear. But let us never fear to negotiate". - "Let us take that first step. Let us, if we can, step back from the shadows of war and seek out the ways of peace. And if that journey is 1.000 miles, or even more, let history record that we, in this land, at this time, took the first step."

(cont.page 2)

"It is never too early to try, and it is never too late to talk. We have the power to make this the best generation of mankind in the history of the world - or to make it the last."

It is my hope that the attitudes expressed in these words may also inspire the youth we are working for in this building. ....."

The family of the late President had been acquainted beforehand through the Danish Ministry of Foreign Affairs of the intention to call the center after President Kennedy. At the inauguration, a message was received from Senator Robert F. Kennedy with greetings and thanks. After the opening, which was attended by Her Majesty the Queen of Denmark, an album containing photographs of the occasion was forwarded to the family by the Social Welfare Mayor.

The Center came into operation in the fall of 1966 and comprises a day nursery for 54 infants, a nursery school for 82 pre-school children, a recreation center for 82 school-agers, a recreation and youth club for about 175 children and adolescents, and a residential hostel for 10 young girls.

Mounted on a seven-foot granite slab placed in front of the Center is a bronze bust in relief of the late President John F. Kennedy, bearing his name below it. The relief is the work of the Danish sculptor Svend Lindhart.

Enclosing some photographs of the Kennedy Center,

yours sincerely,

Egon Weidekamp
President of the Copenhagen City Council

Yad Kennedy in the
John F. Kennedy
Peace Forest, Israel.

John F. Kennedy memorial plaque in
Berlin, Germany.

Memorial fountain in
John F. Kennedy Park,
County Wexford,
Ireland. The fountain
bears the inscription
"Ask not what your
country can do for you
. . . ask what you can
do for your country" in
Irish and English.

Memorial to John F. Kennedy at
Treasury Gardens in Melbourne,
Australia.

International Memorabilia

Paris Mint Club Français de la Medaille Kennedy Medal

Paris Mint issue number 2530 was sculpted by Auguste de Jager and minted in 1966. It measures 68 mm.

K-65-3: Silver on bronze; serial numbers 1 through 400; private issue for Club Français de la Medaille.

K-65-3A: Bronze; undated (probably struck in 1966); no serial number; public issue.

K-65-3B: Silver; dated 1966 on rim; no serial number; public issue.

K-65-3C: Bronze; dated 1967 on rim; no serial number; public issue.

K-65-3D: Bronze; dated 1968 on rim; no serial number; public issue.

K-65-3E: Bronze; dated 1970 on rim; no serial number; public issue.

K-65-3F: Bronze; dated 1970; serial numbers 1 through 100.

K-65-3G: Gold on bronze; dated 1970; serial numbers 1 through 100.

K-65-3H: Bronze; dated 1988; serial numbers 1 through 400; public issue.

K-65-3: Reverse reads, "Our problems are manmade and therefore can be solved by man" in French.

K-65-3A

Asia

Thailand

K-63A-318: General Sarit Thanarat, prime minister of Thailand, died unexpectedly on December 8, 1963, shortly after major economic reforms were announced

Europe

Austria

K-64-17

Vietnam

K-63A-317: Ngo Dinh Diem, the first president of South Vietnam. He was assassinated on November 2, 1963, three weeks before John F. Kennedy.

Azores

K-77-3

Belgium

K-68-55

K-69-2

K-84-3

France

K-68-14A

K-68-14G

K-68-20

K-63A-213: Pope John XXIII is pictured on the reverse.

Germany

K-68-11

K-68-61

K-68-14B

K-68-62

K-68-17

K-68-64

K-68-60

K-68-66

Germany *continued*

K-68-67

K-90-1

K-68-68

K-2010-2

K-68-69

K-63A-111A

K-87-4

K-63A-134B

K-63A-249

K-63A-272

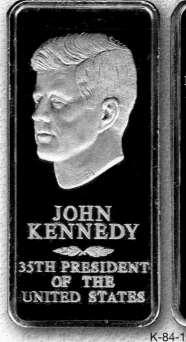 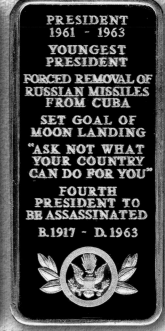

K-84-1

K-63A-333

K-87-1: Isle of Man. *See chapter 16.*

Great Britain

K-74-14

K-88-6

Italy

K-61-22

K-75-5

K-64-6A

The Netherlands

K-70-9

K-68-65

K-63A-87E

K-63A-282: Kennedy-era Lugano cigar bands.

Portugal

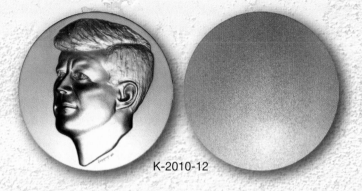

K-2010-12

Slovenia

K-91-3

Russia

K-61-41: International Lenin Peace Medal. Premier Khrushchev of the Soviet Union wore this medal when he met with President Kennedy in Vienna, Austria, on June 4, 1961.

President Kennedy and Premier Khrushchev.

Spain

K-63A-275: Ivory bust.

Switzerland

K-68-59

K-63A-334

The Middle East

Israel

K-66-3

K-66-4

Jordan

K-64-55: Foil stamp set.

President Kennedy greets Golda Meir, foreign minister of Israel, on September 25, 1961, at the United Nations headquarters in New York City.

United Arab Emirates

K-71-55: Ras al-Khaimah two-coin metal stamp set.

K-64-2B and K-64-2C: Sharjah rupee coin stamps.
These commemoratives are from a stamp set of various
denominations. Pictured is an example of an obverse
and an example of a reverse from the set.

K-70-1B

K-81-1

North America

Canada

K-69-9A

Brazil

K-63A-237

South America

Argentina

K-68-60A

Unknown

K-74-8

K-63A-221

K-2008-14

K-63A-223

K-63A-330

K-63A-220

Remembering Kennedy

I am certain that after the dust of centuries has passed

over our cities, we, too, will be remembered not for

victories or defeats in battle or in politics, but for our

contribution to the human spirit.

—*John F. Kennedy, November 29, 1962*

18

March Medals

The Rebirth of a Physical Challenge

From the will of a sick child came the desire to challenge his own physical weakness and to create a body strong enough to carry his creative mind and spirit into adulthood.

Through courage and achievement, Theodore Roosevelt ascended to the presidency of the United States. He believed in creating a healthy, strong military and issued an executive order challenging U.S. Marine officers to walk 50 miles in 20 hours in order to retain their commissions.

Several presidents and years later, following World War II, President Dwight D. Eisenhower, desiring a more healthy American youth, signed Executive Order 10673 on July 16, 1956, which formed the Council on Youth Fitness. Poor organization and no clear guidelines were to prevent the spirit of the program from getting off the ground and receiving any noticeable nationwide success.

K-65-23: Obverse.

For the Collector and Historian

The European Kennedy walk and march medals vary in variety and price. A very limited number of medals are made to commemorate the day; therefore, many march medals are quite rare. Their rarity not only adds to their value but provides an opportunity for a collector to own an interesting piece of Kennedy history of which little is known in the mainstream market.

March medals are a beautiful reflection of JFK's dedication to promoting physical fitness throughout the United States, inspiring other nations to follow suit. However, JFK was not without humor on the subject; a gag gift from Kennedy to his friend David Powers was put up for auction in 2013. The gift, a 50th-birthday "award," is written in Kennedy's own hand: "In recognition of your athletic ability in hiking to my icebox to drink my Heinkens [sic]." It sold for $9,000.

Prior to taking office, President-elect John F. Kennedy had formulated plans in line with his New Frontier philosophy that prompted him to write an article for *Sports Illustrated* called "The Soft American." The article contains four points for overall involvement in physical fitness. Perhaps most important of these was the need for fitness and health programs in public schools nationwide. Kennedy also proposed a national annual convention on youth fitness attended by the governor of each state. The president-elect was making it very clear that healthy citizens would be essential to having a healthy nation.

It is said that in late 1962, Kennedy came across that old executive order issued by Roosevelt challenging military officers. It was after reading that order that Kennedy decided to follow suit, and he presented the challenge of the 50-mile walk to U.S. Marine officers.

Information about the 50-mile hike was published in the media; other branches of the military and citizens nationwide also took up the challenge. In Spring 1963, 50-mile-hike events were held all around the country, a reflection of Kennedy's desire to bring the country back to physical fitness. The New Frontier was now in full swing and America was responding to the idea of becoming a healthy nation. School fitness programs were on the rise and health clubs were opening all across the country.

President Teddy Roosevelt had set the bar very high back in those early years. He, Eisenhower, and Kennedy would be very proud of those runners and hikers who line up today at this worthy event to challenge themselves and honor their intended fitness goals.

After President Kennedy was killed, the large 50-mile-hike event in Washington County, Maryland, changed its name in 1964 from the JFK 50 Mile Challenge to the JFK 50 Mile Memorial. The top military team to finish is awarded the prestigious Kennedy Cup. Each military team is allowed up to ten entries, with the finishing times from the top five combined for the team time, similar to golf and cross country. The lowest time wins. Although open to the public, it is in spirit a military race.

K-2013-8

This event, which draws hundreds each year, is the largest of the Kennedy hike and march events held annually throughout the world. Europeans takes pride in their many JFK and RFK memorial marches, including a Kennedy Mini-March held for children.

K-76-4: Obverse.

K-64-49

K-65-23

K-67-19

K-68-45

K-68-51

K-68-49

K-68-48

K-68-52

K-68-58

K-69-14

K-69-17

K-69-19

K-70-7

K-70-14

K-71-60

K-74-5

K-73-7

K-73-26

K-74-6

K-74-7

K-75-1

K-75-1A

K-75-2

K-75-3

K-76-4

K-75-6

K-75-7

K-79-1

K-82-7

K-83-2

K-83-5

K-89-3

K-2005-1

K-2006-1

K-93-1

K-93-2

K-63A-335

19

Challenge Coins

A Coin, a Medal, a Tribute

Inaccurately named, challenge coins—round pieces of metal bearing a military unit insignia or similar emblem—are actually medals, tokens, or medallions. Perhaps at one time during World War I, challenge coins were actual legal-tender coins with a marking of the serviceman's unit carved or stamped onto them. Alone behind enemy lines, they were a symbol of identification, a way to be recognized when challenged by the allies and to keep from being captured or killed as a spy. The term "coin" stuck and is used in today's collecting field.

From the advent of World War II and the wars in Korea, Vietnam, and the Gulf, military-unit challenge medals—struck, stamped, and cast in various shapes and sizes—have become very popular in the collecting world. They are presented by commanding officers and unit commanders to recognize individual excellence in the performance of duties or heroic unit accomplishments. The medals have now been introduced into occupations well beyond the military, to include law enforcement, fire fighters, and a host of U.S. and foreign government agencies around the world.

The Kennedy-related challenge medals cover a very wide range of the definitions listed above. The crew of the USS *John F. Kennedy* CV-67 aircraft carrier created many challenge medals for the dif-

For the Collector and Historian

A large collection of Kennedy-related challenge coins can be obtained at a reasonable cost and with a little effort. This particular branch of Kennedy medallic art is becoming quite popular and is sure to continue to grow in the years ahead, with many decorative and visually appealing Kennedy-related challenge coins released every year. A "complete" collection will always be a moving target—and an enjoyable pursuit for the collector and historian.

The visually striking designs, colors, sizes, and varieties make challenge coins a fun and educational hobby for military and non-military collectors alike. They can be found easily on Web sites such as eBay for as little as $6, although some specimens are rare or difficult to find depending on their mintage and distribution. Active collectors often trade amongst themselves, swapping duplicates from their collections for pieces they need. This is a collegial niche of the hobby community; old-timers are happy to share information, and newcomers are always welcome.

ferent divisions aboard the ship and cruises around the world during the active term of its service (1967–2007). There are several related military medals that also belong in the listing of this book. The medal illustrating the CIA U-2 spy plane that was flown by Major Rudolph Anderson during the Cuban Missile Crisis is one example. Other units include the U.S. Army John F. Kennedy Special Warfare Center and School and the Navy Seals, organizations which were conceived during and after the Kennedy administration.

The challenge coin series is an interesting and important collection unto itself and worth the effort at a reasonable investment.

KCC-60, the bronze cloisonné JFK CV-67 Judge Advocate General's Office Corps challenge coin, and KCC-88 are not pictured.

USS *John F. Kennedy* (CVA-67)

Authorization for the building of the USS *John F. Kennedy* was provided by the 1963 Shipbuilding and Conversion Program. The laying of the keel began on October 22, 1964. The world's largest warship, the USS *John F. Kennedy* was christened and launched at Newport News, Virginia, on May 27, 1967, just two days before what would have been the late president's 50th birthday. Caroline Kennedy, the daughter of Presi-

USS *John F. Kennedy*.

dent Kennedy, was the christening sponsor. A ceremony commissioning this proud new member of the U.S. Navy fleet was held before a crowd of 10,000 on September 7, 1968. In attendance were the late president's widow, Jacqueline Kennedy, and their children, Caroline and John F. Kennedy Jr.

In 1967, Earl P. Yates, the first commanding officer of the USS *John F. Kennedy*, nicknamed "Big John," commissioned Presidential Art Medals (PAM) to strike 100 bronze 38 mm medals bearing the obverse of the PAM John F. Kennedy memorial medal which had been previously produced. A new reverse of the medal was to bear the official emblem of the USS *John F. Kennedy* CVA-67. While the ship was designated a CV craft (aircraft carrier) in 1974 following a major overhaul, she was originally designated CVA (aircraft carrier, attack) as she was a fixed wing attack carrier. KCC-1 illustrates the original CVA medal.

In 2005, the Northwest Territorial Mint struck a USS *John F. Kennedy* bronze challenge medal bearing the letters CVN (N is the designation for nuclear-powered) in error. The reported original strike was 500 medals. The error was soon corrected and restrikes without the N went into production. The Northwest Territorial designer of KCC-20 through KCC-22 was Justin Michael Ladd.

The statistics of the USS *John F. Kennedy* are as follows:

Weight: 61,450 tons

Length: 1,051 feet

Flight deck: 4-1/2 acres

Crew: 5,200 hands

Maximum speed: 35 knots

Turbine powered 280,000 horsepower

First captain: Earl Yates, USN.

USS *John F. Kennedy* Unit Awards

Award	Start Date	End Date
Armed Forces Expeditionary Medal	11/6/83	11/27/83
	12/2/83	1/21/84
	1/31/84	2/22/84
	2/25/84	2/29/84
	10/31/99*	3/2/00
Armed Forces Service Medal	10/22/92*	10/22/92
	11/25/92*	12/2/92
	1/10/93*	1/12/93
	1/30/93	3/24/93
	6/19/97	6/28/97
Meritorious Unit Commendation	9/29/70	10/1/70
	12/1/77	3/1/79
	7/15/82	4/22/84
	7/1/86	7/6/86
Navy "E" Ribbon	10/1/76	9/30/77
	10/1/77	9/30/78
	1/1/82	12/31/82
	1/1/83	12/31/83
Navy Unit Commendation	1/17/91	2/28/91
Southwest Asia Service Medal	9/14/90	3/2/91
Secretary of the Navy Letter of Commendation	8/4/80	3/28/81
	4/24/88	4/24/88
*one award for multiple dates		

KCC-01

KCC-05

KCC-02

KCC-06

KCC-03

KCC-07

KCC-04

KCC-08

KCC-09

KCC-13

KCC-10

KCC-14

KCC-11

KCC-15

KCC-12

KCC-16

KCC-17

KCC-21

KCC-18

KCC-22

KCC-19

KCC-23

KCC-20

KCC-24

KCC-25

KCC-29

KCC-26

KCC-30

KCC-27

KCC-31

KCC-28

KCC-32

KCC-33

KCC-37

KCC-34

KCC-38

KCC-35

KCC-39

KCC-36

KCC-40

KCC-41

KCC-45

KCC-42

KCC-46

KCC-43

KCC-47

KCC-44

KCC-48

KCC-49

KCC-53

KCC-50

KCC-54

KCC-51

KCC-55

KCC-52

KCC-56

KCC-57

KCC-62

KCC-58

KCC-63

KCC-59

KCC-64

KCC-61

KCC-65

KCC-66

KCC-69

KCC-66A

KCC-70

KCC-67

KCC-71

KCC-68

KCC-72

KCC-73

KCC-75

KCC-74

KCC-77

KCC-76

KCC-78

KCC-82

KCC-79

KCC-83

KCC-80

KCC-84

KCC-81

KCC-85

KCC-86

KCC-90

KCC-87

KCC-91

KCC-89

KCC-92

Sets and Collections

1961 Official John F. Kennedy Inaugural Medal Process Set, K-61-11

The national distributor of the official inaugural medal, the Coin and Currency Institute (of New York City) pulled out all the stops in marketing this issue, designed by Paul Manship. They had forty process sets and twenty 9-1/2–inch plaster models made by the Medallic Art Company for use as promotional display pieces. These sets were placed at various coin counters in major department stores around the country to help sell the official medal. All sets were distributed after the promotional period ended.

Stage One: The Planchet

The alloy is first cast into ingots, which are in turn rolled under great pressure into sheets of proper thickness. These sheets then have individual blanks punched from them. You can tell which side of the planchet was facing up by the deformation of the metal along the edge as it is sheared from the sheet. While this process is similar to that of coin production, several blanks are not punched at once nor are their edges further formed before the blanks are delivered to the press room.

Stage one.

Sets of coins, medals, and tokens have long had pride of place in a Kennedy-related collection. In 1961 the promotional John F. Kennedy inaugural medal process set sold for an issue price of $27.50. Now, when one occasionally shows up at auction or online, it is valued at $650 or more.

More often than not, one item holds as much monetary value as any other within a complete set. The Lincoln Mint series is a good example of this; any individual medal within the set holds the same approximate retail value as any of the other 36 medals. The subject matter of the medal has very little influence on individual retail price if each medal is the same size and has the same bullion content.

Stage Two: First Strike

After the planchets have been washed and annealed (a process of softening), they are ready to receive an impression. The first blow leaves the medal recognizable but very unclear.

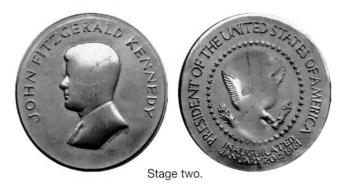

Stage two.

Stage Three: Second Strike

This movement of metal generates great heat which, under the tremendous pressure of the press, causes the planchet to work harden. The medal is again annealed and, after carefully aligning the medal between the dies, another strike is made.

Stage three.

Stage Four: Third and Final Strike

Annealed once more, the medal is struck for the third, and in this case final, time. The total number of strikes required for any art medal can vary from two to twelve or more, depending on the relief of the design. However, for this medal, the third strike reveals the full detail, leaving a proof-like finish. Struck without a collar, the flange is very prominent at this point.

Stage four.

Stage Five: Sizing

The medal is mounted on a turning lathe and machined to the proper size.

Stage five.

Stage Six: Finishing

The finish is sandblasted and a solution that creates an antique finish is applied. A coat of lacquer to protect the bronze is then introduced, thus completing the medal.

Stage six.

Executive Design Presidential Series

The JFK Collection

K-61-17A: Error reverse. Lyndon B. Johnson was the 37th—not 38th—vice president of the United States.

K-61-17D: Correct reverse.

Certificate of Authenticity

The John F. Kennedy Collection

This is to certify that the silver proofs accompanied by this certificate are authentic commemoratives of John F. Kennedy, the 35th President of the United States.

Specifications

Diameter: 38.6 mm	Diameter: 63.00 mm
Weight: 23.33 grams	Weight: 136.08 grams
Composition: .925 fine Sterling Silver	Composition: .925 fine Sterling Silver

Maximum Mintage: 25,000 collections

Designed by Frank Gasparro.

K-61-17A: Rim.

K-88-7: Reverse. The reverse is the same
for all commemoratives in the set.

K-88-10: Obverse.

K-88-7: Obverse.

K-88-11: Obverse.

K-88-8: Obverse.

K-88-12: Obverse.

K-88-9: Obverse.

K-88-13: Obverse.

K-88-14: Obverse.

The End of Camelot, 1963-2003

THE END OF CAMELOT
1963 - 2003

K-88-15: Obverse.

K-88-16: Obverse.

From left to right: K-2003-1A, K-2003-1, K-2003-1B

K-88-17: Obverse.

The Legacy of John F. Kennedy

36 life-event medals struck by the Lincoln Mint in Chicago, Illinois.

The first medal in this series was issued in February 1971. Thirty-five medals followed the first, one issued per month, at a cost of $10.00 each. It took three years to complete the set. Each medal in this set is composed of .999 fine silver and is 39 mm. The album in which the set appears is blue simulated leather with gold lettering. Each collector was assigned a serial number and each medal sent over the course of the three years was stamped with the serial number unique to the collector. The following are additional available versions of the sets.

.925 sterling silver

Size: 39 mm

Brown simulated leather album with gold lettering

Quantity minted: 5,000

Bronze

Size: 39 mm

Date series started: 1971

Quantity minted: 5,000

24k gold over .925 sterling silver

Size: 39 mm

Date of manufacture: 1977

Finish: Cameo Proof

The John F. Kennedy Commemorative Set

While this edition of the set has an alternate title, the obverse and reverse of each medal remains the same.

Brown simulated leather album with gold lettering

Quantity minted: 5,000 sets

The order in which the 36 medals were minted with matching serial numbers:

1. The Inauguration
2. Boyhood of a Legend
3. Cuban Missile Crisis
4. Visit to the Vatican
5. Advisor and Brother
6. The Great TV Debates
7. Jacqueline Bouvier Kennedy
8. Giant Step into Space
9. His Party's Choice
10. Culture in the White House
11. Senator from Massachusetts
12. Krushchev in Vienna
13. Congressman from Boston
14. Sharing of a Dream
15. Ambassador to the World
16. Addressing the United Nations
17. Caroline and John Jr.
18. Blueprint for Reason and Peace
19. Harvard Cum Laude
20. Profiles in Courage
21. Bay of Pigs
22. A New Leader Emerges
23. Victory in the Primaries
24. Medicare Promise
25. A Religious Issue Resolved
26. Birth of the Peace Corps
27. The Kennedy Heritage
28. Rocking Chair President
29. Apprenticeship in Diplomacy
30. Pledge to the Hemisphere
31. PT 109
32. 35th President
33. November 22, 1963
34. The Last March
35. The Eternal Flame
36. The New Frontier

THE LEGACY OF JOHN F. KENNEDY

"...ask not what your country can do for you... ask what you can do for your country."

Inaugural Address January 20, 1961

THE INAUGURATION

K-71-13

ADVISOR AND BROTHER

THE LEGACY OF JOHN F. KENNEDY

JUSTICE

"...(He) saw wrong and tried to right it, saw suffering and tried to heal it, saw war and tried to stop it."

The Attorney General, Robert; President, Kennedy and Edward

K-71-17

THE LEGACY OF JOHN F. KENNEDY

"Mothers may still want their favorite sons to grow up to be President, but... they do not want them to become politicians in the process."

Dexter Academy 1923-26

BOYHOOD OF A LEGEND

K-71-14

THE GREAT TV DEBATES

THE LEGACY OF JOHN F. KENNEDY

The great TV debates of 1960 were considered the single most important factor in advancing John F. Kennedy to the presidency.

Sept. 26, Oct 7, 13, 21, 1960

K-71-18

CUBAN MISSILE CRISIS

ATLANTIC OCEAN

CUBA

THE LEGACY OF JOHN F. KENNEDY

"Neither the United States nor the world community can tolerate deliberate deception and offensive threats on the part of any nation large or small."

October 16-26, 1962

K-71-15

JACQUELINE BOUVIER KENNEDY

THE LEGACY OF JOHN F. KENNEDY

Jacqueline Lee Bouvier born July 28, 1929 Southampton, New York married to John Fitzgerald Kennedy September 12, 1953 Newport, Rhode Island

K-71-19

Visit to the Vatican

THE LEGACY OF JOHN F. KENNEDY

"The making of peace is the noblest work of God-fearing men."

With Pope Paul VI, July 2, 1963

K-71-16

A GIANT STEP INTO SPACE

THE LEGACY OF JOHN F. KENNEDY

"It shall be the goal of my Administration to land a man on the moon and return him safely to earth before this decade is out."

John Glenn and JFK at Cape Canaveral

K-71-20

K-71-21

THE LEGACY OF JOHN F. KENNEDY

As a Congressman J FK followed a course of independent action and thinking, thus gaining recognition and respect throughout Massachusetts
Three terms, 1946 to 1952

K-71-25

K-71-22

K-71-26

K-71-23

K-71-27

K-71-24

K-71-28

K-71-29

BAY
OF
PIGS

THE LEGACY OF JOHN F. KENNEDY

John F. Kennedy
accepted full
responsibility for the
Cuban Exile Brigade's
disastrous invasion
of Cuba.

K-71-33

THE LEGACY OF JOHN F. KENNEDY

The Nuclear Test Ban Treaty...
"It will not resolve all conflicts...
but it is a step away from war...
a step toward peace."

July 25, 1963

K-71-30

A NEW
LEADER
EMERGES

THE LEGACY OF JOHN F. KENNEDY

JFK lost the race for the
1956 Democratic Vice
Presidential nomination
but won nationwide
recognition as a new
party leader.

K-71-34

HARVARD CUM LAUDE

THE LEGACY OF JOHN F. KENNEDY

JFK took his degree,
Cum Laude, in political
science. His thesis,
Why England Slept,
became a best-seller
the same year.

Class of 1940

K-71-31

VICTORY IN THE PRIMARIES

THE LEGACY OF JOHN F. KENNEDY

JFK swept New Hampshire,
and went on to his first
victories outside New
England in Wisconsin.
West Virginia. Indiana
and Oregon.

Spring, 1960

K-71-35

PROFILES IN COURAGE

THE LEGACY OF JOHN F. KENNEDY

Recovering from surgery
JFK wrote of courageous
Americans... "Each man
must decide for himself
the course he
will follow."

Profiles In Courage · Pulitzer Prize 1957

K-71-32

MEDICARE
PROMISE

THE LEGACY OF JOHN F. KENNEDY

In spite of JFK's efforts
to provide health care for
the aged, Medicare was
not enacted until a year
and a half after
his death.

January 20, 1961 – July 30, 1965

K-71-36

A RELIGIOUS ISSUE RESOLVED

THE LEGACY OF JOHN F. KENNEDY

With JFK's eloquent defense of religious liberty during the 1960 campaign, a candidate's religion ceased to be a major political issue.

K-71-37

A APPRENTICESHIP IN DIPLOMACY

THE LEGACY OF JOHN F. KENNEDY

JFK learned world diplomacy during the turbulent pre-war months of 1939 when he assisted his father, the U.S. Ambassador to Britain.

K-71-41

BIRTH OF THE PEACE CORPS

THE LEGACY OF JOHN F. KENNEDY

PEACE CORPS

"A new generation of Americans has taken over this country...working for freedom as servants of peace around the world."

John F. Kennedy, 1960

K-71-38

A PLEDGE TO THE HEMISPHERE

THE LEGACY OF JOHN F. KENNEDY

The Alliance for Progress, a 10 year plan for economic and social development in Latin America. "Our motto is...Progress, yes! Tyranny, no!"

K-71-42

THE KENNEDY HERITAGE

THE LEGACY OF JOHN F. KENNEDY

A trilogy in public service... John Fitzgerald, Mayor Joseph Kennedy Sr., U.S. Ambassador John F. Kennedy, President

K-71-39

PT 109

THE LEGACY OF JOHN F. KENNEDY

Sunk by an enemy destroyer, August 1942. JFK, commander of Navy PT109, led all surviving crewmen to safety through enemy territory.

K-71-43

ROCKING CHAIR PRESIDENT

THE LEGACY OF JOHN F. KENNEDY

JFK's favorite chair, the Colonial rocker in the Oval Office, became a symbol of his administration and the New Frontier.

K-71-40

THE 35TH PRESIDENT

THE LEGACY OF JOHN F. KENNEDY

"Together we shall save our planet...and then shall we earn the eternal thanks of mankind and, as peacemakers, the eternal blessing of God."

Inaugural Address January 20, 1961

K-71-44

THE LEGACY OF JOHN F. KENNEDY

John Fitzgerald Kennedy
35th United States President
Born Brookline, Mass.
May 29.1917. Assassinated
in Dallas, Texas
Nov. 22, 1963
LM

NOVEMBER 22. 1963

K-71-45

THE ETERNAL FLAME

THE LEGACY OF JOHN F. KENNEDY

"Born of the sun they
traveled a short while
towards the sun, and left
the vivid air signed with
their honour."

– Stephen Spender

K-71-47

THE LAST MARCH

THE LEGACY OF JOHN F. KENNEDY

"In Washington, grief was
an agony...the roll of
the drums...will
sound forever..."

LM

K-71-46

THE LEGACY OF JOHN F. KENNEDY

THE NEW FRONTIER

THE LEGACY OF JOHN F. KENNEDY

"...he gave his country back
to its best self...young,
brave, exultant in the
excitement and
potentiality
of history."

LM

K-71-48

Osborne Coinage and Osborne-Style Tokens

K-60-2

K-60-2B

K-60-2A

35TH PRESIDENT, U.S.A.

1961

JOHN F. KENNEDY

THE WHITE HOUSE

INAUGURATED
JANUARY 20, 1961.

K-61-4

K-61-4A

K-61-10C

K-61-4B

K-61-10D

K-61-10

K-61-10E

K-61-10B

K-61-10F

K-61-11

K-61-45

K-61-11A

K-65-2

K-61-27

K-65-2A

K-61-44

K-65-12

K-71-4

K-63A-4E

K-71-4A

K-63A-4F

K-63A-4C

K-63A-9

K-63A-4D

K-63A-9C

K-63A-9D

K-63A-9H

K-63A-9E

K-63A-9I

K-63A-9F

K-63A-9J

K-63A-9G

K-63A-9K

K-63A-10

K-63A-10E

K-63A-10A

K-63A-10F

K-63A-10C

K-63A-11A

K-63A-10D

K-63A-244

K-63A-244A

K-63A-276B

K-63A-244B

K-63A-276C

K-63A-276

K-63A-276D

K-63A-276A

K-63A-277

K-63A-278

K-63A-281

K-63A-279

K-63A-310

K-63A-280

K-63A-313

Profiles in Courage Silver Cameo Set, K-76-29

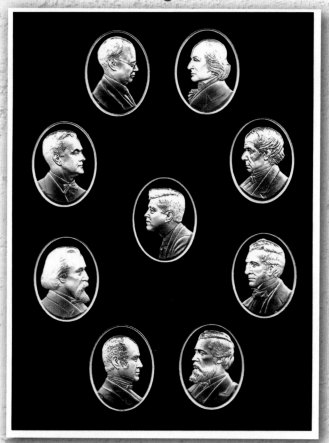

Other Sets

K-65-8: Spoof Proof Set. Created in response to the removal of silver from U.S. coinage.

K-65-24: Wooden Nickel Set.

K-69-3A: Franklin Mint Presidential Mini-Coin Set.

K-92-8: Shell Oil Company coin give-away with gas purchase.

K-2000-16: Sunoco Oil Company coin
give-away with gas purchase.

21

Commemorative Coin Covers and Postage

Commemorative Coin Covers

It is unknown who first put a commemorative coin in a protective mailing envelope, although over time the idea has produced several interesting varieties of this rather limited facet of Kennedy medallic art.

The Great American series, issued by the Postal Commemorative Society, combined a U.S. postage stamp with a gold-plated stamp reproduction. The Famous Americans gold stamp commemorative series, featuring the new Robert F. Kennedy commemorative stamp and accompanying gold reproduction by the Westport Mint, is a fine example of this medallic collectable. Postmasters of America issued a beautiful sterling silver 13-cent reproduction of the official John F. Kennedy 13-cent postage stamp.

Several other private firms, both in the United State and overseas, have produced envelopes and collector showcards that have inserted Kennedy half dollars and various bronze and silver Kennedy medals under see-through plastic windows. Rolled or elongated coins have also proven to be very popular, as they produce a lower profile on a card or envelope and have a strong visual impact.

One great advantage to this collectable has been that the artist is able to add vital information, including background history on the subject, which adds interest to the stamp.

Commemorative coin covers have created an interesting bridge between the worlds of coin and stamp collectors.

For the Collector and Historian

Commemorative coin covers and philatelic Kennedy souvenirs are a small, and very affordable, category of Kennedy memorabilia. Often canceled on key dates in his presidency, these covers present colorful images and interesting factoids about the president's life and time in office.

In 2013, a set of 17 Kennedy-related coin covers housed in a commemorative binder sold for $180. Each cover honors JFK and his achievements, including his inauguration day; a visit to the NASA Manned Spacecraft Center; his family; and his memorable visit to Berlin.

CCC-01

CCC-05

CCC-02

CCC-06

CCC-03

CCC-07

CCC-04

CCC-08

CCC-09

CCC-13

CCC-10

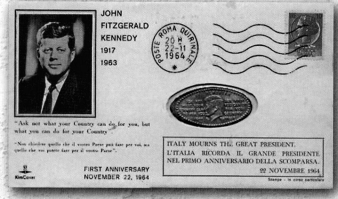

CCC-14

CCC-11

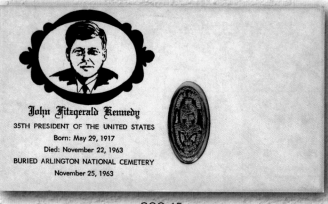

CCC-15

CCC-12

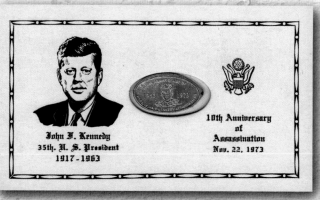

CCC-16

CCC-17

CCC-18

CCC-19

CCC-20

The Cover Mistake Incident

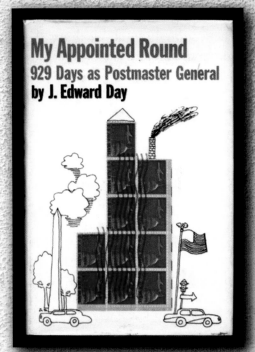

First dust jacket design, with stamps.

Second dust jacket design, without stamps.

The Secret Service must not have heard—or didn't heed—the injunction against judging a book by its cover. As a matter of fact, they didn't even look at the cover; a glimpse of the dust jacket was enough to show them that a federal law had been violated.

The book was a memoir by former postmaster general J. Edward Day, who was selected by President Kennedy to head the nation's post offices. The book went on display in Washington bookstores in June 1965, with a jacket design that included reproductions of eight U.S. airmail stamps in full color.

Embarrassing though it was to a former official whose business was stamps, the color reproductions were illegal. The penalty for this violation was 15 years in prison or a $5,000 fine. The impending crisis was resolved when the publisher, Holt, Rinehart and Winston, ordered the offending jackets destroyed, printed a new design, and noted apologetically that Postmaster Day had not approved the jacket "as it appeared." With that, a spokesman said, the Secret Service considered the incident closed.

Souvenir Stamp Sheets

K-61-14

This souvenir stamp sheet is extremely rare.

22

Other Kennedy Items

Keeping His Memory Alive

Other than medals, medallions, and tokens, there is a multitude of Kennedy items that are not only historical and have enduring cultural value, but are highly commercial in nature.

Perhaps the purpose of the many commercial and artistic items that poured forth shortly after the assassination was to return a lost and admired leader to our grieving society, to bring his persona back in any form possible, and create tangible items to keep his memory alive. Many of these various forms of remembrance demonstrate that he is not really gone.

In *Kitsch: The World of Bad Taste*, Gillo Dorfles describes how people buy bath towels and household items displaying reproductions of the Mona Lisa; however, if the real Mona Lisa is displayed at a nearby art gallery, these same people might not be eager to see it because they already have a version at home. Collecting JFK memorabilia is this same idea but in reverse: Kennedy, and the world of his time, is gone forever and having a deck of cards with his smiling face printed on them can not only bring forth a heartwarming memory as a representation of that time, but this memorabilia can be experienced by future generations.

Americans have always been collectors of one sort or another. Those who lived through the Great Depression remember not having sugar for baking; they remember standing in line for gasoline stamps during World War II. The desire to collect came not only from those difficult times during which people had very little to call their own, but it allowed for a type of freedom, a freedom to possess

For the Collector and Historian

There is no shortage of Kennedy-related items for the unique collector who veers away from mainstream memorabilia. These range from playing cards to paperweights, and everything in between. Many items can be found for less than $20 and some for as little as 10 cents at a flea market.

However, every so often, a Kennedy-related item appears that is so rare it can only be purchased by the most affluent of collectors. One such item was the 1962-era JFK Air Force One bomber jacket, worn by President Kennedy and later loaned to President Ronald Reagan. In 2013, this jacket was valued between $20,000 and $40,000. It sold at auction that year for the incredible amount of $570,000.

more than just the necessities of daily life. A card saved from a pack of cigarettes bearing the image of a favorite movie star; a rock found on a beach you visited when you were a child. We as human beings need the past, not to live in, but to honor the good memories and discard the bad.

President Kennedy believed that past events were the building blocks for the future. The memorial items purchased and saved are themselves a tangible tribute to the memory of this Knight from Camelot who rode through 1,000 days of our history.

K-63A-274: Wedgwood candy dish.

K-62-4: Wedgwood oval.

K-63-18: Game coin.

K-62-4A: Wedgwood oval.

K-63-25: Manufactured when JFK was in office.

K-62-4B: Wedgwood oval.

K-63-25B: Card deck box.

K-64-54: Wood coin plaque with a bright gold finish; uniface.

K-71-61: Face and edge.

K-80-3B: Ingot.

K-66-9

K-80-3C: Ingot.

K-67-11

K-86-6: Belt buckle.

K-2008-1

K-63A-230

K-2011-8: Limited edition.

K-63A-261: 5-cent stamp ingot.

K-63A-121: Mini-medal golf ball marker
given to the author by Ed Rochette.

K-63A-121A: Micro charm
given to the author by Ed Rochette.

K-63A-328: Belt buckle.

Bullion Bars

K-71-56

K-73-8

K-72-10A

K-73-14

K-73-5

K-73-16

K-73-6

K-73-20

K-73-22

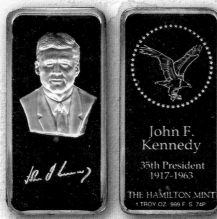

K-74-17

K-74-18

K-75-4

K-76-1

K-76-1A

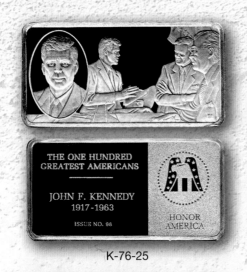

K-76-25

K-2012-3

K-82-4

K-2012-4

Die Hubs

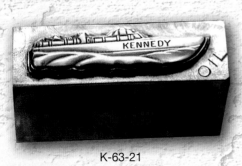

K-63-21

K-95-7

K-95-7

Elongated Coins

Don Adams John F. Kennedy Elongated

The President John F. Kennedy bars were designed by Donald Adams and minted by the Green Duck Mint, which is no longer in existence. The silver bars were issued in 1973 with serial numbers and weigh 1-1/2 ounces. Only 200 silver bars were issued. The bronze bars were also issued in 1973 with serial numbers and weigh 11 ounces. 800 bronze bars were issued. The die was canceled by the mint after the silver and bronze bars were minted.

The Kennedy half dollar elongated nickel was designed and rolled by Don Adams and the die was engraved by Robert Luchtman. This design was part of Adams's elongated coin type series and was rolled in March 1973. Five were rolled on copper cents, five on silver dimes, and 400 were rolled on Jefferson nickels. The die is design number DA-64.

K-73-21

K-73-21A

Angelo Anthony Rosato: Elongated Coin Creator and Collector

Angelo Anthony Rosato.

His 32-year career as a jeweler honed Angelo Rosato's skill and talent for creating and producing some of the finest elongated coins ever made. Prior to his passing at the age of 91 on November 13, 2012, he wrote and published the most detailed reference catalog and guide of elongated coins. The *Encyclopedia of the Modern Elongated* is a fine tribute to his love of the coin-collecting hobby. He designed and hand-engraved the dies and rolled his own elongated coins. Rosato's limited-edition craftsmanship can

Rosato Items On JFK Feature Of Coinarama

On Oct. 23 the Candlewood Valley Association sponsored by the Coin Club of New Milford held its second annual Coinarama. George Mitchell, chairman, and Angelo A. Rosato, co-chairman and president of the Coin Club of New Milford directed the event, which was held at the Danbury Motor Inn.

Numismatic items were given away to registrants as well as copies of the publication "Coin World." An aluminum token commemorating the event was also given free to those who attended. A $5 goldpiece was offered as first prize to those who purchased a ticket for the drawing. With a purchase a specimen $3 note made from the original plates was given free.

Highlighting the event, Angelo Rosato exhibited his "Kennediana" collection. The display contained hundreds of items and JFK medals as well as associated medalic art items. The collection is known, as probably the largest in the New England area.

Discoveries by Mr. Rosato were also shown along with many unique specimens. He has worked in research and has had the pleasure of aiding Edward Rochette, author of the book "Medalic Portraits of John F. Kennedy," whom he met recently at the NENA convention held in Worcester, Mass., while compiling information for Rochette's new supplement.

Many of Mr. Rosato's items will be mentioned in the forthcoming book by Aubrey Mayhew, "The World's Tribute to JFK in Medalic Art."

The *New Milford Times*, October 27, 1965.

be found in this volume as well as the two earlier books on Kennedy medallic art mentioned in the credits.

K-67-23

Memories
From
Bertha
M. Hollars,
Doll Maker,
July 1973

When I was a very small child, I remember my grandmother making me dolls—rag dolls, families of dolls from corn husks and wooden clothes pins.

When I was about four years old, she ordered me a doll from Sears that had a voice box in its head. The doll's head must have been china because one day it broke and it also broke my heart. I had other dolls but they never replaced the doll that my grandmother had given to me.

In 1969, I decided to learn how to make molds, so I found someone to teach me. I am sure that you know how I felt about JFK; he was such a great man in many ways, but I could not find a JFK doll, so I decided to try my luck at making a mold of him. I wanted to make a JFK doll for my niece. I made the mold of JFK, and I hope to make one of each of the children and Mrs. Kennedy soon.

Bertha M. Hollars, California doll maker, finishing her John F. Kennedy doll's head.

K-73-28

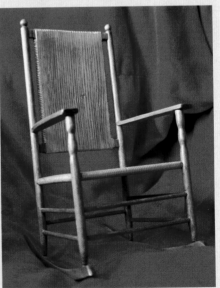

K-73-29

Hobo Coins

The history of the artistic alteration of coinage dates back to the 1700s. Once a nationwide romantic fad, jewelers and artistic metal engravers in the late 1800s also created hobo coins with a wife's or lover's initials decoratively crafted on a dime, quarter, half dollar, or dollar. Wealthier clients had U.S. gold coins initialed in the same manner. Today there are several modern coin-carving artists who practice their craft using a range and variety of world-coin shapes and sizes. Here I have illustrated one such example of a 1974 cupronickel Kennedy half dollar titled JFK Mohawk Skull, by modern-day nickel carver Valerie "Goonie" Vaughan.

K-2013-10: Obverse, hobo half dollar by Pedro Villarrubia.

K-74-20: Obverse, hobo half dollar by Valerie Vaughan.

K-63A-210: Obverse, hobo nickel by Steve Adams.

K-2013-9: Obverse, hobo half dollar by Pedro Villarrubia.

K-63A-211: Obverse, hobo nickel. Artist unknown.

Paper Money

Asian Hell Notes

Many cultures and religions believe that a person lives beyond their mortal life. Therefore, it has been the practice of some of these cultures to provide the departed with money to spend in the afterlife.

In ancient times, the Greeks would place a coin in the mouth of the deceased as payment for the ferryman of Akheron, who would carry the soul across the river to the land of the dead.

Hell notes are examples of a similar practice commonly found in Asia. The reference to hell in the title of these bank notes was introduced by Christian missionaries, who preached that non-Christians who refused to convert to Christianity were destined for an afterlife in hell. These Christians found the native customs blasphemous and sinful.

Hell money bearing a photo of the deceased, in this case John F. Kennedy, is burned and the smoke travels into the spiritual world bank, as depicted on the reverse of the note. This money is then available for use by the departed spirit in order to enjoy a prosperous afterlife. In Asian belief, a higher denomination denotes the importance of the person in life.

For hundreds of years, people have enclosed gifts with their loved one as he or she is laid to rest. These take the form of crosses, wedding rings, spiritual money, and other shared memorials. President Kennedy's wife Jacqueline placed her wedding ring on her husband's finger before his casket was sealed as a way of remaining with him even after he was gone.

Fantasy Notes

Paperweights

Patches

K-63-15B

K-63A-320

K-64-46

K-63-15E

K-65-20

K-69-20

K-76-7

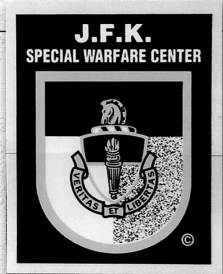

K-76-8

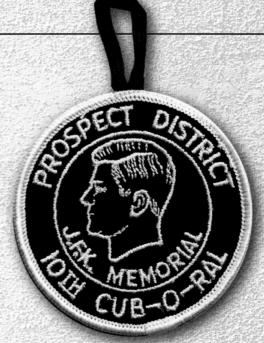

K-63A-226

K-2005-2

K-63A-228

K-63A-227

The Kennedy Catalog

Catalog #	Item Name	Size	Composition	Additional Information
K-00-1	John F. Fitzgerald Old Home Week token, 1907	36 mm	Brass	
K-00-2	Rose Fitzgerald Child of Mary medal, 1913	40 mm	Silver	
K-00-3	Greenbrier Resort room key tag	35 mm	Brass	
K-00-4	John F. Kennedy first birthday medal, 1918	31 mm	Silver	Hallmark: Cg Hallberg; certified 1918
K-00-5	Boston Fire Historical Society Patrick J. Kennedy medal			
K-00-6	John F. Kennedy 1931 Swim Club medal	25 2/5 mm	10K gold	
K-00-7	Navy Cross Award			Posthumous award to Joseph P. Kennedy Jr.
K-00-8	World War II Navy Good Conduct medal			Awarded to JFK
K-00-9	Navy Marine Corps medal			Awarded to JFK for heroism
K-00-10	Purple Heart medal			Awarded to JFK for PT-109 injuries
K-00-11	World War II Victory medal			JFK and RFK are eligible for this medal
K-00-12	Asiatic-Pacific Campaign medal with 3 stars			JFK is eligible for this medal
K-00-13	American Defense medal			JFK is eligible for this medal
K-00-14	American Campaign medal			JFK and RFK are eligible for this medal
K-60-1	"1960 Special Service to the President" JFK-LBJ campaign medal	39 mm	Sterling silver	Edge hallmark: sterling
K-60-1A	"1960 Special Service to the President" JFK-LBJ campaign medal	39 mm	Nickel silver	Plain edge
K-60-1B	"1960 Special Service to the President" JFK-LBJ campaign medal	39 mm	Oxidized nickel silver	Plain edge
K-60-1C	"1960 Special Service to the President" JFK-LBJ campaign medal	39 mm	Oxidized bronze	Plain edge
K-60-1D	"1960 Special Service to the President" JFK-LBJ campaign medal	39 mm	Gold plated	Plain edge
K-60-1D-1	"1960 Special Service to the President" JFK-LBJ campaign medal	39 mm	Aluminum	Plain edge
K-60-1E	"1960 Special Service to the President" Nixon-Lodge campaign medal	39 mm	Sterling silver	Edge hallmark: sterling
K-60-1F	"1960 Special Service to the President" Nixon-Lodge campaign medal	39 mm	Nickel silver	Plain edge
K-60-1G	"1960 Special Service to the President" Nixon-Lodge campaign medal	39 mm	Oxidized nickel silver	Plain edge
K-60-1H	"1960 Special Service to the President" Nixon-Lodge campaign medal	39 mm	Oxidized bronze	Plain edge
K-60-1I	"1960 Special Service to the President" Nixon-Lodge campaign medal	39 mm	Gold plated	Plain edge
K-60-1J	"1960 Special Service to the President" Nixon-Lodge campaign medal	39 mm	Aluminum	Plain edge
K-60-2	1960 Osborne presidential campaign medal	28 mm	Aluminum	Plain edge
K-60-2A	1960 Osborne presidential campaign medal	28 mm	Goldine	Plain edge
K-60-2B	1960 Osborne presidential campaign medal	28 mm	Aluminum	Plain edge; looped
K-60-3	Earl Fankhauser 1960 campaign cent, encased	32 mm	Aluminum copper	Plain edge
K-60-4	Jolle 1960 presidential campaign PT-109 charm	32 mm	Polished bronze	
K-60-4A	1960 presidential PT-109 Wichita Falls, TX, Teenage Chairman medal	32 mm	Polished bronze with a blue background	Reverse: Jackie Kennedy
K-60-5	Inaugural dukaten, Germany	20 mm	.980 fine gold	Reverse: Statue of Liberty
K-60-5A	Inaugural dukaten, Germany	25 mm	.980 fine gold	Reverse: Statue of Liberty
K-60-5B	Inaugural dukaten, Germany	30 mm	.980 fine gold	Reverse: Statue of Liberty
K-60-5C	Inaugural dukaten, Germany	39 mm	.980 fine gold	Reverse: Statue of Liberty
K-60-5D	Inaugural dukaten, Germany	49 mm	.980 fine gold	Reverse: Statue of Liberty
K-60-6	Oleet lithograph portrait of JFK political charm	23 x 30 mm	Gold-plated plastic	Looped; reverse: plain
K-60-6A	Oleet lithograph portrait of JFK political charm	23 x 30 mm	Gold-plated plastic	Clutch pin back
K-60-7	"Kennedy for President" caricature for jewelry	34 mm	Gold-embossed plastic	For insert
K-60-8	JFK rhinestone jewelry pin	53 x 38 mm	Nickel silver with stones	Pin back
K-60-8A	Nixon rhinestone jewelry pin	53 x 38 mm	Nickel silver with stones	Pin back
K-60-9	Map of the United States with JFK in the center	27 x 17 mm	Base metal with red, white, and blue	Pin back
K-60-10	Democratic donkey over Kennedy tie tac pin	26 x 22 mm	Base metal	
K-60-11	PT-109 Kennedy tie tac	28 x 14 mm	Gold-colored base metal	
K-60-12	PT-109 Kennedy tie tac	47 x 18 mm	Gold-colored base metal	
K-60-13	PT-109 Kennedy jewelry pin	30 x 5 mm	Gold-colored base metal	
K-60-14	PT-109 Kennedy 60 pin	45 x 10 mm	Golden brass	
K-60-15	PT-109 Kennedy 60 tie tac	45 x 10 mm	Golden brass	
K-60-16	PT-109 Kennedy 60 pin	45 x 10 mm	Silvered brass	

K-60-17	PT-109 Kennedy 60 tie tac	45 x 10 mm	Silvered brass	
K-60-18	DNC Los Angeles 60 medal	40 mm	Bronze	Looped
K-60-19	Medallic Art "With Appreciation" Richard Nixon campaign medal	63 mm	Bronze	Reverse: three names
K-60-20	Charleston Mint "Echo 1, 1st Communications Satellite" medal	35 1/3 mm	Brass	Serial number; reverse: NASA
K-60-21	PT-109 JK 60 tie tack		Silvered brass	Aligator clip
K-60-21A	PT-109 JK 60 tie pin		Silvered brass	Push pin clasp
K-60-22	JFK presidential campaign K-60 arrow pin	41 3/10 mm	Gold finish	Lock pin
K-60-23	Jack Kennedy campaign jewelry pin	41 1/2 mm	Silver over base metal	Alligator pin
K-60-24	Jack Kennedy campaign jewelry charm	41 1/2 mm	Silver over base metal	Uniface
K-60-25	Kennedy campaign circle wreath jewelry charm	41 1/2 mm	Silver over base metal	Uniface
K-60-26	New Frontier JFK-administration wooden nickel	39 mm	Wood with black lettering	
K-60-27	Los Angeles Democratic 750 Club medal and ribbon	29 mm	Antique silver over bronze	Reverse: union bugs
K-60-28	Heraldic Art 50th anniversary of BSA medal	31 mm	.925 fine silver	Reeded edge; reverse: Scout emblem
K-60-29	Prince Rainier of Monaco 5-franc coin	28 mm	Gold	A gift to President Kennedy from Prince Rainier III; reverse: "With God's Help"
K-60-30	PT-109 necklace		Golden bronze	Looped for a necklace chain
K-61-1	Paul Manship inaugural medal	70 mm	Bronze	53,331 struck
K-61-1A	Paul Manship inaugural medal	70 mm	.999 fine silver	7,500 struck; serial number
K-61-1B	Paul Manship inaugural medal, JFK Library	70 mm	Gold	Unique
K-61-1C	Paul Manship inaugural medal, counterfeit	68 mm	Bronze-plated base metal	
K-61-1D	Paul Manship inaugural medal, copy	64 mm	Porcelain blue glaze	
K-61-1E	Paul Manship inaugural medal, copy	68 mm	Silver-plated base metal	Souvenir from Washington, D.C.; reverse: "Ask Not" credo with sun rays
K-61-1F	Paul Manship inaugural medal	27 mm	Gold	Five struck; a gift for Jacqueline Kennedy
K-61-1G	Paul Manship inaugural medal	24 mm	Gold	Unique; a gift for Jacqueline Kennedy
K-61-1H	Paul Manship inaugural medal	21 mm	Gold	Unique; a gift for Jacqueline Kennedy
K-61-1I	Paul Manship inaugural medal process set	70 mm	Bronze	Six medals in the set; 40 sets made
K-61-1J	Paul Manship inaugural medal	27 mm	Gold	Five struck
K-61-1K	Paul Manship inaugural medal	24 mm	Gold	One struck
K-61-1L	Paul Manship inaugural medal	21 mm	Gold	One struck
K-61-1M	Paul Manship inaugural medal display set	240 mm	Plaster	20 sets cast
K-61-1N	Paul Manship inaugural medal CD label	4 5/8 in	LightScribe	Standard compact disc of secret White House tapes
K-61-2	Inaugural ball charm	25 mm	Gold filled	13,000 struck
K-61-2A	Inaugural ball charm	25 mm	Oxidized silver	13,000 struck
K-61-3	DNC inaugural emblem medal	42 mm	Bronze	Uniface
K-63-3A	DNC inaugural emblem medal with badge	52 x 28 mm	Bronze	Medal is looped
K-63-3B	DNC inaugural emblem medal	48 x 32 mm	Bronze	Looped; reverse: union bugs
K-61-4	Osborne inaugural souvenir medal	35 mm	Goldine	Unlimited
K-61-4A	Osborne inaugural souvenir medal	29 mm	Goldine	Large letters; looped
K-61-4B	Osborne inaugural souvenir medal	29 mm	Brass	Small letters; looped
K-61-5	JFK inaugural tribute medal, type 1, Germany	40 mm	.999 fine silver	Reverse: dove in flight
K-61-5A	JFK inaugural tribute medal, type 1, Germany	20 mm	Gold	Reverse: dove in flight
K-61-5B	JFK inaugural tribute medal, type 1, Germany	26 mm	Gold	Reverse: dove in flight
K-61-5C	JFK inaugural tribute medal, type 1, Germany	32 mm	Gold	Reverse: dove in flight
K-61-5D	JFK inaugural tribute medal, type 1, Germany	40 mm	Gold	Reverse: dove in flight
K-61-5E	JFK inaugural tribute medal, type 1, Germany	50 mm	Gold	Regular size; serial numbers 1–2,500; reverse: dove in flight
K-61-5F	JFK inaugural tribute medal, type 1, Germany	50 mm	Gold	Thick size; serial numbers 1–2,000; reverse: dove in flight
K-61-5G	JFK inaugural tribute medal, type 1, Germany	60 mm	Gold	Regular size; serial numbers 1–1,500; reverse: dove in flight
K-61-5H	JFK inaugural tribute medal, type 1, Germany	60 mm	Gold	Thick size; serial numbers 1–1,000; reverse: dove in flight
K-61-6	JFK inaugural tribute medal, type 2, Germany	65 mm	Silver, Matte Finish	Reverse: White House
K-61-6A	JFK inaugural tribute medal, type 2, Germany	65 mm	Silver, Proof	Reverse: White House
K-61-6B	JFK inaugural tribute medal, type 2, Germany	50 mm	Silver, Matte Finish	Reverse: White House
K-61-6C	JFK inaugural tribute medal, type 2, Germany	40 mm	Silver, Proof	Reverse: White House
K-61-6D	JFK inaugural tribute medal, type 2, Germany	40 mm	Silver, Matte Finish	Reverse: White House
K-61-6E	JFK inaugural tribute medal, type 2, Germany	65 mm	.986 fine gold	Reverse: White House
K-61-6F	JFK inaugural tribute medal, type 2, Germany	50 mm	.900 fine gold	Reverse: White House
K-61-6G	JFK inaugural tribute medal, type 2, Germany	40 mm	.900 fine gold	Reverse: White House
K-61-6H	JFK inaugural tribute medal, type 2, Germany	25 mm	.900 fine gold	Reverse: White House
K-61-6I	JFK inaugural tribute medal, type 2, Germany	22 1/2 mm	.900 fine gold	Reverse: White House
K-61-7	U.S. Mint presidential series	76 mm	Bronze	Reverse: White House
K-61-7A	U.S. Mint at Philadelphia mini-medal	33 mm	Bronze	Reverse: inaugural quote
K-61-7B	U.S. Mint at Denver mini-medal	33 mm	Bronze	Reverse: inaugural quote
K-61-7C	U.S. Mint mini-medal, JFK Library issue	33 mm	Gold-plated bronze	Reverse: inaugural quote

K-61-8	Presidential Art JFK medal	32 mm	Bronze	Reverse: Presidential Seal
K-61-8A	Presidential Art JFK medal	32 mm	.999 fine silver	Serial numbers 1–6,500; reverse: Presidential Seal
K-61-8B	Presidential Art JFK medal	32 mm	Gold	Unique; reverse: Presidential Seal
K-61-8C	Presidential Art JFK medal process set	203 x 140 mm	Bronze	Medal-striking process steps; estimated 300–400 sets made; reverse: Presidential Seal
K-61-9	JFK inaugural tribute medal, type 3, Germany	36 mm	.925 fine sterling silver, Proof	Reverse: version of U.S. Seal
K-61-9A	JFK inaugural tribute medal, type 3, Germany	36 mm	Gold	Reverse: version of U.S. Seal
K-61-10	Osborne JFK-Pulitzer Prize medal	28 mm	Aluminum	
K-61-10A	Osborne JFK-Pulitzer Prize medal	28 mm	Brass-clad on steel	
K-61-10B	Osborne JFK-Pulitzer Prize medal	28 mm	Goldine	Rare; looped
K-61-10C	Osborne Jack-Pulitzer Prize medal	29 mm	Goldine	
K-61-10D	Osborne Jack-Inaugural medal	29 mm	Goldine	
K-61-10E	Osborne JFK-Inaugural medal	29 mm	Goldine	Large bust
K-61-10F	Osborne Jack-Inaugural medal	29 mm	Goldine	Small bust
K-61-11	Osborne Jack-Pulitzer Prize medal, portrait 2	26 mm	Aluminum	
K-61-11A	Osborne Jack-Pulitzer Prize medal, portrait 2	26 mm	Goldine	
K-61-11B	Osborne Jack-Pulitzer Prize medal, portrait 2	26 mm	Brass-clad on steel	
K-61-12	Space achievements medal	38 mm	Base metal, cast	Reverse: space capsule
K-61-13	Cook County, IL, reception dinner medal	27 mm	.925 fine sterling silver	1,500 struck; reverse: date
K-61-13A	Cook County, IL, reception dinner medal	27 mm	Gold	Two struck; reverse: date
K-61-14	1961 postmaster's convention medal	50 mm	Bronze	2,500 struck; reverse: Denver, Colorado, October 26, 1961
K-61-14A	1961 postmaster's convention medal	50 mm	Oxidized sterling silver	15 struck; reverse: Denver, Colorado, October 26, 1961
K-61-14B	1961 postmaster's convention medal	50 mm	14K gold	Unique; reverse: Denver, Colorado, October 26, 1961
K-61-15	R.J. Taylor JFK advertising token	34 mm	Gold-anodized aluminum	2,000 struck; reverse: 50 Stars, "Ask Not" credo, 1961
K-61-16	Beaucraft Jewelers JFK head charm	14 x 18 mm	.925 fine Beau sterling silver	Reverse: "Kennedy 35th President"
K-61-17	Executive Design JFK-LBJ medal, error reverse	70 mm	Bronze	Reverse: presidential and vice-presidential seals, "38th Vice President"
K-61-17A	Executive Design JFK-LBJ medal, error reverse	70 mm	Silver	Reverse: presidential and vice-presidential seals, "38th Vice President"
K-61-17B	Executive Design JFK-LBJ medal, error reverse	70 mm	Platinum	Limited to 25; reverse: presidential and vice-presidential seals, "38th Vice President"
K-61-17C	Executive Design JFK-LBJ medal, correct reverse	70 mm	Bronze	Reverse: presidential and vice-presidential seals, "37th Vice President"
K-61-17D	Executive Design JFK-LBJ medal, correct reverse	70 mm	Silver	Reverse: presidential and vice-presidential seals, "37th Vice President"
K-61-17E	Executive Design JFK-LBJ medal	70 mm	Gold	Unique; a gift for Vice President Lyndon B. Johnson; uniface
K-61-17F	Executive Design JFK-LBJ medal	70 mm	Bronze	Uniface
K-61-17G	Executive Design JFK-LBJ medal, issued in 1969 by the JFK Library	66½ mm	Silver patina over bronze	Reverse: presidential and vice-presidential seals, "38th Vice President"
K-61-18	C. Affer JFK inauguration tribute medal	50 mm	Silver-plated bronze	Reverse: eagle
K-61-18A	C. Affer JFK inauguration tribute medal	50 mm	Silver-plated shell	For plaques
K-61-18B	C. Affer JFK inauguration tribute medal	50 mm	Gold-plated shell	For plaques
K-61-18C	C. Affer JFK inauguration tribute medal	50 mm	Bronze shell	For plaques
K-61-18D	C. Affer JFK inauguration tribute medal	22 mm	Silver shell	For jewelry; uniface
K-61-18E	C. Affer JFK inauguration tribute medal	22 mm	Gold shell	For jewelry; uniface
K-61-18F	C. Affer JFK inauguration tribute medal	22 mm	Bronze shell	For jewelry; uniface
K-61-18G	C. Affer JFK inauguration tribute medal	50 mm	Bronze solid	Reverse: eagle
K-61-18H	C. Affer JFK inauguration tribute medal	50 mm	Gold-plated bronze	Reverse: eagle
K-61-18I	C. Affer JFK inauguration tribute medal	50 mm	.925 fine silver	Reverse: eagle
K-61-18J	Ferri Bros JFK inauguration tribute medal, Italy	49 mm	White metal, cast	Obverse: drill hole
K-61-18K	Ferri Bros JFK inauguration plaque, Italy	161 x 75 mm	Bronze casting	Uniface
K-61-19	Massachusetts marching JFK inaugural parade medal	38 mm	Silver	75 struck; reverse: Jerome O'Connor (full name)
K-61-19A	Massachusetts marching JFK inaugural parade medal	20 mm	Silver	Reverse: Jerome O'Connor (initials only)
K-61-19B	Massachusetts marching JFK inaugural parade medal	38 mm	.925 fine sterling silver	Two struck; reverse: Jerome O'Connor (full name)
K-61-19C	Massachusetts marching JFK inaugural parade medal	20 mm	.925 fine sterling silver	Two struck; reverse: Jerome O'Connor (initials only)
K-61-19D	Massachusetts marching JFK inaugural parade medal	38 mm	Gold	Unique; a gift to JFK on his 44th birthday; reverse: Jerome O'Connor (full name)

K-61-19E	Massachusetts marching JFK inaugural parade medal	20 mm	Gold	Unique; a gift to JFK on his 44th birthday; reverse: Jerome O'Connor (initials only)
K-61-19F	Massachusetts marching JFK inaugural parade medal, trial strike	38 mm	Bronze	No loop; reverse: Jerome O'Connor
K-61-20	E. Monti JFK inauguration tribute medal, Italy	60 mm	Bronze	Reverse: U.S. Capitol
K-61-20A	E. Monti JFK inauguration tribute medal, Italy	60 mm	Ozidized silver on bronze	Reverse: U.S. Capitol
K-61-20B	E. Monti JFK inauguration tribute medal, Italy	60 mm	Gilded bronze	Reverse: U.S. Capitol
K-61-20C	E. Monti JFK inauguration tribute medal, Italy	60 mm	.800 fine silver	Reverse: U.S. Capitol
K-61-21	"JFK-Krushchev Meeting" medal	33 mm	.900 fine silver	Reverse: Schonbrunn Palace
K-61-21A	"JFK-Krushchev Meeting" medal	33 mm	.900 fine gold	Reverse: Schonbrunn Palace
K-61-22	Euronummus JFK medal, Italy	40 mm	.900 fine silver	Reverse: Statue of Liberty
K-61-22A	Euronummus JFK medal, Italy	40 mm	.900 fine gold	Reverse: Statue of Liberty
K-61-22B	Euronummus JFK medal, Italy	50 mm	.900 fine gold	Reverse: Statue of Liberty
K-61-22C	Euronummus JFK medal, Italy	60 mm	.900 fine gold	Reverse: Statue of Liberty
K-61-23	Cape Cod visit token	38 mm	Aluminum	Reverse: "They Came to Cape Cod"
K-61-24	Washington souvenir medal #1, error reverse	32 mm	Base metal, gold finish	Reverse: misquote
K-61-25	Washington souvenir medal #2	32 mm	Brass, gold finish	Lathe reverse
K-61-25A	Washington souvenir medal #2	32 mm	Brass shell	Concave; looped
K-61-26	John Roberts Society Peace Corps medal	50 mm	Bronze	Reverse: dove of peace
K-61-26A	John Roberts Society Peace Corps medal	50 mm	Silver	5,000 struck; reverse: dove of peace
K-61-27	Osborne U.S. Capitol token	28 mm	Goldine	Looped
K-61-28	Osborne Jack-Inaugural medal	28 mm	Goldine	Looped
K-61-29	Paul Manship JFK bust tribute charm	17 $\frac{9}{10}$ mm	Sterling silver	Hallmark: sterling; looped
K-61-30	Franklin Mint "Tribute to LBJ" medal	39 mm	Bronze	2,500 struck; reverse: "Leadership of the Senate"
K-61-30A	Franklin Mint "Tribute to LBJ" medal	39 mm	.925 fine sterling silver	400 struck; reverse: "Leadership of the Senate"
K-61-30B	Franklin Mint "Tribute to LBJ" medal	39 mm	Gold on sterling silver	600 struck; reverse: "Leadership of the Senate"
K-61-31	Harvard University Laetare JFK award medal, JFK Library		Gold	Unique
K-61-32	Frank Gasparro Director Eva Adams medal	76 mm	Bronze	Reverse: flying eagle
K-61-33	Radio and Television Society award medal, JFK Library		Gold	Awarded to JFK for his televised presidential addresses; uniface
K-61-34	MPG White House JFK Medal	37 mm	Nickel silver and base metal	Reverse: White House
K-61-35	Robbins Company Dag Hammarskjöld memorial medal	69 mm	Bronze	Reverse: "Hero of Peace"
K-61-36	Project Mercury Alan Shepard medal	39 $\frac{1}{2}$ mm	Brass	Reverse: "1st American in Space"
K-61-37	Bay of Pigs "Crusade to Free Cuba" memorial medal	36 $\frac{7}{10}$ mm	Cupronickel	Reverse: "There Will Be No End But Victory"
K-61-38	JFK appreciation gift to supporters medal	76 mm	.925 fine sterling silver	Reverse: "Ask Not" credo, engraved with JFK's signature
K-61-39	Parva (PSB) presidential staff badge	50 $\frac{4}{5}$ mm	Multi-colored brass	Serial number
K-61-40	Carlos P. Garcia "LBJ Visit to the Philippines" medal	75 mm	Bronze	
K-61-41	International Lenin Prize for Peace medal		Gold	Worn by Khrushchev during his meeting with JFK in Vienna
K-61-42	Osborne JFK key chain tag	28 mm	Aluminum	Looped; reverse: White House
K-61-43	Osborne JFK key chain tag, large die variety	28 mm	Aluminum	Looped; reverse: White House
K-61-44	Osborne Jack-Inaugural souvenir token	28 mm	Aluminum	Reverse: Jan 20th
K-61-45	Osborne JFK-Inaugural souvenir token	28 mm	Aluminum	Reverse: Jan 20th
K-61-46	Simón Bolívar medal	90 mm	Bronze	Medal mounted; a gift to JFK from Venezuela
K-61-47	French-coin medal chest	203 x 102 x 114 mm		Bears images of Lincoln, Washington, and Lafayette; a gift to JFK during his 1961 visit to Paris
K-61-48	Jose Gervasio Artigas medal	121 x 89 mm	Bronze	A gift to JFK from Uruguay; reverse: "Artigas Libertad"
K-61-49	"100th Anniversary of Italian Unification" medal	67 mm	Gold	A gift to JFK; reverse: four-horse chariot
K-61-50	PT-109 JFK White House–visit giveaway pin	32 mm	Bronze, Proof	Uniface; looped
K-61-51	AMVETS Freedom 7 space capsule key chain tag	25 mm	Gold-colored aluminum	Reverse: the Pledge Of Allegiance
K-61-52	Gonzolo Ximenez medal with ribbon, Belgium	76 mm	18K gold	A gift to JFK from Colombia; red and gold ribbon; reverse: "Santa Fe de Bogota 1538"
K-61-53	Société Arthus-Bertrand medal			Presented to JFK on October 29, 1961; presentation neck ribbon
K-61-54	Playa Giron with soldier and tank square pin, Cuba			Celebrating the Bay of Pigs victory in Cuba
K-61-55	Playa Giron with ship sinking round pin, Cuba			Celebrating the Bay of Pigs victory in Cuba
K-61-56	"CFC Liberation of Brigade 2506" prisoner of war medal	32mm	Bronze	Reverse: Brigade 2506 shield and CFC legend
K-61-57	Grand Cross of the Equestrian Order eight-point cross	80 x 80 mm	Silver, gold, and black enamel	A gift to JFK; Greek Orthodox
K-61-57A	Grand Cross of the Equestrian Order hanging pendant	95 x 41 mm	Silver, gold, and black enamel	A gift to Jacqueline Kennedy; red ribbon

K-61-58	Mesuno three-coin set	19 mm	Gold	3 escudos, circa 1620; a gift to Jacqueline Kennedy from the first lady of Colombia, Bertha Martinez;
K-61-59	Monaco two 25-franc coins and two 2-franc coins gift set	Various sizes	Gold	Bears images of the coat of arms of Monaco, dated 1960; a gift to JFK from Prince Rainier III
K-61-60	White House JFK-administration service medal			Reverse: engraved with recipients name
K-62-1	Frank Gasparro presidential appreciation medal	44 mm	Bronze	300 struck; reverse: "In Appreciation" with JFK's signature
K-62-1A	Frank Gasparro presidential appreciation medal, Smithsonian Institution	44 mm	Bronze	Unique; uniface
K-62-1B	Frank Gasparro presidential appreciation medal, after-issue copy	44 mm	Bronze	Uniface
K-62-2	U.S. Mint Assay Commission annual medal	37 mm	Bronze	Reverse: Mint worker pouring metal
K-62-3	"JFK Visits Philadelphia" elongated U.S. cent	20 x 40 mm	Copper	Reverse: Lincoln Memorial
K-62-3A	"JFK Visits Philadelphia" elongated U.S. nickel	22 x 38 mm	Copper and nickel	Reverse: Monticello
K-62-3B	"JFK Visits Philadelphia" elongated U.S. dime	18 x 40 mm	Copper and nickel	Reverse: lit torch with sprigs of olive and oak
K-62-3C	"JFK Visits Philadelphia" elongated U.S. quarter	26 x 38 mm	Standard coin composition	Reverse: eagle with arrows
K-62-3D	"JFK Visits Philadelphia" elongated U.S. half dollar	30 x 48 mm	Standard coin composition	Reverse: standard Kennedy half dollar
K-62-4	Wedgwood Jasperware JFK medallion	80 x 104 mm	Oval with a blue background	Uniface
K-62-4A	Wedgwood Jasperware JFK medallion	80 x 104 mm	Oval with a black background	Uniface
K-62-4B	Wedgwood Jasperware JFK medallion	80 x 104 mm	Oval with a blue background and a white border	Uniface
K-62-5	U.S. Mint Gilroy Roberts Director Eva Adams medal	76 mm	Bronze	Reverse: Director 1961
K-62-6	JFK mid-term oval pinback with metal donkey	203 mm	Celluloid, cloth, metal	Red ribbon reads "Welcome President John F. Kennedy"
K-62-7	Dag Hammarskjöld tribute medal, Denmark	38 mm	Bronze	Reverse: doves, dated 1962
K-62-8	Indiana Democratic Convention "JFK Visit to Wales" medal	39 x 42 9/20 mm	Stamped brass, cloisonné	Ribbon; uniface
K-62-9	Mexico City Medal of Honor	44 9/20 mm	18K gold	A gift to JFK; inscribed reverse: "Al Presidente John F. Kennedy, La Cuidad de Mexico, June 29 de 1962"
K-62-10	"JFK Visit to Los Alamos, NM" medal	31 mm	Brass	Commemorating JFK's visit to Albuquerque, NM
K-62-11	Huguenot medal	38 mm	.925 fine silver	500 struck; presented to JFK by Beaufort, S.C. Junior COC; reverse: torch and legend with dates 1562–1962
K-62-11A	Huguenot medal	38 mm	Bronze	Very limited; presented to JFK by Beaufort, S.C. Junior COC; reverse: torch and legend with dates 1562–1962
K-62-12	Chaim Weizmann 100-lirot coin	28 6/10 mm	Gold, Proof	Reverse: menorah with wreath, dated 1962; inscription: gift to JFK by David Ben-Gurion
K-63-1	Presidential Art mourning/campaign medallet	18 mm	Gold filled	Uniface
K-63-1A	Presidential Art mourning/campaign medallet	18 mm	14K gold	Looped
K-63-1B	Presidential Art mourning/campaign medallet	18 mm	.925 sterling silver	Looped
K-63-1C	Presidential Art mourning/campaign medallet	18 mm	Bronze embedded in Lucite	No loop
K-63-2	Artcraft JFK campaign mini-medal	11 1/2 mm	Bronze	No loop
K-63-2A	Artcraft JFK campaign mini-medal	11 1/2 mm	Bronze	Looped
K-63-3	"China Lake Presidential Visit" medal, type 1	38 mm	Goldine	Large letters; reverse: "The Presidential Visit, NOTS, June 7, 1963"
K-63-3A	"China Lake Presidential Visit" medal, type 2	38 mm	Goldine	Small letters; reverse: "The Presidential Visit, NOTS, June 7, 1963"
K-63-3B	"China Lake Presidential Visit" medal	38 mm	Goldine	Ten struck; uniface; reverse: "The Presidential Visit, NOTS, June 7, 1963"
K-63-3C	"China Lake Presidential Visit" medal, trial strike	38 mm	Silver	Three struck; irregular bust; reverse: "The Presidential Visit, NOTS, June 7, 1963"
K-63-3D	"China Lake Presidential Visit" medal	38 mm	Gold plated	Six struck; a gift to JFK; reverse: "The Presidential Visit, NOTS, June 7, 1963"
K-63-4	Mexico Alliance For Progress (ALPRO) medal	42 mm	Silver	Reverse: Map of the Americas
K-63-4A	Mexico Alliance For Progress (ALPRO) medal	42 mm	Gold	Reverse: Map of the Americas
K-63-5	"Return of El Chamizal" medal, type 1, Mexico	40 mm	.900 fine silver	Reverse: American and Mexican flags
K-63-5A	"Return of El Chamizal" medal, type 1, Mexico	50 mm	.900 fine silver	Reverse: American and Mexican flags
K-63-5B	"Return of El Chamizal" medal, type 1, Mexico	40 mm	Gold	Reverse: American and Mexican flags
K-63-5C	"Return of El Chamizal" medal, type 1, Mexico	50 mm	Gold	Reverse: American and Mexican flags

K-63-6	"Return of El Chamizal" medal, type 2, Mexico	42 mm	.980 fine silver	Reverse: American and Mexican flags
K-63-6A	"Return of El Chamizal" medal, type 2, Mexico	42 mm	.980 fine silver, frosted	Reverse: American and Mexican flags
K-63-6B	"Return of El Chamizal" medal, type 2, Mexico	42 mm	.925 fine silver, Proof	Reverse: American and Mexican flags
K-63-6C	"Return of El Chamizal" medal, type 2, Mexico	42 mm	Gold	Reverse: American and Mexican flags
K-63-6D	"Return of El Chamizal" medal, type 2, counterfeit, Mexico	42 mm	Silver cast	Small letters; plain edge; reverse: American and Mexican flags
K-63-6E	"Return of El Chamizal" medal, type 2, counterfeit, Mexico	42 mm	Silver cast	Small letters; reed edge; reverse: American and Mexican flags
K-63-7	"JFK-K. Adenauer German Visit" medal	40 mm	.999 fine silver	Reverse: dove and olive branch
K-63-7A	"JFK-K. Adenauer German Visit" medal	20 mm	Gold	Reverse: dove and olive branch
K-63-7B	"JFK-K. Adenauer German Visit" medal	26 mm	Gold	Reverse: dove and olive branch
K-63-7C	"JFK-K. Adenauer German Visit" medal	32 mm	Gold	Reverse: dove and olive branch
K-63-7D	"JFK-K. Adenauer German Visit" medal	40 mm	Gold	Reverse: dove and olive branch
K-63-7E	"JFK-K. Adenauer German Visit" medal	50 mm	Gold	Serial numbers 1–3,000; reverse: dove and olive branch
K-63-7F	"JFK-K. Adenauer German Visit" medal	50 mm	Gold	Thick; reverse: dove and olive branch
K-63-7G	"JFK-K. Adenauer German Visit" medal	60 mm	Gold	Serial numbers 1–2,000; reverse: dove and olive branch
K-63-7H	"JFK-K. Adenauer German Visit" medal	60 mm	Gold	Thick; reverse: dove and olive branch
K-63-8	"Welcome to Germany" medal, Germany	40 mm	.999 fine silver, Matte Finish	Reverse: German eagle
K-63-8A	"Welcome to Germany" medal, Germany	40 mm	Silver, Proof	Reverse: German eagle
K-63-8B	"Welcome to Germany" medal, Germany	50 mm	Silver	Reverse: German eagle
K-63-8C	"Welcome to Germany" medal, Germany	25 mm	.900 fine gold	Reverse: German eagle
K-63-8D	"Welcome to Germany" medal, Germany	40 mm	.900 fine gold	Reverse: German eagle
K-63-8E	"Welcome to Germany" medal, Germany	50 mm	.900 fine gold	100 struck; reverse: German eagle
K-63-9	"JFK-K. Adenauer Visit to Bonn" medal, Germany	50 mm	.925 fine silver	Concave; reverse: "Welcome President Kennedy"
K-63-9A	"JFK-K. Adenauer Visit to Bonn" medal, Germany	77 mm	.925 fine silver	Concave; reverse: "Welcome President Kennedy"
K-63-9B	"JFK-K. Adenauer Visit to Bonn" pin back, Germany	25 2/5 mm	.925 fine silver	Reverse: Hoffstatter Bonn
K-63-10	"I am a Berliner" tribute medal	40 mm	Bronze	Reverse: Berlin Wall
K-63-10A	"I am a Berliner" tribute medal	40 mm	.835 fine silver	Reverse: Berlin Wall
K-63-10B	"I am a Berliner" tribute medal	40 mm	.585 fine gold, 45 g.	Reverse: Berlin Wall
K-63-10C	"I am a Berliner" tribute medal	40 mm	.585 fine gold, 70 g.	Reverse: Berlin Wall
K-63-11	Argenteus JFK tribute medal	35 mm	.1000 fine silver, Proof	Reverse: six-point cross
K-63-11A	Argenteus JFK tribute medal	50 mm	Silver	Reverse: six-point cross
K-63-11B	Argenteus JFK tribute medal	80 mm	Silver	Reverse: six-point cross
K-63-12	Aureus Magnus JFK 1/2 ducat	15 mm	.980 fine gold	Reverse: six-point cross, S
K-63-12A	Aureus Magnus JFK 1 ducat	20 mm	.980 fine gold	Reverse: six-point cross, I
K-63-12B	Aureus Magnus JFK 2-1/2 ducat	26 mm	.980 fine gold	Reverse: six-point cross, II
K-63-12C	Aureus Magnus 5 ducat	35 mm	.980 fine gold	Reverse: six-point cross, V
K-63-12D	Aureus Magnus 10 ducat	44 mm	.980 fine gold	Reverse: six-point cross, X
K-63-12E	Aureus Magnus 20 ducat	50 mm	.980 fine gold	Reverse: six-point cross, XX
K-63-12F	Aureus Magnus 30 ducat	50 mm	.980 fine gold	Thick; reverse: six-point cross, XXX
K-63-12G	Aureus Magnus 100 ducat	80 mm	.980 fine gold	Reverse: six-point cross, C
K-63-13	JFK vertical elongated U.S. cent	20 x 38 mm	Copper	Reverse: Lincoln Memorial
K-63-13A	JFK vertical elongated U.S. cent	20 x 38 mm	Copper	Increased hairlines; reverse: Lincoln Memorial
K-63-13B	JFK vertical elongated U.S. cent	20 x 38 mm	Copper	Sharper image; reverse: Lincoln Memorial
K-63-14	Charles Mullin JFK vertical elongated U.S. cent	20 x 38 mm	Copper	Reverse: Lincoln Memorial
K-63-15	Baccarat JFK sulphide cameo paperweight	70 mm	Glass with a green background	1,200 made; Baccarat-France on the bottom
K-63-15A	Baccarat JFK sulphide cameo paperweight	70 mm	Glass with a blue background	1,200 made; Baccarat-France on the bottom
K-63-15B	Baccarat JFK sulphide cameo paperweight	70 mm	Glass with a red background	1,200 made; Baccarat-France on the bottom
K-63-15C	Baccarat JFK memorial sulphide cameo paperweight	90 mm	Black glass	300 made; Baccarat-France on the bottom
K-63-15D	Baccarat JFK memorial sulphide cameo paperweight	90 mm	Glass, blue with white overlay	300 made; Baccarat-France on the bottom
K-63-15E	Baccarat JFK memorial sulphide cameo paperweight	90 mm	Glass, red with blue overlay	300 made; Baccarat-France on the bottom
K-63-16	"JFK Visit to German Bell of Freedom" medal	40 mm	Bronze	Reverse: German Bell of Freedom
K-63-16A	"JFK Visit to German Bell of Freedom" medal	40 mm	Oxidized .835 fine silver	Reverse: German Bell of Freedom
K-63-16B	"JFK Visit to German Bell of Freedom" medal	40 mm	.333 fine gold	Reverse: German Bell of Freedom
K-63-16C	"JFK Visit to German Bell of Freedom" medal	40 mm	.585 fine gold	Reverse: German Bell of Freedom
K-63-16D	"JFK Visit to German Bell of Freedom" medal	40 mm	.750 fine gold	Reverse: German Bell of Freedom
K-63-16E	"JFK Visit to German Bell of Freedom" medal	40 mm	.900 fine gold	Reverse: German Bell of Freedom
K-63-17	2nd anniversary of ALPRO first-day cover, 1963	58 x 86 mm	Brass plate, gold finish	Standard-size envelope
K-63-18	35th president game coin	29 mm	Gold-anodized aluminum	Reverse: shield and eagle standing on 35 coin

K-63-19	"JFK 35th President" medal, Argentina	27 $^{3/10}$ mm	Silver	Reverse: Presidential Seal, dated 1963
K-63-20	USS Kitty Hawk medal	31½ mm	Bronze	Reverse: "Big E. Commission" dated 1961
K-63-21	PT-109 tie-pin die hub, White House gift edition	53 $^{2/5}$ x 16½mm	Hardened steel	Heavy; uniface
K-63-21A	Jolle PT-109 tie pin, White House gift edition	45 x 10 mm	Golden brass	Reverse: Jolle trademark
K-63-23	U.S. Mint commemorative for Padre Serra	33¾ mm	Silver	Authorized by JFK; reverse: map of California, Frank Gasparro's initials
K-63-23A	U.S. Mint commemorative for Padre Serra	33¾ mm	Bronze	Authorized by JFK; reverse: map of California, Frank Gasparro's initials
K-63-24	"Support Kennedy's Program" key-chain tag	36 mm	Silver on black plastic	Reverse: United Automobile Workers emblem and shield
K-63-25	Original Shasta County, CA, souvenir coin	39 mm	Golden bronze	No serial number; obverse: same as K-65-5; reverse: eagle
K-63A-1	Presidential Art JFK memorial medal	38 mm	Bronze	Reverse: "Three Phases of Public Life"
K-63A-1A	Presidential Art JFK memorial medal	38 mm	.999 fine silver	Reverse: "Three Phases of Public Life"
K-63A-1B	Presidential Art JFK memorial medal	38 mm	Gold	Unique; reverse: Three Phases of Public Life", JFK and Jacqueline
K-63A-1C	Presidential Art Knights of Columbus JFK memorial medal	38 mm	Silver-plated base metal, cast	Scholarship award; serial number 441; looped; reverse: "Champlain Council"
K-63A-2	Heraldic Art "Homage to the Nation" medal	35 mm	.925 fine sterling silver	5,300 struck; reverse: U.S. Capitol
K-63A-3	Capitol Medals memorial medal, error reverse	39 mm	Oxidized bronze	Reverse: 50 stars and a quote
K-63A-3A	Capitol Medals memorial medal, error reverse	39 mm	Oxidized silver-plated bronze	Reverse: 50 stars and a quote
K-63A-3B	Capitol Medals memorial medal, error reverse	39 mm	.999 fine silver	Serial number; 15,000 struck; reverse: 50 stars and a quote
K-63A-3C	Capitol Medals memorial medal, error reverse	39 mm	.999 fine platinum	25 struck; serial number; reverse: 50 stars and a quote
K-63A-3D	Capitol Medals memorial medal, error reverse	39 mm	Aluminum	Presented on a postcard; reverse: 50 stars and a quote
K-63A-3E	Capitol Medals memorial medal for key chain	39 mm	Aluminum	Holed; reverse: 50 stars and a quote
K-63A-4	Wendell's JFK memorial medal	39 mm	Oxidized bronze	Reverse: "Ask Not" credo
K-63A-4A	Wendell's JFK memorial medal	39 mm	.925 fine sterling silver	Reverse: "Ask Not" credo
K-63A-4B	Wendell's JFK memorial medal	28 mm	Antique bronze	5,000 struck; custom; reverse: "Ask Not" credo
K-63A-4C	Wendell's JFK memorial medal	28 mm	Goldine	5,000 struck; reverse: "Ask Not" credo
K-63A-4D	Wendell's JFK memorial medal	28 mm	Goldine, thick planchet	Reverse: "Ask Not" credo
K-63A-4E	Wendell's JFK memorial medal	28 mm	Goldine	Reverse: same as obverse
K-63A-4F	Wendell's JFK memorial medal	28 mm	Silver aluminum	Recut reverse die: larger lettering and wreath
K-63A-5	James Ryan Association placer JFK medal	39 mm	24K gold	Reverse: wreath and quote
K-63A-5A	James Ryan Association JFK medal, trial strike	39 mm	Aluminum	Reverse: wreath and quote
K-63A-5B	James Ryan Association JFK medal, trial strike	39 mm	Aluminum	Uniface; reverse: wreath and quote
K-63A-6	National Commemorative Society JFK medal	39 mm	.925 fine sterling silver	5,249 struck; serial number; reverse: eternal flame
K-63A-6A	National Commemorative Society JFK medal	39 mm	.999 fine platinum	Three struck; reverse: eternal flame
K-63A-7	NY World's Fair Hall Of Education JFK medal	36 mm	.925 fine sterling silver	Reverse: Kennedy family crest
K-63A-7A	NY World's Fair Hall Of Education JFK medal	26 mm	.925 fine sterling silver	Reverse: Kennedy family crest
K-63A-7B	NY World's Fair Hall Of Education JFK medal	20 mm	.925 fine sterling silver	Reverse: Kennedy family crest
K-63A-7C	NY World's Fair Hall Of Education JFK medal	26 mm	.900 fine gold	Reverse: Kennedy family crest
K-63A-7D	NY World's Fair Hall Of Education JFK medal	20 mm	.986 fine gold	Reverse: Kennedy family crest
K-63A-7E	NY World's Fair Hall Of Education Jacqueline Kennedy medal	26 mm	.925 fine sterling silver	Reverse: Kennedy family crest
K-63A-7F	NY World's Fair Hall Of Education Jacqueline Kennedy medal	20 mm	.986 fine gold	Reverse: Kennedy family crest
K-63A-8	Klitzner JFK tribute medal	30 mm	Antique bronze	Reverse: "Ask Not" credo
K-63A-8A	Klitzner JFK tribute medal	30 mm	Silver	Reverse: "Ask Not" credo
K-63A-8B	Klitzner JFK tribute medal	29 mm	Sterling silver	Looped; reverse: "Ask Not" credo
K-63A-8C	Klitzner JFK tribute medal	30 mm	Antique bronze	Looped; reverse: "Ask Not" credo
K-63A-9	Osborne presidential series JFK medal	26 mm	Aluminum	Reverse: "JFK Originator of Peace Corps"
K-63A-9A	Osborne presidential series JFK medal	26 mm	Goldine	Reverse: JFK
K-63A-9B	Osborne presidential series JFK medal	26 mm	Rolled brass on steel	Reverse: JFK
K-63A-9C	Osborne presidential series JFK medal, Dallas Museum	28 mm	Goldine	Small letters; reverse: "JFK Originator of Peace Corps"
K-63A-9D	Osborne presidential series JFK medal, Dallas Museum	28 mm	Goldine	Change of lettering; reverse: "JFK Originator of Peace Corps"
K-63A-9E	Osborne-Slater presidential series JFK medal	28 mm	Goldine	Reverse: same as obverse
K-63A-9F	Osborne JFK-Ritz Theater admission coin	28 mm	Aluminum	Reverse: "Good For One Admission"
K-63A-9G	Osborne JFK-Taylor Drug Store coin	28 mm	Goldine	Reverse: "Taylor Drug Store"
K-63A-9H	Osborne JFK-George Washington medal	28 mm	Goldine	Reverse: portrait of George Washington
K-63A-9I	Osborne JFK-Peace Corps medal	28 mm	Goldine	Reverse: "JFK Originator of Peace Corps"
K-63A-9J	Osborne JFK portrait souvenir medal	28 mm	Aluminum	Reverse: "JFK Originator of Peace Corps"

K-63A-9K	Osborne JFK portrait souvenir medal	28 mm	Goldine	Large letters; reverse: "JFK Originator of Peace Corps"
K-63A-10	Osborne president game series JFK medal	28 mm	Aluminum	Reverse: "JFK Originator of Peace Corps"
K-63A-10A	Osborne president game series JFK medal	28 mm	Nickel silver	Heavy gauge; reverse: "JFK Originator of Peace Corps"
K-63A-10B	Osborne president game series JFK medal	28 mm	Rolled brass on steel	Reverse: "JFK Originator of Peace Corps"
K-63A-10C	Osborne president game series JFK medal	28 mm	Goldine	Reverse: "JFK Originator of Peace Corps"
K-63A-10D	Osborne president game series JFK medal	28 mm	Goldine	Heavy gauge; reverse: "JFK Originator of Peace Corps"
K-63A-10E	Osborne JFK mule medal	28 mm	Bronze	5,000 struck; special order; obverse: K-63A-10; reverse: K-61-10
K-63A-10F	Osborne JFK plastic game piece	28 mm	Chrome on red plastic	Reverse: "JFK Originator of Peace Corps"
K-63A-11	Osborne-Capsco JFK souvenir medal	35 mm	Goldine	Reverse: wreath and JFK's signature
K-63A-11A	Osborne-Capsco JFK souvenir medal	35 mm	Goldine	Reverse die change: small wreath and JFK's signature
K-63A-12	R.J. Taylor "JFK Credo" medal	34 mm	Gold-anodized aluminum	7,655 struck, reverse: stars and JFK quote
K-63A-12A	R.J. Taylor "JFK Credo" medal	34 mm	Bronze	4,872 struck, reverse: stars and JFK quote
K-63A-12B	R.J. Taylor "JFK Credo" medal	34 mm	.925 fine sterling silver	189 struck, reverse: stars and JFK quote
K-63A-12C	R.J. Taylor "JFK Credo" medal	34 mm	.999 fine silver	1,112 struck, reverse: stars and JFK quote
K-63A-13	Stafford World's Fair JFK-Lincoln souvenir medal	38 mm	Bronze chemical etch	Reverse: Abraham Lincoln
K-63A-14	"JFK Credo" medal	30 mm	Bronze	Reverse: "Ask Not" credo
K-63A-14A	"JFK Credo" medal	30 mm	Silver	Looped; reverse: "Ask Not" credo
K-63A-14B	"JFK Credo" medal	30 mm	Bronze	Looped; reverse: "Ask Not" credo
K-63A-14C	"JFK Credo" medal	76 mm	Pewter	Reverse: "Ask Not" credo
K-63A-15	Charles Naimot Labor of Honor medal, JFK Library	38 mm	Silver	Unique; reverse: self discipline
K-63A-16	Lindsey Morris Prize JFK plaque	240 mm	Bronze	Unique; uniface
K-63A-16A	Lindsey Morris Prize JFK medal	76 mm	Bronze	Uniface
K-63A-16B	Lindsey Morris Prize JFK medallion, Hyannis, MA, JFK Memorial	1219 1/5 mm	Bronze	Uniface
K-63A-17	President and First Lady series medal	27 mm	Bronze, Proof	20,000 struck; reverse: goddess of liberty
K-63A-17A	President and First Lady series medal	27 mm	Sterling silver	Serial number; reverse: goddess of liberty
K-63A-17B	President and First Lady series medal	27 mm	Platinum	Serial number; reverse: goddess of liberty
K-63A-17C	President and First Lady series medal, restrike	27 mm	Sterling silver	No serial number; reverse: goddess of liberty
K-63A-18	Southern California Trophy JFK medal	36 mm	Oxidized silver finish	Looped; reverse: quote
K-63A-18A	Southern California Trophy JFK medal	36 mm	Gold-anodized aluminum	Looped; reverse: quote
K-63A-19	American Pacific Stamp JFK tribute medal	31 mm	Bronze	Looped; reverse: quote
K-63A-20	Washington, D.C., JFK souvenir medal	32 mm	Copper plate on base metal	Reverse: quote and dove with olive branch
K-63A-20A	Washington, D.C., JFK souvenir medal	32 mm	Bronze plate on base metal	Reverse: quote and dove with olive branch
K-63A-20B	Washington, D.C., JFK souvenir medal	32 mm	Copper plate on base metal	Looped; reverse: quote and dove with olive branch
K-63A-20C	Washington, D.C., JFK souvenir medal	32 mm	Bronze plate on base metal	Looped; reverse: quote and dove with olive branch
K-63A-21	Green Duck JFK memorial medal	30 mm	Bronze antique satin	Looped; reverse: quote
K-63A-22	Janon Washington, D.C., JFK tribute medal	29 mm	Brass	Looped; reverse: "Ask Not" credo
K-63A-22A	Janon Washington, D.C., JFK tribute medal for key chain	29 mm	Solid bronze	Looped; reverse: "Ask Not" credo
K-63A-22B	Janon Washington, D.C., JFK tribute medal	29 mm	Base metal, gold finish	Looped; reverse: "Ask Not" credo
K-63A-22C	Janon Washington, D.C., JFK tribute medal, illegal copy	29 mm	Britannia metal, cast	Looped; reverse: quote
K-63A-22D	Janon Washington, D.C., JFK tribute medal	29 mm	Base metal, gold finish, cast	Looped; reverse: quote
K-63A-22E	Janon Washington, D.C., JFK tribute medal	29 mm	Silver finish	Looped; reverse: "Ask Not" credo
K-63A-22F	Janon Washington, D.C., JFK tribute medal, copy	29 mm	Bronze	750 struck; reverse: quote
K-63A-22G	Janon Washington, D.C., JFK tribute medal, Dallas Museum	29 mm	Gold finish	Revised die
K-63A-22H	Janon Washington, D.C., JFK tribute medal, Dallas Museum	29 mm	Polished silver finish	Revised die
K-63A-22I	Janon Washington, D.C., JFK tribute medal	29 mm	Silver-plated brass, machined finish	Uniface
K-63A-22J	Janon Washington, D.C., "35th President" tribute medal	32 mm	Antiqued bronze	Looped; reverse: "Ask Not" credo
K-63A-23	MPG JFK birth- and death-date memorial medal	38 mm	Bronze-colored base metal, cast	Reeded edge; reverse: quote
K-63A-23A	MPG JFK birth- and death-date memorial medal	38 mm	Base metal, gold finish, cast	Reeded edge; reverse: quote
K-63A-24	JFK novelty souvenir medal	33 mm	Base metal, gold finish	Looped; reverse: quote
K-63A-24A	JFK novelty souvenir medal	33 mm	Antique Bronze on base metal	No loop; reverse: quote
K-63A-24B	JFK novelty souvenir medal	33 mm	Base metal, silver finish	No loop; reverse: quote
K-63A-25	Don Howden JFK tribute medal	32 mm	Base metal, gold finish	Looped; reverse: fallen dove
K-63A-25A	Don Howden JFK tribute medal	32 mm	Base metal, gold finish	Uniface cut-out; looped; reverse: stippled
K-63A-26	Washington, D.C., brass-shell key-chain medal	28 mm	Polished brass	Concave; looped

K-63A-26A	Washington, D.C., brass-shell key-chain medal	28 mm	Chrome plated	Concave; looped
K-63A-27	Teena Creations JFK charm	24 mm	.925 fine sterling silver	Looped; reverse: "Ask Not" credo
K-63A-27A	Teena Creations JFK charm, type 1	24 mm	14K gold	Looped; reverse: "Ask Not" credo
K-63A-27B	Teena Creations JFK charm, type 2	24 mm	14K gold	Looped; reverse: "Ask Not" credo
K-63A-28	Michele JFK medalet	21 mm	Sterling silver	Looped; reverse: "Ask Not" credo
K-63A-28A	Michele JFK medalet	21 mm	Sterling silver, cast	Looped; reverse: "Ask Not" credo
K-63A-29	Aetna Jewelers JFK charm	19 mm	Sterling silver	Looped; reverse: "Our Goal" quote
K-63A-29A	Aetna Jewelers JFK charm	24 mm	Sterling silver	Looped; reverse: "Our Goal" quote
K-63A-29B	Aetna Jewelers JFK charm	29 mm	Sterling silver	Looped; reverse: "Our Goal" quote
K-63A-29C	Aetna Jewelers JFK charm	19 mm	14K gold	Looped; reverse: "Our Goal" quote
K-63A-29D	Aetna Jewelers JFK charm	24 mm	14K gold	New design
K-63A-29E	Aetna Jewelers JFK charm	29 mm	14K gold	Looped; reverse: "Our Goal" quote
K-63A-29F	Aetna Jewelers JFK charm	26 mm	Soft plastic	Looped; reverse: "Our Goal" quote, no initials
K-63A-29G	Aetna Jewelers JFK charm	19 mm	Sterling silver	Uniface; no loop
K-63A-29H	Aetna Jewelers JFK charm	22 mm	Sterling silver	Uniface; no loop
K-63A-29I	Aetna Jewelers JFK charm	24 mm	Sterling silver	Uniface; no loop
K-63A-29J	Aetna Jewelers JFK charm	29 mm	Sterling silver	Uniface; no loop
K-63A-29K	Aetna Jewelers JFK charm	19 mm	14K gold	Uniface; no loop
K-63A-29L	Aetna Jewelers JFK charm	22 mm	14K gold	Uniface; no loop
K-63A-29M	Aetna Jewelers JFK charm	24 mm	14K gold	Uniface; no loop
K-63A-29N	Aetna Jewelers JFK charm	29 mm	14K gold	Uniface; no loop
K-63A-29O	Aetna Jewelers JFK charm	22 mm	Sterling silver	Obverse and reverse change; looped; reverse: "Our Goal" quote
K-63A-29P	Aetna Jewelers JFK charm	22 mm	14K gold	Obverse and reverse change; looped; reverse: "Our Goal" quote
K-63A-29Q	Aetna Jewelers JFK charm	25 mm	Sterling silver	Looped; reverse: "Our Goal" quote
K-63A-29R	Aetna Jewelers JFK charm	25 mm	14K gold	Looped; reverse: "Our Goal" quote
K-63A-30	Aetna Jewelers JFK charm	19 mm	Sterling silver	Hallmark: AE sterling; reverse: "Ask Not" credo
K-63A-30A	Aetna Jewelers JFK charm	24 mm	Sterling silver	Bust change; hallmark: AE sterling; reverse: "Ask Not" credo
K-63A-30B	Aetna Jewelers JFK charm	29 mm	Sterling silver	Bust change; hallmark: AE sterling; reverse: "Ask Not" credo
K-63A-30C	Aetna Jewelers JFK charm	19 mm	14K gold	Hallmark: AE sterling; reverse: "Ask Not" credo
K-63A-30D	Aetna Jewelers JFK charm	24 mm	14K gold	Hallmark: AE sterling; reverse: "Ask Not" credo
K-63A-30E	Aetna Jewelers JFK charm	29 mm	14K gold	Hallmark: AE sterling; reverse: "Ask Not" credo
K-63A-30F	Aetna Jewelers JFK charm	28 mm	Plastic, multi colored	Reverse: "Ask Not" credo, no initials
K-63A-30G	Aetna Jewelers JFK charm	19 mm	Sterling silver	Uniface; no loop
K-63A-30H	Aetna Jewelers JFK charm	22 mm	Sterling silver	Uniface; no loop
K-63A-30I	Aetna Jewelers JFK charm	24 mm	Sterling silver	Uniface; no loop
K-63A-30J	Aetna Jewelers JFK charm	29 mm	Sterling silver	Uniface; no loop
K-63A-30K	Aetna Jewelers JFK charm	19 mm	14K gold	Uniface; no loop
K-63A-30L	Aetna Jewelers JFK charm	22 mm	14K gold	Uniface; no loop
K-63A-30M	Aetna Jewelers JFK charm	24 mm	14K gold	Uniface; no loop
K-63A-30N	Aetna Jewelers JFK charm	29 mm	14K gold	Uniface; no loop
K-63A-30O	Aetna Jewelers JFK charm	22 mm	Sterling silver	Obverse and reverse change; looped; reverse: "Ask Not" credo
K-63A-30P	Aetna Jewelers JFK charm	22 mm	14K gold	Obverse and reverse change; looped; reverse: "Ask Not" credo
K-63A-30Q	Aetna Jewelers JFK charm	23 mm	Sterling silver	Die variations; looped; reverse: "Ask Not" credo
K-63A-30R	Aetna Jewelers JFK charm	29 mm	Sterling silver	Looped; reverse: "Ask Not" credo, stamped
K-63A-31	Wells JFK medalet	22 mm	Sterling silver	Looped; reverse: birth and death dates
K-63A-31A	Wells JFK medalet	22 mm	Gold plated	Looped; reverse: birth and death dates
K-63A-31B	Wells JFK medalet, die test	22 mm	Bronze	Looped; reverse: birth and death dates
K-63A-31C	Wells Jacqueline Kennedy medalet	22 mm	Sterling silver	Looped; reverse: birth and death dates
K-63A-31D	Wells Jacqueline Kennedy medalet	22 mm	Gold plated	Looped; reverse: birth and death dates
K-63A-31E	Wells Jacqueline Kennedy medalet, die test	22 mm	Bronze	Untrimmed; uniface
K-63A-31F	Wells Kennedy children medalet	22 mm	Sterling silver	Looped; reverse: birth and death dates
K-63A-31G	Wells Kennedy children medalet	22 mm	Gold plated	Looped; reverse: birth and death dates
K-63A-31H	Wells Kennedy children medalet - die test	22 mm	Bronze	Untrimmed; uniface
K-63A-32	JFK key-chain link	14 x 20 mm	Painted base metal	Looped ends; reverse: U.S. Capitol and flame
K-63A-33	Fort Jewelry JFK head charm	14 x 16 mm	Sterling silver	Looped; reverse: "Ask Not" credo
K-63A-34	Dawn Creations JFK tribute head charm	12 x 18 mm	Sterling silver	Looped; reverse: "Ask Not" credo
K-63A-35	Fort Jewelry JFK head charm spinner	14 mm	Sterling silver	With axle pins; uniface

K-63A-35A	Fort Jewelry spoon insert coin	14 mm	Sterling silver	Uniface
K-63A-35B	Fort Jewelry spoon insert coin	14 mm	Gold plated	Uniface
K-63A-36	Kennedy half dollar jewelry filler coin	30 mm	Bronze-plated shell, cast	Uniface
K-63A-36A	Kennedy half dollar jewelry filler coin	30 mm	Silver-plated base metal	Uniface
K-63A-37	Ralph Menconi JFK bust charm	25 x 32 mm	Base metal, gold finish	Uniface
K-63A-37A	Ralph Menconi JFK bust charm	25 x 32 mm	Base metal, silver finish	Uniface
K-63A-38	The Menconi JFK head	13 x 23 mm	Base metal, gold finish	Cut-out for jewelry application; uniface
K-63A-38A	The Menconi JFK head	13 x 23 mm	Base metal, silver finish	Cut-out for jewelry application; uniface
K-63A-39	Kennedy half dollar foil key-chain insert	30 mm	Embossed silver foil	Reverse: instructions
K-63A-39A	Kennedy half dollar foil key-chain insert	30 mm	Foil variation	Reverse: instructions
K-63A-39B	Kennedy half dollar foil key-chain insert	30 mm	Thick foil	Reverse: instructions
K-63A-39C	Kennedy half dollar (spelling error) foil key-chain insert	30 mm		Reverse: instructions
K-63A-39D	Kennedy half dollar foil key-chain insert	30 mm		Reverse: new instructions
K-63A-39E	Kennedy half dollar foil key-chain insert	30 mm	Heavy metallic foil	Reverse: profile of JFK
K-63A-39F	Kennedy half dollar foil key-chain insert	30 mm	Heavy metallic foil	Reverse: new instructions, smaller JFK bust
K-63A-39G	Kennedy half dollar plastic key-chain tag	35 mm	Gold-embossed black plastic	Uniface
K-63A-40	Barton's Bonbonniere JFK 25-dollar chocolate coin	76 mm	Gold-colored foil	Reverse: "To-From"
K-63A-41	Penny Mementos JFK vertical elongated U.S. cent	20 x 34 mm		Reverse: Lincoln Memorial
K-63A-42	Ralph Jones "JFK Assassinated" elongated U.S. cent	20 x 40 mm		Horizontal script; Reverse: Lincoln Memorial
K-63A-42A	Ralph Jones "JFK Assassinated" elongated U.S. cent	20 x 40 mm		Without RJ initials; reverse: Lincoln Memorial
K-63A-42B	Ralph Jones "JFK Assassinated" elongated U.S. nickel	22 x 38 mm		Reverse: Monticello
K-63A-42C	Ralph Jones "JFK Assassinated" elongated U.S. dime	18 x 40 mm		Reverse: lit torch with sprigs of olive and oak
K-63A-42D	Ralph Jones "JFK Assassinated" elongated U.S. quarter	26 x 38 mm		Reverse: eagle with arrows
K-63A-42E	Ralph Jones "JFK Assassinated" elongated U.S. half dollar	30 x 48 mm		Reverse: heraldic eagle
K-63A-43	Ralph Jones JFK bust and credo elongated U.S. cent	20 x 40 mm		Horizontal bust; reverse: Lincoln Memorial
K-63A-43A	Ralph Jones JFK bust and credo elongated U.S. nickel	22 x 38 mm	Standard coin composition	Reverse: Monticello
K-63A-43B	Ralph Jones JFK bust and credo elongated U.S. dime	18 x 40 mm	Standard coin composition	Reverse: lit torch with sprigs of olive and oak
K-63A-43C	Ralph Jones JFK bust and credo elongated U.S. quarter	26 x 38 mm	Standard coin composition	Reverse: eagle with arrows
K-63A-43D	Ralph Jones JFK bust and credo elongated U.S. half dollar	30 x 48 mm	Standard coin composition	Reverse: standard Kennedy half dollar
K-63A-44	Pontiac Press JFK counterstamped U.S. cent	19 mm		Obverse: JFK facing Lincoln; reverse: Lincoln Memorial
K-63A-44A	Pontiac Press Littleton Coin Company promotional JFK counterstamped U.S. cent	19 mm		Finer detail on obverse; reverse: Lincoln Memorial
K-63A-44B	Management Consultants Association JFK cent	19 mm		On a card, 177.8 x 76.2 mm, "Lincoln Lives"
K-63A-44C	Management Consultants Association JFK cent	19 mm		On a card, 146.1 x 76.2 mm, "Lincoln Lives"
K-63A-45	American Coin, NJ, JFK facing Lincoln, 1963 coin	19 mm		Reverse: JFK above, 1963 below
K-63A-45A	Nicholas Salimbene JFK facing Lincoln, 1963 coin	19 mm		1,250 struck; NS monogram below the neck
K-63A-45B	American Coin, NJ, JFK facing Lincoln, 1964 coin	19 mm		Reverse: JFK above, 1963 below
K-63A-46	Del Schuler Kennedy half dollar coin sculpture	56 x 60 mm		Unique; two fused Kennedy half dollars
K-63A-47	Earl Fankhauser JFK memorial cent, encased	32 mm	Standard coin composition with aluminum ring	Standard Lucky Design U.S. cent
K-63A-48	Kennedy half dollar key-chain ornament	39 mm	Silver on base metal	Reverse: U.S. Capitol and flame
K-63A-48A	Kennedy half dollar key-chain ornament	39 mm	Base metal, gold finish	Reverse: U.S. Capitol and flame
K-63A-48B	Kennedy half dollar money clip	39 mm	Silver base metal with clip	Uniface
K-63A-49	Kennedy half dollar encased key-chain ornament	39 mm	Silver base metal with a black background	Looped
K-63A-49A	Kennedy half dollar encased key-chain ornament	39 mm	Gold base metal	Looped
K-63A-50	Dawn Creations JFK-Jacqueline Kennedy heart charm	30 mm	Sterling silver	Uniface; looped
K-63A-51	"JFK Credo" Kennedy half dollar holder	30 mm	Brass	Reversed shell
K-63A-51A	"JFK Credo" Kennedy half dollar holder filler insert	30 mm	Thin brass	Reverse: reversed "Ask Not" credo
K-63A-52	Erie Publishers JFK medal	38 mm	.999 fine silver	15,000 struck; serial number; reverse: wreath and flame
K-63A-52A	Erie Publishers JFK medal	38 mm	Bronze	No serial number; reverse: wreath and flame
K-63A-53	Green Duck JFK credo medal	39 mm	Antique silver on bronze	Reverse: upright flame with hyphen
K-63A-53A	Green Duck JFK credo medal	39 mm	18K-gold–plated bronze	Reverse: upright flame with hyphen
K-63A-54	Shields JFK lighter	38 mm	Oxidized silver-plated tin	Flip the head to light; inscribed with "In God We Trust"
K-63A-54A	Shields JFK lighter	38 mm	Rhodium-plated nickel	Flip the head to light; inscribed with "In God We Trust"
K-63A-54B	Shields JFK lighter	38 mm	Dull, coarse surface	Flip the head to light; inscribed with "In God We Trust"

K-63A-55	Kennedy half dollar foil insert for key chain	30 mm	Embossed foil insert	Reverse: instructions
K-63A-55A	Kennedy half dollar foil insert for key chain	30 mm	Embossed foil insert	Instructions changed
K-63A-55B	Kennedy half dollar foil insert for key chain	30 mm	Embossed foil insert	Uniface
K-63A-56	"Tell JFK" chocolate medal	80 mm	Gold-colored foil	Reverse: Capitol
K-63A-57	"Tell JFK" chocolate coin	31 mm	Silver-colored foil	Reverse: 50 cents
K-63A-58	Star JFK chocolate novelty coin	32 mm	Silver-colored foil	Reverse: "Nation's Capitol"
K-63A-58A	Star JFK chocolate novelty coin	32 mm	Gold-colored foil	Reverse: "Nation's Capitol"
K-63A-59	Lloyd E. Wagaman elongated Kennedy half dollar cameo bust	36 x 32 mm		118 rolled; die destroyed
K-63A-59A	Lloyd E. Wagaman elongated Kennedy half dollar cameo bust	36 x 32 mm		Three rolled; cancelled
K-63A-59B	Lloyd E. Wagaman elongated Kennedy half dollar cameo bust, trial roll	36 x 32 mm		Six rolled; shallow JFK
K-63A-60	In memoriam souvenir medallion	36 mm	Brass, silk screen process	Uniface; looped
K-63A-61	"Defensor Liberatis" JFK medal	20 mm	.925 fine sterling silver	Reverse: Statue of Liberty
K-63A-61A	"Defensor Liberatis" JFK medal	32 mm	.925 fine sterling silver	Reverse: Statue of Liberty
K-63A-61B	"Defensor Liberatis" JFK medal	40 mm	.925 fine sterling silver	Reverse: Statue of Liberty
K-63A-61C	"Defensor Liberatis" JFK medal	50 mm	.925 fine sterling silver	Reverse: Statue of Liberty
K-63A-61D	"Defensor Liberatis" JFK medal	20 mm	.900 fine gold	Reverse: Statue of Liberty
K-63A-61E	"Defensor Liberatis" JFK medal	32 mm	.900 fine gold	Reverse: Statue of Liberty
K-63A-61F	"Defensor Liberatis" JFK medal	50 mm	.900 fine gold	Reverse: Statue of Liberty
K-63A-61G	"Defensor Liberatis" JFK medal, U.S. issue	21 mm	Sterling silver	Reverse: Statue of Liberty
K-63A-61H	"Defensor Liberatis" JFK medal, U.S. issue	30 mm	Sterling silver	Reverse: Statue of Liberty
K-63A-62	S.M. Federit JFK medal	12½ mm	.900 fine gold	Reverse: flying eagle
K-63A-62A	S.M. Federit JFK medal	20 mm	.900 fine gold	Reverse: flying eagle
K-63A-62B	S.M. Federit JFK medal	33 mm	.900 fine gold	Reverse: flying eagle
K-63A-62C	S.M. Federit JFK medal	40 mm	.900 fine gold	Reverse: flying eagle
K-63A-62D	S.M. Federit JFK medal	55 mm	.900 fine gold	Reverse: flying eagle
K-63A-62E	S.M. Federit JFK medal	55 mm	.900 fine silver	Reverse: flying eagle
K-63A-63	Eurocommerce JFK medal	32 mm	Base metal, antique silver finish	Looped; reverse: Prestdental Seal
K-63A-63A	Eurocommerce JFK medal	32 mm	Gold plated	Looped; reverse: Presidental Seal
K-63A-63B	Eurocommerce JFK medal	32 mm	Antique silver finish	Looped; reverse: Presidental Seal
K-63A-63C	Eurocommerce JFK medal	32 mm	Heavy gold plating	Looped; reverse: Presidental Seal
K-63A-63D	Eurocommerce JFK medal	32 mm	Gold-plated base metal	Looped; reverse: Presidental Seal
K-63A-63E	Eurocommerce JFK medal	24 mm	Gold-plated base metal	Looped; reverse: Presidental Seal
K-63A-63F	Eurocommerce JFK medal	20 mm	Gold-plated base metal	Looped; reverse: Presidental Seal
K-63A-63G	Eurocommerce JFK medal	17 mm	Gold-plated base metal	Looped; reverse: Presidental Seal
K-63A-63H	Eurocommerce JFK medal	12 mm	Gold-plated base metal	Looped; reverse: Presidental Seal
K-63A-63I	Eurocommerce JFK medal	24 mm	Heavy gold plating	Looped; reverse: Presidental Seal
K-63A-63J	Eurocommerce JFK medal	20 mm	Heavy gold plating	Looped; reverse: Presidental Seal
K-63A-63K	Eurocommerce JFK medal	17 mm	Heavy gold plating	Looped; reverse: Presidental Seal
K-63A-64	Austrian Mint issue medal	20 mm	.900 fine gold	Reverse: feather
K-63A-64A	Austrian Mint issue medal	32 mm	.900 fine gold	Reverse: feather
K-63A-64B	Austrian Mint issue medal	40 mm	.900 fine gold	Reverse: feather
K-63A-64C	Austrian Mint issue medal	40 mm	.900 fine silver	Reverse: feather
K-63A-65	JFK memorial medal, Canada	40 mm	Bronze	Reverse: draped cross
K-63A-65A	JFK memorial medal, Canada	40 mm	.835 fine silver	Reverse: draped cross
K-63A-65B	JFK memorial medal, Canada	40 mm	.585 fine gold, 45 g.	Reverse: draped cross
K-63A-65C	JFK memorial medal, Canada	40 mm	.986 fine gold, 70 g.	Reverse: draped cross
K-63A-66	JFK tribute medal, Canada	40 mm	Copper	Reverse: maple leaves
K-63A-66A	JFK tribute medal, Canada	40 mm	Copper, antique finish	Reverse: maple leaves
K-63A-66B	JFK tribute medal, Canada	40 mm	.999 fine silver	Reverse: maple leaves
K-63A-66C	JFK tribute medal, Canada	40 mm	24K gold	Reverse: maple leaves
K-63A-66D	JFK tribute medal, Canada	40 mm	.999 fine platinum	Reverse: maple leaves
K-63A-67	Wellings JFK memorial medal	52 mm	Bronze	Reverse: open hands
K-63A-67A	Wellings JFK memorial medal	52 mm	.999 fine silver	1,000 struck; serial number; reverse: open hands
K-63A-67B	Wellings JFK memorial medal	52 mm	.999 fine gold	Ten struck; serial number; reverse: open hands
K-63A-68	Nickel Monument JFK medal, variety 1	40 mm	Nickel silver	Reverse: eternal flame
K-63A-68A	Nickel Monument JFK medal, variety 1	40 mm	Bronze	Reverse: eternal flame
K-63A-68B	Nickel Monument JFK medal, variety 1	40 mm	.999 fine silver	Serial number; reverse: eternal flame
K-63A-68C	Nickel Monument JFK medal, variety 1	40 mm	24K gold	Serial number; reverse: eternal flame
K-63A-68D	Nickel Monument JFK medal, variety 1	40 mm	.999 fine platinum	Serial number; reverse: eternal flame
K-63A-68E	Nickel Monument JFK medal, variety 2	40 mm	Bronze	Die change
K-63A-68F	Nickel Monument JFK medal, variety 2	40 mm	Nickel silver	Reverse: name
K-63A-68G	Nickel Monument JFK medal, variety 2	40 mm	.999 fine silver	Reverse: name
K-63A-69	French Mint Kennedy half dollar, copy	32 mm	Gold-plated bronze	Reverse: Presidential Seal
K-63A-70	Bavarian Mint JFK memorial medal	40 mm	Silver	Reverse: "We Lost Him"

K-63A-70A	Bavarian Mint JFK memorial medal	60 mm	Silver	Reverse: "We Lost Him"
K-63A-70B	Bavarian Mint JFK memorial medal	50 mm	Silver	Reverse: "We Lost Him"
K-63A-70C	Bavarian Mint JFK memorial medal three-piece set	40 mm	Silver	Reverse: "We Lost Him"
K-63A-70D	Bavarian Mint JFK memorial medal	20 mm	Gold	Reverse: "We Lost Him"
K-63A-70E	Bavarian Mint JFK memorial medal	26 mm	Gold	Reverse: "We Lost Him"
K-63A-70F	Bavarian Mint JFK memorial medal	32 mm	Gold	Reverse: "We Lost Him"
K-63A-70G	Bavarian Mint JFK memorial medal	40 mm	Gold	Reverse: "We Lost Him"
K-63A-70H	Bavarian Mint JFK memorial medal	50 mm	Gold	Thin planchet; reverse: "We Lost Him"
K-63A-70I	Bavarian Mint JFK memorial medal	50 mm	Gold	2,000 struck; thick planchet; reverse: "We Lost Him"
K-63A-70J	Bavarian Mint JFK memorial medal	60 mm	Gold	1,500 struck; thin planchet; reverse: "We Lost Him"
K-63A-70K	Bavarian Mint JFK memorial medal	60 mm	Gold	1,000 struck; thick planchet; reverse: "We Lost Him"
K-63A-71	"Freedom in a Free World" medal	20 mm	Silver	Reverse: Liberty Bell
K-63A-71A	"Freedom in a Free World" medal	20 mm	Gold	Reverse: Liberty Bell
K-63A-71B	"Freedom in a Free World" medal	26 mm	Gold	Reverse: Liberty Bell
K-63A-71C	"Freedom in a Free World" medal	32 mm	Gold	Reverse: Liberty Bell
K-63A-71D	"Freedom in a Free World" medal	40 mm	Gold	Reverse: Liberty Bell
K-63A-71E	"Freedom in a Free World" medal	50 mm	Gold	Thin planchet; reverse: Liberty Bell
K-63A-71F	"Freedom in a Free World" medal	50 mm	Gold	Thick planchet; reverse: Liberty Bell
K-63A-71G	"Freedom in a Free World" medal	60 mm	Gold	Thin planchet; reverse: Liberty Bell
K-63A-71H	"Freedom in a Free World" medal	60 mm	Gold	Thick planchet; reverse: Liberty Bell
K-63A-71I	"Freedom in a Free World" medal	40 mm	Silver	Reverse: Liberty Bell
K-63A-72	"Righteousness" medal	40 mm	.999 fine silver, Matte Finish	Reverse: "Righteousness" quote
K-63A-72A	"Righteousness" medal	40 mm	Silver, Proof	Reverse: "Righteousness" quote
K-63A-72B	"Righteousness" medal	50 mm	Silver, Matte Finish	Reverse: "Righteousness" quote
K-63A-72C	"Righteousness" medal	65 mm	Silver, Proof	Reverse: "Righteousness" quote
K-63A-72D	"Righteousness" medal	65 mm	Silver, Matte Finish	Reverse: "Righteousness" quote
K-63A-72E	"Righteousness" medal	75 mm	Silver, Proof	Reverse: "Righteousness" quote
K-63A-72F	"Righteousness" medal	75 mm	Silver, Matte Finish	Reverse: "Righteousness" quote
K-63A-72G	"Righteousness" medal	85 mm	Silver, Proof	Reverse: "Righteousness" quote
K-63A-72H	"Righteousness" medal	85 mm	Silver, Matte Finish	Reverse: "Righteousness" quote
K-63A-72I	"Righteousness" medal	22 1/2 mm	.900 fine gold	Reverse: "Righteousness" quote
K-63A-72J	"Righteousness" medal	25 mm	.900 fine gold	Reverse: "Righteousness" quote
K-63A-72K	"Righteousness" medal	40 mm	.900 fine gold	Reverse: "Righteousness" quote
K-63A-72L	"Righteousness" medal	50 mm	.900 fine gold	Reverse: "Righteousness" quote
K-63A-72M	"Righteousness" medal	65 mm	.986 fine gold	Reverse: "Righteousness" quote
K-63A-72N	"Righteousness" medal	75 mm	.986 fine gold	Reverse: "Righteousness" quote
K-63A-72O	"Righteousness" medal	85 mm	.986 fine gold	Reverse: "Righteousness" quote
K-63A-73	Argenteus series medal	35 mm	.999 fine silver, Proof	Reverse: "Righteousness" quote
K-63A-73A	Argenteus series medal	50 mm	.999 fine silver, Proof	Reverse: "Righteousness" quote
K-63A-74	Aureus Magnus JFK series coin	15 mm	Gold	Reverse: S
K-63A-74A	Aureus Magnus JFK series coin	20 mm	Gold	Reverse: I
K-63A-74B	Aureus Magnus JFK series 2-1/2-ducat coin	26 mm	Gold	Reverse: II
K-63A-74C	Aureus Magnus JFK series 5-ducat coin	35 mm	Gold	Reverse: V
K-63A-74D	Aureus Magnus JFK series 10-ducat coin	44 mm	Gold	Reverse: X
K-63A-74E	Aureus Magnus JFK series 20-ducat coin	50 mm	Gold	Reverse: XX
K-63A-74F	Aureus Magnus JFK series 30-ducat coin	50 mm	Gold	Thick planchet; reverse: XXX
K-63A-74G	Aureus Magnus JFK series 100-ducat coin	80 mm	Gold	Reverse: C
K-63A-75	Tenfold Argenteus JFK medal	80 mm	.1000 fine silver	2,000 struck; serial number on the edge; reverse: X
K-63A-75A	Tenfold Argenteus JFK 100-ducat medal	80 mm	Gold	150 struck; reverse: X
K-63A-76	JFK-Oswald assassination medal, Germany	60 mm	Silver, Matte Finish	Export only; reverse: Oswald killing
K-63A-76A	JFK-Oswald assassination medal, Germany	60 mm	Silver, Proof	10,000 struck; reverse: Oswald killing
K-63A-76B	JFK-Oswald assassination medal, trial strike, Germany	60 mm	Silver	Three struck; reverse: Oswald killing, dated 1963
K-63A-76C	JFK-Oswald assassination medal, trial strike, Germany	30 mm	Silver	Three struck; reverse: Oswald killing, dated 1963
K-63A-76D	JFK-Oswald assassination medal, Italy	30 mm	Silver	Reeded edge; reverse: Oswald killing
K-63A-76E	JFK-Oswald assassination medal, Italy	14 mm	Gold	Reeded edge; reverse: Oswald killing
K-63A-76F	JFK-Oswald assassination medal, Italy	21 mm	Gold	Reeded edge; reverse: Oswald killing
K-63A-76G	JFK-Oswald assassination medal, Germany	25 mm	Gold	Plain edge; reverse: Oswald killing
K-63A-76H	JFK-Oswald assassination medal, Germany	30 mm	Gold	Plain edge; reverse: Oswald killing
K-63A-76I	JFK-Oswald assassination medal, Italy	30 mm	Gold	Reeded edge; reverse: Oswald killing
K-63A-76J	JFK-Oswald assassination medal, Germany	60 mm	Gold	300 struck; thin planchet; serial number; reverse: Oswald killing

K-63A-76K	JFK-Oswald assassination medal, Germany	60 mm	Gold	150 struck; regular planchet; serial number; reverse: Oswald killing
K-63A-76L	JFK-Oswald assassination medal, Germany	60 mm	Gold	50 struck; thick planchet; reverse: Oswald killing
K-63A-76M	JFK-Oswald assassination medal, Venezuela	50 mm	.900 fine gold	Reeded edge; reverse: Oswald killing
K-63A-76N	JFK-Oswald assassination medal, Venezuela	50 mm	.1000 fine silver	Reeded edge; reverse: Oswald killing
K-63A-77	Deutsche Numismatik JFK-Oswald medal	60 mm	Silver, Matte Finish	Reverse: "In Honorem"
K-63A-77A	Deutsche Numismatik JFK-Oswald medal	60 mm	Silver, Proof	Reverse: "In Honorem"
K-63A-77B	Deutsche Numismatik JFK-Oswald medal	25 mm	Gold	Reverse: "In Honorem"
K-63A-77C	Deutsche Numismatik JFK-Oswald medal	30 mm	Gold	Reverse: "In Honorem"
K-63A-77D	Deutsche Numismatik JFK-Oswald medal	60 mm	Gold	300 struck; thin planchet; reverse: "In Honorem"
K-63A-77E	Deutsche Numismatik JFK-Oswald medal	60 mm	Gold	150 struck; regular planchet; reverse: "In Honorem"
K-63A-77F	Deutsche Numismatik JFK-Oswald medal	60 mm	Gold	50 struck; thick planchet; reverse: "In Honorem"
K-63A-77G	Deutsche Numismatik JFK-Oswald medal	60 mm	Silver, Proof	Rare; reverse: "Cusus Ut Memoria"
K-63A-78	JFK-Lincoln medal	20 mm	.900 fine gold	Reverse: a family; "You Can Stop Men"
K-63A-78A	JFK-Lincoln medal	24 mm	.900 fine gold	Reverse: a family; "You Can Stop Men"
K-63A-78B	JFK-Lincoln medal	28 mm	.900 fine gold	Reverse: a family; "You Can Stop Men"
K-63A-78C	JFK-Lincoln medal	32 mm	.900 fine gold	Reverse: a family; "You Can Stop Men"
K-63A-78D	JFK-Lincoln medal	40 mm	.900 fine gold	Reverse: a family; "You Can Stop Men"
K-63A-78E	JFK-Lincoln medal	32 mm	Heavy bronze, gilded	Promo; reverse: a family; "You Can Stop Men"
K-63A-78F	JFK-Lincoln medal	12 mm	Gold	Used in jewelry; reverse: a family; "You Can Stop Men"
K-63A-78G	JFK-Lincoln medal	40 mm	Heavy bronze, gilded	Promo; reverse: a family; "You Can Stop Men"
K-63A-79	"Catholic Men of the Century" medal	32 mm	Gold-anodized aluminum	No loop; reverse: Pope John
K-63A-79A	"Catholic Men of the Century" medal	32 mm	Polished aluminum	No loop; reverse: Pope John
K-63A-79B	"Catholic Men of the Century" medal	32 mm	Gold-anodized aluminum	No loop; reverse: Pope John
K-63A-79C	"Catholic Men of the Century" medal	32 mm	Polished aluminum	No loop; reverse: Pope John
K-63A-79D	"Catholic Men of the Century" medal	32 mm	Gold-anodized aluminum	Reverse: Pope John, Germany letters
K-63A-80	Bavarian Mint JFK memorial medal	13 mm	.890 fine gold	Reverse: roses
K-63A-80A	Bavarian Mint JFK memorial medal	15 1/2 mm	.890 fine gold	Reverse: roses
K-63A-80B	Bavarian Mint JFK memorial medal	20 mm	.890 fine gold	Reverse: roses
K-63A-80C	Bavarian Mint JFK memorial medal	34 mm	.890 fine gold	Reverse: roses
K-63A-80D	Bavarian Mint JFK memorial medal	13 mm	.585 fine gold	Reverse: roses
K-63A-80E	Bavarian Mint JFK memorial medal	15 1/2 mm	.585 fine gold	Reverse: roses
K-63A-80F	Bavarian Mint JFK memorial medal	20 mm	.585 fine gold	Reverse: roses
K-63A-80G	Bavarian Mint JFK memorial medal	34 mm	.585 fine gold	Reverse: roses
K-63A-81	JFK memorial medal, Hong Kong	30 mm	Chrome-plated aluminum	Reverse: "Ask Not" credo
K-63A-81A	JFK memorial medal, Hong Kong	30 mm	Gold-anodized aluminum	Reverse: "Ask Not" credo
K-63A-81B	JFK memorial medal, Hong Kong	30 mm	Gold-anodized aluminum	Looped; reverse: "Ask Not" credo
K-63A-81C	JFK memorial medal, Hong Kong	30 mm	Chrome-plated aluminum	Reverse: "Ask Not" credo
K-63A-81D	JFK memorial medal, Hong Kong	30 mm	Gold-anodized aluminum	Letter variation; reverse: "Ask Not" credo
K-63A-82	JFK memorial medal, series 1, Italy	50 mm	Silver-plated brass	Obverse: JFK facing left; reverse: "Ask Not" credo
K-63A-82A	JFK memorial medal, series 1, Italy	50 mm	Bronze	Obverse: JFK facing left; reverse: "Ask Not" credo
K-63A-82B	JFK memorial medal, series 1, Italy	32 mm	Silver-plated brass	Looped; obverse: JFK facing left; reverse: "Ask Not" credo
K-63A-82C	JFK memorial medal, series 1, Italy	32 mm	Gold-plated brass	Looped; obverse: JFK facing left; reverse: "Ask Not" credo
K-63A-82D	JFK memorial medal, series 1, Italy	32 mm	Bronze	Looped; obverse: JFK facing left; reverse: "Ask Not" credo
K-63A-82E	JFK memorial medal, series 1, Italy	32 mm	Sterling silver	Looped; obverse: JFK facing left; reverse: "Ask Not" credo
K-63A-82F	JFK memorial medal, series 1, Italy	50 mm	Sterling silver	No loop; obverse: JFK facing left; reverse: "Ask Not" credo
K-63A-82G	JFK memorial medal, series 1, Italy	50 mm	Gold-plated brass	No loop; obverse: JFK facing left; reverse: "Ask Not" credo
K-63A-82H	JFK memorial medal, series 1, Italy	49 mm	Base metal Cast Copy	Obverse: Italy removed, JFK facing left; reverse: quote
K-63A-83	JFK memorial medal, series 2, Italy	50 mm	Silver-plated brass	Obverse: JFK facing front; reverse: eagle
K-63A-83A	JFK memorial medal, series 2, Italy	50 mm	Gold-plated brass	Obverse: JFK facing front; reverse: eagle
K-63A-83B	JFK memorial medal, series 2, Italy	50 mm	Sterling silver	Obverse: JFK facing front; reverse: eagle
K-63A-83C	JFK memorial medal, series 2, Italy	50 mm	Bronze	Obverse: JFK facing front; reverse: eagle
K-63A-83D	JFK memorial medal, series 2, Italy	32 mm	Sterling silver	Square loop at the top; obverse: JFK facing front; reverse: eagle

K-63A-83E	JFK memorial medal, series 2, Italy	32 mm	Silver-plated brass	Looped; obverse: JFK facing front; reverse: eagle
K-63A-83F	JFK memorial medal, series 2, Italy	28 mm	Sterling silver	Square loop at the top; obverse: variations, JFK facing front
K-63A-83G	JFK memorial medal, series 2, Italy	28 mm	Silver-plated brass	Obverse: variations, JFK facing front
K-63A-83H	JFK memorial medal, series 2, Italy	36 mm	Gold-plated brass shell	For desk top; obverse: JFK facing front
K-63A-83I	JFK memorial medal, series 2, Italy	50 mm	Silver-plated brass, mule	Obverse: JFK facing front; reverse: same as K-61-18
K-63A-83J	JFK memorial medal, series 2, Italy	50 mm	Gold-plated brass, mule	Obverse: JFK facing front; reverse: same as K-61-18
K-63A-83K	JFK memorial medal, series 2, Italy	50 mm	Bronze, mule	Obverse: JFK facing front; reverse: same as K-61-18
K-63A-83L	JFK memorial medal, series 2, Italy	32 mm	Silver plated	Obverse: JFK facing front; reverse: eagle
K-63A-83M	JFK memorial medal, series 2, Italy	32 mm	Gold plated	Obverse: JFK facing front; reverse: eagle
K-63A-83N	JFK memorial medal, series 2, Italy	32 mm	Bronze	Obverse: JFK facing front; reverse: eagle
K-63A-83O	JFK memorial medal, series 2, Italy	32 mm	Silver plated	Square loop at the top; obverse: JFK facing front; reverse: eagle
K-63A-83P	JFK memorial medal, series 2, Italy	32 mm	Gold plated	Square loop at the top; obverse: JFK facing front; reverse: eagle
K-63A-83Q	JFK memorial medal, series 2, Italy	32 mm	Bronze	Square loop at the top; obverse: JFK facing front; reverse: eagle
K-63A-83R	JFK memorial medal, series 2, Italy	28 mm	Silver plated	Square loop at the top; obverse: JFK facing front; reverse: eagle
K-63A-83S	JFK memorial medal, series 2, Italy	28 mm	Gold plated	Square loop at the top; obverse: JFK facing front; reverse: eagle
K-63A-83T	JFK memorial medal, series 2, Italy	32 mm	Silver plated	Shell, obverse only; JFK facing front
K-63A-83U	JFK memorial medal, series 2, Italy	28 mm	Silver plated	Shell, obverse only; JFK facing front
K-63A-83V	JFK memorial medal, series 2, Italy	21 mm	Silver plated	Shell, obverse only; JFK facing front
K-63A-83W	JFK memorial medal, series 2, Italy	100 mm	Silver-plated bronze, mule	Obverse: JFK facing front; reverse: eagle
K-63A-84	JFK memorial medal, series 3, Italy	12 mm	.750 fine gold	Obverse: JFK facing left; reverse: 750 under eagle
K-63A-84A	JFK memorial medal, series 3, Italy	21 mm	.750 fine gold	Obverse: JFK facing left; reverse: 750 under eagle
K-63A-84B	JFK memorial medal, series 3, Italy	21 mm	Sterling silver	Obverse: JFK facing left; reverse: eagle
K-63A-84C	JFK memorial medal, series 3, Italy	21 mm	Silver-plated brass	Obverse: JFK facing left; reverse: eagle
K-63A-84D	JFK memorial medal, series 3, Italy	21 mm	Gold-plated brass	Obverse: JFK facing left; reverse: eagle
K-63A-84E	JFK memorial medal, series 3, Italy	21 mm	Bronze	Obverse: JFK facing left; reverse: eagle
K-63A-84F	JFK memorial medal, series 3, Italy	12 mm	Sterling silver	Obverse: JFK facing left; reverse: eagle
K-63A-84G	JFK memorial medal, series 3, Italy	12 mm	Silver-plated brass	Obverse: JFK facing left; reverse: eagle
K-63A-85	Aurea Numismatica JFK medal	45 mm	Bronze	Reverse: U.S. Capitol
K-63A-85A	Aurea Numismatica JFK medal	45 mm	.999 fine silver	Reverse: U.S. Capitol
K-63A-85B	Aurea Numismatica JFK medal	45 mm	.900 fine gold	1,000 struck; reverse: U.S. Capitol
K-63A-85C	Aurea Numismatica JFK medal	30 mm	.900 fine gold	Reverse: U.S. Capitol
K-63A-85D	Aurea Numismatica JFK medal	20 mm	.900 fine gold	Thick planchet; reverse: U.S. Capitol
K-63A-85E	Aurea Numismatica JFK medal	20 mm	.900 fine gold	Thin planchet; reverse: U.S. Capitol
K-63A-85F	Aurea Numismatica JFK medal	60 mm	Bronze	Reverse: U.S. Capitol
K-63A-85G	Aurea Numismatica JFK medal	60 mm	Possibly silver	Reverse: U.S. Capitol
K-63A-86	Franco-Tedesca JFK medal	38 mm	.925 fine silver	Reverse: "Man Does What He Must"
K-63A-86A	Franco-Tedesca JFK medal	25 mm	Gold	Reverse: "Man Does What He Must"
K-63A-86B	Franco-Tedesca JFK medal	38 mm	Gold	Reverse: "Man Does What He Must"
K-63A-86C	Franco-Tedesca JFK medal	50 mm	Gold	Reverse: "Man Does What He Must"
K-63A-86D	Franco-Tedesca JFK medal	60 mm	Gold	Reverse: "Man Does What He Must"
K-63A-87	Franco Fossa JFK memorial medal	180 mm	Bronze	Reverse: seal, stars, and eagle
K-63A-87A	Franco Fossa JFK memorial medal	22 mm	Gold	Reverse: seal, stars, and eagle
K-63A-87B	Franco Fossa JFK memorial medal	26 mm	Gold	Reverse: seal, stars, and eagle
K-63A-87C	Franco Fossa JFK memorial medal	32 mm	Gold	Reverse: seal, stars, and eagle
K-63A-87D	Franco Fossa JFK memorial medal	40 mm	Gold	Reverse: seal, stars, and eagle
K-63A-87E	Franco Fossa JFK memorial medal	50 mm	Gold	Reverse: seal, stars, and eagle
K-63A-87F	Franco Fossa JFK memorial medal	60 mm	Gold	Reverse: seal, stars, and eagle
K-63A-87G	Franco Fossa JFK memorial medal	32 mm	Gold-plated bronze	Reverse: seal, met under tail feathers
K-63A-87H	Franco Fossa JFK memorial medal	22 mm	Gold	Serial number; reverse: seal, stars, eagle, London
K-63A-87I	Franco Fossa JFK memorial medal	32 mm	Gold	Serial number; reverse: seal, stars, eagle, London
K-63A-87J	Franco Fossa JFK memorial medal	38 mm	Gold	Serial number; reverse: seal, stars, eagle, London
K-63A-88	Zinn original JFK medal	38 mm	Gilder's brass	Reverse: beaded border

K-63A-88A	Zinn original JFK medal	38 mm	Gilder's brass	Uniface
K-63A-89	Naigai cloisonné JFK flag charm	22 x 20 mm	Nickel-plated brass	Reverse: JFK head
K-63A-90	JFK memorial series, English-language, Mexico	30 mm	.900 fine silver	Reverse: English legend
K-63A-90A	JFK memorial series, English-language, Mexico	40 mm	.900 fine silver	Reverse: English legend
K-63A-90B	JFK memorial series, English-language, Mexico	50 mm	.900 fine silver	Reverse: English legend
K-63A-90C	JFK memorial series, English-language, Mexico	30 mm	Gold	Reverse: English legend
K-63A-90D	JFK memorial series, English-language, Mexico	40 mm	Gold	Reverse: English legend
K-63A-90E	JFK memorial series, English-language, Mexico	50 mm	Gold	Reverse: English legend
K-63A-90F	JFK memorial series, English-language, Mexico	20 mm	.900 fine silver	Reverse: English legend
K-63A-90G	JFK memorial series, English-language, Mexico	20 mm	Gold	Reverse: English legend
K-63A-91	JFK memorial series, Spanish-language, Mexico	30 mm	.900 fine silver	Reverse: Spanish legend
K-63A-91A	JFK memorial series, Spanish-language, Mexico	40 mm	.900 fine silver	Reverse: Spanish legend
K-63A-91B	JFK memorial series, Spanish-language, Mexico	50 mm	.900 fine silver	Reverse: Spanish legend
K-63A-91C	JFK memorial series, Spanish-language, Mexico	30 mm	Gold	Reverse: Spanish legend
K-63A-91D	JFK memorial series, Spanish-language, Mexico	40 mm	Gold	Reverse: Spanish legend
K-63A-91E	JFK memorial series, Spanish-language, Mexico	50 mm	Gold	Reverse: Spanish legend
K-63A-91F	JFK memorial series, Spanish-language, trial strike, Mexico	50 mm	Silver	Reverse: rejected Spanish legend
K-63A-92	JFK memorial series, Italian-language, Mexico	40 mm	.900 fine silver	Reverse: Italian legend
K-63A-92A	JFK memorial series, Italian-language, Mexico	40 mm	Gold	Reverse: Italian legend
K-63A-93	JFK memorial series, German-language, Mexico	40 mm	.900 fine silver	Reverse: German legend
K-63A-93A	JFK memorial series, German-language, Mexico	40 mm	Gold	Reverse: German legend
K-63A-94	JFK memorial series, French-language, Mexico	40 mm	.900 fine silver, Matte Finish	Reverse: French legend
K-63A-94A	JFK memorial series, French-language, Mexico	40 mm	Gold	Reverse: French legend
K-63A-94B	JFK memorial series, French-language, Mexico	50 mm	.900 fine silver	Reverse: French legend
K-63A-94C	JFK memorial series, French-language, Mexico	50 mm	Gold	Reverse: French legend
K-63A-95	JFK memorial series, Russian-language, Mexico	40 mm	.900 fine silver	Reverse: Russian legend
K-63A-95A	JFK memorial series, Russian-language, Mexico	40 mm	Gold	Reverse: Russian legend
K-63A-96	JFK memorial series, Hebrew-language, Mexico	50 mm	.900 fine silver	Reverse: Hebrew legend
K-63A-96A	JFK memorial series, Hebrew-language, Mexico	50 mm	Gold	Reverse: Hebrew legend
K-63A-97	JFK memorial series, Finnish-language, Mexico	40 mm	.900 fine silver	Reverse: Finnish legend
K-63A-97A	JFK memorial series, Finnish-language, Mexico	40 mm	Gold	Reverse: Finnish legend
K-63A-98	"JFK Visit to U.S. Air Force Academy" medal	32 mm	Silver-plated brass	Looped; reverse: "Some of You"
K-63A-98A	"JFK Visit to U.S. Air Force Academy" medal	32 mm	24K gold plating	Five struck; serial number; reverse: "Some of You"
K-63A-98B	"JFK Visit to U.S. Air Force Academy" medal	32 mm		Unique; approval shell; uniface; reverse: "Some of You"
K-63A-99	JFK-Pope John medal	50 mm	Sterling silver	Obverse: JFK facing front; reverse: Pope John
K-63A-99A	JFK-Pope John medal	50 mm	Silver-plated brass	Obverse: JFK facing front; reverse: Pope John
K-63A-99B	JFK-Pope John medal	50 mm	Gold-plated brass	Obverse: JFK facing front; reverse: Pope John
K-63A-99C	JFK-Pope John medal	50 mm	Bronze	Obverse: JFK facing front; reverse: Pope John
K-63A-99D	JFK-Pope John medal	32 mm	Sterling silver	Looped; obverse: JFK facing front; reverse: Pope John
K-63A-99E	JFK-Pope John medal	32 mm	Silver-plated brass	Looped; obverse: JFK facing front; reverse: Pope John
K-63A-99F	JFK-Pope John medal	32 mm	Gold-plated brass	Looped; obverse: JFK facing front; reverse: Pope John
K-63A-99G	JFK-Pope John medal	32 mm	Bronze	Looped; obverse: JFK facing front; reverse: Pope John
K-63A-99H	JFK-Pope John medal	28 mm	Sterling silver	Looped; obverse: JFK facing front; reverse: Pope John
K-63A-99I	JFK-Pope John medal	28 mm	Silver-plated brass	Looped; obverse: JFK facing front; reverse: Pope John
K-63A-99J	JFK-Pope John medal	28 mm	Gold-plated brass	Looped; obverse: JFK facing front; reverse: Pope John
K-63A-99K	JFK-Pope John medal	28 mm	Bronze	Looped; obverse: JFK facing front; reverse: Pope John
K-63A-99L	JFK-Pope John medal	21 mm	Sterling silver	Looped; obverse: JFK facing front; reverse: Pope John
K-63A-99M	JFK-Pope John medal	21 mm	Silver-plated brass	Looped; obverse: JFK facing front; reverse: Pope John
K-63A-99N	JFK-Pope John medal	21 mm	Gold-plated brass	Looped; obverse: JFK facing front; reverse: Pope John
K-63A-99O	JFK-Pope John medal	21 mm	Bronze	Looped; obverse: JFK facing front; reverse: Pope John
K-63A-99P	JFK-Pope John medal	50 mm	Silver-plated brass	Obverse: JFK facing front; reverse: Pope John, Affer removed
K-63A-99Q	JFK-Pope John medal	32 mm	Silver-plated brass	Obverse: JFK facing front; reverse: Pope John, Affer removed

K-63A-100	Nebraska Numismatics "Martyrs to Freedom" medal	32 mm	Silver-plated brass	No loop; reverse: Statue of Liberty
K-63A-100A	Nebraska Numismatics "Martyrs to Freedom" medal	32 mm	Silver-plated brass	Looped; reverse: Statue of Liberty
K-63A-101	Peace Corps medal, Netherlands	70 mm	Bronze	Reverse: man on a horse
K-63A-101A	Peace Corps medal, Netherlands	40 mm	Bronze	Reverse: man on a horse
K-63A-101B	Peace Corps medal, Netherlands	40 mm	Silver	Reverse: man on a horse
K-63A-101C	Peace Corps medal, Netherlands	25 mm	Silver	Reverse: man on a horse
K-63A-101D	Peace Corps medal, Netherlands	25 mm	Gold	Reverse: man on a horse
K-63A-101E	Peace Corps medal, Netherlands	18½ mm	Gold	Reverse: man on a horse
K-63A-102	Huguenin Médailleurs JFK medal	60 mm	Bronze	Obverse: JFK facing right; reverse: 1917–1961–1963
K-63A-102A	Huguenin Médailleurs JFK medal	60 mm	.925 fine silver	Obverse: JFK facing right; reverse: 1917–1961–1963
K-63A-102B	Huguenin Médailleurs JFK medal	60 mm	.750 fine gold	Obverse: JFK facing right; reverse: 1917–1961–1963
K-63A-102C	Huguenin Médailleurs JFK medal plaque	60 mm	Bronze shell	Obverse: JFK facing right; reverse: mirror image of the obverse
K-63A-103	JFK memorial medal, Taiwan	26 mm	Sterling silver	Reverse: Profiles in Courage
K-63A-103A	JFK memorial medal, Taiwan	26 mm	Bronze	Reverse: Profiles in Courage
K-63A-103B	JFK memorial medal, Taiwan	26 mm	Aluminum	Reverse: Profiles in Courage
K-63A-104	JFK memorial pin, Taiwan	15 x 18 mm	Sterling silver	Pin has been soldered
K-63A-105	Presidential series JFK medal, type 1, Venezuela	30 mm	Silver	Reverse: Presidential Seal
K-63A-105A	Presidential series JFK medal, type 1, Venezuela	14 mm	.900 fine gold	Reverse: Presidential Seal
K-63A-105B	Presidential series JFK medal, type 1, Venezuela	21 mm	.900 fine gold	Reverse: Presidential Seal
K-63A-105C	Presidential series JFK medal, type 1, Venezuela	30 mm	.900 fine gold	Reverse: Presidential Seal
K-63A-106	JFK vending-machine token	22 mm	Gold-anodized aluminum	Looped; reverse: eagle
K-63A-106	JFK vending-machine token	22 mm	Gold-anodized aluminum	Minor die variety; reverse: eagle
K-63A-107	JFK vending-machine premium small photo insert	18 x 30 mm	Plastic with gold lettering	Reverse: three lines of legend
K-63A-108	World personalities series JFK medal	20 mm	Bronze	Reverse: "Peace and Freedom Don't Come"
K-63A-108A	World personalities series JFK medal	20 mm	Gold plated	Reverse: "Peace and Freedom Don't Come"
K-63A-108B	World personalities series JFK medal	20 mm	.999 fine silver	Reverse: "Peace and Freedom Don't Come"
K-63A-108C	World personalities series JFK medal, special order	20 mm	24K gold	Reverse: "Peace and Freedom Don't Come"
K-63A-109	Reichs-Gold-Munze JFK medal	22½ mm	Gold	Reverse: "In Memoriam"
K-63A-109A	Reichs-Gold-Munze JFK medal	33 mm	Gold	Reverse: "In Memoriam"
K-63A-110	"I am a Berliner" medal	32 mm	Gold-plated base metal	Looped; reverse: bear
K-63A-110A	"I am a Berliner" medal	24 mm	Gold-plated base metal	Looped; reverse: bear
K-63A-110B	"I am a Berliner" medal	20 mm	Gold-plated base metal	Looped; reverse: bear
K-63A-110C	"I am a Berliner" medal	17 mm	Gold-plated base metal	Looped; reverse: bear
K-63A-110D	"I am a Berliner" medal	12 mm	Gold-plated base metal	Looped; reverse: bear
K-63A-110E	"I am a Berliner" medal	32 mm	Silver-plated bronze	Looped; reverse: bear
K-63A-110F	"I am a Berliner" medal	32 mm	Silver-plated bronze	Reverse: Presidential Seal
K-63A-110G	"I am a Berliner" medal	32 mm	Bronze	Obverse: shell; reverse: impression
K-63A-111	JFK commemorative stamp medal, Germany	21 x 24 mm	.986 fine gold	Reverse: "Freedom" quote
K-63A-111A	JFK commemorative stamp medal, Germany	21 x 24 mm	Silver	Reverse: "Freedom" quote
K-63A-112	Corwill JFK charm	19 x 30 mm	Silver plated	Uniface; looped
K-63A-113	Pirrone JFK memorial medal	120 mm	Bronze	Uniface
K-63A-114	Mayer JFK memorial medal	40 mm	Bronze	Reverse: "Be Always the First"
K-63A-114A	Mayer JFK memorial medal	40 mm	Oxidized .835 fine silver	Reverse: "Be Always the First"
K-63A-114B	Mayer JFK memorial medal	40 mm	.333 fine gold	Reverse: "Be Always the First"
K-63A-114	Mayer JFK memorial medal	40 mm	.585 fine gold	Reverse: "Be Always the First"
K-63A-114D	Mayer JFK memorial medal	40 mm	.750 fine gold	Reverse: "Be Always the First"
K-63A-114E	Mayer JFK memorial medal	40 mm	.900 fine gold	Reverse: "Be Always the First"
K-63A-115	Kennedy half dollar chocolate coin, Israel	32 mm	Gold-colored foil	
K-63A-116	Ermanno Massa JFK memorial medal	104 mm	Bronze	Two known; uniface
K-63A-117	Japanese novelty JFK medallion	38 mm	Copper	Reverse: Statue of Liberty
K-63A-117A	Japanese novelty JFK medallion	38 mm	Brass	Reverse: Statue of Liberty
K-63A-117B	Japanese novelty JFK medallion	38 mm	Chrome plated	Reverse: Statue of Liberty
K-63A-118	Presidential series JFK medal, type 2, Venezuela	30 mm	.1000 fine silver	Reverse: Statue of Liberty
K-63A-118A	Presidential series JFK medal, type 2, Venezuela	14 mm	.900 fine gold	Reverse: Statue of Liberty
K-63A-118B	Presidential series JFK medal, type 2, Venezuela	21 mm	.900 fine gold	Reverse: Statue of Liberty
K-63A-118C	Presidential series JFK medal, type 2, Venezuela	30 mm	.900 fine gold	Reverse: Statue of Liberty
K-63A-119	JFK memorial medal, Yugoslavia	54 mm	Dark bronze, rough finish	Croatian metal casting; reverse: E. Markham verse, 1852
K-63A-119A	JFK memorial medal, Yugoslavia	54 mm	Light bronze patina, smooth finish	Croatian metal casting; reverse: E. Markham verse, 1852
K-63A-119B	JFK memorial medal, Yugoslavia	54 mm	Dark green patina, smooth finish	Croatian metal casting; reverse: E. Markham verse, 1852
K-63A-119C	JFK memorial medal, Yugoslavia	120 mm	Bronze	Croatian metal casting; reverse: E. Markham verse, 1852

K-63A-120	C. Affer JFK memorial medal	32 mm	Silver-plated brass	Obverse: JFK facing left; reverse: blank for engraving
K-63A-120A	C. Affer JFK memorial medal	32 mm	Gold-plated brass	Obverse: JFK facing left; reverse: blank for engraving
K-63A-120B	C. Affer JFK memorial medal	32 mm	Bronze	Obverse: JFK facing left; reverse: blank for engraving
K-63A-120C	C. Affer JFK memorial medal	32 mm	Sterling silver	Obverse: JFK facing left; reverse: blank for engraving
K-63A-120D	C. Affer JFK memorial medal	21 mm	Silver-plated brass	Obverse: JFK facing left; reverse: blank for engraving
K-63A-120E	C. Affer JFK memorial medal	21 mm	Gold-plated brass	Obverse: JFK facing left; reverse: blank for engraving
K-63A-120F	C. Affer JFK memorial medal	21 mm	Bronze	Obverse: JFK facing left; reverse: blank for engraving
K-63A-120G	C. Affer JFK memorial medal	21 mm	Sterling silver	Obverse: JFK facing left; reverse: blank for engraving
K-63A-121	Ed Rochette JFK mini-medal golf ball marker	12 mm	Silver-plated brass	500 struck; reverse: Denver, Colorado
K-63A-121A	Ed Rochette JFK micro charm	12 mm	Silver-plated brass	100 struck; Looped; reverse: Denver
K-63A-122	President and flag memorial medal, Italy	46 x 28 mm	Silver-plated brass	Reverse: wreath and legend
K-63A-122A	President and flag memorial medal, Italy	46 x 28 mm	Silver-plated brass	Reverse: wreath without legend
K-63A-123	"JFK United Nations Address" medal	50 mm	Bronze	Reverse: "Ask Not" credo
K-63A-123A	"JFK United Nations Address" medal	50 mm	Silver-plated brass	Reverse: "Ask Not" credo
K-63A-123B	"JFK United Nations Address" medal	50 mm	Sterling silver	Reverse: "Ask Not" credo
K-63A-123C	"JFK United Nations Address" medal	50 mm	Gold-plated brass	Reverse: "Ask Not" credo
K-63A-124	Classic shield key-chain ornament	32 x 42 mm	Silver-plated brass	Looped; reverse: plain
K-63A-124A	Classic shield key-chain ornament	32 x 42 mm	Bronze	Looped; reverse: plain
K-63A-124B	Classic shield key-chain ornament	32 x 42 mm	Gold-plated brass	Looped; reverse: plain
K-63A-125	Classic eagle key-chain ornament	32 x 38 mm	Silver-plated brass	Looped; reverse: plain
K-63A-125A	Classic eagle key-chain ornament	32 x 38 mm	Bronze	Looped; reverse: plain
K-63A-125B	Classic eagle key-chain ornament	32 x 38 mm	Gold-plated brass	Looped; reverse: plain
K-63A-125C	Classic eagle key-chain pin	32 x 38 mm	Silver plated	No loop; reverse: plain
K-63A-125D	Classic eagle key-chain pin	32 x 38 mm	Bronze	No loop; reverse: plain
K-63A-125E	Classic eagle key-chain pin	32 x 38 mm	Gold plated	No loop; reverse: plain
K-63A-126	Kennedy Space Center medal	32 mm	Silver-plated brass	Reverse: "Moon Speech" quote
K-63A-127	Medallic portraits bookmark	22 x 34 mm	Plastic	12 issued
K-63A-128	"Catholic Leaders of the Century" medal	32 mm	Gold-anodized aluminum	Reverse: Pope Paul
K-63A-129	JFK candy premium token, Philippines	23 mm	Base metal, gold finish	Reverse: Mrs. Jacqueline Kennedy
K-63A-130	JFK key-ring ornament, France	36 mm	Base metal	Looped; reverse: "Ask Not" credo
K-63A-131	Creations Fauvre JFK key ring, type 1, France	35 mm	Antique silver	Looped; "35th President"
K-63A-132	Creations Fauvre JFK key ring, type 2, France	35 mm	Silver	Poor lettering; looped; reverse: SAA
K-63A-133	World personalities series medal, second edition	20 mm	Bronze	Reverse: "Peace and Freedom"
K-63A-133A	World personalities series medal, second edition	20 mm	Gold plated	Reverse: "Peace and Freedom"
K-63A-133B	World personalities series medal, second edition	20 mm	.999 fine silver	Reverse: "Peace and Freedom"
K-63A-133C	World personalities series medal, second edition	20 mm	24K gold	Special order; reverse: "Peace and Freedom"
K-63A-133D	World personalities series medal, second edition	20 mm	Lead trial-piece sheets	Ten struck; reverse: "Peace and Freedom"
K-63A-134	"I am a Berliner" medal	36 mm	Gold	Reverse: "Ich Bin Ein Berliner" on a scroll
K-63A-134A	"I am a Berliner" medal	26 mm	.900 fine gold	Reverse: "Ich Bin Ein Berliner" on a scroll
K-63A-134B	"I am a Berliner" medal	20 mm	.986 fine gold	Reverse: "Ich Bin Ein Berliner" on a scroll
K-63A-135	Bradshaw & Darlington JFK medal	51 mm	Sterling silver	2,000 struck; serial number; reverse: JFK in a chair
K-63A-135A	Bradshaw & Darlington JFK medal	38 mm	Sterling silver	3,500 struck; reverse: JFK in a chair
K-63A-135B	Bradshaw & Darlington JFK medal	45 mm	Gold-plated sterling silver	3,500 struck; reverse: JFK in a chair
K-63A-135C	Bradshaw & Darlington JFK medal	38 mm	Gold-plated sterling silver	200 struck; reverse: JFK in a chair
K-63A-136	Preissler JFK medal	20 mm	Silver	Uniface; looped
K-63A-137	Solidus Mint–series JFK medal	34 mm	Silver	Reverse: Statue of Liberty
K-63A-137A	Solidus Mint–series JFK medal	50 mm	Silver	2,000 struck; serial number; reverse: Statue of Liberty
K-63A-138	"Kennedy Memorial at Arlington" medal	50 mm	Sterling silver	Reverse: Kennedy grave
K-63A-138A	"Kennedy Memorial at Arlington" medal	32 mm	Sterling silver	Reverse: Kennedy grave
K-63A-138B	"Kennedy Memorial at Arlington" medal	50 mm	.900 fine gold	600 struck; serial number; reverse: Kennedy grave
K-63A-138C	"Kennedy Memorial at Arlington" medal	32 mm	.900 fine gold	3,000 struck; serial number; reverse: Kennedy grave
K-63A-138D	"Kennedy Memorial at Arlington" medal	25 mm	.900 fine gold	Reverse: Kennedy grave
K-63A-138E	"Kennedy Memorial at Arlington" medal	20 mm	.900 fine gold	20,000 struck; reverse: Kennedy grave
K-62A-138F	"Kennedy Memorial at Arlington" medal	20 mm	.900 fine gold	Thin planchet; reverse: Kennedy grave
K-63A-139	Paris Mint JFK memorial series medal	34 mm	Silver	Reverse: eagle, United States of America
K-63A-139A	Paris Mint JFK memorial series medal	50 mm	Silver	Reverse: eagle, United States of America

K-63A-139B	Paris Mint JFK memorial series medal	34 mm	Gold	Reverse: eagle, United States of America
K-63A-139C	Paris Mint JFK memorial series medal	26 mm	Gold	Reverse: eagle, United States of America
K-63A-139D	Paris Mint JFK memorial series medal	21 mm	Gold	Reverse: eagle, United States of America
K-63A-139E	Paris Mint JFK memorial series medal	15½ mm	Gold	Reverse: eagle, United States of America
K-63A-140	Rheingold-series JFK medal	30 mm	.900 fine gold	Reverse: six-bar cross
K-63A-140A	Rheingold-series JFK medal	26 mm	.900 fine gold	Reverse: six-bar cross
K-63A-140B	Rheingold-series JFK medal	22½ mm	.900 fine gold	Reverse: six-bar cross
K-63A-140C	Rheingold-series JFK medal	20 mm	.900 fine gold	Reverse: six-bar cross
K-63A-140D	Rheingold-series JFK medal	15½ mm	.900 fine gold	Reverse: six-bar cross
K-63A-140E	Rheingold-series JFK medal	13 mm	.900 fine gold	Reverse: six-bar cross
K-63A-140F	Rheingold-series JFK medal	22½ mm	.585 fine gold	Reverse: six-bar cross
K-63A-140G	Rheingold-series JFK medal	20 mm	.585 fine gold	Reverse: six-bar cross
K-63A-140H	Rheingold-series JFK medal	15½ mm	.585 fine gold	Reverse: six-bar cross
K-63A-140I	Rheingold-series JFK medal	13 mm	.585 fine gold	Reverse: six-bar cross
K-63A-140J	Rheingold-series JFK medal	30 mm	.333 fine gold	Reverse: six-bar cross
K-63A-140K	Rheingold-series JFK medal	26 mm	.333 fine gold	Reverse: six-bar cross
K-63A-140L	Rheingold-series JFK medal	22½ mm	.333 fine gold	Reverse: six-bar cross
K-63A-140M	Rheingold-series JFK medal	20 mm	.333 fine gold	Reverse: six-bar cross
K-63A-140N	Rheingold-series JFK medal	15½ mm	.333 fine gold	Reverse: six-bar cross
K-63A-140O	Rheingold-series JFK medal	13 mm	.333 fine gold	Reverse: six-bar cross
K-63A-140P	Rheingold-series JFK medal	10 mm	.333 fine gold	Reverse: six-bar cross
K-63A-141	Franklin Mint JFK medal, England	57 mm	Gold	500 struck, reverse: eagle on a flag
K-63A-141A	Franklin Mint JFK medal, England	38 mm	Gold	1,000 struck, reverse: eagle on a flag
K-63A-141B	Franklin Mint JFK medal, England	22 mm	Gold	3,000 struck, reverse: eagle on a flag
K-63A-141C	Franklin Mint JFK medal, England	57 mm	Britannia silver	5,000 struck, reverse: eagle on a flag
K-63A-141D	Franklin Mint JFK medal, England	38 mm	Britannia silver	5,000 struck, reverse: eagle on a flag
K-63A-141E	Franklin Mint JFK medal, England	57 mm	Platinum	Ten struck, reverse: eagle on a flag
K-63A-141F	Franklin Mint JFK medal, England	38 mm	Platinum	Ten struck, reverse: eagle on a flag
K-63A-141G	Franklin Mint JFK medal, England, sales sample	38 mm	Gold plated, Proof	Serial number; reverse: eagle on a flag
K-63A-142	Argor Swiss JFK memorial medal	33 mm	.900/.1000 fine silver	Reverse: eagle, flag, and wheat
K-63A-142A	Argor Swiss JFK memorial medal, revised die variety	33 mm	.900/.1000 fine silver	Sharper image; reverse: eagle, flag, and wheat
K-63A-142B	Argor Swiss JFK memorial medal	33 mm	.900 fine gold, 15 g.	Revised die, sharper image; reverse: eagle, flag, and wheat
K-63A-142C	Argor Swiss JFK memorial medal	33 mm	.900 fine gold, 30 g.	Revised die, sharper image; thick planchet; reverse: eagle, flag, and wheat
K-63A-143	"10th Anniversary of JFK's Death" medal, Switzerland	33 mm	.999 fine silver	3,000 struck; reverse: Presidential Seal
K-63A-143A	"10th Anniversary of JFK's Death" medal, Switzerland	55 mm	.999 fine silver	1,000 struck; reverse: Presidential Seal
K-63A-143B	"10th Anniversary of JFK's Death" medal, Switzerland	33 mm	.999 fine gold	300 struck; reverse: Presidential Seal
K-63A-143C	"10th Anniversary of JFK's Death" medal, Switzerland	55 mm	.999 fine gold	50 struck; reverse: Presidential Seal
K-63A-144	Intercoins JFK medal	43 mm	.925 fine silver	Reverse: Presidential Seal
K-63A-144A	Intercoins JFK medal	10 mm	Gold, 1 g.	Reverse: Presidential Seal
K-63A-144B	Intercoins JFK medal	18 mm	Gold, 3 g.	Reverse: Presidential Seal
K-63A-144C	Intercoins JFK medal	22 mm	Gold, 6 g.	Reverse: Presidential Seal
K-63A-144D	Intercoins JFK medal	26 mm	Gold, 9 g.	Reverse: Presidential Seal
K-63A-144E	Intercoins JFK medal	32 mm	Gold, 15 g.	Reverse: Presidential Seal
K-63A-144F	Intercoins JFK medal	43 mm	Gold, 30 g.	Reverse: Presidential Seal
K-63A-145	Sudbury Kennedy half dollar coin memorial	38 mm	Goldine	Replica Kennedy half dollar with ring
K-63A-145A	Sudbury Kennedy half dollar coin memorial	38 mm	Nickel silver	Replica Kennedy half dollar with ring
K-63A-146	Delaware Turnpike JFK Memorial Hwy. token	27 mm	Steel	Hole in the center
K-63A-146A	Delaware Turnpike JFK Memorial Hwy. token	27 mm	Steel	Black center
K-63A-146B	Delaware Turnpike JFK Memorial Hwy. token	27 mm	Steel	Red center
K-63A-146C	Delaware Turnpike JFK Memorial Hwy. token	27 mm	Steel	Blue center
K-63A-147	Maryland Transportation Authority JFK Hwy. token	28 mm	Steel	Obverse: official duty
K-63A-148	JFK-Pope John XXIII key chain medal	32 mm	Silver-plated brass	Spelling error; looped; reverse: Pope John
K-63A-148A	JFK-Pope John XXIII key chain medal	32 mm	Brass	Spelling error; looped; reverse: Pope John
K-63A-149	JFK-Pope John XXIII key chain medal	32 mm	Silver-plated brass	Looped; reverse: Pope John
K-63A-150	Vincenzo Liverno JFK coral cameo	45 mm	Coral shell, white and black	Uniface
K-63A-151	Spencer JFK head charm	14 x 20 mm	Sterling silver	Looped; obverse: JFK facing left; reverse: "Ask Not" credo
K-63A-151A	Spencer JFK head charm	14 x 20 mm	Gold-plated sterling silver	Looped; obverse: JFK facing left; reverse: "Ask Not" credo
K-63A-152	American Charm Corporation JFK head charm	25 mm	Sterling silver	Looped; reverse: "Ask Not" credo
K-63A-152A	American Charm Corporation JFK head charm	25 mm	14K gold	Thin planchet; looped; reverse: "Ask Not" credo
K-63A-152B	American Charm Corporation JFK head charm	25 mm	14K gold	Heavy weight; looped; reverse: "Ask Not" credo

K-63A-153	Coronet Jewelry JFK charm	26 mm	14K gold	Reverse: Plain with 14K at the loop
K-63A-153A	Coronet Jewelry JFK charm	32 mm	14K gold	Head is the same size; reverse: plain with 14K at the loop
K-63A-154	Zolnier Jewelry JFK memorial charm	24 mm	Sterling silver	Looped; reverse: "Ask Not" credo
K-63A-154A	Zolnier Jewelry JFK memorial charm	24 mm	14K gold	Looped; reverse: "Ask Not" credo
K-63A-154B	Zolnier Jewelry JFK memorial charm	24 mm	Sterling silver	No loop; reverse: "Ask Not" credo
K-63A-154C	Zolnier Jewelry JFK memorial charm	24 mm	14K gold	No loop; reverse: "Ask Not" credo
K-63A-155	Paramount Watch "Birth and Death Dates" jewelry link	12 x 16 mm	Goldine	Holed top and bottom
K-63A-155A	Paramount Watch "Birth and Death Dates" jewelry link	12 x 16 mm	Goldine	Reverse: JFK
K-63A-156	R.L. Griffith JFK charm	24 mm	Sterling silver	Looped
K-63A-156A	R.L. Griffith JFK charm	24 mm	12K filled gold	Looped
K-63A-157	Gold Mine JFK charm	19 mm	Sterling silver	Looped; reverse: "Ask Not" credo
K-63A-157A	Gold Mine JFK charm	25 mm	Sterling silver	Looped; reverse: "Ask Not" credo
K-63A-157B	Gold Mine JFK charm	19 mm	14K gold	Looped; reverse: "Ask Not" credo
K-63A-157C	Gold Mine JFK charm	25 mm	14K gold	Looped; reverse: "Ask Not" credo
K-63A-158	Fort Jewelry JFK shield emblem	13 x 15 mm	Polished bronze	Uniface
K-63A-159	Vanguard JFK memorial medal	38 mm	Antique bronze	Reverse: Oswald and Ruby
K-63A-159A	Vanguard JFK memorial medal	38 mm	.999 fine silver	1,000 struck; serial number; reverse: Oswald and Ruby
K-63A-159B	Vanguard JFK memorial medal	38 mm	14K gold	Illegal at the time of release; 25 struck; serial number; reverse: Oswald and Ruby
K-63A-160	Artcraft JFK Manship bust campaign piece	23 mm	Bronze	Reverse: John F. Kennedy
K-63A-160A	Artcraft JFK Manship bust campaign piece	23 mm	Antique bronze	Reverse: John F. Kennedy
K-63A-160B	Artcraft JFK Manship bust campaign piece	23 mm	Copper finish	Reverse: John F. Kennedy
K-63A-160C	Artcraft JFK Manship bust campaign piece	23 mm	Silver	Reverse: John F. Kennedy
K-63A-161	Artcraft JFK Manship bust campaign piece	23 mm	Bronze	Looped; reverse: John F. Kennedy
K-63A-161A	Artcraft JFK Manship bust campaign piece	23 mm	Antique bronze	Looped; reverse: John F. Kennedy
K-63A-161B	Artcraft JFK Manship bust campaign piece	23 mm	Copper finish	Looped; reverse: John F. Kennedy
K-63A-161C	Artcraft JFK Manship bust campaign piece	23 mm	Silver	Looped; reverse: John F. Kennedy
K-63A-162	Artcraft JFK Manship bust "Birth and Death Date" campaign piece	23 mm	Bronze	Looped; reverse: John F. Kennedy
K-63A-162A	Artcraft JFK Manship bust "Birth and Death Date" campaign piece	23 mm	Antique bronze	Looped; reverse: John F. Kennedy
K-63A-162B	Artcraft JFK Manship bust "Birth and Death Date" campaign piece	23 mm	Copper finish	Looped; reverse: John F. Kennedy
K-63A-162C	Artcraft JFK Manship bust "Birth and Death Date" memorial medal	23 mm	Silver	Looped; reverse: John F. Kennedy
K-63A-162D	Artcraft JFK Manship bust "Birth and Death Date" memorial medal	23 mm	Bronze	Reverse: John F. Kennedy
K-63A-162E	Artcraft JFK Manship bust "Birth and Death Date" memorial medal	23 mm	Silver	Reverse: John F. Kennedy
K-63A-163	Artcraft JFK Manship bust memorial medal	23 mm	Bronze	Looped; reverse: Arlington eternal flame
K-63A-163A	Artcraft JFK Manship bust memorial medal	23 mm	Antique bronze	Looped; reverse: Arlington eternal flame
K-63A-163B	Artcraft JFK Manship bust memorial medal	23 mm	Copper	Looped; reverse: Arlington eternal flame
K-63A-163C	Artcraft JFK Manship bust memorial medal	23 mm	Silver	Looped; reverse: Arlington eternal flame
K-63A-164	Artcraft JFK heraldic eagle paperweight		Bronze on base metal	Uniface
K-63A-164A	Artcraft JFK heraldic eagle paperweight		Silver-plated base metal	Uniface
K-63A-165	Krause premium key-chain link	11½ x 32 mm	Steel	Looped at both ends
K-63A-165A	Krause premium key-chain link	11½ x 32 mm	Steel	Copy change; looped at both ends
K-63A-165B	Krause premium key-chain link	11½ x 32 mm	Steel	Oval shaped; looped at both ends
K-63A-166	Jewish National Fund John F. Kennedy Peace Award medal	76 mm	Bronze	26 struck
K-63A-166A	Jewish National Fund John F. Kennedy Peace Award medal	76 mm	Sterling silver	Six struck
K-63A-166B	Jewish National Fund John F. Kennedy Peace Award medal	76 mm	14K gold	11 struck
K-63A-167	Eternal flame key-chain ornament	33 mm	Base metal, cast	Reverse: flame and capitol
K-63A-167A	Eternal flame key-chain ornament	33 mm	Bronze-plated, cast	Reverse: flame and capitol
K-63A-168	International Coin medal	39 mm	.999 fine silver	Reverse: Presidential Seal
K-63A-168A	International Coin medal	39 mm	Pewter	Reverse: Presidential Seal
K-63A-168B	International Coin medal	39 mm	Silver-plated	Reverse: Presidential Seal
K-63A-168C	International Coin medal	39 mm	Bronze, golden finish	Reverse: Presidential Seal
K-63A-168D	International Coin medal	39 mm	Bronze, antique finish	Reverse: Presidential Seal
K-63A-168E	International Coin medal	39 mm	Aluminum	Reverse: Presidential Seal
K-63A-169	JFK-Lincoln error medal	39 mm	.999 fine silver	Reverse: Lincoln
K-63A-169A	JFK-Lincoln error medal	39 mm	Pewter	Reverse: Lincoln
K-63A-169B	JFK-Lincoln error medal	39 mm	Silver-plated	Reverse: Lincoln
K-63A-169C	JFK-Lincoln error medal	39 mm	Bronze, golden finish	Reverse: Lincoln
K-63A-169D	JFK-Lincoln error medal	39 mm	Bronze, antique finish	Reverse: Lincoln
K-63A-169E	JFK-Lincoln error medal	39 mm	Aluminum	Reverse: Lincoln
K-63A-169F	JFK-Lincoln error medal	39 mm	Silver Proof pideforts	Double thickness; reverse: Lincoln
K-63A-170	JFK cent	20 mm	Copper	Reverse: Presidential Seal
K-63A-170A	JFK cent	20 mm	Golden bronze	Reverse: Presidential Seal
K-63A-170B	JFK cent	20 mm	Antique bronze	Reverse: Presidential Seal

K-63A-170C	JFK cent	20 mm	Pewter	Reverse: Presidential Seal
K-63A-170D	JFK cent	20 mm	.999 fine silver	Reverse: Presidential Seal
K-63A-170E	JFK cent trial die strike bar	78 x 26 mm	Bronze	Uniface
K-63A-171	International JFK pocket piece	32 mm	Golden bronze	Reverse: Presidential Seal
K-63A-171A	International JFK pocket piece	32 mm	Golden bronze	Looped; reverse: Presidential Seal
K-63A-172	Elongated JFK charm	11 x 24 mm	Bronze	Uniface
K-63A-173	Folz Vending JFK token	30 mm	Base metal and plastic	Uniface
K-63A-173A	Folz Vending JFK head charm	2 x 14 mm	Base metal, gold finish	Round head
K-63A-174	Denlinger JFK memorial medal, type 1	38 mm	Aluminum	Reverse: "In Memory of"
K-63A-174A	Denlinger JFK memorial medal, type 2	38 mm	Bronze	Obverse die change; reverse: "In Memory of"
K-63A-175	"35th President U.S. Capitol" medal	30½ mm	Nickel	Reverse: credo and Capitol
K-63A-175A	"35th President U.S. Capitol" medal	30½ mm	Brass	Reverse: credo and Capitol
K-63A-176	"JFK Visit to Redding, CA" good-luck token	34 mm	Silver-colored aluminum	Reverse: Horseshoe
K-63A-177	"JFK Visit to Whiskeytown" good-luck token	34 mm	Gold-colored aluminum	Reverse: Horseshoe
K-63A-178	"John Kennedy 1961-1963 35th President" tribute medal	38½ mm	Brass	Reverse: eagle with stars
K-63A-179	Franklin Mint presidential series medal, first edition	39 mm	Sterling silver	Reverse: eagle
K-63A-179A	Franklin Mint presidential series medal, first edition	32 mm	Sterling silver, Proof	Reverse: eagle
K-63A-180	Franklin Mint "Presidential Hall of Fame" medal	26 mm	.925 fine sterling silver	Reverse: biography of JFK
K-63A-180A	Franklin Mint "Presidential Hall of Fame" medal	26 mm	Platinum .999 fine	32 struck; reverse: biography of JFK
K-63A-180B	Franklin Mint "Presidential Hall of Fame" Shell Oil premium	26 mm	Bronze	1,377,324 struck; reverse: biography JFK
K-63A-180C	Franklin Mint "Presidential Hall of Fame" collector medal	32 mm	Golden bronze	Reeded edge; reverse: biography JFK
K-63A-181	Franklin Mint mini-medal series JFK medal	10 mm	.925 fine sterling silver	88,750 struck; reverse: eagle
K-63A-181A	Franklin Mint mini-medal series JFK medal	10 mm	.999 fine platinum	540 struck; reverse: eagle
K-63A-182	Eagle Mold presidential heritage series plastic token	43 mm	Silver-colored styrene	Reverse: dates
K-63A-182A	Eagle Mold presidential heritage series plastic token	43 mm	Bronze-colored styrene	Reverse: dates
K-63A-183	JFK jewelry insert	34½ mm	Gold-tone finish	Uniface
K-63A-184	Hannan Brown presidential series JFK vertical elongated U.S. cent	19 x 33 mm	Bronze	JB by name
K-63A-185	O'Hara JFK vertical elongated U.S. cent	20 x 38 mm	Bronze	Obverse: JFK facing left; reverse: four lines of type
K-63A-185A	O'Hara JFK vertical elongated U.S. dime	18 x 36 mm	.900 fine silver	Obverse: JFK facing left
K-63A-186	Ralph Jones "First Catholic President" horizontal elongated U.S. cent	40 x 20 mm	Bronze	
K-63A-187	Angelo Rosato JFK famous quote vertical elongated U.S. cent	19 x 33 mm	Bronze	348 rolled
K-63A-187A	Angelo Rosato JFK famous quote vertical elongated pre-1964 U.S. dime	18 x 32 mm	.900 fine silver	
K-63A-188	Angelo Rosato elongated Kennedy half dollar	35 x 43 mm	Cupronickel-clad	27 rolled sets
K-63A-188A	Angelo Rosato elongated Kennedy half dollar	35 x 43 mm	Aluminum planchet	Five rolled sets
K-63A-188B	Angelo Rosato "JFK Senate" elongated coin, type 2	35 x 43 mm	Cupronickel-clad	27 rolled sets
K-63A-188C	Angelo Rosato "JFK Senate" elongated coin, type 2	35 x 43 mm	Aluminum planchet	Five rolled sets
K-63A-188D	Angelo Rosato "JFK Inaugural Address" elongated coin	35 x 43 mm	Cupronickel-clad	27 rolled sets
K-63A-188E	Angelo Rosato "JFK Inaugural Address" elongated coin	35 x 43 mm	Aluminum planchet	Five rolled sets
K-63A-188F	Angelo Rosato "JFK Message to Congress" elongated coin	35 x 43 mm	Cupronickel-clad	27 rolled sets
K-63A-188G	Angelo Rosato "JFK Message to Congress" elongated coin	35 x 43 mm	Aluminum planchet	Five rolled sets
K-63A-188H	Angelo Rosato "JFK Message to Congress" elongated coin, type 2	35 x 43 mm	Cupronickel-clad	27 rolled sets
K-63A-188I	Angelo Rosato "JFK Message to Congress" elongated coin, type 2	35 x 43 mm	Aluminum planchet	Five rolled sets
K-63A-188J	Angelo Rosato "JFK Peace Corps" elongated coin	35 x 43 mm	Cupronickel-clad	27 rolled sets
K-63A-188K	Angelo Rosato "JFK Peace Corps" elongated coin	35 x 43 mm	Aluminum planchet	Five rolled sets
K-63A-188L	Angelo Rosato "JFK Message to Congress" elongated coin, type 3	35 x 26 mm	Cupronickel-clad	27 rolled sets
K-63A-188M	Angelo Rosato "JFK Message to Congress" elongated coin, type 3	35 x 43 mm	Aluminum planchet	Five rolled sets
K-63A-188N	Angelo Rosato "JFK United Nations Address" elongated coin	35 x 43 mm	Cupronickel-clad	27 rolled sets
K-63A-188O	Angelo Rosato "JFK United Nations Address" elongated coin	35 x 24 mm	Aluminum planchet	Five rolled sets
K-63A-188P	Angelo Rosato "JFK State of the Union" elongated coin	35 x 43 mm	Cupronickel-clad	27 rolled sets
K-63A-188Q	Angelo Rosato "JFK State of the Union" elongated coin	35 x 43 mm	Aluminum planchet	Five rolled sets
K-63A-188R	Angelo Rosato "JFK State of the Union" elongated coin, type 2	35 x 43 mm	Cupronickel-clad	27 rolled sets
K-63A-188S	Angelo Rosato "JFK State of the Union" elongated coin, type 2	35 x 43 mm	Aluminum planchet	Five rolled sets
K-63A-188T	Angelo Rosato "JFK Privilege of American" elongated coin	35 x 43 mm	Cupronickel-clad	27 rolled sets
K-63A-188U	Angelo Rosato "JFK Privilege of American" elongated coin	35 x 43 mm	Aluminum planchet	Five rolled sets
K-63A-188V	Angelo Rosato "JFK Miss the Future" elongated coin	35 x 43 mm	Cupronickel-clad	27 rolled sets
K-63A-188W	Angelo Rosato "JFK Miss the Future" elongated coin	35 x 43 mm	Aluminum planchet	Five rolled sets
K-63A-188X	Angelo Rosato "JFK Desire for Liberty" elongated coin	35 x 43 mm	Cupronickel-clad	27 rolled sets
K-63A-188Y	Angelo Rosato "JFK Desire for Liberty" elongated coin	35 x 43 mm	Aluminum planchet	Five rolled sets
K-63A-188 Z	Angelo Rosato "JFK Freedom is Indivisible" elongated coin	35 x 43 mm	Cupronickel-clad	27 rolled sets
K-63A-188AA	Angelo Rosato "JFK Freedom is Indivisible" elongated coin	35 x 43 mm	Aluminum planchet	Five rolled sets
K-63A-188AB	Angelo Rosato "JFK Italian People Address" elongated coin	35 x 43 mm	Cupronickel-clad	27 rolled sets
K-63A-188AC	Angelo Rosato "JFK Italian People Address" elongated coin	35 x 43 mm	Aluminum planchet	Five rolled sets
K-63A-188AD	Angelo Rosato "JFK Community Without Law" elongated coin	35 x 43 mm	Cupronickel-clad	27 rolled sets
K-63A-188AE	Angelo Rosato "JFK Community Without Law" elongated coin	35 x 43 mm	Aluminum planchet	Five rolled sets
K-63A-188AF	Angelo Rosato "JFK Avenue for Peace" elongated coin	35 x 43 mm	Cupronickel-clad	27 rolled sets
K-63A-188AG	Angelo Rosato "JFK Avenue for Peace" elongated coin	35 x 43 mm	Aluminum planchet	Five rolled sets
K-63A-188AH	Angelo Rosato "JFK Peace Does Not Rest" elongated coin	35 x 43 mm	Cupronickel-clad	27 rolled sets

K-63A-188AI	Angelo Rosato "JFK Peace Does Not Rest" elongated coin	35 x 43 mm	Aluminum planchet	Five rolled sets
K-63A-188AJ	Angelo Rosato "JFK No Faith in Tomorrow" elongated coin	35 x 43 mm	Cupronickel-clad	27 rolled sets
K-63A-188AK	Angelo Rosato "JFK No Faith in Tomorrow" elongated coin	35 x 43 mm	Aluminum planchet	Five rolled sets
K-63A-188AL	Angelo Rosato "JFK Mourning Ceases" elongated coin	35 x 43 mm	Cupronickel-clad	27 rolled sets
K-63A-188AM	Angelo Rosato "JFK Mourning Ceases" elongated coin	35 x 43 mm	Aluminum planchet	Five rolled sets
K-63A-189	Angelo Rosato JFK memorial elongated U.S. cent #128			
K-63A-190	Don Sabo JFK elongated U.S. cent	20 x 42 mm	Bronze	62 rolled
K-63A-190A	Don Sabo JFK elongated U.S. dime		Standard coin composition	5 rolled, die destroyed
K-63A-190B	Don Sabo JFK elongated U.S. cent	20 x 42 mm	Bronze	Cancelled die
K-63A-190C	Don Sabo JFK elongated U.S. cent	20 x 42 mm	Bronze	Die trial, no initials
K-63A-190D	Don Sabo JFK elongated coin, lead strip die trial	48 x 24 mm	Bronze	Four rolled, die trial
K-63A-190E	Don Sabo JFK elongated Kennedy half dollar		Standard coin composition	Six rolled
K-63A-191	Don Sabo JFK elongated Apollo VIII medallion	27 x 53 mm	Aluminum	Obverse: JFK facing right; reverse: "Ye Be Lucky Forever"
K-63A-192	Don Sabo JFK elongated Franklin half dollar	31½ x 67 mm	.900 fine silver	Rolled; obverse: JFK facing right
K-63A-192A	Don Sabo JFK elongated medallion	39 x 52 mm	Bronze	Obverse: JFK facing right
K-63A-193	Ralph Jobe PT-109 elongated U.S. cent	40 x 20 mm	Bronze	Rolled Lincoln bust
K-63A-193A	Ralph Jobe PT-109 elongated 1943 U.S. cent	40 x 20 mm	Zinc	Rolled Lincoln bust
K-63A-193B	Ralph Jobe PT-109 elongated U.S. nickel	38 x 22 mm	Standard coin composition	Rolled Jefferson nickel
K-63A-193C	Ralph Jobe PT-109 elongated U.S. dime	40 x 18 mm	Standard coin composition	Rolled Roosevelt dime
K-63A-193D	Ralph Jobe PT-109 elongated U.S. quarter	38 x 26 mm	Standard coin composition	Rolled Washington quarter
K-63A-193E	Ralph Jobe PT-109 elongated Kennedy half dollar	41 x 31 mm	Standard coin composition	Rolled Kennedy half dollar
K-63A-193F	Ralph Jobe PT-109 elongated Philippine centavo	38 x 25 mm	Philippine centavo	Rolled coat of arms
K-63A-193G	Ralph Jobe PT-109 elongated U.S. cent		Standard coin composition	Rolled Lincoln cent; die trial; reverse: one line
K-63A-194	Elmer Anderson "JFK Final Salute" vertical elongated U.S. cent	20 x 39 mm	Bronze	Rolled Lincoln cent
K-63A-195	JFK Hospital parking-lot token	25 mm	Brass	Reverse: plain
K-63A-196	Wagaman JFK elongated U.S. nickel	38 x 22 mm	Standard coin composition	135 rolled
K-63A-196A	Wagaman JFK elongated U.S. cent		Bronze	13 rolled
K-63A-196B	Wagaman JFK elongated coin, progression Proof	44 x 27 mm	Aluminum	13 rolled
K-63A-196C	Wagaman JFK elongated Franklin Mint token, progression Proof	44 x 27 mm	Aluminum	13 rolled; die change
K-63A-196D	Wagaman JFK elongated coin	38 x 22 mm	Aluminum	13 rolled; die cancelled; defaced die example
K-63A-197	Jack Meccariello JFK elongated U.S. cent	45 x 20 mm	Bronze	36 rolled
K-63A-197A	Jack Meccariello JFK elongated U.S. cent	43 x 20 mm	Bronze	100 rolled
K-63A-197B	Jack Meccariello JFK elongated Kennedy half dollar	45 x 32 mm	Cupronickel-clad	20 rolled
K-63A-198	MPG JFK memorial medal, counterstamped	36 mm	Base metal	Reverse: White House, dates added
K-63A-199	John F. Kennedy Museum, Dallas, TX, medal	41 mm	Antique bronze, black insert	Reverse: "Ask Not" credo
K-63A-199A	John F. Kennedy Museum, Dallas, TX, medal	41 mm	Antique bronze, blue insert	Reverse: "Ask Not" credo
K-63A-200	Jayposon JFK charm	25 mm	Sterling silver	Looped
K-63A-200A	Jayposon JFK charm	25 mm	1/2K gold	Looped
K-63A-200B	Jayposon JFK charm	31 mm	Sterling silver	Looped
K-63A-200C	Jayposon JFK charm	31 mm	1/2K gold	Looped
K-63A-200D	Jayposon JFK charm	20 mm	Sterling silver	Looped
K-63A-201	Huguenin Médailleurs JFK medal	40 mm	Silver	First edition reverse; uniface; obverse: JFK facing right
K-63A-202	Huguenin Médailleurs JFK medal	60 mm	Bronze	Second edition; uniface; obverse: JFK facing left
K-63A-202A	Huguenin Médailleurs JFK medal	40 mm	Bronze	Second edition; uniface; obverse: JFK facing left
K-63A-203	Huguenin Médailleurs JFK medal	60 mm	Bronze	Second edition reverse; uniface; obverse: dates added, JFK facing left
K-63A-203A	Huguenin Médailleurs JFK medal	60 mm	.925 fine silver	Second edition reverse; obverse: JFK facing left
K-63A-203B	Huguenin Médailleurs JFK medal	60 mm	18K .750 fine gold	Second edition reverse; obverse: JFK facing left
K-63A-203C	Huguenin Médailleurs JFK medal	40 mm	.925 fine gold	Second edition reverse; uniface; obverse: JFK facing left
K-63A-203D	Huguenin Médailleurs JFK medal	30 mm	.925 fine silver	Second edition reverse; uniface; obverse: JFK facing left

K-63A-203E	Huguenin Médailleurs JFK medal	22 mm	.925 fine silver	Second edition reverse; uniface; obverse: JFK facing left
K-63A-203F	Huguenin Médailleurs JFK medal	44 mm	.925 fine silver with gold rim	Second edition reverse; uniface; no loop; obverse: JFK facing left
K-63A-203G	Huguenin Médailleurs JFK medal	50 mm	.925 fine silver	Heavy; uniface
K-63A-204	Huguenin Médailleurs "President Kennedy and First Lady" medal	60 mm	Bronze	Uniface; no loop
K-63A-204A	Huguenin Médailleurs "President Kennedy and First Lady" medal	40 mm	Bronze	Uniface; no loop
K-63A-205	Paul Kramer march medal with wreath	42 x 50 mm	.925 fine silver	Holed; reverse: stippled
K-63A-206	L. Morini Manship inaugural medal, copy	30 mm	Bronze	No loop
K-63A-207	"Ask Not" JFK key chain	32 mm	Goldine brass	Holed; reverse: "Ask Not" credo
K-63A-208	Kennedy half dollar look-alike	33 mm	Brass, silver finish	Holed; reverse: "Ask Not" credo
K-63A-209	JFK bronze bust	65 x 47 mm	Bronze, bright Cast	Uniface; JFK facing right
K-63A-210	Steve Adams JFK hobo 1937 nickel	U.S. 5 cent	Standard coin composition	Reverse: buffalo
K-63A-211	RFK hobo 1937 nickel	U.S. 5 cent	Standard coin composition	Artist unknown; reverse: buffalo
K-63A-212	Ancient Order of Hibernians JFK medal, trial strike	51 mm	Gold-plated bronze	Unique; uniface
K-63A-213	JFK-Pope key chain, France		Bronze	
K-63A-214	JFK plaque medal, type 1	53 mm	Brass	Uniface
K-63A-215	JFK plaque medal, type 2	101³/₅ mm	Brass	Uniface
K-63A-216	Gerald Steinberg JFK tribute medal #1	39 mm	.999 fine silver	Gerald Perry/Gerald Steinberg; collector names; serial number
K-63A-216A	Gerald Steinberg JFK tribute medal #1	39 mm	Oxidized bronze	Gerald Perry/Gerald Steinberg; collector names; serial number
K-63A-217	Gerald Steinberg JFK Tribute Medal #2	39 mm	.999 fine silver	Gerald Steinberg; collector names; serial number
K-63A-217A	Gerald Steinberg JFK Tribute Medal #2	39 mm	Oxidized bronze	Gerald Steinberg; collector names; serial number
K-63A-218	Stylized Manship JFK inaugural medal, copy	66 mm	Antiqued bronze	Reverse: "Ask Not" error, large reeds
K-63A-219	"China Lake NOTS Visit" good-luck token	34 mm	Silver-colored aluminum	Reverse: horseshoe
K-63A-220	Foreign Freedom medal	32 mm	Bronze	Presented during the Kennedy administration; reverse: Liberty Bell, USA
K-63A-221	Universidad de Buenos Aires JFK award, Argentina	66 mm	Bronze	Reverse: plain
K-63A-222	American Mint "I am a Berliner" medal	40 mm	Silver-plated copper	Reverse: eagle
K-63A-223	Universidad de Buenos Aires JFK award, Argentina	30¹/₂ mm	Silver-plated bronze	Reverse: three blank spaces for engraving
K-63A-224	Woodmen of the World JFK-RFK tribute medal	30 mm	Silver	Reeded edge; reverse: axe in trees
K-63A-225	Boston, MA, VFW convention badge with ribbon	114 x 57 mm	Antique bronze	Plain with pin
K-63A-226	BSA Prospect District JFK memorial fabric patch	76¹/₅ mm	White and black cloth	Cloth loop at the top
K-63A-227	JFK Memorial Hospital fabric patch	76¹/₅ mm	White cloth with red lettering	Reverse: plain
K-63A-228	John F. Kennedy commanders anchor fabric patch	76¹/₅ mm	Blue background with green lettering and gold anchor	Reverse: plain
K-63A-229	U.S. Mint Gilroy Roberts LBJ inaugural medal	76 mm	Bronze	Reverse designed by Frank Gasparro
K-63A-230	Medallic Art East Coast memorial "Who Died in the Ocean" medal	63¹/₂ mm	Bronze	Reverse: JFK inauguration quote
K-63A-231	WRR "JFK Assassinated" good-luck token	33¹/₂ mm	Aluminum	Reverse: good luck
K-63A-232	WRR JFK "Good Luck, the Rices Remember You" token	33¹/₂ mm	Aluminum	Reverse: good luck
K-63A-233	Arthur Blumenthal Kennedy half dollar, replica	47⁷/₁₀ mm	.999 fine silver	Serial number; reverse: marked "Copy"
K-63A-234	AMVETS Washington-Lincoln-JFK American veterans medal	30 x 38 mm	Polished nickel with gold emblem	Green, black, and red ribbon; uniface
K-63A-235	AU Mining mini 1964 Kennedy half dollar	17¹/₄ mm	.999 fine silver, 2⁴/₅ g.	Reverse: torch
K-63A-236	"He Worked for the Common Good" JFK medal	20¹/₄ mm	Gold	Reverse: Presidential Seal
K-63A-237	JFK-Arnaldo Galluzzi medal, Brazil	40³/₅ mm	Silver	Reverse: Spanish-language memorial text
K-63A-238	1964 Kennedy half dollar, copy	31 mm	Silver	Reverse: heraldic eagle
K-63A-239	"He Worked for the Common Good" JFK medal, France	35¹/₂ mm	.999 fine silver	
K-63A-240	American Currencies Kennedy half dollar medal	50 mm	.999 fine silver with gold-plated half dollar	Reverse: Capitol and eagle
K-63A-241	Nummismundi JFK in memoriam medal	34 mm	.925 fine silver	Reverse: coat of arms
K-63A-242	JFK "Freedom More Than the Rejection of Tyranny" medal	40 mm	.999 fine silver	Reverse: Frankfurt government building
K-63A-243	Aurum-S JFK tribute medal	26 mm	.999 fine silver	Reverse: Aurum-S shield
K-63A-244	Osborne "LBJ Became President" medal	25⁷/₂₀ mm	Aluminum	Reverse: "Upon Death of"
K-63A-244A	Osborne "LBJ Became President" medal	28¹/₂ mm	Brass	Reverse: "Upon Death of"
K-63A-244B	Osborne "LBJ Became President" medal	28³/₅ mm	Aluminum	Reverse: "Upon Death of"
K-63A-245	Danbury Mint JFK funeral medal	40 mm	Sterling silver	Reverse: text 1963
K-63A-245A	Danbury Mint JFK funeral medal	40 mm	Pewter	Reverse: text 1963
K-63A-246	JFK "Man on the Moon" tribute medal	39 mm	.999 fine silver	Reverse: astronaut saluting
K-63A-247	High-relief JFK bust memorial medal, New Orleans	40³/₁₀ mm	.999 fine silver	Reverse: Presidential Seal
K-63A-248	JFK silver round	38⁴/₅ mm	.999 fine silver	Reverse: wreath
K-63A-248A	JFK silver round	38⁴/₅ mm	.999 fine silver	Reverse: Great Seal

K-63A-248B	JFK-Marilyn Monroe silver round	39 mm	.999 fine silver	Plain edge; reverse: Marilyn Monroe
K-63A-248C	JFK-Marilyn Monroe round	39 mm	Cupronickel	Reeded edge; reverse: Marilyn Monroe
K-63A-248D	JFK-Marilyn Monroe round	40 mm	.999 fine silver	Reeded edge; reverse: Marilyn Monroe
K-63A-249	American Mint JFK memorial coin, Germany	30 mm	.999 fine silver	Reverse: stylized Presidential Seal
K-63A-250	JFK wooden nickel	38 9/10 mm	Wood with black ink	Reverse: "Equality for All Americans"
K-63A-251	JFK "1955 Senator in Washington" medal, Germany	14 mm	Gold, 1 1/10 g.	
K-63A-252	Sherwood B. Stolp JFK presidential ingot	63 1/2 x 38 mm	.925 sterling silver, 324 g.	Hallmark; reverse: Seal
K-63A-253	JFK wood-coin wall plaque	406 2/5 x 406 2/5 mm	Golden-colored wood	Uniface
K-63A-254	C. Affer JFK-Pope John XXIII mule medal	50 mm	Silvered bronze	Obverse: same as K-61-18; reverse: Pope
K-63A-255	John F. Kennedy Award plaque shell medal, Italy	62 mm	Silver-plated base metal	Uniface shell
K-63A-256	JFK-Jacqueline Kennedy charm	27 1/2 mm	Gold chrome on base metal	Reverse: same as obverse
K-63A-256A	JFK-Jacqueline Kennedy charm	27 3/4 mm	Copper on base metal	Reverse: same as obverse
K-63A-257	Hall Of Education JFK medal, Germany	20 mm	.900 fine gold	Reverse: stylized American eagle
K-63A-258	"Sic Transit Gloria Mundi" JFK gold medal, Italy	12 7/10 mm	.900 fine gold, Proof	Reverse: four-bar cross, legend
K-63A-259	Dieges & Clust JFK profile medal plaque, Providence, RI	197 mm	Bronze circular, cast	Hallmark: Dieges & Clust
K-63A-260	BPO Elks JFK Boston lodge #10 medal	39 mm	Aluminum	Reeded edge; reverse: "Ask Not" credo
K-63A-261	Southampton Mint 5 cent JFK stamp ingot	26 x 39 mm	Gold plated	Reverse: blank and smooth
K-63A-262	U.S. Mint JFK inaugural medal, mule copy	38 mm	Bronze	Obverse: mule; reverse: inauguration
K-63A-263	JFK tribute medal	32 mm	Antique silvered base metalshield with stars	Obverse: JFK facing left; reverse: eagle on
K-63A-264	Astro MFG large Kennedy half dollar bank, Michigan	152 x 127 x 13 mm	Base metal, chrome finish	Reverse: eternal flame
K-63A-265	First Lady Jacqueline Bouvier Kennedy medal	39 mm	Bronze	Reverse: Capitol statue
K-63A-266	JFK anniversary coin lapel pin	17 mm	Gold-colored base metal	Reverse: plain
K-63A-267	Cuban Missile Crisis 1962 JFK medal	39 mm	.999 fine silver	Reverse: eagle on shield
K-63A-268	JFK-RFK tribute medal	40 mm	.999 fine silver	Plain edge; reverse: Statue of Liberty
K-63A-269	JFK 1917-1963 medal	26 mm	.925 fine silver	Plain edge; reverse: 35 stars, Presidential Seal
K-63A-270	JFK "In God We Trust" token	30 4/5 mm	Bronzed base metal	Reverse: "In God We Trust", JFK
K-63A-270A	JFK "In God We Trust" token	30 4/5 mm	Silvered base metal	Reverse: "In God We Trust", JFK
K-63A-271	JFK memorial charm	29 mm	Sterling silver	Looped; reverse: "Ask Not" credo
K-63A-272	JFK in memoriam medal, Germany	20 mm	Gold	Reverse: 35 presidents over the U.S. legend
K-63A-273	Wedgwood Jasperware large JFK bust cameo, England	76 x 102 mm	Blue and white	Hallmark; reverse: plain
K-63A-273A	Wedgwood Jasperware large JFK bust cameo, England	76 x 102 mm	Black and white	Hallmark; reverse: plain
K-63A-274	Wedgwood Jasperware JFK change dish, England	114 mm	Blue and white	Hallmark; reverse: plain
K-63A-275	United Ivory Artists hand-carved JFK bust, Madrid, Spain	33 x 60 mm	White ivory, glass frame	Frame: convex glass oval
K-63A-276	Osborne JFK-Peace Corps token	28 mm	Aluminum	Reverse: "Originator of the Peace Corps"
K-63A-276A	Osborne JFK-Peace Corps token	28 mm	Aluminum	Die change; reverse: mini letters
K-63A-276B	Osborne JFK-Peace Corps token	28 mm	Aluminum	Reverse: large letters
K-63A-276C	Osborne JFK-Peace Corps token	28 mm	Aluminum	Face change
K-63A-276D	Osborne JFK-Pulitzer Prize token	28 mm	Aluminum	Reverse: "Pulitzer Prize"
K-63A-277	Osborne JFK-Clarksburg token	28 mm	Aluminum	Reverse: "Ritz Theatre Admission"
K-63A-278	Osborne JFK two-headed token	28 mm	Goldine	Reverse: same as obverse
K-63A-279	Osborne JFK-Taylor Drug Store token	28 mm	Goldine	Reverse: "Taylor Drug Store, 1879"
K-63A-280	Osborne JFK-Washington token	28 mm	Goldine	Reverse: George Washington
K-63A-281	Osborne JFK-Great Seal token	28 mm	Goldine	Reverse: Great Seal of the United States
K-63A-282	Kennedy-era Lugano cigar bands, Holland	Various sizes	Various metallic colors	Series numbers and information
K-63A-283	JFK 1917–1963 tie tac	20 mm	Goldine	Uniface
K-63A-284	JFK commemorative medallion	83 mm	Gray base metal	Reverse: accomplishments and quote
K-63A-285	JFK commemorative jewelry coin, Germany	15 3/10 mm	Gold	Reverse: American eagle
K-63A-286	JFK paper insert for Kennedy half dollar key chain	30 mm	Paper with cardboard back	Loosen screw at top
K-63A-287	JFK paper insert for Kennedy half dollar key chain	29 mm	Paper	Twist cap to open and remove black image
K-63A-288	JFK aluminum insert for Kennedy half dollar key chain	30 mm	Foil paper with a black portrait	Blank
K-63A-289	Danbury Mint "JFK-Nixon TV debates" medal	40 mm	Sterling silver	Reverse: text 1960
K-63A-290	Danbury Mint Cuban Missile Crisis medal	40 mm	.925 fine silver	Reverse: eagle, eight lines, legend
K-63A-291	Las Vegas Freemont Hotel JFK key-chain medal	39 mm	Gold base metal	Reverse: hotel building and legend
K-63A-292	Ralph Menconi JFK bust "Life-Liberty" key-chain medal	38 mm	Silver-plated base metal	Reverse: eagle, life and liberty
K-63A-293	JFK key chain two-part pivot locket medal	27 mm	Brass	Heavy, fine engraving
K-63A-294	JFK memorial key-chain medallion	29 mm	Brass	Looped; reverse: "Ask Not" credo, eternal flame
K-63A-295	Nickel Monument Numismatic Park medal, Canada	40 1/2 mm	Nickel	See K-63A-68; reverse: the Big Nickel monument, JFK

K-63A-296	"The Kennedys: JFK-Jacqueline Kennedy" charm	22 mm	Sterling silver	Hallmark: Elmar
K-63A-297	JFK bust looped charm	10 x 18 mm	Sterling silver	Uniface
K-63A-298	JFK bust on gold heart charm	34 x 38 mm	Gold-plated sterling silver	Uniface
K-63A-299	JFK rectanglular silver bar necklace	11 x 24 mm	.999 fine silver, 2 g.	Serial number 04903
K-63A-300	JFK memorial looped charm	23 mm	Sterling silver	Reverse: "Ask Not" credo
K-63A-301	JFK poker chip	39 mm	Clay and plastic, red and yellow	Reverse: photo of JFK
K-63A-302	JFK poker chip with JFK-Lawford photo	39 mm	Clay, black	Reverse: photo of Bugsy Siegel, 1946
K-63A-303	JFK poker chip with JFK-Lawford photo	39 mm	Clay, grey	Reverse: photo of Debbie Reynolds, 1977
K-63A-304	JFK New Frontier wooden nickel	39 mm	Wood	Reverse: "The New Frontier"
K-63A-305	Pontiac Press JFK in memoriam wood nickel	38 mm	Wood with black ink	Reverse: Jefferson image, 1950-D
K-63A-305A	Pontiac Press JFK in memoriam wood nickel	38 mm	Wood with red ink	Reverse: Jefferson image, 1950-D
K-63A-306	Locica milk chocolate Kennedy half dollar coin, Italy	29 mm	Silver-colored foil	
K-63A-307	JFK round pocket knife key chain	40 mm	Goldine	Plastic pearl insert
K-63A-308	JFK Airport silver charm	32 mm	Enameled sterling silver	Uniface
K-63A-309	JFK tribute medal	38 mm	Antique bronze	Reverse: "Originator of Peace Corps"
K-63A-310	JFK-Washington medal	29 mm	Golden bronze	Reverse: George Washington, date reversed
K-63A-311	Danbury Mint JFK Peace Corps medal	40 mm	Pewter	Reverse: text 1961
K-63A-312	U.S. Mint JFK bust medal	27 1/2 mm	Bronze-colored foil with white paper	
K-63A-313	Osborne JFK memorial medal	34 mm	Goldine	Reverse: "Ask Not" credo with JFK's signature
K-63A-314	Kennedy Space Center key chain tag	21 1/4 x 41mm	Base metal with blue background and gold	Looped; reverse: rocket launch lettering, cast
K-63A-315	JFK tribute medal, large head variety	39 mm	Silver aluminum	Reverse: JFK's signature and biographical information
K-63A-316	JFK tribute medal	36 mm	.999 fine silver, Proof	Obverse: same as K-63A-134, portrait only; Reverse: same as K-61-9, revised Presidential Seal
K-63A-317	Ngo Dinh Diem 50-xu coin, Vietnam	30 mm	Aluminum	Reeded edge; reverse: bamboo plants, dated 1963
K-63A-318	General Sarit Thanarat coin, Thailand	35 mm	Nickel silver	Plain edge; revers: five stars, sword, wreath, torch, and legend
K-63A-319	"Assassin's Challenge" coin	30 mm	.900 fine silver	Reverse: Presidential Seal, tail feathers stamped with #4
K-63A-320	JFK-Jacqueline Kennedy Crystal d'Albret sulphide paperweight, France	76 1/5 x 44 1/2 mm	Lead crystal glass with green overlay	Star burst pattern on bottom, signed trunnion
K-63A-321	PT-109 JFK tribute man's ring	Size 11	Sterling silver	Hallmarked inside; size marked
K-63A-322	PT-109 tie clip	45 x 10 mm	Polished golden brass	Aligator clasp; unpainted PT-109 on the bow
K-63A-323	PT-109 tie clip	45 x 10 mm	Golden brass	PT-109 on the bow painted black
K-63A-324	PT-109 tie clip		Golden brass	Unpainted PT-109, raised number
K-63A-325	BSA "JFK Tribute to Courage" patch	235 x 127 mm	Embroidered cloth	BSA 1917–1963, Native American on horseback
K-63A-326	PT-boat cloth patch	50 4/5 mm	Embroidered cloth, black and silver	PT torpedo in silver
K-63A-327	"JFK-LBJ-HST-FDR Great American Presidents" medal	32 mm	Silvered base metal	Reverse: U.S. Capitol, "Pride in the Future"
K-63A-328	Rainy Mountain Design "JFK An American" limited-edition brass belt buckle	94 x 70 mm	Solid brass	First edition; serial number; "Oklahoma City, OK"
K-63A-329	FBI JFK taskforce identification pin			
K-63A-330	Kennedy half dollar with double date, Argentina	32 mm	Base metal, cast	Reverse: seated Liberty figure
K-63A-331	Franklin Mint Cuban Missile Crisis medal	39 mm	.925 fine sterling silver	Reverse: six lines of text
K-63A-332	JFK metal plaque	304 4/5 mm diameter	Metal, high-relief cast	Mounted on finished-wood wall mount; uniface
K-63A-333	JFK coin flip-out magnifying glass, West Germany	40 mm	Bronze with plastic magnifying glass insert	Reverse: eagle and stars
K-63A-334	JFK Swiss incabloc coin pendant watch	35 mm	Gold plated with golden time-piece dial and hands	Bears image of JFK; reeded edge; looped
K-63A-335	"Germany-USA Friendship Through Sports" medal	81 x 47 mm	Gold-colored base metal painted red, white, and blue	Two-piece medal; uniface; obverse: five-point star with JFK round insert
K-63A-336	Illinois Tollway Kennedy half dollar	30 mm	.900 fine silver,	Illinois Tollway giveaway following the release protective packaging of the Kennedy half dollar; reverse: Presidential Seal
K-64-1	U.S. Mint at Philadelphia Kennedy half dollar	30 mm	.900 fine silver, Uncirculated	Reverse: Presidential Seal
K-64-1A	U.S. Mint at Denver Kennedy half dollar	30 mm	.900 fine silver, Uncirculated	Reverse: Presidential Seal
K-64-1B	U.S. Mint at Philadelphia Kennedy half dollar	30 mm	.900 fine silver, Proof	Reverse: Presidential Seal

K-64-1C	U.S. Mint at Philadelphia Kennedy half dollar	30 mm	Gold-plated .900 fine silver	Privately plated
K-64-1D	U.S. Mint at Denver Kennedy half dollar	30 mm	Gold-plated .900 fine silver	Privately plated
K-64-1E	Kennedy half dollar	30 mm	Embossed aluminum foil	For embedding; uniface
K-64-1F	Two-sided obverse 1964 Kennedy half dollar	30 mm	.900 fine silver	Magician's coin
K-64-1G	Two-sided reverse Kennedy half dollar	30 mm	.900 fine silver	Magician's coin
K-64-1H	Enlarged Kennedy half dollar	35 mm	.900 fine silver	Standard Kennedy half dollar reverse
K-64-1I	Gilroy Roberts Kennedy half dollar, original design		Plaster galvano	Uniface
K-64-1J	Kennedy half dollar with accented hair	30 mm	.900 fine silver, Proof	50,000 struck; reverse: Presidential Seal
K-64-1K	Kennedy half dollar, cloisonnéd	30 mm	.900 fine silver	Reverse: Presidential Seal
K-64-1L	Kennedy half dollar holder Capitol Hill jewelry tag	30 x 24 mm	Silver- and blue-colored foil	3 dollars plus tax
K-64-1M	Kennedy half dollar holder paper filler with photo of JFK	30½ mm	Paper	
K-64-1N	Kennedy half dollar, counterfeit reverse, overstrike on obverse	31 mm	.900 fine silver	Called a sandwich coin by Ken Potter; original with fake overstrike
K-64-1O	Gilroy Roberts Kennedy half dollar gift, first strike	73 x 69 x 25 mm	Clear Lucite	Reverse of Kennedy half dollar with inscription
K-64-2	Paris Mint JFK 5-rupee coin, Sharjah	36 mm	.720 fine silver	14,900 survived melt
K-64-2A	Paris Mint JFK 5-rupee coin, Sharjah	36 mm	.720 fine silver, Proof	7,000 survived melt
K-64-2B	JFK rupee-coin stamps, Sharjah	Various sizes	Silver aluminum on paper	Watermarked; obverses with various denominations
K-64-2C	JFK rupee-coin stamps, Sharjah	Various sizes	Silver aluminum on paper	Watermarked; reverses with various denominations
K-64-3	JFK-Shriver Peace Corps medal	40 mm	.999 fine silver	Reverse: dove of peace
K-64-3A	JFK-Shriver Peace Corps medal	40 mm	.999 fine silver, Proof	Reverse: dove of peace
K-64-3B	JFK-Shriver Peace Corps medal	50 mm	.900 fine gold, 175 g.	150 struck
K-64-3C	JFK-Shriver Peace Corps medal	50 mm	.900 fine gold, 140 g.	200 struck
K-64-3D	JFK-Shriver Peace Corps medal	50 mm	.900 fine gold, 105 g.	500 struck
K-64-3E	JFK-Shriver Peace Corps medal	50 mm	.900 fine gold, 70 g.	500 struck
K-64-3F	JFK-Shriver Peace Corps medal	40 mm	.900 fine gold	Reverse: dove of peace
K-64-3G	JFK-Shriver Peace Corps medal	32 mm	.900 fine gold	Reverse: dove of peace
K-64-3H	JFK-Shriver Peace Corps medal	26 mm	.900 fine gold	Reverse: dove of peace
K-64-3I	JFK-Shriver Peace Corps medal	20 mm	.900 fine gold	Reverse: dove of peace
K-64-4	"Political Leaders of the World" medal, Germany	50 mm	Silver, Matte Finish	Reverse: globe with flags
K-64-4A	"Political Leaders of the World" medal, Germany	50 mm	.1000 fine silver, Proof	Reverse: globe with flags
K-64-4B	"Political Leaders of the World" medal, Italy	50 mm	.925 fine silver, Proof	Reverse: globe with flags
K-64-4C	"Political Leaders of the World" medal, Germany	40 mm	.1000 fine silver, Matte Finish	Reverse: globe with flags
K-64-4D	"Political Leaders of the World" medal, Germany	40 mm	.1000 fine silver, Proof	Reverse: globe with flags
K-64-4E	"Political Leaders of the World" medal, Italy	40 mm	.925 fine silver, Proof	Reverse: globe with flags
K-64-4F	"Political Leaders of the World" medal, Germany	30 mm	.1000 fine silver, Matte Finish	Reverse: globe with flags
K-64-4G	"Political Leaders of the World" medal, Germany	30 mm	.1000 fine silver, Proof	Reverse: globe with flags
K-64-4H	"Political Leaders of the World" medal, Italy	30 mm	.925 fine silver, Proof	Reverse: globe with flags
K-64-4I	"Political Leaders of the World" medal, Germany	50 mm	.900 fine gold	Reverse: globe with flags
K-64-4J	"Political Leaders of the World" medal, France	50 mm	.920 fine gold	Reverse: globe with flags
K-64-4K	"Political Leaders of the World" medal, Germany	40 mm	.900 fine gold	Reverse: globe with flags
K-64-4L	"Political Leaders of the World" medal, France	40 mm	.920 fine gold	Reverse: globe with flags
K-64-4M	"Political Leaders of the World" medal, Germany, Italy, and Venezuela	30 mm	.900 fine gold	Reverse: globe with flags
K-64-4N	"Political Leaders of the World" medal, Venezuela	30 mm	.900 fine gold	Thick planchet; reverse: globe with flags
K-64-4O	"Political Leaders of the World" medal, France	30 mm	.920 fine gold	Reverse: globe with flags
K-64-4P	"Political Leaders of the World" medal, Germany, Italy, and Venezuela	21 mm	.900 fine gold	Reverse: globe with flags
K-64-4Q	"Political Leaders of the World" medal, France	21 mm	.920 fine gold	Reverse: globe with flags
K-64-4R	"Political Leaders of the World" medal, Venezuela	15 mm	.900 fine gold	Early issue; reverse: globe with flags
K-64-4S	"Political Leaders of the World" medal, Germany and Venezuela	14 mm	.900 fine gold	Later issue; reverse: globe with flags
K-64-4T	"Political Leaders of the World" medal, France	14 mm	.920 fine gold	Reverse: globe with flags
K-64-4U	Paris Mint "Political Leaders of the World" display medal	30 mm	Bronze, Proof	Very scarce; reverse: globe with flags
K-64-4V	"Grandes Estadistas do Mundo" medal, variety sample	30 mm	Oxidized silver	No lettering
K-64-5	Sachs Outstanding Citizenship Award medal, Sachs Quality	76 mm	Bronze	295 presented; uniface; reverse for engraving
K-64-5A	Sachs Outstanding Citizenship Award medal, Sachs New York	76 mm	Bronze	Uniface; reverse for engraving
K-64-6	President Kennedy Sport Center medal, Italy	42 mm	Silver	Reverse: shield of Milan
K-64-6A	President Kennedy Sport Center medal, Italy	42 mm	Gold	Reverse: shield of Milan
K-64-7	"JFK Death Anniversary" medal, Italy	32 mm	Bronze	Reverse: White House
K-64-7A	"JFK Death Anniversary" medal, Italy	43 mm	Silver	Reverse: White House
K-64-7B	"JFK Death Anniversary" medal, Italy	21 mm	Gold	10,000 struck; reverse: White House
K-64-7C	"JFK Death Anniversary" medal, Italy	26 mm	Gold	7,000 struck; reverse: White House
K-64-7D	"JFK Death Anniversary" medal, Italy	32 mm	Gold	5,000 struck; reverse: White House

K-64-7E	"JFK Death Anniversary" medal, Italy	43 mm	Gold	2,000 struck; reverse: White House
K-64-7F	"JFK-Jacqueline Kennedy Death Anniversary" medal, Italy	32 mm	Bronze	Reverse: White House
K-64-8	JFK traffic safety medal, Japan	30 mm	Nickel silver	Looped; reverse: eagle
K-64-8A	JFK traffic safety medal, Japan	28 mm	Nickel silver	Looped; reverse: eagle
K-64-9	Civil Rights Act of 1964 medal, Holland	38 mm	Sterling	Reverse: torch and Seal
K-64-9A	Civil Rights Act of 1964 medal, Holland	38 mm	Bronze	Reverse: torch and Seal
K-64-9B	Civil Rights Act of 1964 medal, Holland	18½ mm	Gold, 4⅕ g.	Reverse: torch and Seal
K-64-9C	Civil Rights Act of 1964 medal, Holland	22 mm	Gold, 7 g.	Reverse: torch and Seal
K-64-9D	Civil Rights Act of 1964 medal, Holland	25 mm	Gold, 8⅕ g.	Reverse: torch and Seal
K-64-9E	Civil Rights Act of 1964 medal, Holland	38 mm	Gold, 50 g.	Reverse: torch and Seal
K-64-9F	Civil Rights Act of 1964 medal, Holland	18½ mm	Silver	Reverse: torch and Seal
K-64-9G	Civil Rights Act of 1964 medal, Holland	22 mm	Silver	Reverse: torch and Seal
K-64-9H	Civil Rights Act of 1964 medal, Holland	25 mm	Silver	Reverse: torch and Seal
K-64-9I	Civil Rights Act of 1964 medal, Holland	50 mm	Silver	Reverse: torch and Seal
K-64-9J	Civil Rights Act of 1964 medal, Holland	50 mm	Bronze	Reverse: torch and Seal
K-64-10	Proposed JFK campaign rocking-chair charm	25 mm	Gold wash on base metal, textured finish	Looped
K-64-10A	Proposed JFK campaign rocking-chair tie tac	16 mm	Gold wash on base metal, textured finish	With pin lock
K-64-11	Sculptored Coins embossed Kennedy half dollar	30 mm	.900 fine silver	Reverse: indentation of U.S. Seal
K-64-11A	Sculptored Coins embossed Kennedy half dollar, copy	30 mm	Silver-colored base metal	Looped; reverse: indentation of U.S. Seal
K-64-11B	Sculptored Coins embossed Kennedy half dollar, copy	30 mm	Silver-colored base metal	No loop; reverse: indentation of U.S. Seal
K-64-12	Stafford JFK World's Fair souvenir, type 1	70 mm	Bronze chemical etch	Reverse: A. Lincoln
K-64-13	Stafford JFK World's Fair souvenir, type 2	35 mm	Bronze with deep etch	Holed; reverse: A. Lincoln
K-64-13A	Stafford JFK World's Fair souvenir, type 3	31 mm	Bronze with deep etch	No hole; reverse: A. Lincoln
K-64-14	Klefot JFK coin jewelry	18 x 22 mm	.900 fine silver	JFK cutout; uniface
K-64-14A	Schuler JFK coin jewelry	18 x 22 mm	.900 fine silver	Convex JFK cutout; uniface
K-64-15	Presidential Novelty Company first family portrait charm	24 mm	Gold-plated base metal	Uniface; radiant lines
K-64-15A	Abon MFG "First Family Portrait" charm	24 mm	Base metal, silver finish	Uniface; radiant lines
K-64-15B	Abon MFG "First Family Portrait" charm	24 mm	.925 fine sterling silver	Uniface; radiant lines
K-64-15C	Abon MFG "First Family Portrait" charm	24 mm	Gold-plated .925 fine sterling silver	Uniface; radiant lines
K-64-15D	Abon MFG "First Family Portrait" charm	24 mm	14K gold	Uniface; radiant lines
K-64-16	1964 Kennedy half dollar Assay Commission medal	57 mm	Bronze	33 struck; reverse: hand holding Kennedy half dollar
K-64-17	JFK commemorative postage-stamp medal, Austria	26 x 40 mm	.900 fine silver	15,000 struck; reverse: info on JFK and stamp
K-64-17A	JFK commemorative postage-stamp medal, Austria	26 x 40 mm	Gold	Limited edition; reverse: info on JFK and stamp
K-64-18	Eternal flame elongated U.S. cent	42 x 20 mm	Bronze	25 rolled
K-64-18A	Eternal flame elongated U.S. cent	42 x 20 mm	Bronze	150 rolled; JFK added
K-64-18B	Eternal flame elongated 1943 U.S. cent	42 x 20 mm	Steel	25 rolled
K-64-18C	Eternal flame elongated pre-1959 U.S. cent	42 x 20 mm	Bronze	Words added
K-64-18D	Eternal flame elongated post-1959 U.S. cent	42 x 20 mm	Bronze	Reverse: Lincoln Memorial
K-64-18E	Eternal flame elongated 1943 U.S. cent	42 x 20 mm	Steel	Reverse: Lincoln Memorial
K-64-18F	Eternal flame elongated U.S. nickel		Nickel	Jefferson nickel
K-64-18G	Eternal flame elongated U.S. dime		Dime	Roosevelt dime
K-64-18H	Eternal flame elongated U.S. quarter		Silver	Washington quarter
K-64-18I	Eternal flame elongated U.S. quarter		Clad metal	Washington quarter
K-64-18J	Eternal flame elongated Kennedy half dollar		Silver	
K-64-18K	Eternal flame elongated Kennedy half dollar		Clad metal	
K-64-18L	Eternal flame elongated Canadian cent			
K-64-18M	Eternal flame elongated Canadian nickel			
K-64-19	Louis Zahn Jewish National Fund JFK memorial medal	29 mm	Bronze	
K-64-20	M.J. Hatfield JFK memorial medal	70 mm	White metal, gold finish	Reverse: eternal flame and credo
K-64-20A	M.J. Hatfield JFK memorial medal	70 mm	Silver finish	100 cast; reverse: eternal flame and credo
K-64-20B	M.J. Hatfield JFK memorial medal	70 mm	Copper Finish	100 cast; reverse: eternal flame and credo
K-64-20C	M.J. Hatfield JFK memorial medal	70 mm	Gold finish	300 cast; reverse: eternal flame and credo
K-64-20D	M.J. Hatfield JFK memorial medal	70 mm	Silver finish, one coat	300 cast; reverse: eternal flame and credo
K-64-20E	M.J. Hatfield JFK memorial medal	70 mm	Copper finish, one coat	300 cast; reverse: eternal flame and credo
K-64-20F	M.J. Hatfield JFK memorial medal	70 mm	Gold finish	100 cast; reverse: "Will Do"
K-64-20G	M.J. Hatfield JFK memorial medal	70 mm	Silver finish	100 cast; reverse: "Will Do"
K-64-20H	M.J. Hatfield JFK memorial medal	70 mm	Copper finish	100 cast; reverse: "Will Do"
K-64-20I	M.J. Hatfield JFK memorial medal	70 mm	Chrome plated	50 cast; reverse: "Will Do"
K-64-20J	M.J. Hatfield JFK memorial medal	70 mm	Copper plated	50 cast; reverse: "Will Do"
K-64-20K	M.J. Hatfield JFK memorial medal, original trial piece	70 mm	Copper finish	Reverse: eternal flame and credo
K-64-21	Kennedy half dollar, copy, Argentina	29 mm	Silver base metal, cast	Looped
K-64-22	Kennedy half dollar, struck copy, Argentina	30 mm	Nickel silver	No loop

K-64-23	Kennedy half dollar, insert copy, Argentina	29 mm	Bronze	Looped
K-64-24	Kennedy half dollar, stamped insert copy, Argentina	24 mm	Brass	Uniface
K-64-25	Kennedy half dollar, copy, Japan	30 mm	Plastic	Looped; reverse: U.S. Seal
K-64-26	Mini Kennedy half dollar, Japan	18 mm	Silver	Uniface
K-64-26A	Mini Kennedy half dollar, Japan	18 mm	Copper	Uniface
K-64-26B	Mini Kennedy half dollar, Japan	14 mm	Silver	Uniface
K-64-26C	Mini Kennedy half dollar, Japan	14 mm	Copper	Uniface
K-64-27	Royal Athena embossed Kennedy half dollar	30 mm	.900 fine silver	Reverse: indentation of Seal
K-64-28	Victor Capo embossed Kennedy half dollar	30 mm	Clad metal	Reverse: indentation of Seal
K-64-28A	Victor Capo embossed Kennedy half dollar	30 mm	Gold plated	Reverse: indentation of Seal
K-64-29	Temple Coins embossed Kennedy half dollar	30 mm	Clad metal	Reverse: indentation of Seal
K-64-30	Embossed Kennedy half dollar	29 mm	Base metal, cast	No detail, rough pattern
K-64-31	AAU sports JFK memorial medal	140 mm	Bronze-plated zinc alloy, cast	Reverse: AAU inscription
K-64-32	VFW 1964 Chicago convention badge	40 x 32 mm	Bronze	Reverse: union bugs
K-64-32A	VFW 1964 Pittsburgh convention badge, post 8795	40 x 32 mm	Bronze	Red, white, and blue delegate ribbon; reverse: union bugs
K-64-33	United Rubber Workers 1964 24th convention badge	34 mm	Bronze	Red, white, and blue ribbon with logo; reverse: "URCL and PW of A", union bugs
K-64-33A	United Rubber Workers 1964 convention badge	34 mm	Bronze	Reverse: "URCL and PW of A"
K-64-33B	United Rubber Workers 1964 convention badge	34 mm	Bronze	Reverse: "URCL and PW of A"
K-64-34	First Union Health Center anniversary medal	77 mm	Bronze	10,000 struck; reverse: cupped hand
K-64-34A	First Union Health Center anniversary medal	77 mm	Silver	Unique; reverse: cupped hand
K-64-35	Kennedy Society of Denmark medal	30 mm	Silver	Looped; reverse: Kennedy half dollar
K-64-36	Kennedy half dollar with Japanese quotation	39 mm	Antique silver	Looped; reverse: map of America
K-64-37	Jack Meccariello elongated Kennedy half dollar paperweight	45 x 32 mm	Lead	
K-64-38	Half Dollar Novelties Kennedy half dollar, copy	57 mm	Bronze, cast	Uniface
K-64-39	Kennedy half dollar belt buckle, copy	74 mm	Nickel-plated base metal	Uniface
K-64-40	Kennedy half dollar	77 mm	Zinc, Matte Finish, inflated cast	Reverse: U.S. Seal
K-64-40A	Kennedy half dollar	77 mm	Zinc, Chrome Finish, inflated cast	Reverse: U.S. Seal
K-64-40B	Kennedy half dollar	77 mm	Zinc, Matte Finish, inflated cast	Holed; reverse: U.S. Seal
K-64-40C	Kennedy half dollar bank	77 mm	Zinc, Matte Finish, inflated cast	Holed; reverse: U.S. Seal
K-64-41	Presidential Novelty Company Jacqueline Kennedy charm	24 mm	24K gold on base metal	Uniface; looped
K-64-41A	Abon MFG Jacqueline Kennedy charm	24 mm	Base metal, silver finish	Uniface; looped
K-64-41B	Abon MFG Jacqueline Kennedy charm	24 mm	Sterling silver	Uniface; looped
K-64-41C	Abon MFG Jacqueline Kennedy charm	24 mm	24K gold plating on sterling silver	Uniface; looped
K-64-41D	Abon MFG Jacqueline Kennedy charm	24 mm	14K gold	Uniface; looped
K-64-42	Abon MFG Caroline Kennedy charm	24 mm	Base metal, silver finish	Uniface; looped
K-64-42A	Abon MFG Caroline Kennedy charm	24 mm	Sterling silver	Uniface; looped
K-64-42B	Abon MFG Caroline Kennedy charm	24 mm	24K gold plating on sterling silver	Uniface; looped
K-64-42C	Abon MFG Caroline Kennedy charm	24 mm	14K gold	Uniface; looped
K-64-43	Abon MFG JFK Jr. charm	24 mm	24K gold on base metal	Uniface; looped
K-64-43A	Abon MFG JFK Jr. charm	24 mm	Base metal, silver finish	Uniface; looped
K-64-43B	Abon MFG JFK Jr. charm	24 mm	Sterling silver	Uniface; looped
K-64-43C	Abon MFG JFK Jr. charm	24 mm	24K gold plating on sterling silver	Uniface; looped
K-64-43D	Abon MFG JFK Jr. charm	24 mm	14K gold	Uniface; looped
K-64-44	Danbury Mint JFK commemorative medal and first-day cover	40 mm	Sterling silver	Serial number; reverse: JFK bio and credo
K-64-44A	Danbury Mint JFK commemorative medal and first-day cover	40 mm	Bronze	Reverse: JFK bio and credo
K-64-45	American Legion 1964 Syracuse convention badge	40 x 32 mm	White bronze with blue logo	Red and blue ribbon; reverse: union bugs
K-64-45A	American Legion 1964 Syracuse convention badge	40 x 32 mm	White bronze, unpainted	Red and blue ribbon; reverse: union bugs
K-64-46	"JFK 1st Physical Fitness Winter Camporee" fabric patch	89 x 101³⁄₅ mm	Blue background with white letters and a red trim	Reverse: plain
K-64-47	Golden Artcraft PT-109 Kennedy 64 pin	44¹⁄₂ mm	Heavy bright brass	Alligator clasp
K-64-48	Massachusetts Historical Society JFK award medal	90 mm	Bronze	Reverse: liberty, learning
K-64-49	Huguenin Médailleurs "Kennedy-Lauf Mosnang 1964" march medal	40 mm	.925 fine silver	Ribbon; uniface; reverse: stippled
K-64-50	Cape Kennedy Florida state medal	26 mm	Goldine	Reeded edge; reverse: Florida statistics
K-64-51	Kennedy half dollar, copy, Argentina	31 mm	Nickel silver	Reverse: stylized eagle
K-64-52	1964 World's Fair JFK-Jacqueline Kennedy souvenir medal	40 mm	Brass	Reeded edge; reverse: Jacqueline $1.00 with rays

K-64-52A	1964 World's Fair JFK-Jacqueline Kennedy postage stamp souvenir medal	40 mm	Nickel silver	Reeded edge; reverse: NY with F postage stamp
K-64-52B	1964 World's Fair JFK-Jacqueline Kennedy souvenir medal	31 mm	Nickel silver	Reeded edge; reverse: Jacqueline 50 cent
K-64-52C	1964 World's Fair JFK-Jacqueline Kennedy souvenir medal	40 mm	Brass	Reverse: Jacqueline $1.00 without rays
K-64-53	"Ask Not" JFK memorial key-chain tag	31³/₁₀ mm	Silvered base metal	Reverse: "Ask Not" credo
K-64-54	JFK wood coin plaque	406²/₅ mm diameter	Bright gold finish	Obverse: JFK facing left; reverse: plain
K-64-55	JFK coin foil stamp set, Jordan	Various sizes	Golden aluminum base	Watermarked; various postage
K-64-56	California Collectors of Elongateds "5th Year" Kennedy half dollar	Various sizes	Cupronickel	Reverse: obverse of the 1971 Kennedy half dollar
K-64-57	1964 Kennedy half dollar round, copy		.999 fine silver, 2 Troy oz.	
K-64-58	1964 Kennedy half dollar, first issue	30 mm	Gold on silver, Uncirculated, encased	Standard Kennedy half dollar reverse
K-65-1	Numismundi series JFK medal, Germany	34 mm	.999 fine silver	Reverse: coat of arms
K-65-1A	Numismundi series JFK medal, Germany	50 mm	.999 fine silver	Reverse: coat of arms
K-65-1B	Numismundi series JFK medal, Germany	20 mm	24K gold	Reverse: coat of arms
K-65-1C	Numismundi series JFK medal, Germany	26 mm	24K gold	Reverse: coat of arms
K-65-1D	Numismundi series JFK medal, Germany	34 mm	24K gold	Reverse: coat of arms
K-65-1E	Numismundi series JFK medal, Germany	34 mm	24K gold	Thick planchet; reverse: coat of arms
K-65-1F	Numismundi series JFK medal, Germany	50 mm	24K gold	Reverse: coat of arms
K-65-2	Osborne Coin Collectors of America JFK token, type 1 obverse	28 mm	Aluminum	Reverse: "Member CCOA 1965"
K-65-2A	Osborne Coin Collectors of America JFK token, type 2 obverse	28 mm	Aluminum	Revised die; reverse: "Member CCOA 1965"
K-65-3	French Medal Club JFK medal, private issue, France	68 mm	Silver on bronze	Serial numbers 1–400; reverse: "Man's Problems" quote
K-65-3A	French Medal Club JFK medal, public issue, France	68 mm	Bronze	No serial number; reverse: "Man's Problems" quote
K-65-3B	French Medal Club JFK medal, public issue, France	68 mm	Silver	No serial number; 1966 on rim; reverse: "Man's Problems" quote
K-65-3C	French Medal Club JFK medal, public issue, France	68 mm	Bronze	No serial number; 1967 on rim; reverse: "Man's Problems" quote
K-65-3D	French Medal Club JFK medal, public issue, France	68 mm	Bronze	No serial number; 1968 on rim; reverse: "Man's Problems" quote
K-65-3E	French Medal Club JFK medal, public issue, France	68 mm	Bronze	No serial number; 1970 on rim; reverse: "Man's Problems" quote
K-65-3F	French Medal Club JFK medal, France	105 mm	Bronze, 538³/₅ g., cast	Serial numbers 1–100; 1970 on rim; reverse: "Man's Problems" quote
K-65-3G	French Medal Club JFK medal, France	105 mm	Golden bronze, cast	Serial numbers 1–100; 1970 on rim; reverse: "Man's Problems" quote
K-65-3H	French Medal Club JFK medal, public issue, France	68 mm	Bronze	Serial numbers 1–400; 1988 on rim; reverse: "Man's Problems" quote
K-65-4	JFK-Lincoln medal, Mexico	42 mm	.925 fine silver	Serial numbers 1–20,000; reverse: Lincoln
K-65-4A	JFK-Lincoln medal, trial piece, Mexico	42 mm	.980 fine silver	No serial number; reverse: Lincoln
K-65-5	JFK Whiskeytown memorial dedication medal	39 mm	Golden bronze	No serial number; reverse: gold panner
K-65-5A	JFK Whiskeytown memorial dedication medal	39 mm	Nickel silver	Serial numbers 1–300; reverse: gold panner
K-65-5B	JFK Whiskeytown memorial dedication medal	39 mm	Nickel silver	Six known; no serial number; revers: gold panner
K-65-6	Elongated Kennedy half dollar cut-out	42 x 56 mm	Silver	Unique
K-65-7	"RFK for President Club" JFK medal	39 mm	Silver-plated bronze	Serial number to 99,999; reverse: "Ask Not" credo
K-65-7A	"RFK for President Club" JFK medal, sales sample	39 mm	Silver-plated bronze	No serial number; reverse: "Ask Not" credo
K-65-7B	"RFK For President Club" RFK medal	39 mm	Silver-plated bronze	Serial number to 99,999; reverse: "Destined to Become"
K-65-7C	"RFK for President Club" RFK medal, sales sample	39 mm	Silver-plated bronze	No serial number; reverse: "Destined to Become"
K-65-8	U.S. Mint 1965 Kennedy half dollar spoof set	26 mm	Nickel silver	Reverse: "Half Enough Silver"
K-65-9	Northern Textile Association award medal	64 mm	Gold	Unique; reverse: wreath
K-65-9A	Northern Textile Association award medal	64 mm	Bronze	Reverse: wreath
K-65-9B	Northern Textile Association award medal	64 mm	Silver	Unique; reverse: wreath
K-65-10	"Pope Paul's NY Visit" medal	20 mm	Gold	Reverse: Statue of Liberty
K-65-10A	"Pope Paul's NY Visit" medal	24 mm	Gold	Reverse: Statue of Liberty
K-65-10B	"Pope Paul's NY Visit" medal	28 mm	Gold	Reverse: Statue of Liberty
K-65-10C	"Pope Paul's NY Visit" medal	32 mm	Gold	Reverse: Statue of Liberty
K-65-10D	"Pope Paul's NY Visit" medal	40 mm	Gold	Reverse: Statue of Liberty
K-65-10E	"Pope Paul's NY Visit" medal, sales sample	40 mm	Gold plated	Reverse: Statue of Liberty
K-65-10F	"Pope Paul's NY Visit" medal, sales sample	32 mm	Gold plated	Reverse: Statue of Liberty
K-65-10G	"Pope Paul's NY Visit" medal	13 mm	.585 fine gold	Reverse: torch and flame
K-65-11	JFK-Pope John memorial peace medal	64 mm	Bronze	3,500 struck; reverse: White House and the Vatican

K-65-11A	JFK-Pope John memorial peace medal	64 mm	Silver	200 struck; reverse: White House and the Vatican
K-65-11B	JFK-Pope John memorial peace medal	64 mm	Gold	Unique; a gift for the Pope; reverse: White House and the Vatican
K-65-12	Papillion Post Office JFK medal, Nebraska	28 mm	Bronze	Reverse: JFK dedication
K-65-13	"Four Assassinated Presidents" medal	70 mm	Bronze	Reverse: names of presidents
K-65-13A	"Four Assassinated Presidents" medal	70 mm	Silver	Serial numbers 1–1,000; reverse: names of presidents
K-65-14	"Three Presidents" medal, Germany	40 mm	.1000 fine silver	Reverse: "For Peace and Liberty"
K-65-14A	"Three Presidents" medal, Germany	30 mm	.1000 fine silver	Reverse: "For Peace and Liberty"
K-65-15	JFK college charm	16 mm	Sterling silver	Reverse: college seal
K-65-15A	JFK college charm	16 mm	Sterling silver with a blue background	Reverse: college seal
K-65-15B	JFK college school key	9 mm	Sterling silver with an enameled border	
K-65-15C	JFK college school key	9 mm	Sterling silver	Antique school jewelry
K-65-16	North American Studies Award medal, Barcelona, Spain	38 mm	Silver	
K-65-17	JFK-Churchill memorial medal, England	25 mm	.999 fine silver	Four struck; reverse: bust of JFK
K-65-17A	JFK-Churchill memorial medal, England	25 mm	Copper	Four struck; reverse: bust of JFK
K-65-17B	JFK-Churchill memorial medal, England	25 mm	Aluminum	Four struck; reverse: bust of JFK
K-65-18	Wendell's JFK memorial medal	39 mm	Oxidized bronze	New reverse die: wreath and quote with Wendell removed
K-65-18A	Wendell's JFK memorial medal	39 mm	Nickel silver	500 struck; new reverse die: wreath and quote with Wendell removed
K-65-19	"JFK Lucky Play" money, 1 dollar	44 mm	Dark brown plastic	Reverse: "Lucky Play Dollar $"
K-65-20	BSA "JFK Camporee Bethlehem" area patc	76 1/5 x 31 1/4 mm	Blue background with gold edge	Reverse: plain
K-65-21	JFK memorial medal, England	22 mm	18K gold, 7 3/10 g.	
K-65-22	Warner Williams JFK galvano	279 2/5 mm diameter	Plaster	Unique; uniface
K-65-23	"JFK-Jacqueline Kennedy Marsch Oberwangen 1965" march medal	40 mm	.925 fine silver	Huguenin Le Locle with ribbon; uniface; reverse: stippled
K-65-24	Wheaton Coin Club Dupage Coin Festival wooden mint set	152 2/5 x 114 3/10 mm	Wood	Six pieces in the set; serial number on the reverse of the identity mint tag
K-66-1	"Medallic Portraits of JFK" medal	38 mm	Aluminum	Serial number 1–1,000; reverse: "Good for Trade"
K-66-1A	"Medallic Portraits of JFK" medal	38 mm	Goldine	Six struck for presentation
K-66-1B	"Medallic Portraits of JFK" medal	38 mm	Aluminum	No serial number; reverse: "Good for Trade"
K-66-2	"A Father's Love" medal	26 mm	Bronze	
K-66-3	Kennedy Memorial Peace Forest medal, Israel	59 mm	Bronze	12,000 struck; reverse: memorial column
K-66-3A	Kennedy Memorial Peace Forest medal, Israel	59 mm	.999 fine silver	3,000 struck; serial number; reverse: memorial column
K-66-3B	Kennedy Memorial Peace Forest medal, Israel	35 mm	.999 fine silver	5,000 struck; serial number; reverse: memorial column
K-66-3C	Kennedy Memorial Peace Forest medal, Israel	35 mm	22K gold	2,000 struck; serial number; reverse: memorial column
K-66-3D	Kennedy Memorial Peace Forest medal, Israel	23 mm	22K gold	2,000 struck; serial number; reverse: memorial column
K-66-3E	Kennedy Memorial Peace Forest medal, Israel	23 mm	Platinum	50 struck with a serial number, 50 struck without a serial number; reverse: memorial column
K-66-4	Kennedy Memorial Peace Forest medal, Israel	38 mm	.999 fine silver	10,000 struck; serial number; reverse: JFK Memorial
K-66-4A	Kennedy Memorial Peace Forest medal, Israel	57 mm	.999 fine silver	5,000 struck; serial number; reverse: JFK Memorial
K-66-4B	Kennedy Memorial Peace Forest medal, Israel	38 mm	24K gold	2,000 struck; serial number; reverse: JFK Memorial
K-66-4C	Kennedy Memorial Peace Forest medal, Israel	57 mm	24K gold	250 struck; serial number; reverse: JFK Memorial
K-66-4D	Kennedy Memorial Peace Forest medal, Israel	38 mm	Platinum	100 struck; serial number; reverse: JFK Memorial
K-66-5	Kennedy Memorial Peace Forest shell, Israel	69 mm	Brass	Uniface
K-66-6	Jack Meccariello elongated U.S. cent	35 x 20 mm	Bronze	173 rolled
K-66-6A	Jack Meccariello elongated U.S. cent	35 x 20 mm	Steel	15 rolled
K-66-6B	Jack Meccariello elongated U.S. nickel		Standard coin composition	13 rolled
K-66-6C	Jack Meccariello elongated U.S. dime		Standard coin composition	12 rolled

K-66-6D	Jack Meccariello elongated U.S. quarter		Standard coin composition	Ten rolled
K-66-6E	Jack Meccariello elongated Kennedy half dollar		Standard coin composition	Ten rolled
K-66-6F	Jack Meccariello elongated dollar coin		Standard coin composition	Five rolled
K-66-6G	Jack Meccariello elongated coin, blank		Aluminum	Blank; Seven rolled
K-66-6H	Jack Meccariello elongated coin, blank		Lead	Blank; Five rolled
K-66-6I	Jack Meccariello elongated token		Aluminum	36 rolled
K-66-6J	American Heritage elongated U.S. cent	37 x 20 mm	Bronze	1,003 rolled; reverse: rifle and star
K-66-6K	Jack Meccariello store card, U.S. cent	39 x 20 mm	Bronze	105 rolled; reverse: "We Buy Sell"
K-66-6L	Jack Meccariello store card, U.S. cent	39 x 20 mm	Steel	16 rolled
K-66-6M	Jack Meccariello store card, U.S. nickel		Standard coin composition	Ten rolled
K-66-6N	Jack Meccariello store card, U.S. dime		Standard coin composition	Ten rolled
K-66-6O	Jack Meccariello store card, U.S. quarter		Standard coin composition	Ten rolled
K-66-6P	Jack Meccariello store card, Kennedy half dollar		Standard coin composition	Ten rolled
K-66-6Q	Jack Meccariello store card, dollar coin		Standard coin composition	One rolled
K-66-6R	Jack Meccariello store card, dollar coin		Aluminum	39 rolled
K-66-6S	Designer's initials elongated U.S. cent	39 x 21 mm	Bronze	107 rolled
K-66-6T	The Peace Ship elongated U.S. cent	36 x 20 mm	Bronze	1,001 rolled
K-66-7	Kennedy Memorial Peace Forest simulated elongated coin	35 x 21 mm	White metal	15 rolled; reverse: minute man
K-66-8	Our Lady of the Skies Chapel shell, Italy	62 mm	Brass	Sold at the JFK Airport; uniface
K-66-9	California state-fair pin with Hong Kong JFK medal	30 mm	Gold-anodized aluminum	Purple ribbon; reverse: JFK quote
K-66-10	Friends of the Kennedy Center medal	38 mm	22K gold plating on bronze	Reverse: Kennedy Center, D.C.
K-66-11	"JFK Bidingen German Peoples" march medal	26 mm	.899 fine silver	Looped; reverse: "3. International Bidingen" dated 1966
K-66-12	JFK Airport DEA U.S. Customs wallet badge	37 x 25 mm	Goldine	Alligator pinback; uniface
K-66-13	JFK hand-carved bust, Spain	127 x 127 mm	Ivory with a gold-plated wood frame and convex glass	
K-66-14	JFK School of Government Harvard lapel pin	22 mm	Goldine with black, red, and white cloisonné	Spike with push pin lock
K-67-1	"50th Anniversary of JFK's Birth" medal, France	68 mm	Bronze	50 struck; reverse: "50th Anniversary"
K-67-1A	"50th Anniversary of JFK's Birth" medal, France	68 mm	Gold-plated bronze	50 struck; reverse: "50th Anniversary"
K-67-1B	"50th Anniversary of JFK's Birth" medal, France	68 mm	.950 fine silver	50 struck; reverse: "50th Anniversary"
K-67-1C	"50th Anniversary of JFK's Birth" medal, France	68 mm	Silver-plated Bronze	50 struck; reverse: "50th Anniversary"
K-67-1D	"50th Anniversary of JFK's Birth" medal, 1968 date, France	68 mm	Bronze	50 replacements struck; reverse: "50th Anniversary"
K-67-1E	"50th Anniversary of JFK's Birth" medal, 1968 date, France	68 mm	Gold-plated bronze	50 replacements struck; reverse: "50th Anniversary"
K-67-1F	"50th Anniversary of JFK's Birth" medal, 1968 date, France	68 mm	.950 fine silver	50 replacements struck; reverse: "50th Anniversary"
K-67-1G	"50th Anniversary of JFK's Birth" medal, 1968 date, France	68 mm	Silver-plated Bronze	50 replacements struck; reverse: "50th Anniversary"
K-67-2	"Wendell's 50th Birthdate" medal	38 mm	Aluminum	2,500 struck; reverse: wreath, "50th"
K-67-2A	"Wendell's 50th Birthdate" medal	38 mm	Antique bronze	500 struck; reverse: wreath, "50th"
K-67-2B	"Wendell's 50th Birthdate" medal	38 mm	Golden bronze	500 struck; reverse: wreath, "50th"
K-67-2C	"Wendell's 50th Birthdate" medal	38 mm	.999 fine silver	25 struck; reverse: wreath, "50th"
K-67-3	Nebraska JFK College medal	34 mm	Goldine	400 struck; reverse: JFK College
K-67-3A	Nebraska JFK College medal	34 mm	Oxidized bronze	600 struck; reverse: JFK College
K-67-3B	Nebraska JFK College medal	34 mm	Nickel silver	1,000 struck; reverse: JFK College
K-67-3C	Nebraska JFK College medal	34 mm	Sterling silver	150 struck; reverse: JFK College
K-67-3D	Nebraska JFK College medal	34 mm	Oxidized silver	15 struck; reverse: JFK College
K-67-4	Kennedy High School senior prom 1967 medal	27 mm	Goldine	200 struck; reverse: "Senior Prom"
K-67-5	Satellite JFK commemorative medal	34 mm	Bronze	Reverse: JFK quote
K-67-5A	Satellite JFK commemorative medal	34 mm	.999 fine silver	Serial numbers 1–1,000; reverse: JFK quote
K-67-6	JFK "Prominent American" series 13-cent stamp	64 x 76 mm	.999 fine silver, copper finish	Uniface
K-67-6A	JFK "Prominent American" series 13-cent stamp	64 x 76 mm	Silver plated, oxidized finish	Uniface
K-67-6B	JFK "Prominent American" series 13-cent stamp	64 x 76 mm	24K gold over copper, Proof	Five struck; uniface

K-67-7	Kennedy National Life Insurance medal with hyphen	39 mm	Antique silver plating	2,000 struck; reverse: eternal flame
K-67-7A	Kennedy National Life Insurance medal with hyphen	39 mm	Golden bronze	2,000 struck; reverse: eternal flame
K-67-7B	Kennedy National Life Insurance medal with semicolon	39 mm	Antique silver and bronze	Reverse: eternal flame
K-67-7C	Kennedy National Life Insurance medal with semicolon	39 mm	Antique silver plating	Reverse: eternal flame
K-67-8	"Miccosukee Tribe Treaty" medal	39 mm	.999 fine silver, Proof	401 struck; reverse: eagle in flight
K-67-8A	"Miccosukee Tribe Treaty" medal	39 mm	.925 fine silver, Proof	602 struck; reverse: eagle in flight
K-67-8B	"Miccosukee Tribe Treaty" medal	39 mm	Franklin bronze, Proof	801 struck; reverse: eagle in flight
K-67-8C	"Miccosukee Tribe Treaty" medal, mint run	39 mm	Franklin bronze	2,740 struck; reverse: eagle in flight
K-67-9	WRR JFK torch has been passed good-luck token	33$\frac{1}{2}$ mm	Aluminum	Reverse: good luck
K-67-10	Franklin Mint presidential series JFK medal	39 mm	Sterling silver, Proof	2,525 struck; reverse: eagle on shield
K-67-11	Franklin Mint Gilroy Roberts JFK fine-art plaque	495$\frac{3}{10}$ x 368$\frac{3}{10}$ mm	Wood-mounted silver, 31 Troy oz.	50 created; $750 issue price; serial number; uniface
K-67-12	Chase Commemorative Society JFK medal	38 mm	.999 fine silver	Reverse: glow from fire
K-67-13	JFK-K. Adenauer tribute medal, Netherlands	50 mm	Silver	Reverse: K. Adenauer
K-67-14	Trafford Realty Kennedy Space Center medal	32 mm	Goldine	Reverse: "50 Years of Service"
K-67-15	JFK stamp first-day issue Boston medal with Germany	34$\frac{1}{5}$ mm	Brass	First day of issue; edge marked with German
K-67-16	Miami Medals Cape Kennedy medal	38 mm	Bronze	Reverse: vehicle building
K-67-16A	Miami Medals Cape Kennedy medal	38 mm	Cupronickel	Reverse: vehicle building
K-67-16B	Miami Medals Cape Kennedy medal	38 mm	Silver	100 struck; reverse: vehicle building
K-67-16C	Miami Medals Cape Kennedy medal, wording changed	38 mm	Bronze	Reverse: vehicle building
K-67-16D	Miami Medals Cape Kennedy medal, wording changed	38 mm	Cupronickel	Reverse: vehicle building
K-67-17	Chris Mueller Disneyland JFK galvano	304$\frac{4}{5}$ mm		Blank
K-67-18	JFK-Andy Wilkison medal, Spain	76$\frac{1}{5}$ mm		Reverse: inscribed 11 lines
K-67-19	"JFK-Gedenk Lauf Walk Cross Square" medal, Germany	40 x 44 mm	Bronze with .800 fine silver insert	Reverse: "4 Int. Volks Undwald-Lauf-Bidin-gen"
K-67-20	WRR "JFK Birth and Death Date" good-luck token	33$\frac{1}{2}$ mm	Aluminum	Reverse: American flag in the center
K-67-21	"Ich Bin Ein Berliner" flame JFK medal	39 mm	Silvered bronze	Reverse: eternal flame, "Ich Bin Ein Berliner"
K-67-22	"Ask Not" JFK eternal flame medal	39 mm	Silvered bronze	Reverse: eternal flame and "Ask Not" credo
K-67-23	Angelo Rosato elongated Proof set with Kennedy half dollar	152$\frac{2}{5}$ x 88$\frac{9}{10}$ mm		Rolled on a U.S. Mint coin set; reverse: JFK bust over eternal flame
K-68-1	Kennedy Whiskeytown memorial medal	39 mm	Golden bronze	5,000 struck
K-68-1A	Kennedy Whiskeytown memorial medal	39 mm	Nickel silver	300 struck; serial number 1–300
K-68-1B	Kennedy Whiskeytown memorial medal	39 mm	Oxidized bronze	Unique
K-68-2	JFK-RFK Whiskeytown medal	39 mm	Golden bronze	Reverse: RFK
K-68-2A	JFK-RFK Whiskeytown medal	39 mm	Nickel silver	300 struck; serial numbers 1–300; reverse: RFK
K-68-3	American Airlines Kennedy sports memorial medal	140 mm	Bronze-plated zinc alloy	25,000 struck; hole for hanging
K-68-3A	American Airlines Kennedy sports memorial medal	140 mm	Bronze-plated zinc alloy	First issue removed
K-68-4	"50th Anniversary of JFK Assassination" medal	30 mm	Silver	Reverse: eagle on globe
K-68-5	"JFK Birthplace" medal	37$\frac{1}{2}$ mm	Nickel silver	Unlimited; reverse: Beal St. house
K-68-5A	"JFK Birthplace" medal	37$\frac{1}{2}$ mm	.999 fine silver	Serial number on the edge; reverse: Beal St. house
K-68-6	Kennedy brothers medal, Italy	32 mm	Silver-plated brass	Looped
K-68-7	"The Kennedys" jugate medal	32 mm	Silver-plated brass	Reverse: Pope John
K-68-8	"Two Martyrs" medal, Germany	32 mm	Silver-plated brass	Reverse: eagle
K-68-9	JFK-RFK "Martyrs to Freedom" medal	32 mm	Silver-plated brass	Reverse: Statue of Liberty
K-68-9A	JFK-RFK "Martyrs to Freedom" medal	32 mm	Brass	Unfinished trial strike; no loop; reverse: Statue of Liberty
K-68-9B	JFK-RFK "Martyrs to Freedom" medal	32 mm	Silver-plated brass	Looped; reverse: Statue of Liberty
K-68-9C	JFK-RFK "Martyrs to Freedom" medal, final die trim	32 mm	Brass	Unfinished trial strike; no loop; reverse: Statue of Liberty
K-68-10	JFK-RFK-MLK medal	32 mm	Silver-plated brass	Looped; reverse: MLK
K-68-10A	JFK-RFK-MLK medal	32 mm	Gold-plated brass	Looped; reverse: MLK
K-68-10B	RFK-MLK tribute medal	32$\frac{7}{10}$ mm	Silver-plated brass	Looped; reverse: MLK
K-68-11	JFK-RFK liberty medal, Germany	60 mm	.1000 fine silver, Proof	Reverse: Statue of Liberty
K-68-11A	JFK-RFK liberty medal, Germany	30 mm	.1000 fine silver	Reverse: Statue of Liberty
K-68-11B	JFK-RFK liberty medal, Germany	60 mm	.986 fine gold	Thick planchet; serial numbers 1–100; reverse: Statue of Liberty
K-68-11C	JFK-RFK liberty medal, Germany	60 mm	.986 fine gold	Regular planchet; serial numbers 1–150; reverse: Statue of Liberty
K-68-11D	JFK-RFK liberty medal, Germany	60 mm	.986 fine gold	Thin planchet; serial numbers 1–250; reverse: Statue of Liberty
K-68-11E	JFK-RFK liberty medal, Germany	30 mm	.986 fine gold	Reverse: Statue of Liberty
K-68-11F	JFK-RFK liberty medal, Germany	23 mm	.986 fine gold	Reverse: Statue of Liberty
K-68-11G	JFK-RFK liberty medal, Germany	18 mm	.986 fine gold	Reverse: Statue of Liberty
K-68-11H	JFK-RFK liberty medal, Venezuela	50 mm	.900 fine gold	Reverse: Statue of Liberty
K-68-11I	JFK-RFK liberty medal, Venezuela	30 mm	.900 fine gold	Reverse: Statue of Liberty
K-68-11J	JFK-RFK liberty medal, Venezuela	21 mm	.900 fine gold	Reverse: Statue of Liberty

K-68-11K	JFK-RFK liberty medal, Venezuela	14 mm	.900 fine gold	Reverse: Statue of Liberty
K-68-11L	JFK-RFK liberty medal, Venezuela	50 mm	.999 fine silver	Reverse: Statue of Liberty
K-68-12	JFK-RFK elongated Kennedy half dollar	47 x 30 mm	Silver-clad	Standard Kennedy half dollar reverse
K-68-12A	JFK-RFK elongated Kennedy half dollar medal	47 x 30 mm	Brass planchet	Kennedy half dollar die
K-68-12B	JFK-RFK elongated Kennedy half dollar medal	47 x 30 mm	Aluminum planchet	Kennedy half dollar die
K-68-13	"The Three Martyrs" medal, Netherlands	30 mm	Silver	Reverse: eagle on globe
K-68-14	JFK-RFK "In Memoriam" medal, Germany and France	34 mm	Goldine	Reverse: eagle
K-68-14A	JFK-RFK "In Memoriam" medal, Germany and France	34 mm	.999 fine silver	Reverse: eagle
K-68-14B	JFK-RFK "In Memoriam" medal, Germany	36 mm	Gold plated	Beaded edge; reverse: eagle
K-68-14C	JFK-RFK "In Memoriam" medal, Germany	50 mm	.999 fine silver	Reverse: eagle
K-68-14D	JFK-RFK "In Memoriam" medal, France	15½ mm	24K gold	Reverse: eagle
K-68-14E	JFK-RFK "In Memoriam" medal, Germany	20 mm	24K gold	Reverse: eagle
K-68-14F	JFK-RFK "In Memoriam" medal, France	21¹¹⁄₁₀ mm	24K gold	Reverse: eagle
K-68-14G	JFK-RFK "In Memoriam" medal, Germany and France	26 mm	Gold	Reverse: eagle
K-68-14H	JFK-RFK "In Memoriam" medal, Germany	34 mm	Gold, 16 g.	Reverse: eagle
K-68-14I	JFK-RFK "In Memoriam" medal, France	34 mm	Gold, 17 g.	Reverse: eagle
K-68-14J	JFK-RFK "In Memoriam" medal, Germany	34 mm	Gold, 30 g.	Reverse: eagle
K-68-14K	JFK-RFK "In Memoriam" medal, Germany	50 mm	Gold	Reverse: eagle
K-68-14L	JFK-RFK "In Memoriam" medal, Germany	34 mm	.999 fine silver	Reverse: eagle
K-68-15	JFK-RFK-MLK "United by Death" medal	35 mm	Sterling silver	Reverse: eternal flame
K-68-15A	JFK-RFK-MLK "United by Death" medal	23 mm	.900 fine gold	Reverse: eternal flame
K-68-15B	JFK-RFK-MLK "United by Death" medal	28 mm	.900 fine gold	Reverse: eternal flame
K-68-15C	JFK-RFK-MLK "United by Death" medal	35 mm	.900 fine gold	Reverse: eternal flame
K-68-16	JFK-RFK key-chain medal	38 mm	Aluminum	10,000 struck; looped; reverse: JFK
K-68-16A	JFK-RFK key-chain medal	38 mm	Zinc	10,100 struck; looped; reverse: JFK
K-68-17	Bavarian Mint JFK-RFK tribute medal	40 mm	Silver	Reverse: eagle
K-68-17A	Bavarian Mint JFK-RFK tribute medal	20 mm	Gold	Reverse: eagle
K-68-17B	Bavarian Mint JFK-RFK tribute medal	26 mm	Gold	Reverse: eagle
K-68-17C	Bavarian Mint JFK-RFK tribute medal	32 mm	Gold	Reverse: eagle
K-68-17D	Bavarian Mint JFK-RFK tribute medal	40 mm	Gold	Reverse: eagle
K-68-17E	Bavarian Mint JFK-RFK tribute medal	50 mm	Gold	Regular planchet; reverse: eagle
K-68-17F	Bavarian Mint JFK-RFK tribute medal	50 mm	Gold	Thick planchet; reverse: eagle
K-68-17G	Bavarian Mint JFK-RFK tribute medal	60 mm	Gold	Regular planchet; reverse: eagle
K-68-17H	Bavarian Mint JFK-RFK tribute medal	60 mm	Gold	Thick planchet; reverse: eagle
K-68-18	Rheingold JFK-RFK medal, Germany	30 mm	.900 fine gold	Reverse: six-bar cross
K-68-18A	Rheingold JFK-RFK medal, Germany	26 mm	.900 fine gold	Reverse: six-bar cross
K-68-18B	Rheingold JFK-RFK medal, Germany	22½ mm	.900 fine gold	Reverse: six-bar cross
K-68-18C	Rheingold JFK-RFK medal, Germany	20 mm	.900 fine gold	Reverse: six-bar cross
K-68-18D	Rheingold JFK-RFK medal, Germany	15½ mm	.900 fine gold	Reverse: six-bar cross
K-68-18E	Rheingold JFK-RFK medal, Germany	13 mm	.900 fine gold	Reverse: six-bar cross
K-68-18F	Rheingold JFK-RFK medal, Germany	22½ mm	.585 fine gold	Reverse: six-bar cross
K-68-18G	Rheingold JFK-RFK medal, Germany	20 mm	.585 fine gold	Reverse: six-bar cross
K-68-18H	Rheingold JFK-RFK medal, Germany	15½ mm	.585 fine gold	Reverse: six-bar cross
K-68-18I	Rheingold JFK-RFK medal, Germany	13 mm	.585 fine gold	Reverse: six-bar cross
K-68-18J	Rheingold JFK-RFK medal, Germany	30 mm	.333 fine gold	Reverse: six-bar cross
K-68-18K	Rheingold JFK-RFK medal, Germany	26 mm	.333 fine gold	Reverse: six-bar cross
K-68-18L	Rheingold JFK-RFK medal, Germany	22½ mm	.333 fine gold	Reverse: six-bar cross
K-68-18M	Rheingold JFK-RFK medal, Germany	20 mm	.333 fine gold	Reverse: six-bar cross
K-68-18N	Rheingold JFK-RFK medal, Germany	15½ mm	.333 fine gold	Reverse: six-bar cross
K-68-18O	Rheingold JFK-RFK medal, Germany	13 mm	.333 fine gold	Reverse: six-bar cross
K-68-18P	Rheingold JFK-RFK medal, Germany	10 mm	.333 fine gold	Reverse: six-bar cross
K-68-18Q	Rheingold JFK-RFK medal, Germany	20 mm	.900 fine gold	Reverse: walking Liberty
K-68-19	"The Kennedys" medal, Switzerland	33 mm	.925 fine sterling silver	Reverse: RFK
K-68-19A	"The Kennedys" medal, Switzerland	33 mm	.900 fine gold	12,000 struck; reverse: RFK
K-68-20	JFK-RFK memorial medal, France	64 mm	Bronze	Reverse: "Peace and Justice"
K-68-20A	JFK-RFK memorial medal, France	64 mm	Silver	Reverse: "Peace and Justice"
K-68-21	Ettore Maggi "The Kennedys" medal, Italy	32 mm	Silver-plated brass	Looped; reverse: RFK
K-68-22	Ettore Maggi "The Kennedys-Pope John" medal	32 mm	Silver-plated brass	Reverse: RFK
K-68-23	Emilio Senesi "The Kennedys" medal	32 mm	Silver-plated brass	Reverse: RFK
K-68-24	"Two Kennedys, Two Popes" medal, Italy	32 mm	Silver-plated brass	Looped; two popes
K-68-25	JFK-RFK-Pope John medal, Italy	32 mm	Silver-plated brass	Looped; reverse: "Ave Maria"
K-68-25A	JFK-RFK and Ave Maria medal	32 mm	Silver-plated brass	Looped; reverse: "Ave Maria"
K-68-26	Josef Preissler "The Kennedys" memorial medal	26 mm	Antique silver finish	Looped
K-68-26A	Josef Preissler "The Kennedys" memorial medal	30 mm	Antique silver finish	No loop
K-68-27	Paul Kramer Kennedy pendant	45 mm	Silver	Looped
K-68-28	Kennedy High School "Class of 1968" medal	35 mm	Gold-anodized aluminum	Reverse: "Senior Prom"
K-68-28A	Kennedy High School "Class of 1968" medal	35 mm	Blue-anodized aluminum	Reverse: "Senior Prom"
K-68-28B	Kennedy High School "Class of 1969" medal	35 mm	Wooden nickels	Reverse: "Senior Prom"

K-68-29	JFK-RFK souvenir charm spin photo bubble	32 mm	Brass and plastic	Spins
K-68-30	JFK-MLK souvenir charm spin photo bubble	32 mm	Brass and plastic	Spins
K-68-31	JFK-RFK-MLK souvenir charm spin photo bubble	32 mm	Brass and plastic	Spins
K-68-32	JFK-RFK "Brothers United" charm	14 x 17 mm	.925 fine sterling silver	Reverse: dates
K-68-33	"The Brothers Kennedy" medal	29½ mm	Base metal, gold finish	Looped; reverse: "They Gave"
K-68-33A	"The Brothers Kennedy" medal	29½ mm	Antique bronze	Looped; reverse: "They Gave"
K-68-33B	"The Brothers Kennedy" medal	29½ mm	Chrome finish	Looped; reverse: "They Gave"
K-68-33C	"The Brothers Kennedy" medal	29½ mm	Bright gold finish	Looped; reverse: "They Gave"
K-68-33D	"The Brothers Kennedy" medal	23³/₁₀ mm	Bright gold finish	Looped; reverse: "They Gave"
K-68-34	JFK-RFK "They Died for America" key-chain tag	37 mm	Black plastic, gold-colored foil	Reverse: plain
K-68-35	Kennedy memorial medal, Italy	30 mm	Silver-plated bronze	Reverse: RFK
K-68-36	King Kennedy memorial medal, Italy	30 mm	Silver-plated bronze	Reverse: MLK
K-68-37	RFK memorial medal, Canada	39 mm	Nickel silver	Reverse: "He Saw Wrong" quote
K-68-37A	RFK memorial medal, Canada	39 mm	Golden bronze	Reverse: "He Saw Wrong" quote
K-68-38	Goldey Philatelic Society medal	39 mm	Aluminum	No serial number; reverse: "End of Terror" quote
K-68-38A	Goldey Philatelic Society medal	39 mm	Antique bronze	100 struck; serial number; reverse: "End of Terror" quote
K-68-38B	Goldey Philatelic Society medal	39 mm	Golden bronze	100 struck; serial number; reverse: "End of Terror" quote
K-68-39	Goldey Philatelic Society medal	39 mm	Golden bronze	100 struck; serial number; reverse: 15 names
K-68-39A	Goldey Philatelic Society medal	39 mm	Golden bronze	No serial number; reverse: 15 names
K-68-39B	Goldey Philatelic Society medal	39 mm	Silver	First known in 2013; no serial number; reverse: 15 names, including Penn Jones Jr.
K-68-40	Goldey Philatelic Society medal	39 mm	Golden bronze	100 struck; serial number; reverse: 17 names
K-68-40A	Goldey Philatelic Society medal	39 mm	Antique bronze	No serial number; reverse: 17 names
K-68-41	Goldey Philatelic Society medal	39 mm	Golden bronze	No serial number; reverse: "Some Men" quote
K-68-42	Goldey Philatelic Society medal	39 mm	Golden bronze	No serial number; reverse: USS JFK and CV-67 information
K-68-42A	Goldey Philatelic Society medal	39 mm	Golden bronze	100 struck; serial number; reverse: USS JFK and CV-67 information
K-68-43	JFK embossed coin, Ireland	31 mm	Golden bi-metal	Reverse: "Eire 1968"
K-68-44	Embossed Kennedy half dollar charm	35 mm	Silver base metal, cast	Looped
K-68-44A	Embossed Kennedy half dollar charm	35 mm	Golden base metal, cast	Looped
K-68-45	"SV Bidingen Kennedy Lauf Bidingen" march medal, type 2	30 x 37 mm	.800 fine silver	Gold and black ribbon; reverse: light stippling
K-68-46	JFK-RFK-MLK "For Peace and Justice" medal	50 mm	Silver over bronze	Reverse: Lincoln Memorial
K-68-47	Knights of Columbus 86th convention JFK memorial chalice badge	29 x 57 mm	Bronze, gold finish	Red and white ribbon; reverse: Blackinton
K-68-47A	Knights of Columbus 86th convention JFK memorial chalice badge		Gold-plated bronze, embeded in Lucite	Universal view; convention of August 20–22, 1968, in California
K-68-48	JFK-RFK "Gebrüder Gedachtnismarsch" medal	43 x 46 mm	Bronze rim with gold finish, silver medal	Reverse: Bear, 1968, "Meitinger Herbstmarsch"
K-68-48A	JFK-RFK "Gebrüder Gedachtnismarsch" medal	43 x 46 mm	Bronze rim with gold finish, bronze medal	Reverse: Bear, 1968, "Meitinger Herbstmarsch"
K-68-49	JFK-RFK "Königsland Aschbach" march medal	50 mm	Silver with gold rim	Reverse: U.S. Seal
K-68-50	JFK-RFK-MLK tribute medal with chain	49 mm	Polished gold finish	Reverse: MLK and quote
K-68-51	Huguenin Médailleurs RFK march medal	44 mm	.925 fine silver with gold rim	Ribbon; obverse: RFK facing left; reverse: stippled, Huguenin Le Locle
K-68-52	"Kennedy Gedenkmarsch" JFK-RFK memorial march, Germany	50 mm	Antique silvered bronze	Red and blue ribbon; reverse: coat of arms
K-68-53	Hughes House JFK-RFK tribute medal	39 mm	.999 fine silver	Serial number; obverse: JFK; reverse: RFK
K-68-53A	Hughes House JFK-RFK tribute medal	39 mm	Antique silvered bronze	Obverse: JFK; reverse: RFK
K-68-53B	Hughes House JFK-RFK tribute medal	39 mm	Antique bronze	Obverse: JFK; reverse: RFK
K-68-53C	Hughes House JFK-RFK tribute medal	39 mm	Goldine	Obverse: JFK; reverse: RFK
K-68-53D	Hughes House JFK-RFK tribute medal	39 mm	Aluminum	Obverse: JFK; reverse: RFK
K-68-54	Franklin Mint presidential series JFK medal	32 mm	Sterling silver, Proof	1,088 struck; reverse: eagle on shield
K-68-54A	Franklin Mint presidential series JFK medal	26 mm	Sterling, prooflike	19,942 struck; changed reverse
K-68-54B	Franklin Mint presidential series JFK medal	26 mm	Platinum, prooflike	32 struck; changed reverse
K-68-54C	Franklin Mint presidential series JFK medal, mint run	26 mm	Bronze	1,377,324 struck; changed reverse
K-68-55	Belgium JFK-RFK tribute medal	31½ mm	Bronze	Uniface
K-68-56	RFK Medical Center security fabric patch	95¼ x 101³/₅ mm	White background with silver and black letters	Reverse: plain
K-68-57	Jack Gladfelter souvenir Kennedy half dollar	108 x 63½ mm	Wood	Serial number; reverse: six-line legend, dated 1968
K-68-58	JFK-RFK "Gedenkmarsch Wangen b/O" medal, Switzerland	45 mm	Silver with gold rim	Red and white ribbon; hallmark: Heuri-Welschenrohr
K-68-59	Huguenin Médailleurs JFK-RFK tribute medal, Switzerland	40 mm	.999 fine silver	Jugated bust; reverse: JFK RFK

K-68-60	JFK-RFK memorial medal, Germany	35⁷/₁₀ mm	Silver	Obverse: JFK-RFK facing right; reverse: eagle breaking a chain
K-68-60A	JFK-RFK memorial medal, Argentina	35 mm	Silver	Die variety; obverse: JFK-RFK facing right; reverse: eagle breaking a chain
K-68-61	JFK-RFK memorial medal, Germany	44¹/₅ mm	Nickel silver	Uniface; obverse: JFK-RFK facing right; reverse: stippled
K-68-62	JFK-RFK medal, Germany	21 mm	.999 fine silver, Proof	Obverse: JFK-RFK facing each other; reverse: shield and liberty
K-68-63	JFK-RFK "Angel on Shoulder" memorial medal	29 mm	Goldine	Reverse: open Bible
K-68-63A	JFK-RFK "Angel on Shoulder" memorial medal	29 mm	Goldine	Reverse: open Bible with initials BG
K-68-64	JFK-RFK memorial jewelry medal, Germany	15¹/₂ mm	Gold, possibly .585 fine	Reverse: six-bar cross
K-68-65	JFK-RFK "To Seek a Newer World" medal, Italy	26 mm	Silver	Reverse: Senate and presidential seals
K-68-66	JFK-RFK walking Liberty memorial medal, Germany	38 mm	Silver	Reverse: walking Liberty
K-68-67	JFK-RFK headless Liberty memorial medal, Germany	26 mm	Silver	Reverse: in memoriam
K-68-68	JFK-RFK In Memoriam Dallas" medal, Germany	30²/₅ mm	Silver	Reverse: seated Liberty with flag
K-68-69	Rheingold JFK-RFK memorial medal, Germany	30 mm	.999 fine silver, Proof	Reverse: six-bar cross
K-68-70	JFK-RFK double eagle coin memorial medal	36 mm	Silver	Standard double eagle reverse
K-68-71	JFK-RFK "World Leaders" medal	35¹/₅ mm	Silver	Obverse: JFK-RFK facing left; reverse: eagle breaking a chain
K-68-72	JFK-RFK "Brothers United" medal	28¹/₂ mm	Bronze	Uniface
K-68-72A	JFK-RFK "Brothers United" medal, Puerto Rico	28¹/₂ mm	Bronze	Reverse: Puerto Rico advertisement
K-68-72B	JFK-RFK "Brothers United" medal, Florida Police	28¹/₂ mm	Bronze	Reverse: New London Lodge
K-68-73	JFK-RFK memorial medal, Rhode Island	30¹/₂ mm	Silvered base metal	Looped; reverse: RFK
K-68-73A	JFK-RFK memorial medal, Rhode Island	38 mm	Bronze	No loop; hole for chain; reverse: RFK
K-68-74	JFK-RFK "Death-Date Only" Kennedy half dollar, copy	30³/₅ mm	Silver	Reeded edge; reverse: RFK
K-68-75	JFK-RFK "Great Patriots" key-chain tag medal	32 mm	Gold-anodized aluminum with silver rim	Reverse: St. Christopher
K-68-76	JFK-image wooden 1968 half dollar	38 mm	Wood	Uniface
K-68-77	JFK-Lincoln 1968 U.S. cent	19 mm	Bronze	Reverse: Lincoln Memorial
K-68-78	JFK-RFK high-relief tribute medal	30 mm	Silvered base metal	Looped; reverse: RFK with dates
K-68-79	JFK-RFK medalette	32¹/₂ mm	Brass	Looped; reverse: RFK with legend around the portrait
K-68-80	JFK-RFK duel portrait "In Memory of" key chain tag	39 mm	Brass	Looped; reverse: two olive branches
K-68-81	Presidential Arts JFK-RFK duel set	38 mm (each)	Bronze, mounted in black fold-up stand	Standard PAM JFK memorial medal and PAM RFK memorial medal; struck by Medallic Art
K-69-1	Franklin Mint "175th Anniversary of the U.S. Half Dollar" medal	39 mm	Goldine	Reverse: Lady Liberty
K-69-2	JFK Tunnel, Antwerp medal, Belgium	70 mm	Bronze	500 struck; reverse: four shields
K-69-3	Franklin Mint presidential series JFK mini-medal, mint run	10 mm	Sterling silver	88,750 struck; changed from large size
K-69-3A	Franklin Mint presidential mini medal set	10 mm	Sterling silver	Changed from large size
K-69-4	Karen Worth Apollo 11 JFK medal	63 mm	.999 fine silver	10,000 struck; reverse: JFK face and quote
K-69-5	Cape Kennedy launching site medal	39 mm	.999 fine silver	Serial number; reverse: vehicle assembly building
K-69-6	Gerald Steinberg JFK "Man on Moon" medal	31 mm	Bronze	Serial number; reverse: "I Believe" quote
K-69-6A	Gerald Steinberg JFK "Man on Moon" medal	31 mm	Bronze	No serial number; reverse: "I Believe" quote
K-69-6B	Gerald Steinberg JFK "Man on Moon" medal	31 mm	Sterling silver	Serial number; reverse: "I Believe" quote
K-69-7	JFK-RFK 200 francs guineens, Republic of Guinea	30 mm	.999 fine silver	Reverse: elephant, shield
K-69-8	Apollo "JFK Quote" medal	32 mm	Bronze	Reverse: "We Choose the Moon"
K-69-9	"Man's First Lunar Landing" JFK medal, Canada	38²/₅ mm	.999 fine silver	Hallmark; reverse: JFK and rocket
K-69-9A	"Man's First Lunar Landing" JFK medal, Canada	38²/₅ mm	Bronze	Reverse: JFK and rocket
K-69-10	JFK-MLK-Einstein "Tribute to the 20th Century", Germany	40 mm	Cupronickel	Plain edge; reverse: "Man on Moon XX"
K-69-11	JFK High School junior prom "Class of '70" token	39 mm	Gold-anodized aluminum	Reverse: The Rivergate, April 11, 1969
K-69-11A	JFK High School junior prom "Class of '70" token	39 mm	Blue-anodized aluminum	Reverse: The Rivergate, April 11, 1969
K-69-12	Apollo 11 commemorative medal, Venezuela	30 mm	.900 fine gold	Reverse: rocket and capsule
K-69-12A	Apollo 11 commemorative medal, Venezuela	30 mm	Bronze	Unique; reverse: rocket and capsule
K-69-13	Kennedy half dollar stamp set, Ras al-Khaima	69⁴/₅ x 69⁴/₅ mm	Gold Foil	500 sets were made, 18 gold-foil stamps in the set
K-69-13A	Kennedy half dollar stamp set, Ras al-Khaima	69⁴/₅ x 69⁴/₅ mm	Silver Foil	500 sets were made, 18 silver-foil stamps in the set
K-69-14	JFK-RFK "Gedenkmarsch 1969" march, Germany	50 mm	Silver over bronze	Red and blue ribbon; reverse: coat of arms, DJK-SG-Ellwangen
K-69-15	JFK-RFK "Liberty for All" key-chain tag medal	32²/₅ mm	Brass	Looped; reverse: Statue of Liberty
K-69-16	Democratic Party of Michigan RFK memorial tie tac	22 mm	Base metal	
K-69-17	JFK "Gedenk-Lauf" medal, Germany	30 x 26 mm	.800 fine silver	Yellow and black ribbon; reverse: "Rettenmaier Schw.gmünd"
K-69-18	Apollo 11 "JFK In This Decade" medal	35 mm	Nickel silver	Reverse: "Dream Fulfilled", Apollo 11 mission
K-69-19	JFK-RFK Swiss popular march	45 mm	Bronze-luster patina, high polish with gold rim	Red, white, and blue ribbon; uniface; reverse: P. Kramer, Neuchatel
K-69-20	Murano JFK sulphide paperweight, Italy	81 x 55 mm	Sulphide figure in fine glass with yellow overlay	Smooth bottom

K-70-1	Lombardo peace medal, Canada	39 mm	Bronze, antique finish	Reverse: peace sign
K-70-1A	Lombardo peace medal, Canada	39 mm	Bronze	Serial numbers 1–3,000; reverse: peace sign
K-70-1B	Lombardo peace medal, Canada	39 mm	Silver	Serial numbers 1–3,000; reverse: peace sign
K-70-1C	Lombardo peace medal, Canada	39 mm	Aluminum	No serial number; reverse: peace sign
K-70-2	JFK-RFK memorial march medal, Switzerland	40 mm	Silver	Reverse: stippled
K-70-3	John Roberts Society JFK Peace Corps medal	50 mm	Bronze	Reverse: dove and people
K-79-3A	John Roberts Society JFK Peace Corps medal	50 mm	.999 fine silver	Reverse: dove and people
K-70-4	Franklin Mint-American Express presidential series JFK medal	39 mm	Sterling silver, prooflike	60,709 struck; reverse: eagle and shield
K-70-5	Ohio state Special Olympics medal	56 mm	Bronze	Reverse: Kennedy Foundation
K-70-6	"JFK Assassinated, LBJ Sworn In" medal	45 mm	Golden bronze Fm	Reverse: Texas under six flags
K-70-7	JFK-RFK "Volksmarsch Brigels 1970" march medal, Switzerland	44 mm	Silver, polished outer ring	Insert medal; reverse: stippled
K-70-8	Ralph Menconi Apollo 12 moon landing medal	63 mm	Bronze	Reverse: ocean of storms
K-70-8A	Ralph Menconi Apollo 12 moon landing medal	63 mm	.999 fine silver	10,000 struck; serial number; reverse: "Ocean of Storms"
K-70-9	Numint JFK-Jules Verne Apollo 12 medal	50 mm	.925 fine silver	Reverse: JFK and planets
K-70-10	Franklin Mint "Landmarks of America Cape Kennedy" medal	26 mm	Aluminum	Reverse: map of the USA, no Sunoco
K-70-10A	Franklin Mint "Landmarks of America Cape Kennedy" medal	26 mm	Aluminum	Reverse: map of the USA, Sunoco added
K-70-10B	Franklin Mint "Landmarks of America Cape Kennedy" medal	26 mm	Bronze	Prize set; 100,000 made; reverse: map of the USA, Sunoco added
K-70-11	JFK-RFK 1000-francs coin, Republic of Guinea	17 mm	.900 fine gold, 4 g.	Reverse: Guinea coat of arms
K-70-12	1963 Kennedy half dollar replica medal, Spain	20 mm	18K gold	Stylized reverse
K-70-13	JFK Foundation dinner medal, England			Reverse: legend, September 8, 1970
K-70-14	JFK-K. Adenauer-R.Schuman "Freindschafismarsch 1970" medal	55 x 39 mm	Bronze and pewter	Red and blue ribbon; uniface; reverse: stippled
K-70-15	"10th Anniversary of Independence" JFK 300-francs coin, Chad	42 mm	.925 fine silver, Proof	504 struck in Brussels; obverse: JFK and moon; reverse: map of Africa
K-71-1	JFK Center for the Performing Arts dedicatory medal	62 mm	Bronze, 1/10 filled with 14K gold	Reverse: JFK Center for the Performing Arts building
K-71-1A	JFK Center for the Performing Arts dedicatory medal	62 mm	.999 fine silver	Serial number 1–5,000; reverse: JFK Center for the Performing Arts building
K-71-1B	JFK Center for the Performing Arts dedicatory medal	62 mm	Gold	Given to L. Bernstein; reverse: JFK Center for the Performing Arts building
K-71-1C	JFK Center for the Performing Arts dedicatory medal, gift shop	62 mm	Bronze	Serial number; reverse: JFK Center for the Performing Arts building
K-71-1D	JFK Center for the Performing Arts dedicatory medal	42 mm	Gold-filled bronze	Serial number 1–5,000; reverse: JFK Center for the Performing Arts building
K-71-1E	JFK Center for the Performing Arts dedicatory medal	42 mm	.999 fine silver	Serial number 1–5,000; reverse: JFK Center for the Performing Arts building
K-71-1F	JFK Center for the Performing Arts dedicatory medal	42 mm	Gold-filled bronze	Unlimited; reverse: JFK Center for the Performing Arts building
K-71-1G	JFK Center for the Performing Arts dedicatory medal	42 mm	.999 fine silver	Unlimited; reverse: JFK Center for the Performing Arts building
K-71-1H	JFK Center for the Performing Arts dedicatory medal	42 mm	Bronze	Unlimited; reverse: JFK Center for the Performing Arts building
K-71-1I	C. P. Jennewein JFK relief plaque	304 4/5 mm diameter	Plaster	Unique
K-71-2	Lincoln Mint "Performing Arts" medal	45 mm	.999 fine silver	Serial number 1–5,000; reverse: various arts
K-71-3	Amherst College Theatre Festival JFK medal	64 mm	Bronze	Reverse: comedy and tragedy masks, winner's name engraved
K-71-3A	Amherst College Theatre Festival JFK medal	64 mm	Silver	Looped; reverse: comedy and tragedy masks, winner's name engraved
K-71-3B	Amherst College Theatre Festival JFK medal	64 mm	Gold	Looped; reverse: comedy and tragedy masks, winner's name engraved
K-71-3C	Amherst College Theatre Festival JFK medal, dated 1972	64 mm	Bronze	Serial number; no loop; reverse: Amherst Oil Co., winner's name engraved
K-71-4	Osborne JFK Center for the Performing Arts medal, type 1 obverse	28 mm	Goldine	Looped; reverse: building
K-71-4A	Osborne JFK Center for the Performing Arts key-chain tag, type two obverse	28 mm	Goldine	Looped; obverse: dates by head; reverse: building
K-71-5	JFK Center for the Performing Arts medallet	24 mm	Sterling silver	Looped; reverse: plain
K-71-6	Silco JFK Center souvenir charm	20 mm	Sterling silver	Looped; reverse: sterling
K-71-7	Rosecraft JFK Center souvenir shield charm	18 x 16 mm	Enameled sterling silver	Looped; reverse: sterling
K-71-8	JFK Center half dollar holder, encased	47 mm	Lucite with black lettering	Looped with eye screw
K-71-9	Silberne JFK Center souvenir key-chain tag	38 mm	Brass with a gold and white background	34 mm insert
K-71-9A	Silberne JFK Center souvenir key-chain tag	38 mm	Brass	Blue disc; looped; 34 mm insert
K-71-9B	Silberne JFK Center souvenir key-chain tag	38 mm	Brass	Red disc; looped; 34 mm insert
K-71-10	Wendell's JFK Center souvenir	39 mm	Goldine	Reverse: Building with clouds
K-71-11	"U.S. Conference of Mayors 38th Annual Meeting" JFK token	39 mm	Sterling silver	700 struck; obverse: JFK; reverse: City Hall

K-71-12	Knights of Columbus "JFK Council" Manship bust 15 cent coin	28 3/10 mm	Brass	Reverse: 15 cents
K-71-13	Lincoln Mint "The Inauguration" medal	39 mm	.999 fine silver	Serial number: JFK event information
K-71-13A	Lincoln Mint "The Inauguration" medal	39 mm	Sterling silver	Reverse: JFK event information
K-71-13B	Lincoln Mint "The Inauguration" medal	39 mm	Bronze	Reverse: JFK event information
K-71-13C	Lincoln Mint "The Inauguration" medal	39 mm	Gold over sterling silver	Reverse: JFK event information
K-71-14	Lincoln Mint "Boyhood of a Legend" medal	39 mm	.999 fine silver	Reverse: JFK event information
K-71-14A	Lincoln Mint "Boyhood of a Legend" medal	39 mm	Sterling silver	Reverse: JFK event information
K-71-14B	Lincoln Mint "Boyhood of a Legend" medal	39 mm	Bronze	Reverse: JFK event information
K-71-14C	Lincoln Mint "Boyhood of a Legend" medal	39 mm	Gold over sterling silver	Reverse: JFK event information
K-71-15	Lincoln Mint "Cuban Missile Crisis" medal	39 mm	.999 fine silver	Reverse: JFK event information
K-71-15A	Lincoln Mint "Cuban Missile Crisis" medal	39 mm	Sterling silver	Reverse: JFK event information
K-71-15B	Lincoln Mint "Cuban Missile Crisis" medal	39 mm	Bronze	Reverse: JFK event information
K-71-15C	Lincoln Mint "Cuban Missile Crisis" medal	39 mm	Gold over sterling silver	Reverse: JFK event information
K-71-16	Lincoln Mint "Visit to the Vatican" medal	39 mm	.999 fine silver	Reverse: JFK event information
K-71-16A	Lincoln Mint "Visit to the Vatican" medal	39 mm	Sterling silver	Reverse: JFK event information
K-71-16B	Lincoln Mint "Visit to the Vatican" medal	39 mm	Bronze	Reverse: JFK event information
K-71-16C	Lincoln Mint "Visit to the Vatican" medal	39 mm	Gold over sterling silver	Reverse: JFK event information
K-71-17	Lincoln Mint "Advisor and Brother" medal	39 mm	.999 fine silver	Reverse: JFK event information
K-71-17A	Lincoln Mint "Advisor and Brother" medal	39 mm	Sterling silver	Reverse: JFK event information
K-71-17B	Lincoln Mint "Advisor and Brother" medal	39 mm	Bronze	Reverse: JFK event information
K-71-17C	Lincoln Mint "Advisor and Brother" medal	39 mm	Gold over sterling silver	Reverse: JFK event information
K-71-18	Lincoln Mint "The Great TV Debates" medal	39 mm	.999 fine silver	Reverse: JFK event information
K-71-18A	Lincoln Mint "The Great TV Debates" medal	39 mm	Sterling silver	Reverse: JFK event information
K-71-18B	Lincoln Mint "The Great TV Debates" medal	39 mm	Bronze	Reverse: JFK event information
K-71-18C	Lincoln Mint "The Great TV Debates" medal	39 mm	Gold over sterling silver	Reverse: JFK event information
K-71-19	Lincoln Mint "Jacqueline Bouvier Kennedy" medal	39 mm	.999 fine silver	Reverse: JFK event information
K-71-19A	Lincoln Mint "Jacqueline Bouvier Kennedy" medal	39 mm	Sterling silver	Reverse: JFK event information
K-71-19B	Lincoln Mint "Jacqueline Bouvier Kennedy" medal	39 mm	Bronze	Reverse: JFK event information
K-71-19C	Lincoln Mint "Jacqueline Bouvier Kennedy" medal	39 mm	Gold over sterling silver	Reverse: JFK event information
K-71-20	Lincoln Mint "A Giant Step into Space" medal	39 mm	.999 fine silver	Reverse: JFK event information
K-71-20A	Lincoln Mint "A Giant Step into Space" medal	39 mm	Sterling silver	Reverse: JFK event information
K-71-20B	Lincoln Mint "A Giant Step into Space" medal	39 mm	Bronze	Reverse: JFK event information
K-71-20C	Lincoln Mint "A Giant Step into Space" medal	39 mm	Gold over sterling silver	Reverse: JFK event information
K-71-21	Lincoln Mint "His Party's Choice" medal medal	39 mm	.999 fine silver	Reverse: JFK event information
K-71-21A	Lincoln Mint "His Party's Choice" medal medal	39 mm	Sterling silver	Reverse: JFK event information
K-71-21B	Lincoln Mint "His Party's Choice" medal medal	39 mm	Bronze	Reverse: JFK event information
K-71-21C	Lincoln Mint "His Party's Choice" medal medal	39 mm	Gold over sterling silver	Reverse: JFK event information
K-71-22	Lincoln Mint "Culture in the White House" medal	39 mm	.999 fine silver	Reverse: JFK event information
K-71-22A	Lincoln Mint "Culture in the White House" medal	39 mm	Sterling silver	Reverse: JFK event information
K-71-22B	Lincoln Mint "Culture in the White House" medal	39 mm	Bronze	Reverse: JFK event information
K-71-22C	Lincoln Mint "Culture in the White House" medal	39 mm	Gold over sterling silver	Reverse: JFK event information
K-71-23	Lincoln Mint "Senator from Massachusetts" medal	39 mm	.999 fine silver	Reverse: JFK event information
K-71-23A	Lincoln Mint "Senator from Massachusetts" medal	39 mm	Sterling silver	Reverse: JFK event information
K-71-23B	Lincoln Mint "Senator from Massachusetts" medal	39 mm	Bronze	Reverse: JFK event information
K-71-23C	Lincoln Mint "Senator from Massachusetts" medal	39 mm	Gold over sterling silver	Reverse: JFK event information
K-71-24	Lincoln Mint "With Khrushchev in Vienna" medal	39 mm	.999 fine silver	Reverse: JFK event information
K-71-24A	Lincoln Mint "With Khrushchev in Vienna" medal	39 mm	Sterling silver	Reverse: JFK event information
K-71-24B	Lincoln Mint "With Khrushchev in Vienna" medal	39 mm	Bronze	Reverse: JFK event information
K-71-24C	Lincoln Mint "With Khrushchev in Vienna" medal	39 mm	Gold over sterling silver	Reverse: JFK event information
K-71-25	Lincoln Mint "Congressman from Boston" medal	39 mm	.999 fine silver	Reverse: JFK event information
K-71-25A	Lincoln Mint "Congressman from Boston" medal	39 mm	Sterling silver	Reverse: JFK event information
K-71-25B	Lincoln Mint "Congressman from Boston" medal	39 mm	Bronze	Reverse: JFK event information
K-71-25C	Lincoln Mint "Congressman from Boston" medal	39 mm	Gold over sterling silver	Reverse: JFK event information
K-71-26	Lincoln Mint "Sharing of a Dream" medal	39 mm	.999 fine silver	Reverse: JFK event information
K-71-26A	Lincoln Mint "Sharing of a Dream" medal	39 mm	Sterling silver	Reverse: JFK event information
K-71-26B	Lincoln Mint "Sharing of a Dream" medal	39 mm	Bronze	Reverse: JFK event information
K-71-26C	Lincoln Mint "Sharing of a Dream" medal	39 mm	Gold over sterling silver	Reverse: JFK event information
K-71-27	Lincoln Mint "Ambassador to the World" medal	39 mm	.999 fine silver	Reverse: JFK event information
K-71-27A	Lincoln Mint "Ambassador to the World" medal	39 mm	Sterling silver	Reverse: JFK event information
K-71-27B	Lincoln Mint "Ambassador to the World" medal	39 mm	Bronze	Reverse: JFK event information
K-71-27C	Lincoln Mint "Ambassador to the World" medal	39 mm	Gold over sterling silver	Reverse: JFK event information
K-71-28	Lincoln Mint "Addressing the United Nations" medal	39 mm	.999 fine silver	Reverse: JFK event information
K-71-28A	Lincoln Mint "Addressing the United Nations" medal	39 mm	Sterling silver	Reverse: JFK event information
K-71-28B	Lincoln Mint "Addressing the United Nations" medal	39 mm	Bronze	Reverse: JFK event information
K-71-28C	Lincoln Mint "Addressing the United Nations" medal	39 mm	Gold over sterling silver	Reverse: JFK event information
K-71-29	Lincoln Mint "Caroline and JFK Jr." medal	39 mm	.999 fine silver	Reverse: JFK event information
K-71-29A	Lincoln Mint "Caroline and JFK Jr." medal	39 mm	Sterling silver	Reverse: JFK event information
K-71-29B	Lincoln Mint "Caroline and JFK Jr." medal	39 mm	Bronze	Reverse: JFK event information

K-71-29C	Lincoln Mint "Caroline and JFK Jr." medal	39 mm	Gold over sterling silver	Reverse: JFK event information
K-71-30	Lincoln Mint "Blueprint for Reason and Peace" medal	39 mm	.999 fine silver	Reverse: JFK event information
K-71-30A	Lincoln Mint "Blueprint for Reason and Peace" medal	39 mm	Sterling silver	Reverse: JFK event information
K-71-30B	Lincoln Mint "Blueprint for Reason and Peace" medal	39 mm	Bronze	Reverse: JFK event information
K-71-30C	Lincoln Mint "Blueprint for Reason and Peace" medal	39 mm	Gold over sterling silver	Reverse: JFK event information
K-71-31	Lincoln Mint "Harvard cum laude" medal	39 mm	Silver	Reverse: JFK event information
K-71-31A	Lincoln Mint "Harvard cum laude" medal	39 mm	Sterling silver	Reverse: JFK event information
K-71-31B	Lincoln Mint "Harvard cum laude" medal	39 mm	Bronze	Reverse: JFK event information
K-71-31C	Lincoln Mint "Harvard cum laude" medal	39 mm	Gold over sterling silver	Reverse: JFK event information
K-71-32	Lincoln Mint "Profiles in Courage" medal	39 mm	.999 fine silver	Reverse: JFK event information
K-71-32A	Lincoln Mint "Profiles in Courage" medal	39 mm	Sterling silver	Reverse: JFK event information
K-71-32B	Lincoln Mint "Profiles in Courage" medal	39 mm	Bronze	Reverse: JFK event information
K-71-32C	Lincoln Mint "Profiles in Courage" medal	39 mm	Gold over sterling silver	Reverse: JFK event information
K-71-33	Lincoln Mint "Bay of Pigs" medal	39 mm	.999 fine silver	Reverse: JFK event information
K-71-33A	Lincoln Mint "Bay of Pigs" medal	39 mm	Sterling silver	Reverse: JFK event information
K-71-33B	Lincoln Mint "Bay of Pigs" medal	39 mm	Bronze	Reverse: JFK event information
K-71-33C	Lincoln Mint "Bay of Pigs" medal	39 mm	Gold over sterling silver	Reverse: JFK event information
K-71-34	Lincoln Mint "A New Leader Emerges" medal	39 mm	.999 fine silver	Reverse: JFK event information
K-71-34A	Lincoln Mint "A New Leader Emerges" medal	39 mm	Sterling silver	Reverse: JFK event information
K-71-34B	Lincoln Mint "A New Leader Emerges" medal	39 mm	Bronze	Reverse: JFK event information
K-71-34C	Lincoln Mint "A New Leader Emerges" medal	39 mm	Gold over sterling silver	Reverse: JFK event information
K-71-35	Lincoln Mint "Victory in the Primaries" medal	39 mm	.999 fine silver	Reverse: JFK event information
K-71-35A	Lincoln Mint "Victory in the Primaries" medal	39 mm	Sterling silver	Reverse: JFK event information
K-71-35B	Lincoln Mint "Victory in the Primaries" medal	39 mm	Bronze	Reverse: JFK event information
K-71-35C	Lincoln Mint "Victory in the Primaries" medal	39 mm	Gold over sterling silver	Reverse: JFK event information
K-71-36	Lincoln Mint "Medicare Promise" medal	39 mm	.999 fine silver	Reverse: JFK event information
K-71-36A	Lincoln Mint "Medicare Promise" medal	39 mm	Sterling silver	Reverse: JFK event information
K-71-36B	Lincoln Mint "Medicare Promise" medal	39 mm	Bronze	Reverse: JFK event information
K-71-36C	Lincoln Mint "Medicare Promise" medal	39 mm	Gold over sterling silver	Reverse: JFK event information
K-71-37	Lincoln Mint "A Religious Issue Resolved" medal	39 mm	.999 fine silver	Reverse: JFK event information
K-71-37A	Lincoln Mint "A Religious Issue Resolved" medal	39 mm	Sterling silver	Reverse: JFK event information
K-71-37B	Lincoln Mint "A Religious Issue Resolved" medal	39 mm	Bronze	Reverse: JFK event information
K-71-37C	Lincoln Mint "A Religious Issue Resolved" medal	39 mm	Gold over sterling silver	Reverse: JFK event information
K-71-38	Lincoln Mint "Birth of the Peace Corps" medal	39 mm	.999 fine silver	Reverse: JFK event information
K-71-38A	Lincoln Mint "Birth of the Peace Corps" medal	39 mm	Sterling silver	Reverse: JFK event information
K-71-38B	Lincoln Mint "Birth of the Peace Corps" medal	39 mm	Bronze	Reverse: JFK event information
K-71-38C	Lincoln Mint "Birth of the Peace Corps" medal	39 mm	Gold over sterling silver	Reverse: JFK event information
K-71-39	Lincoln Mint "The Kennedy Heritage" medal	39 mm	.999 fine silver	Reverse: JFK event information
K-71-39A	Lincoln Mint "The Kennedy Heritage" medal	39 mm	Sterling silver	Reverse: JFK event information
K-71-39B	Lincoln Mint "The Kennedy Heritage" medal	39 mm	Bronze	Reverse: JFK event information
K-71-39C	Lincoln Mint "The Kennedy Heritage" medal	39 mm	Gold over sterling silver	Reverse: JFK event information
K-71-40	Lincoln Mint "Rocking Chair President" medal	39 mm	.999 fine silver	Reverse: JFK event information
K-71-40A	Lincoln Mint "Rocking Chair President" medal	39 mm	Sterling silver	Reverse: JFK event information
K-71-40B	Lincoln Mint "Rocking Chair President" medal	39 mm	Bronze	Reverse: JFK event information
K-71-40C	Lincoln Mint "Rocking Chair President" medal	39 mm	Gold over sterling silver	Reverse: JFK event information
K-71-41	Lincoln Mint "Apprenticeship in Diplomacy" medal	39 mm	.999 fine silver	Reverse: JFK event information
K-71-41A	Lincoln Mint "Apprenticeship in Diplomacy" medal	39 mm	Sterling silver	Reverse: JFK event information
K-71-41B	Lincoln Mint "Apprenticeship in Diplomacy" medal	39 mm	Bronze	Reverse: JFK event information
K-71-41C	Lincoln Mint "Apprenticeship in Diplomacy" medal	39 mm	Gold over sterling silver	Reverse: JFK event information
K-71-42	Lincoln Mint "A Pledge to the Hemisphere" medal	39 mm	.999 fine silver	Reverse: JFK event information
K-71-42A	Lincoln Mint "A Pledge to the Hemisphere" medal	39 mm	Sterling silver	Reverse: JFK event information
K-71-42B	Lincoln Mint "A Pledge to the Hemisphere" medal	39 mm	Bronze	Reverse: JFK event information
K-71-42C	Lincoln Mint "A Pledge to the Hemisphere" medal	39 mm	Gold over sterling silver	Reverse: JFK event information
K-71-43	Lincoln Mint PT-109 medal	39 mm	.999 fine silver	Reverse: JFK event information
K-71-43A	Lincoln Mint PT-109 medal	39 mm	Sterling silver	Reverse: JFK event information
K-71-43B	Lincoln Mint PT-109 medal	39 mm	Bronze	Reverse: JFK event information
K-71-43C	Lincoln Mint PT-109 medal	39 mm	Gold over sterling silver	Reverse: JFK event information
K-71-44	Lincoln Mint "The 35th President" medal	39 mm	.999 fine silver	Reverse: JFK event information
K-71-44A	Lincoln Mint "The 35th President" medal	39 mm	Sterling silver	Reverse: JFK event information
K-71-44B	Lincoln Mint "The 35th President" medal	39 mm	Bronze	Reverse: JFK event information
K-71-44C	Lincoln Mint "The 35th President" medal	39 mm	Gold over sterling silver	Reverse: JFK event information
K-71-45	Lincoln Mint "November 22, 1963" medal	39 mm	Silver	Reverse: JFK event information
K-71-45A	Lincoln Mint "November 22, 1963" medal	39 mm	Sterling silver	Reverse: JFK event information
K-71-45B	Lincoln Mint "November 22, 1963" medal	39 mm	Bronze	Reverse: JFK event information
K-71-45C	Lincoln Mint "November 22, 1963" medal	39 mm	Gold over sterling silver	Reverse: JFK event information
K-71-46	Lincoln Mint "The Last March" medal	39 mm	.999 fine silver	Reverse: JFK event information
K-71-46A	Lincoln Mint "The Last March" medal	39 mm	Sterling silver	Reverse: JFK event information
K-71-46B	Lincoln Mint "The Last March" medal	39 mm	Bronze	Reverse: JFK event information

K-71-46C	Lincoln Mint "The Last March" medal	39 mm	Gold over sterling silver	Reverse: JFK event information
K-71-47	Lincoln Mint "The Eternal Flame" medal	39 mm	.999 fine silver	Reverse: JFK event information
K-71-47A	Lincoln Mint "The Eternal Flame" medal	39 mm	Sterling silver	Reverse: JFK event information
K-71-47B	Lincoln Mint "The Eternal Flame" medal	39 mm	Bronze	Reverse: JFK event information
K-71-47C	Lincoln Mint "The Eternal Flame" medal	39 mm	Gold over sterling silver	Reverse: JFK event information
K-71-48	Lincoln Mint "The New Frontier" medal	39 mm	.999 fine silver	Reverse: JFK event information
K-71-48A	Lincoln Mint "The New Frontier" medal	39 mm	Sterling silver	Reverse: JFK event information
K-71-48B	Lincoln Mint "The New Frontier" medal	39 mm	Bronze	Reverse: JFK event information
K-71-48C	Lincoln Mint "The New Frontier" medal	39 mm	Gold over sterling silver	Reverse: JFK event information
K-71-49	Franklin Mint first-ladies series Jacqueline Kennedy medal	39 mm	Sterling silver, Proof	7,373 struck; reverse: White House
K-71-50	Franklin Mint "10th-Aanniversary Peace Corps" medal	39 mm	Sterling silver	6,356 struck; reverse: events of 1961
K-71-50A	Franklin Mint "10th-Aanniversary Peace Corps" medal	39 mm	Franklin bronze	1,926 struck; reverse: events of 1961
K-71-51	Franklin Mint "Decade of Space Achievement, Cape Kennedy" medal	39 mm	Sterling silver, Proof	24,641 struck; hallmarked edge; reverse: eagle on shield
K-71-52	John Roberts Society Peace Corps medal	50 mm	.925 fine sterling silver	Reverse: dove and peace
K-71-53	Danbury Mint Postal Commemorative Society Alan Shepard medal	36 mm	.999 fine silver	Reeded edge; obverse: 1961–1971; reverse: JFK "Moon" quote, moon and earth
K-71-54	Osborne "JFK Signs Test Ban Treaty" medal	39 mm	Bronze	Reverse: JFK signs treaty
K-71-54A	Osborne "JFK Signs Test Ban Treaty" medal	39 mm	Sterling silver	Reverse: JFK signs treaty
K-71-55	Metal 2-coin stamp set, Ras al-khaima	31¼ mm	Paper back aluminum foil	Watermarked
K-71-56	Kennedy Mint JFK silver bar		.999 fine silver, 20 g.	Reverse: 20 grams silver
K-71-57	Catholic Digest JFK memorial medal, trial strike	47 mm	.925 fine silver	Untrimmed; reverse: "Ask Not" credo
K-71-57A	Catholic Digest JFK memorial medal	40 mm	Sterling silver	Very limited; reverse: John F. Kennedy and credo
K-71-58	Franklin Mint "10th Anniversary of America in Space" silver bar	23 x 45 mm	Sterling silver, 1000 g.	Reverse: mission names
K-71-59	Slidell Coin Club Mardi Gras NASA Computer Center at Cape Kennedy medal	39 mm	Bronze	Reverse: Slidell NASA Computer Center, dated 1971
K-71-60	JFK-RFK "Volksmarsch 1971" march medal	45 mm	.925 fine silver with gold rim	Black and white ribbon; reverse: Huguenin Le Locle
K-71-61	JFK flat paperweight, Belgium	76 x 102 x 89 mm	Lead crystal	Serial number; JFK portrait with signature, dated
K-71-62	JFK Center for the Performing Arts medal	39 mm	Goldine	No loop; reverse: Building with clouds
K-72-1	Knights of Columbus elongated mule cent	20½ x 38 mm	Bronze	1,000 struck; Reverse: KOC, Peace Forest
K-72-1A	Knights of Columbus elongated JFK cent	20½ x 38 mm	Bronze	1,118 struck; reverse: standard U.S. cent
K-72-1B	Knights of Columbus without JFK side burnished die	20½ x 38 mm	Bronze	
K-72-2	JFK "55th Birthday" wooden dollar	50⅘ mm	Lacquered wood	
K-72-3	U.S. Mint J. Edgar Hoover memorial medal	76 mm	Bronze	Reverse: director
K-72-4	White House Historical Association Gilroy Roberts presidential JFK medal	45 mm	Sterling silver, Proof	7,864 struck; reverse: eagle on shield
K-72-4A	White House Historical Association presidential JFK medal	45 mm	Gold on sterling silver	5,999 struck; reverse: eagle on shield
K-72-5	Franklin Mint first-ladies series Jacqueline Kennedy medal	39 mm	Sterling silver, prooflike	2,913 struck; reverse: White House
K-72-6	Franklin Mint "Postmaster of American Peace Corps" medal	38½ mm	Sterling silver, Proof	Reverse: eagle on shield
K-72-7	Hobo Kennedy half dollar	30⅗ mm	Cupronickel, Matte Finish	Reverse: eagle, Confederate smoking
K-72-8	Wittnauer JFK PT-109 medal	40 mm	Sterling silver	Serial number on rim; reverse: crossed swords
K-72-9	Wittnauer "Great American Triumphs" JFK medal	40 mm	.999 fine silver	Numbered edge
K-72-9A	Wittnauer "Great American Triumphs" JFK medal	40 mm	.925 fine silver	Numbered edge
K-72-9B	Wittnauer "Great American Triumphs" JFK medal	40 mm	Gold-plated sterling silver	Numbered edge
K-72-9C	Wittnauer "Great American Triumphs" JFK medal	40 mm	Pewter	Numbered edge
K-72-9D	Wittnauer "Great American Triumphs" JFK medal	40 mm	Bronze	Numbered edge
K-72-10	Madison Mint JFK silver collectors bar	49¾ x 29 mm	.999 fine silver, 28⅖ g.	No serial number; reverse: plain with indentation
K-72-10A	Madison Mint JFK silver collectors bar	49¾ x 29 mm	.999 fine silver, 28⅖ g.	Serial number; plain with indentation
K-72-11	JFK Physical Fitness Award medal	55 mm	Bronze	Reverse: blank for engraving
K-72-12	Wittnauer presidential signature series Arco gas card	40 mm	.925 fine silver	Serial number; reverse: eagle and JFK's signature
K-72-13	Years of Lightning key-chain medal	30½ mm	Base metal, cast	Looped; reverse: "KTLA commemorative Showing Sponsored by Harris and Frank"
K-72-13A	Years of Lightning key-chain medal	30½ mm	Base metal, cast	Looped; reverse: "WNAC-TV Commemorative Showing Sponsored by Kennedy's"
K-72-13B	Years of Lightning key-chain medal	30½ mm	Base metal, cast	Looped; reverse: "Commemorative Showing Sponsored by Blake's, 1972"
K-72-13C	Years of Lightning key-chain medal	30½ mm	Base metal, cast	Looped; reverse: "Commemorative Showing Sponsored by Hamburgers, 1972–73"
K-72-14	Rose Kennedy limited-edition Caritas anniversary plate	152⅖ mm	White porcelain china	Reverse: inscription by Rose Kennedy

K-73-1	JFK-DDE Mardi Gras doubloon	39 mm	Blue-anodized aluminum	Reverse: krewe emblem
K-73-1A	JFK-DDE Mardi Gras doubloon	39 mm	Gold-anodized aluminum	Reverse: krewe emblem
K-73-1B	JFK-DDE Mardi Gras doubloon	39 mm	Tri-color–anodized aluminum	Reverse: krewe emblem
K-73-1C	JFK-DDE Mardi Gras doubloon	39 mm	Bronze-anodized aluminum	Reverse: krewe emblem
K-73-1D	JFK-DDE Mardi Gras doubloon	39 mm	Silver-anodized aluminum	Reverse: krewe emblem
K-73-1E	JFK-DDE Mardi Gras doubloon	39 mm	.999 fine silver	Reverse: krewe emblem
K-73-1F	JFK-DDE Mardi Gras doubloon charm		Silver	Reduced size; reverse: krewe emblem
K-73-1G	JFK-DDE Mardi Gras ball-favor hexagon doubloon medal		Bright bronze	Reverse: token of youth, emblem, dated 1967
K-73-2	American Coin Club 10th-anniversary JFK memorial medal	39 mm	Goldine, heavy gauge	Reverse: ACC emblem
K-73-3	International Numismatic Agency JFK memorial medal, type 1	30 mm	.925 fine silver	Limited to 2,000; reverse: "Commander PT"
K-73-3A	International Numismatic Agency JFK memorial medal, type 1	39 mm	Bronze	Limited to 2,500; reverse: "Commander PT"
K-73-4	International Numismatic Agency JFK memorial medal, type 2	39 mm	.925 fine silver	Limited to 2,500; reverse: funeral caisson
K-73-4A	International Numismatic Agency JFK memorial medal, type 2	39 mm	Bronze	Limited to 2,500; reverse: funeral caisson
K-73-5	Silver Creations JFK bar	26 x 48 1/2 mm	.999 fine silver	4,000 struck
K-73-5A	Silver Creations JFK bar	26 x 48 1/2 mm	Gold and silver	1,000 struck
K-73-5B	Silver Creations JFK bar	26 x 48 mm	Bronze	1,000 struck
K-73-6	Medali-Craft Mint JFK 10th-anniversary bar	50 x 29 1/2 mm	.999 fine silver	2,300 struck; reverse: plain
K-73-6A	Medali-Craft Mint JFK 10th-anniversary bar	50 x 29 1/2 mm	Gold-plated .999 fine silver	200 struck; reverse: plain
K-73-7	"Kennedy Mars Someren" march medal, Netherlands	33 x 50 1/2 mm	Silver	Reverse: dated 1973
K-73-8	Colonial Mint "JFK Day of Remembrance" bar	29 x 50 mm	.999 fine silver, 28 2/5 g.	Serial number; reverse: "One ounce"
K-73-9	Franklin Mint Gilroy Roberts JFK memorial medal	51 mm	.925 fine sterling silver	Reverse: JFK walking
K-73-9A	Franklin Mint Gilroy Roberts JFK memorial medal, England	38 1/2 mm	.925 fine sterling silver	Reverse: JFK walking
K-73-10	Franklin Mint presidential JFK ingot	54 2/5 x 27 1/4 mm	Sterling silver, 64 4/5 g.	2,360 struck; reverse: eagle on shield, "1,000 grains"
K-73-11	Mini 1973 Kennedy half dollar	16 mm	Base metal, silver finish	Reverse: Presidential Seal
K-73-12	Micro-mini 1964 Kennedy half dollar	8 1/2 mm	Silver	Reverse: Presidential Seal
K-73-13	Mini Kennedy half dollar copy without date	10 3/5 mm	Base metal, silver finish	Reverse: Presidential Seal
K-73-14	Hamilton Mint "Our Greatest Americans" JFK art bar		Silver, 28 2/5 g.	Reverse: "Travel to the Stars in Peace"; "1 Oz."
K-73-15	Paul Vincze JFK memorial plaque, trial strike	110 x 155 mm	Lead	Signed etch pen
K-73-16	American Silver Editions JFK silver bar	50 x 29 mm	.999 fine silver, 28 2/5 g.	Limited edition; serial number on edge; hallmark; reverse: "one ounce .999"
K-73-17	Lincoln Mint "Great Leaders of WWII" JFK art bar		Silver, 28 2/5 g.	
K-73-18	Minimint JFK bust Bicentennial mini art bar		Sterling silver, 9 2/5 g.	Reverse: blank
K-73-19	Minimint Kennedy half dollar replica mini art bar		Sterling silver, 9 2/5 g.	Reverse: blank
K-73-20	Ceeco Mint "JFK-Nixon Debate" silver bar		Silver, 28 2/5 g.	Reverse: type 6, "1 oz."
K-73-21	Don Adams JFK elongated bar		.999 fine silver, 42 1/2 g.	200 struck by Green Duck; serial number on edge; reverse: blank
K-73-21A	Don Adams JFK elongated bar		Bronze, 28 2/5 g.	800 struck by Green Duck; serial number on edge; reverse: blank
K-73-21B	Don Adams JFK elongated U.S. nickel	37 1/2 x 22 mm	Standard coin composition	400 rolled
K-73-21C	Don Adams JFK elongated U.S. dime		Standard coin composition	Five rolled
K-73-21D	Don Adams JFK elongated U.S. cent		Copper	Five rolled
K-73-22	Washington Mint JFK silver bar		.999 fine silver, 20 g.	Reverse: George Washington and monument
K-73-23	JFK tribute key-chain tag, Asia	25 x 25 mm	Brass, red cloisonné	Holed; uniface; obverse: JFK profile
K-73-24	JFK assassination 10th-anniversary key-chain tag	33 1/2 mm	Red-anodized aluminum	Reverse: "Variety for the Nation"
K-73-24A	JFK assassination 10th-anniversary key-chain tag	33 1/2 mm	Blue-anodized aluminum	Reverse: "Variety for the Nation"
K-73-25	JFK "Outstanding Young Men of America" medal	38 mm	.999 fine silver	Reverse: "Let the Word go Forth" quote
K-73-26	JFK "Wanderfreunde Ebermannstadt Walk 1973" march medal, Germany	45 x 53 mm	Silvered bronze with silver finish, gold-plated ring	Looped; reverse: stippled
K-73-27	Ralph Menconi tribute medal	70 mm	.999 fine silver	Reverse: Menconi engraving a medal
K-73-28	Bertha Hollars JFK porcelain doll	457 1/5 mm	Porcelain	White shirt, black suit, with a necktie
K-73-29	JFK rocking chair, hand-carved	292 x 165 mm	Wood	One made; hallmark: PF; made for Bertha Hollars and her JFK doll (see K-73-28)
K-74-1	1983 ANA convention souvenir bar	28 1/2 x 50 mm	.999 fine silver	Reverse: 83 anniversary ANA
K-74-2	Mardi Gras JFK "Profiles in Courage" medal	39 mm	Gold-anodized aluminum	Reverse: krewe coat of arms
K-74-2A	Mardi Gras JFK "Profiles in Courage" medal	39 mm	Aluminum	Reverse: krewe coat of arms
K-74-2B	Mardi Gras JFK "Profiles in Courage" medal	39 mm	Green-anodized aluminum	Reverse: krewe coat of arms
K-74-2C	Mardi Gras JFK "Profiles in Courage" medal	39 mm	Purple-anodized aluminum	Reverse: krewe coat of arms

K-74-2D	Mardi Gras JFK "Profiles in Courage" medal	39 mm	Blue-anodized aluminum	Reverse: krewe coat of arms
K-74-2E	Mardi Gras JFK "Profiles in Courage" medal	39 mm	Red-anodized aluminum	Reverse: krewe coat of arms
K-74-2F	Mardi Gras JFK "Profiles in Courage" medal	39 mm	Copper-anodized aluminum	Reverse: krewe coat of arms
K-74-2G	Mardi Gras JFK "Profiles in Courage" medal	39 mm	Duel-color–anodized aluminum	Reverse: krewe coat of arms
K-74-2H	Mardi Gras JFK "Profiles in Courage" medal	39 mm	.999 fine silver	Reverse: krewe coat of arms
K-74-2I	Mardi Gras JFK "Profiles in Courage" medal	39 mm	Silver-and-gold–anodized aluminum	Reverse: krewe coat of arms in gold
K-74-3	Mardi Gras JFK "Profiles in Courage" medal, type 2	39 mm	Blue-anodized aluminum	Reverse: "Sunday Nite at the Movies"
K-74-4	JFK Youth Olympics medal	39 mm	Brass	Reverse: "Founded June 74"
K-74-5	"Kennedy-Tocht Menaldum - 5-10-15-20-35 k/18-5-1974" medal, Netherlands	33 x 44 mm	Brass	Medal is in the shape of a map; looped; reverse: plain
K-74-6	JFK-K. Adenauer-T. Heuss "Wanderfreunde Weiltal TS" march medal	55 x 39 mm	Bronze and pewter	USA-Germany colored ribbon; uniface; square loop; reverse: stippled
K-74-7	JFK "Weltfriedensmarsch" march medal, Europe	60 x 60 mm	Multi-colored enamel	Reverse: "Reu and Co. Heubach"
K-74-8	JFK charm, Europe	32 x 23 mm	Bronze	Reverse: eternal flame and "Ask Not" credo
K-74-9	JFK-Lady Liberty embossed Kennedy half dollar	31 mm	Clad	Reverse: indentation of Kennedy half dollar
K-74-10	Franklin Mint presidential JFK ingot		Sterling silver, 324 g.	960 struck
K-74-11	White House Historical Association presidential JFK medal	44 mm	Sterling silver, Proof	Reverse: eagle on shield
K-74-11A	White House Historical Association presidential JFK medal	44 mm	Gold on sterling silver	4,088 struck; reverse: eagle on shield
K-74-12	JFK trial medal	40 mm	Matte image on polished bronze	Possibly designed by Arnold Machin; uniface
K-74-13	Wittnauer presidential signature series JFK medal	40 mm	Sterling silver	Serial number on the rim; reverse: JFK's signature
K-74-14	JFK-Churchill Honorable Citizenship medal, England	38 mm	Gold-plated sterling silver	Trustees edition written on the rim
K-74-15	JFK 150-guaranies coin, Paraguay	40²/₅ mm	.999 fine silver	Reverse: wreath and star
K-74-16	Roger Williams Mint JFK silver art bar		.999 fine silver, 226⁴/₅ g.	500 struck; reverse: "8 oz."
K-74-17	Hamilton Mint JFK presidential art bar		.999 fine silver, 1 Troy oz.	Reverse: flying eagle circled by stars, "1 Troy oz."
K-74-17A	Hamilton Mint JFK presidential art bar		Gold-plated silver, 1 Troy oz.	Reverse: flying eagle circled by stars, "1 Troy oz."
K-74-18	World Mint JFK-Jacqueline Kennedy silver bar, type 2		.999 fine silver, 28²/₅ g.	Reverse: "World Mint"
K-74-19	Ultra-mini Kennedy half dollar charm	10 mm	Silver base metal	Looped; reverse: standard Kennedy half dollar
K-74-20	JFK carved-skull mohawk hobo 1974 Kennedy half dollar coin	30 mm	Copper-clad	Reverse: standard 1974 Kennedy half dollar
K-75-1	German-American Wander Club medal	46 mm	Cloisonné, antique silver finish	German-American flags ribbon; obverse: Kennedy half dollar insert
K-75-1A	German-American Wander Club medal	46 mm	Cloisonné, antique gold finish	German-American flags ribbon; obverse: Kennedy half dollar insert
K-75-2	JFK-RFK march medal, Europe	49 x 43¹/₂ mm	Antique silver finish	Yellow and blue ribbon; reverse: Willy Krafft Eupen
K-75-3	"WSV-de-Vrijbuiters-Beverwijk-JFK Wandeltocht" march medal, Holland	33 x 48¹/₂ mm	Antique silver on brass	Obverse: circle atop pyramid; looped; brass reverse: plain
K-75-4	Colonial Mint "A Day to Remember" JFK bar	29 x 50 mm	.999 fine silver	Serial number
K-75-5	JFK award medal and ribbon, Italy	26 mm	Gold finish	Obverse: wreath around JFK's head; reverse: wreath
K-75-6	JFK "80 km-Wandeltocht-S.V. de L.A.T." medal and ribbon, Holland	34 x 50 mm	Silvered bronze	Blue and white ribbon; uniface; silver reverse: plain
K-75-7	"Munich, Germany, to Houston, Texas" J.P. Kennedy Foundation run	37 mm	Silvered bronze	Ribbon with torch; reverse: "Run for the Handicapped, NCOA"
K-75-8	Franklin Mint Bicentennial "30 Great Americans" medal	63 mm	Sterling silver, 129³/₅ g.	Serial number; reverse: "We the People"
K-75-8A	Franklin Mint Bicentennial "30 Great Americans" medal	63 mm	Bronze, 129³/₅ g.	Serial number; reverse: "We the People"
K-75-9	Pacific Mint Jackie O nude silver round medal	39 mm	.999 fine silver, 28²/₅ g.	Reverse: JFK and Aristotle Onassis
K-75-9A	Pacific Mint Jackie O nude silver round medal, trial strike	39¹/₂ mm	Pewter	Reeded edge, reverse: JFK and Aristotle Onassis
K-75-10	American Mint Canaveral Space Center silver bar	54 x 27 mm	.999 fine silver	Renamed for JFK
K-75-11	Franklin Mint JFK cameo medal	12¹/₂ mm	24K gold	Reverse: White House and dates
K-75-12	Bicentennial Kennedy half dollar, error	31 mm	Standard coin composition	Double-struck reverse
K-76-1	Madison Mint presidential JFK cameo bar	29 x 50 mm	.999 fine silver	Reverse: bi-cent eagle
K-76-1A	Madison Mint presidential JFK cameo bar	29 x 50 mm	.999 fine silver	Reverse: Madison Mint logo
K-76-2	Letcher Mint "12 Great Americans" JFK medal	39 mm	24K gold on .999 fine silver	9,800 total issue sets
K-76-3	Bicentennial JFK-walking Liberty embossed Kennedy half dollar	31 mm	Clad gold plating	Reverse: indentation of JFK
K-76-4	JFK-K. Adenauer "Wanderlun" march medal	65 x 64 mm	Cloisonné flags, antique silver finish	Color twine support; reverse: plain, light stipple pattern
K-76-5	Bicentennial JFK liberty bell embossed Kennedy half dollar	31 mm	Standard coin composition	Reverse: indentation of JFK

K-76-6	Lewis King "Black Jack 1947–1976" tribute medal	45 mm	Bronze, silver finish	Uniface; reverse: plain
K-76-7	JFK Knights of Columbus Pittsburgh 14th annual 3-mile run fabric patch	76 1/5 x 82 1/2 mm	White background with blue letters and a red border	Reverse: plain
K-76-8	JFK Special Warfare Center decal	57 1/5 x 70 mm	Various colors on a black background	Reverse: plain
K-76-9	JFK Special Forces official insignia fabric patch	50 4/5 x 76 1/5 mm	Various colors with a gold border	Reverse: plain
K-76-10	Franklin Mint Freedom Foundation "Valley Forge" JFK medal	38 1/2 mm	Sterling silver, Proof	Reverse: George Washington praying
K-76-11	Franklin Mint Freedom Foundation "Valley Forge" Frost medal	38 1/2 mm	Sterling silver, Proof	Reverse: George Washington praying
K-76-12	Hamilton Mint Bicentennial JFK medal	62 mm	.999 fine silver	Reverse: 13 original state maps
K-76-12A	Hamilton Mint Bicentennial JFK medal	62 mm	Pewter	Reverse: 13 original state maps
K-76-13	Karen Worth Bicentennial presidential commemorative medal	63 1/2 mm	Bronze	Reverse: all of the presidents' names
K-76-14	Kennedy half dollar large paperweight	77 mm	Base metal	Bicentennial Kennedy half dollar
K-76-15	Franklin Mint "America Mourns" JFK assassination medal	44 mm	Bronze, Proof	Reverse: Capitol and funeral
K-76-16	Franklin Mint "One Man One Vote" Warren Commission release medal	44 mm	Bronze, Proof	Reverse: Warren Commission
K-76-17	Franklin Mint "LBJ Refuses to Run, MLK-RFK Assassinated" medal	44 mm	Bronze, Proof	Reverse: MLK-RFK shot
K-76-18	Franklin Mint "First Orbital Flight, Cuban Missile Crisis" medal	44 mm	Bronze, Proof	Reverse: Cuban Missile
K-76-19	Franklin Mint "Great TV Debates, Fall 1960" medal	44 mm	Bronze, Proof	Reverse: Nixon and JFK
K-76-19A	Franklin Mint "Great TV Debates, Fall 1960" mini-medal	12 mm	Sterling silver, Proof	Reverse: text
K-76-20	Franklin Mint "RFK-LBJ Civil Rights Signing 1964" medal	44 mm	Bronze, Proof	Reverse: "Civil Rights" text
K-76-21	Franklin Mint "Medicare Aids in Reducing Medical Cost" medal	44 mm	Bronze, Proof	Reverse: Medicare start
K-76-22	Bicentennial Kennedy Space Center "Expo on Science and Technology" medal	39 mm	Bronze	Reverse: JFK
K-76-23	Bicentennial 1975 Lincoln cent with JFK bust, trial strike	20 2/5 mm	Brass	
K-76-23A	Bicentennial 1975 Lincoln cent with JFK bust, dated 1976	21 mm	Brass	
K-76-23B	Bicentennial JFK bust, no lettering	17 3/5 mm	Sterling silver	
K-76-23C	Bicentennial mini 1964 Kennedy half dollar	17 1/2 mm	.999 fine silver	
K-76-23D	Bicentennial mini 1964 Kennedy half dollar	19 mm	Sterling silver	Octagonal background
K-76-23E	Bicentennial mini 1964 Kennedy half dollar on 1975 cent	21 mm	Copper and zinc	
K-76-24	Pacific Mint "JFK-RFK 1776–1976, a Time to Remember" memorial medal	39 mm	.999 fine silver, 28 2/5 g., Proof	Reverse: wreath and torch
K-76-25	Franklin Mint "100 Greatest Americans" #98 JFK bar	54 3/10 x 27 1/4 mm	Sterling silver	Reverse: honor America, eagle
K-76-26	"200 Years of Greatness" three presidents medal	44 2/5 mm	Bronze	Reverse: sword and quill pen
K-76-27	Kroger Bicentennial Cape Kennedy medal	40 mm	Antique bronze	10,000 struck; reverse: 12-lined legend
K-76-27A	Kroger Bicentennial Cape Kennedy medal	40 mm	.925 fine silver	50 struck; reverse: 12-lined legend
K-76-28	"Ted Kennedy for President" key-chain good-luck token	34 mm	Colored aluminum	Reverse: blank
K-76-29	Profiles in Courage cameo collection	35 x 44 1/2 mm	.925 fine silver, Proof	9 cameos; reverse: name, date, state
K-76-30	U.S. Bicentennial Kennedy half dollar, error	31 mm	Clad	Reverse: Independence Hall error
K-76-31	Numistamp Mort Reed Kennedy half dollar metal stamp	57 3/4 x 35 3/5 mm	Possibly burnished	Serial number
K-76-31A	Numistamp Mort Reed Bicentennial Kennedy half dollar metal stamp	57 3/4 x 35 3/5 mm	Burnished	Serial number
K-76-32	Knights of Equity Bicentennial JFK-J. Barry medal	38 mm	Antique bronze	Looped; reverse: "A United Ireland"
K-77-1	"Concorde First Flight to JFK, NY" medal	38 1/2 mm	Sterling silver	5,000 struck; reverse: Statue of Liberty
K-77-1A	"Concorde First Flight to JFK, NY" medal	38 1/2 mm	Gold and sterling silver	2,500 struck; reverse: Statue of Liberty
K-77-2	Franklin Mint Gilroy Roberts JFK mini-medal	12 2/5 mm	Sterling silver	Reverse: White House
K-77-3	Açores Humanitarian Services JFK medal, JFK Library	39 mm	Gold	Unique; reverse: 5-lined legend
K-77-4	JFK-RFK uniface medal	36 mm	Bronze	Uniface
K-77-5	Franklin Mint "Jacqueline Kennedy First Lady" mini medal	12 1/2 mm	Sterling silver, Proof	Reverse: White House, 1961–1963
K-78-1	U.S. Mint Hubert H. Humphrey Congressional Award medal	76 mm	Bronze	Reverse: "He Cared"
K-79-1	JFK "First International Volkswandertag TSV Hütschenhausen" march medal	57 x 92 mm	Antique pewter insert, cast metal, gold finish	Red ribbon
K-79-2	JFK Library JFK-RFK memorial medal	63 mm	Bronze	Reverse: JFK Library building
K-79-3	JFK University Award medal	76 mm	Bronze	Revolving stand; unique; obverse: same as K-63A-16; reverse: "H. Downie U.S. Steel Award 1979"
K-79-4	1979 elongated Kennedy half dollar with Lord's Prayer	42 x 31 mm	Standard coin composition	Reverse: Lord's prayer
K-79-5	PT-109 tie clasp with JFK Library inscription on bow	45 x 10 mm	Golden brass	Aligator clasp
K-80-1	"EMK for President" Madison Square Garden medal	39 1/5 mm	Bronze	Obverse: portrait only; reverse: "1980 Kennedy 4 President"
K-80-2	Empire Mint "39 Presidents" medal	33 3/5 mm	Electroplated gold	Reverse: 39 presidents names
K-80-3	American Mint JFK half-stamp medal set		Electroplated gold	Three pieces; various designs
K-80-3A	American Mint JFK half-stamp medal set medal	38 3/5 mm	Electroplated gold	Reverse: eagle and "Ask Not" credo
K-80-3B	American Mint JFK half-stamp medal set bar stamp ingot	41 1/2 x 28 mm	Electroplated-gold base metal	Reverse: blank

K-80-3C	American Mint JFK half-stamp medal set scroll quote ingot	38 x 33 mm	Electroplated-gold base metal	Reverse: blank
K-80-4	National Historical Society JFK with football pewter figure	63 1/2 mm tall	Pewter	Hallmark on the bottom
K-80-5	"20th Anniversary of Election" overstamped 1980 Kennedy half dollar	30 mm	Gold-plated copper	Reverse: standard Kennedy half dollar
K-80-6	JFK figure standing in suit, name on base reads Kennedy	63 1/2 mm tall	Polished silvered metal	No hallmark
K-80-7	JFK figure standing in suit, Walt Disney Hall of Presidents	133 2/5 mm tall	Pewter	Serial number; hallmark; reverse: signed Calhouns
K-81-1	Lombardo Mint JFK 5-cent U.S. postage-stamp art bar	39 x 24 mm	.999 fine silver	Serial number
K-81-2	Gold Standard Corporation JFK gold round medal	35 mm	.903 fine gold	Reverse: "one Troy ounce gold" in large letters
K-81-3	"39 Presidents" steel die hub		Hardened steel	Round
K-81-4	World's Smallest Coins miniature Kennedy half dollar	8 3/10 mm	Silver-colored base metal	Reverse: standard Kennedy half dollar
K-82-1	ANA 1982 JFK Library, Boston, metal pass	71 x 46 mm	Gold-anodized aluminum	Reverse: marked Italy
K-82-2	Franklin Mint "One Hundred Greatest Americans" JFK bar	27 x 54 mm	Sterling silver	Reverse: "100 Greatest" dated 1982
K-82-2A	Franklin Mint "One Hundred Greatest Americans" JFK bar	27 x 54 mm	Franklin bronze	Reverse: "100 Greatest" dated 1982
K-82-3	"STS-5 Space Shuttle 11-11-82" Kennedy Space Center, type 1	39 mm	Bronze	Reverse: small "New Era"
K-82-3A	"STS-5 Space Shuttle 11-11-82" Kennedy Space Center, type 2	39 mm	Bronze	Reverse: large "New Era"
K-82-4	Franklin Mint air and space series JFK art bar		Sterling silver, 28 2/5 g.	Serial number; reverse: "Kennedy Expands American Space Program"
K-82-5	Georgia State Exonumia Association rolled Kennedy half dollar	31 x 45 mm	Standard coin composition	Obverse: standard Kennedy half dollar
K-82-6	Maryland Token and Medal Society 3rd-rolled Kennedy half dollar	31 x 45 mm	Standard coin composition	Obverse: 1971 Kennedy half dollar
K-82-7	"German Wandertag in Memory of our 4 Fallen Presidents"	90 x 60 mm	Red, white, and blue cloisonné, cast medal with chains	Reverse: Carl Poellath name and address, U.S. map
K-82-8	Kennedy Space Center launch scene state of Florida dollar	28 mm	Nickel silver	No serial number: state of Florida seal
K-83-1	Jacki Mauviel JFK 20th-anniversary medal, France	21 mm	.999 fine silver	Reverse: presidential eagle seal
K-83-1A	Jacki Mauviel JFK 20th-anniversary medal, France	21 mm	Platinum	1,000 struck; reverse: presidential eagle seal
K-83-2	JFK International Games medal	42 mm	Silver base metal with white and black plastic insert	Red ribbon; reverse: plain
K-83-3	Franklin Mint Bicentennial "History of U.S., JFK assassination" bar #95	37 x 55 1/2 mm	Pewter	Reverse: Bicentennial symbol
K-83-4	Franklin Mint Bicentennial "History of U.S., Cuban Missile" bar	37 x 55 1/2 mm	Pewter	Reverse: Bicentennial symbol
K-83-5	"Kennedy Mars-Someren" march medal, Netherlands	45 x 62 mm	Bronze	Uniface; looped; reverse: dated 1983
K-83-6	National Historic Mint JFK 20th-anniversary assassination medal	38 3/4 mm	Silver-layered bronze	Reverse: double eagle
K-83-6A	National Historic Mint JFK 25th-anniversary medal	38 3/5 mm	Silver- and gold-plated bronze	Reverse: double eagle
K-83-7	Franklin Mint Postal Commemorative Society U.S. Mint JFK medal	33 mm	Electroplated gold over bronze	Reverse: same as K-61-7A
K-83-7A	Franklin Mint Postal Commemorative Society U.S. Mint JFK medal	33 mm	Electroplated gold over bronze	Reverse: same as K-61-7B
K-84-1	Danbury Mint JFK presidential ingot, England	25 x 51 mm	24K gold on bronze, 28 2/5 g.	Reverse: brief biography, "4 president", assassination
K-84-1A	Danbury Mint JFK presidential ingot, England	25 x 51 mm	.999 fine silver, Proof	Reverse: brief biography
K-84-1B	Danbury Mint JFK presidential ingot, England	25 x 51 mm	Bronze, Proof	Reverse: brief biography
K-84-2	Ho-Ho Art Craft JFK American flag Fairfax, VA, Lions Club pin	63 x 42 mm	Multi-colored cloisonné-enameled brass	Double pin clasp
K-84-3	JFK home medal, Belgium	60 mm	Bronze	500 struck; serial number; reverse: Belgian home
K-84-4	JFK award medal, Brazil	37 mm	Nickel silver	Reverse: mount marks V
K-84-5	National Historic Mint first lady series Jacqueline Kennedy medal	38 1/2 mm	Silver-layered bronze	Reverse: double eagle
K-84-6	Columbia Mint Kennedy half dollar, replica	Possibly 10 mm	24K gold	Reverse: eagle
K-84-7	Franklin Mint "One Hundred Greatest Americans" JFK bar	27 x 54 mm	Franklin bronze	Reverse: "100 Greatest" dated 1984
K-84-8	Kennedy Space Center rocket charm	20 mm	Sterling silver	Looped
K-85-1	Boston Mint JFK 25th-anniversary "1960–1985" medal	39 mm	Silver-layered bronze	Reverse: U.S. Capitol dome
K-85-2	National Historic Mint JFK 25th-anniversary medal, obverse dated 1985	38 3/5 mm	Silver- and gold-plated bronze	Reverse: double eagle
K-85-2A	National Historic Mint JFK 25th-anniversary medal, obverse dated 1985	38 3/5 mm	Nickel plated	Reverse: double eagle
K-85-2B	National Historic Mint JFK 25th-anniversary medal, dated 1983	38 3/5 mm		Reverse: double eagle
K-86-1	JFK Center for the Performing Arts 20th-anniversary medal	38 mm	Brass	Reverse: JFK Center for the Performing Arts building
K-86-2	Frank Gasparro "Statue of Liberty Centennial 1886–1986" JFK medal	38 mm	.925 fine silver	Reverse: Statue of Liberty
K-86-3	Franklin Mint JFK inaugural commemorative medal	70 mm	Bronze, Proof	Reverse: 25th anniversary inauguration
K-86-4	JFK "25th Anniversary of Inauguration" medal	31 3/4 mm	Nickel silver	Reverse: 25th anniversary inauguration

K-86-5	Alpha 66 "Bay of Pigs 25th Anniversary" token	30 mm		Reverse: 25th anniversary Bay of Pigs invasion
K-86-6	Arroyo Grande limited JFK tribute belt buckle	77 x 55 mm	Hard pewter	Hallmark; serial number; reverse: dated and signed
K-86-7	Statue of Liberty Kennedy half dollar overstamp	31 mm	Silver-clad with silver insert coin	Reverse: 1886–1986 coin insert on Kennedy half dollar
K-87-1	Isle of Man "Bicentennial of American Constitution" presidential medal	38 3/5 mm	Cupronickel	Reeded edge; reverse: Queen Elizabeth
K-87-2	Wooden Kennedy half dollar	40 mm	Wood	Obverse: wooden Kennedy half dollar; reverse: wooden nickel
K-87-3	"Ich Bin Ein Berliner" medal, Germany	40 mm	.999 fine silver	Reverse: Berlin shield
K-87-4	JFK "750 year anniversary of Berlin, Germany" medal	27 mm	.999 fine silver	Reverse: 750 jahre, Berlin shield
K-88-1	Magnes Museum Paul Vincze "1963–1988" JFK medal	57 mm	.999 fine silver	100 struck; reverse: JFK quote
K-88-1A	Magnes Museum Paul Vincze "1963–1988" JFK medal	57 mm	Bronze	Reverse: JFK quote
K-88-2	Franklin Mint official presidential portrait medal	38 mm	.925 fine sterling silver	Reverse: American eagle
K-88-3	Pobjoy Mint "Ich Bin Eln Berliner" 5-dollar coin, Niue	38 3/5 mm	Cupronickel	Reverse: state emblem
K-88-4	Pobjoy Mint "Ich Bin Ein Berliner" 50-dollar coin, Niue	38 3/5 mm	Sterling silver	Reverse: state emblem
K-88-4A	Pobjoy Mint "Ich Bin Ein Berliner" 100-dollar coin, Niue	65 mm	Sterling silver	Reverse: state emblem
K-88-4B	Pobjoy Mint "Ich Bin Ein Berliner" 250-dollar coin, Niue	27 mm	.916 fine gold	Reverse: state emblem
K-88-5	1988 JFK silver round		.999 fine silver, 1 Troy lb.	Reverse: Kennedy half dollar
K-88-6	Kennedy Memorial Trust Appeal medal, England	44 1/2 mm	Cupronickel	Reverse: "Ask Not" credo
K-88-7	Frank Gasparro JFK German collection tribute medal	63 mm	Sterling silver, Proof	Reverse: eagle
K-88-8	JFK German collection "Oath of Office" medal	38 3/5 mm	Sterling silver, Proof	Reverse: eagle
K-88-9	JFK German collection "Start of Space Program" medal	38 3/5 mm	Sterling silver, Proof	Reverse: eagle
K-88-10	JFK German collection JFK-MLK medal	38 3/5 mm	Sterling silver, Proof	Reverse: eagle
K-88-11	JFK German collection JFK-C. de Gaulle medal	38 3/5 mm	Sterling silver, Proof	Reverse: eagle
K-88-12	JFK German collection JFK-Khrushchev medal	38 3/5 mm	Sterling silver, Proof	Reverse: eagle
K-88-13	JFK German collection "JFK Visit to Germany" medal	38 3/5 mm	Sterling silver, Proof	Reverse: eagle
K-88-14	JFK German collection "JFK in Berlin" medal	38 3/5 mm	Sterling silver, Proof	Reverse: eagle
K-88-15	JFK German collection "JFK and the Berlin Wall" medal	38 3/5 mm	Sterling silver, Proof	Reverse: eagle
K-88-16	JFK German collection "Ich Bin Ein Berliner" medal	38 3/5 mm	Sterling silver, Proof	Reverse: eagle
K-88-17	JFK German collection "JFK Jr. Salutes" medal	38 3/5 mm	Sterling silver, Proof	Reverse: eagle
K-88-18	Republic of Panama JFK $1.00 VN Balboa coin, Germany	33 mm	Cupronickel	Reverse: eagle and shield
K-88-19	JFK Greers "Ferry Dam Dedication 25th-Anniversary" lapel pin	20 mm	Enameled	Push clasp
K-88-20	Adejaeger JFK memorial medal, Paris, France	68 mm	Silver-plated bronze	Serial numbers 1–400; reverse: JFK quote in French
K-88-21	Racine Numismatic Society "50 years 1938-1988" Kennedy half dollar	31 mm	Copper-nickel-clad	Reverse; fancy RNS lettering
K-89-1	Crown Mint "Three Kennedy Brothers" medal	39 mm	.999 fine silver, 28 2/5 g.	Reverse: presidential eagle
K-89-2	Federal Coin Fund "Presidents Bicentennial" medal		.999 fine silver, 12 Troy oz.	Reverse: president's names
K-89-3	"17 Int. Freundschafts Wanderung RVB Hohenöllen 1989" march medal	74 7/10 x 74 1/2 mm	Silvered, cast	Pin clip; Reverse: E. Adelmann Lauterecken with photo, ribbon, and flags
K-89-4	JFK-Willy Brandt "40 years German Federal Republic" medal	40 mm	.999 fine silver	Reverse: German Republic eagle, .999
K-89-4A	JFK-Willy Brandt "40 years German Federal Republic" medal	40 mm	Cupronickel	Reverse: German Republic eagle
K-89-5	JFK-Reagan-Bush-Gorbachev Berlin Wall medal	45 mm	Sterling silver over bronze	Reverse: "Ich Bin Ein Berliner"/"Tear Down This Wall"
K-89-5A	JFK-Reagan-Bush-Gorbachev Berlin Wall medal	45 mm	Bronze	Reverse: "Ich Bin Ein Berliner"/"Tear Down This Wall"
K-89-6	"The 39 Presidents of the United States" medal	39 mm	Brass	Reeded edge; reverse: U.S. Capitol, 1789–1989
K-90-1	"Ich Bin Ein Berliner" medal and stamp	65 mm	.999 fine silver	Reverse: Berlin gate
K-91-1	"Ich Bin Ein Berliner" medal, Germany	30 mm	Gilt bronze	Reverse: eagle with stars
K-91-2	JFK CV-67 aircraft carrier 5-dollar commemorative coin	39 mm	Cupronickel	Reeded edge; reverse: "Hutt River Prov."
K-91-3	JFK tribute medal, Slovenija	63 2/5 mm	Thick aluminum	Reverse: "Ask Not" credo
K-91-4	Brandenburg Gate 200 year anniversary JFK medal	40 mm	Gold, Proof	Reverse: German eagle
K-91-5	Pobjoy Mint ANA 100th-anniversary Kennedy half dollar	39 mm	Cupronickel, Proof	Reeded edge; reverse: Isle of Man
K-92-1	U.S. Mint "Bicentennial 1792–1992" medal	76 mm	High-polish bronze	Reverse: 15 U.S. coins, including the Kennedy half dollar
K-92-1A	U.S. Mint "Bicentennial 1792–1992" medal	38 mm	High-polish bronze	Reverse: 15 U.S. coins, including the Kennedy half dollar
K-92-2	Michael Gode JFK medal, type 1, Germany	30 mm	.999 fine silver	Reverse: eagle, president
K-92-3	Michael Gode JFK medal, type 2, Germany	30 mm	.999 fine silver	Reverse: eagle, death Dallas
K-92-4	Michael Gode Jacqueline and John medal, Germany	30 mm	.999 fine silver	Reverse: married Jacqueline Bouvier
K-92-5	Michael Gode JFK medal, type 3, Germany	30 mm	.999 fine silver	Reverse: eagle, Berlin visit
K-92-6	JFK memorial medal, Germany	13 1/2 mm	.585 fine gold, 1 2/5 g.	Reverse: treasure chest
K-92-7	JFK Berlin tribute medal, Germany	30 mm	Gold-plated .800 fine silver	Reverse: JFK and Berlin
K-92-8	Shell Gas presidential eight-coin set	32 mm	Brass	Reverse: 10 lines of text on JFK coin

K-93-1	"Kennedy 1993 Mars Someren" march medal	55 mm	Black plastic with bronze insert	Looped; reverse: plain
K-93-2	JFK "80 km Wien-Tulln-Krems" march medal, Austria	34 mm	Bronze	Reverse: R. Souval Wien VII
K-93-3	JFK Medical HMO Center award two-piece medal	26 mm	Bronze	Blue and white ribbon; reverse: overall over subscription
K-93-4	JFK commemorative medal, Argentina	80 mm	Bronze	Reverse: family releasing a dove
K-93-5	Pobjoy Mint "Statesmen of the World" JFK coin	32 1/4 mm	.999 fine silver, 1 2/5 g.	50,000 struck; Reverse: Republic of Liberia coat of arms
K-93-5A	Pobjoy Mint "Statesmen of the World" JFK 10-dollar coin	38 3/5 mm	.999 fine silver, 28 2/5 g.	25,000 struck; Reverse: Republic of Liberia coat of arms
K-93-5B	Pobjoy Mint "Statesmen of the World" JFK coin	65 mm	.999 fine silver, 141 4/5 g.	5,000 struck; Reverse: Republic of Liberia coat of arms
K-93-5C	Pobjoy Mint "Statesmen of the World" JFK coin	75 mm	.999 fine silver, 283 1/2 g.	5,000 struck; Reverse: Republic of Liberia coat of arms
K-93-6	JFK-Apollo 50-dollar coin, Niue	65 mm	.999 fine silver, 155 1/2 g.	Reverse: Republic of Liberia coat of arms
K-93-7	JFK-Statue of Liberty 20-dollar coin, Niue	38 3/5 mm	.925 fine sterling silver, Proof	Reverse: Niue coat of arms
K-93-8	JFK inauguration 50-dollar coin, Niue	25 mm	.583 fine gold, 7 7/10 g.	Reverse: Niue coat of arms
K-93-9	JFK "Berlin Speech" coin, Republic of Liberia	14 mm	.999 fine gold, 1 1/10 g.	15,000 struck; reverse: Republic of Liberia coat of arms
K-93-9A	JFK "Berlin Speech" coin, Republic of Liberia	18 mm	.999 fine gold, 2 4/5 g.	10,000 struck; reverse: Republic of Liberia coat of arms
K-93-9B	JFK "Berlin Speech" coin, Republic of Liberia	22 mm	.999 fine gold, 5 7/10 g.	7,500 struck; reverse: Republic of Liberia coat of arms
K-93-9C	JFK "Berlin Speech" coin, Republic of Liberia	32 mm	.999 fine gold, 14 1/5 g.	5,000 struck; reverse: Republic of Liberia coat of arms
K-93-9D	JFK "Berlin Speech" coin, Republic of Liberia	38 mm	.999 fine gold, 28 2/5 g.	2,500 struck; reverse: Republic of Liberia coat of arms
K-93-9E	JFK "Berlin Speech" coin, Republic of Liberia	50 mm	.999 fine gold, 141 4/5 g.	250 struck; reverse: Republic of Liberia coat of arms
K-93-9F	JFK "Berlin Speech" coin, Republic of Liberia	65 mm	.999 fine gold, 283 1/2 g.	250 struck; reverse: Republic of Liberia coat of arms
K-93-9G	JFK "Berlin Speech" coin, Republic of Liberia	70 mm	.999 fine gold, 425 1/5 g.	250 struck; reverse: Republic of Liberia coat of arms
K-93-9H	JFK "Berlin Speech" coin, Republic of Liberia	75 mm	.999 fine gold, 567 g.	250 struck; reverse: Republic of Liberia coat of arms
K-93-9I	JFK "Berlin Speech" coin, Republic of Liberia	80 mm	.999 fine gold, 708 7/10 g.	250 struck; reverse: Republic of Liberia coat of arms
K-93-10	JFK inaugural medal signed by Evelyn Lincoln	70 mm	Bronze	Unique; reverse: Presidential Seal
K-94-1	JFK "First Man on Moon" 10-dollar coin, Marshall Islands	34 3/5 mm	Brass, Proof	Reverse: Marshall Islands coat of arms
K-94-2	JFK inaugural 25-dollar coin, Niue	14 mm	.999 fine gold	25,000 struck; Reverse: Niue coat of arms
K-94-3	Kennedy half dollar silver round, replica	89 mm	.999 fine silver, 8 Troy oz.	Reverse: standard Kennedy half dollar
K-94-4	NY Municipal Art Society Jacqueline Kennedy Onassis Award medal	102 mm	Bronze	Unique, struck for the author; reverse: Jacqueline Kennedy Onassis anniversary award
K-94-5	1994 Kennedy half dollar with mini 1977 Kennedy half dollar	30 1/2 mm	Silver alloy with mini half dollar insert, cast	Mini Kennedy half dollar; Kennedy half dollar insert
K-95-1	JFK "A New Generation" 5-dollar coin, Marshall Islands	38 7/10 mm	Cupronickel	Reverse: Marshall Islands coat of arms
K-95-1A	JFK "A New Generation" 10-dollar coin, Marshall Islands	38 7/10 mm	Brass	Reverse: Marshall Islands coat of arms
K-95-1B	JFK "A New Generation" 50-dollar coin, Marshall Islands	38 7/10 mm	.999 fine silver, 28 2/5 g.	Reverse: Marshall Islands coat of arms
K-95-2	JFK "Meet Any Hardship" 5-dollar coin, Marshall Islands	38 7/10 mm	Cupronickel	Reverse: Marshall Islands coat of arms
K-95-2A	JFK "Meet Any Hardship" 10-dollar coin, Marshall Islands	38 7/10 mm	Brass	Reverse: Marshall Islands coat of arms
K-95-2B	JFK "Meet Any Hardship" 50-dollar coin, Marshall Islands	38 7/10 mm	.999 fine silver, 28 2/5 g.	Reverse: Marshall Islands coat of arms
K-95-3	JFK "Bear Any Burden" 5-dollar coin, Marshall Islands	38 7/10 mm	Cupronickel	Reverse: Marshall Islands coat of arms
K-95-3A	JFK "Bear Any Burden" 10-dollar coin, Marshall Islands	38 7/10 mm	Brass	Reverse: Marshall Islands coat of arms
K-95-3B	JFK "Bear Any Burden" 50-dollar coin, Marshall Islands	38 7/10 mm	.999 fine silver, 28 2/5 g.	Reverse: Marshall Islands coat of arms
K-95-4	JFK "Support Any Friend" 5-dollar coin, Marshall Islands	38 7/10 mm	Cupronickel	Reverse: Marshall Islands coat of arms
K-95-4A	JFK "Support Any Friend" 10-dollar coin, Marshall Islands	38 7/10 mm	Brass	Reverse: Marshall Islands coat of arms
K-95-4B	JFK "Support Any Friend" 50-dollar coin, Marshall Islands	38 7/10 mm	.999 fine silver, 28-2/5 g.	Reverse: Marshall Islands coat of arms
K-95-5	JFK "Oppose Any Foe" 5-dollar coin, Marshall Islands	38 7/10 mm	Cupronickel	Reverse: Marshall Islands coat of arms
K-95-5A	JFK "Oppose Any Foe" 10-dollar coin, Marshall Islands	38 7/10 mm	Brass	Reverse: Marshall Islands coat of arms
K-95-5B	JFK "Oppose Any Foe" 50-dollar coin, Marshall Islands	38 7/10 mm	.999 fine silver, 28 2/5 g.	Reverse: Marshall Islands coat of arms
K-95-6	JFK "Assure Liberty" 5-dollar coin, Marshall Islands	38 7/10 mm	Cupronickel	Reverse: Marshall Islands coat of arms
K-95-6A	JFK "Assure Liberty" 10-dollar coin, Marshall Islands	38 7/10 mm	Brass	Reverse: Marshall Islands coat of arms
K-95-6B	JFK "Assure Liberty" 50-dollar coin, Marshall Islands	38 7/10 mm	.999 fine silver, 28 2/5 g.	25,000 struck; reverse: Marshall Islands coat of arms
K-95-7	JFK "Assure the Success" die hub, Marshall Islands	63 1/4 x 54 mm	Hardened steel	Round

K-95-8	JFK "Ich Bin Ein Berliner" 20-dollar coin, Republic of Liberia	13 9/10 mm	.999 fine gold, 1 1/10 g., Proof	Reverse: Republic of Liberia coat of arms
K-95-9	1995 Kennedy half dollar silver round	89 mm	.999 fine silver, 8 Troy oz.	Reverse: standard Kennedy half dollar
K-95-10	Special Olympics Eunice Kennedy U.S. commemorative silver dollar	38 mm	.900 fine silver	Reverse: "As We Hope for the Best" Eunice Kennedy quote
K-96-1	JFK Center for the Performing Arts 25th-anniversary medal	40 mm	Bronze	Reverse: "Twenty-Fifth Anniversary"
K-96-2	Collector's Mint Kennedy half dollar, replica	89 mm	.999 fine silver, 6 Troy oz., Proof	Reverse: standard Kennedy half dollar
K-98-1	American Mint JFK commemorative medal	30 mm	.999 fine silver	20,000 struck; reverse: eagle
K-98-2	Paris Mint Jacki Mauviel JFK mememorial medal	41 mm	Cupronickel	Reeded edge; reverse: Presidential Seal
K-98-3	American Discovery JFK Arlington memorial medal	44 1/2 mm	Antique bronze	Plain edge; reverse: Casson and JFK Jr.
K-98-4	American Discovery Jacqueline Kennedy medal	44 1/2 mm	Antique bronze	Plain edge; reverse: Arlington grave site
K-98-5	U.S. Mint JFK-RFK commemorative Matte coin set	31 mm and 40 mm	Silver Matte Finish	Reverse: standard coin
K-98-6	JFK 50-mile hike medal	68 mm	Polished nickel silver	Red, white, and blue ribbon; looped; reverse: blank for engraving
K-98-7	U.S. commemorative Uncirculated RFK silver dollar	38 mm	.900 fine silver	S mint mark; reeded edge; reverse: U.S. Senate Seal, eagle
K-98-7A	U.S. commemorative RFK silver dollar	38 mm	.900 fine silver, Proof	S mint mark; reeded edge; reverse: U.S. Senate Seal, eagle
K-98-7B	U.S. commemorative Uncirculated RFK silver and Kennedy half dollars set	38 mm and 30 mm	.900 fine silver, burnished finish	Reeded edge
K-98-7C	U.S. commemorative RFK silver dollars two-coin set	38 mm	.900 fine silver, Proof and Uncirculated	S mint mark; reeded edge; reverse: U.S. Senate Seal, eagle
K-99-1	Washington Monetary Authority JFK Jr. commemorative medal	39 mm	.999 fine silver	Reverse: John Jr. saluting
K-99-2	Caroline Bessette-Kennedy memorial medal	39 mm	.999 fine silver	Reverse: John Jr. saluting
K-99-3	JFK Jr. 10-dollar coin, Republic of Liberia	40 mm	.999 fine silver	Reverse: Republic of Liberia coat of arms
K-99-3A	JFK Jr. 5-dollar coin, Republic of Liberia	38 mm	Cupronickel	Reverse: Republic of Liberia coat of arms
K-99-4	JFK-JFK Jr. 10-dollar coin, Republic of Liberia	30 3/5 mm	.999 fine silver, 14 1/5 g.	Reverse: Republic of Liberia coat of arms
K-99-4A	JFK-JFK Jr. 250-dollar coin, Republic of Liberia		.999 fine gold, 14 1/5 g.	375 struck; reverse: Republic of Liberia coat of arms
K-99-4B	JFK-JFK Jr. 150-dollar coin, Republic of Liberia		.999 fine platinum, 7 1/10 g.	Reverse: Republic of Liberia coat of arms
K-99-5	JFK-JFK Jr. 1-dollar coin, Republic of Liberia	22 mm	.999 fine silver	Reverse: Republic of Liberia coat of arms
K-99-6	National Parks JFK pin	25 2/5 mm	Blue and gold base metal	Push-lock pin
k-99-7	JFK-K. Adenauer-Brandt "50th Anniversary of the German Republic" medal	41 mm	.999 fine silver	Reverse: map of Germany, eagle in a circle
K-2000-1	JFK tribute 20-dollar coin, Republic of Liberia	40 mm	.999 fine silver	Reverse: Republic of Liberia coat of arms
K-2000-2	JFK Air Force One 5-dollar coin, Republic of Liberia	40 mm	Cupronickel	Reverse: Republic of Liberia coat of arms
K-2000-2A	JFK Air Force One 10-dollar coin, Republic of Liberia	30 mm	.999 fine silver	20,000 struck; reverse: Republic of Liberia coat of arms
K-2000-3	JFK Jr. tribute 20-dollar coin, Republic of Liberia	39 mm	.999 fine silver	Reverse: Republic of Liberia coat of arms
K-2000-3A	JFK Jr. tribute 20-dollar coin, Republic of Liberia	39 mm	.999 fine Silver, Proof	Reverse: Republic of Liberia coat of arms
K-2000-4	JFK Jr. tribute 10-dollar coin, Republic of Liberia	37 mm	Cupronickel	Reverse: Republic of Liberia coat of arms
K-2000-5	JFK memorial 20-dollar coin, Republic of Liberia	40 mm	.999 fine silver, Proof	Reverse: Republic of Liberia coat of arms
K-2000-6	"Thirteen Days Film Cast Present" medal and 1964 Kennedy half dollar set	31 4/5 mm	Silver	Reverse: Thirteen Days
K-2000-7	"The Presidents" JFK 10-dollar coin, Republic of Liberia	33 mm	Cupronickel	Reverse: Republic of Liberia coat of arms
K-2000-8	JFK tribute 5-dollar coin, Republic of Liberia	31 1/4 mm	Cupronickel	Reverse: Republic of Liberia coat of arms
K-2000-9	JFK Jr. memorial 50-dollar coin, Republic of Liberia	40 mm	Gold	Reverse: Republic of Liberia coat of arms
K-2000-10	JFK memorial 25-dollar coin, Republic of Liberia	40 mm	.999 fine gold	Reverse: Republic of Liberia coat of arms
K-2000-11	American Historical Society JFK-Jacqueline-JFK Jr. half dollar	30 mm	Cupronickel	Reverse: standard Kennedy half dollar
K-2000-12	JFK Berlin tribute 100-dollar coin, Republic of Liberia	40 mm	.999 fine silver	Reverse: Republic of Liberia coat of arms
K-2000-13	Highland Mint JFK bullion three-medal set		Gold-plated silver, 170 1/10 g.	Reverse: 1 half lb. silver
K-2000-14	JFK tribute 25-dollar coin, Republic of Liberia	13 1/2 mm	.585 fine gold	Reeded edge; reverse: Republic of Liberia coat of arms
K-2000-15	JFK-JFK Jr. bi-metal 500-dollar coin, Republic of Liberia	88 9/10 mm	.999 fine gold and .999 fine silver, 1 Troy lb., Proof	Reverse: Republic of Liberia coat of arms
K-2000-16	Sunoco Gas 1950–2000 presidential coin series	31 1/2 mm	Golden brass	Reeded edge; reverse: Sunoco logo, 10 presidents
K-2001-1	JFK-Khrushchev-Castro medal, Republic of Liberia	40 mm	.999 fine silver	Reverse: Republic of Liberia coat of arms
K-2001-2	American Mint JFK tribute 10-dollar coin, Republic of Liberia	33 mm	Gold-plated copper, Proof	Reverse: Republic of Liberia coat of arms
K-2001-3	American Mint Jacqueline Kennedy 10-dollar coin, Republic of Liberia	33 mm	Gold-plated copper, Proof	Reverse: Republic of Liberia coat of arms

K-2001-4	Knights of Malta St. John of Jerusalem JFK medal	38 3/5 mm	24K gold, 31 1/10 g., Proof	Reverse: 5,000 liras
K-2001-5	U.S. Mint Henrietta Holsman Ford medal	70 mm	Bronze	Reverse: standard Kennedy half dollar
K-2002-1	JFK 5-cent U.S. Post Office stamp, replica		Electroplated gold over .999 fine silver	2,002 struck
K-2002-3	Jacqueline Kennedy without hat 10-dollar coin, Republic of Liberia	40 mm	Cupronickel	50,000 struck; reverse: Republic of Liberia coat of arms
K-2002-4	Jacqueline Kennedy with hat 10-dollar coin, Republic of Liberia	40 mm	Cupronickel	Reverse: Republic of Liberia coat of arms
K-2003-1	The End of Camelot JFK medal	46 4/5 mm	.999 fine silver with gold rim, 56 7/10 g.	Reverse: Ghana 200 sika
K-2003-1A	The End of Camelot JFK-Jacqueline Kennedy medal	46 4/5 mm	.999 fine silver, 56 7/10 g.	Reverse: Ghana 200 sika
K-2003-1B	The End of Camelot JFK Jr. medal	46 4/5 mm	.999 fine silver, 56 7/10 g.	Reverse: Ghana 200 sika
K-2003-2	JFK 40th-anniversary 10-dollar coin, British Virgin Islands	38 3/5 mm	Sterling silver, Proof	Reverse: Queen Elizabeth
K-2003-2A	JFK 40th-anniversary 20-dollar coin, British Virgin Islands	13 9/10 mm	Gold, Proof	Reverse: Queen Elizabeth
K-2003-2B	JFK 40th-anniversary 50-dollar coin, British Virgin Islands	18 mm	Gold, Proof	Reverse: Queen Elizabeth
K-2003-2C	JFK 40th-anniversary 100-dollar coin, British Virgin Islands	22 mm	Gold, Proof	Reverse: Queen Elizabeth
K-2003-2D	JFK 40th-anniversary 250-dollar coin, British Virgin Islands	30 mm	Gold, Proof	Reverse: Queen Elizabeth
K-2003-3	JFK "In God We Trust" 10-dollar coin, Republic of Liberia	33 mm	.999 fine silver	Reverse: Republic of Liberia coat of arms
K-2003-4	JFK 2-dollar coin, Cook Islands	30 mm	.999 fine silver	Reverse: Queen Elizabeth
K-2003-5	JFK 1-dollar coin, British Virgin Islands	38 1/2 mm	Cupronickel	Reverse: Queen Elizabeth
K-2003-6	JFK-Liberty silver round	39 mm	.999 fine silver	Reverse: JFK and U.S. Capitol
K-2003-7	JFK 10-dollar West Samoa coin, Germany	13 9/10 mm	.999 fine gold, Proof	Reverse: Samoa coat of arms
K-2003-8	JFK 25-dollar coin, Republic of Liberia	11 mm	.999 fine gold, Proof	Reverse: Republic of Liberia coat of arms
K-2003-9	University College Dublin Eunice Kennedy-Shriver medal			
K-2003-10	"Inauguration of JFK" 20-dollar coin, Republic of Liberia	40 mm	.925 fine silver, Proof	Reverse: Republic of Liberia coat of arms
K-2004-1	Knights of Malta St. John of Jerusalem JFK medal	38 3/5 mm	.999 fine silver	Reverse: 500 liras
K-2004-2	"Ask Not" JFK silver round	39 mm	.999 fine silver	Reverse: "Ask Not" credo
K-2004-3	Kuchler's Hawaii craft fair Kennedy half dollar, encased		Cupronickel with aluminum ring	Reverse: 2004 Merry Christmas
K-2004-4	JFK president 1-dollar coin, Micronesia	35 mm	Cupronickel	Reverse: federated states
K-2004-5	"America's Peace Corps Founded 1961" 20-dollar coin, Republic of Liberia	40 mm	.925 fine silver	Reverse: Republic of Liberia coat of arms, dated 2004
K-2005-1	JFK 50-mile hike medal	51 mm	Silvered bronze	No loop; reverse: plain
K-2005-2	National Capital Area Council BSA "JFK Grave" fabric patch	127 x 57 1/5 mm	Multi-colored with gold border	Reverse: plain
K-2005-3	JFK ultra mini-medal, Germany	10 mm	Gold	Reverse: eagle and rays
K-2006-1	JFK 50-mile hike medal	68 mm	Polished nickel silver	Red, white, and blue ribbon; looped; reverse: plain
K-2006-2	American Mint JFK tribute 5-dollar coin, Republic of Liberia	40 mm	Cupronickel	Obverse: photo of JFK; reverse: Republic of Liberia coat of arms
K-2006-3	American Mint JFK president medal	11 mm	.585 fine gold	Reverse: coat of arms
K-2006-4	Kennedy half dollar silver round	39 mm	.999 fine silver	Reverse: eagle
K-2006-5	JFK-W. Brandt-K. Adenauer medal, Germany	40 mm	Silver, 40 g.	Reverse: German eagle
K-2006-6	JFK 1-dollar coin, Palau	11 mm	.999 fine gold, Proof	Reverse: republic shield
K-2007-1	American Mint JFK commemorative medal	40 mm	Silver-plated copper	Reverse: eagle
K-2007-2	American Mint JFK photo commemorative coin	33 mm	Cupronickel	Reverse: eagle with portrait
K-2007-3	Charleston Mint JFK-Great Seal medal set, type 1	34 mm	Brass	Reverse: U.S. Seal
K-2007-4	Charleston Mint JFK-Great Seal medal set, type 2	28 1/2 mm	Brass	Reverse: U.S. Seal
K-2007-5	American Mint JFK inaguration (spelling error) medal	40 mm	Cupronickel	Plain edge; reverse: life and legacy
K-2007-5A	American Mint JFK inaguration (spelling error) medal	40 mm	.999 fine silver-plated copper, Proof	Reverse: life and legacy
K-2007-5B	American Mint JFK inauguration (correct spelling) medal	40 mm	Cupronickel	Plain edge; reverse: life and legacy
K-2007-5C	American Mint JFK inauguration (correct spelling) medal	40 mm	.999 fine silver-plated copper, Proof	Reverse: life and legacy
K-2007-6	Swiss Mint JFK speaker 500-tugrik coin, Mongolia	40 mm	.925 fine silver	5,000 struck; reverse: "500 torpor"
K-2007-7	JFK-Pope John commemorative medal, Italy	21 mm	.900 fine gold, 0.1166 Troy oz.	Obverse: JFK; reverse: Pope John
K-2007-8	JFK photo medal with color sticker	33 mm	Cupronickel, Proof	Reverse: stylized Presidential Seal
K-2007-9	JFK 90th birthday memorial 1-dollar coin, Palau	11 mm	Gold, Proof	Reverse: Palau coat of arms
K-2007-10	American Mint JFK nomination acceptance medal	40 mm	.999 fine silver-plated copper, Proof	Reverse: life and legacy
K-2007-10A	American Mint JFK nomination acceptance medal	40 mm	24K gold-plated copper over cupronickel	Reverse: life and legacy
K-2008-1	JFK Library Christmas ornament	58 mm	Pewter	Reverse: "© Fort"
K-2008-2	American Mint JFK commemorative medal	33 mm	Gold-toned cupronickel	Reverse: eagle
K-2008-3	American Mint JFK commemorative medal	33 mm	Gold-plated	Reverse: eagle
K-2008-4	American Mint JFK "Berlin Speech" medal	40 mm	Silver-plated copper	Reverse: life and legacy
K-2008-5	American Mint JFK "Moon Speech" medal	40 mm	Silver-plated copper	Reverse: life and legacy

K-2008-6	American Mint JFK "Oath of Office" medal	40 mm	Silver-plated copper	Reverse: "Great Leaders"
K-2008-7	American Mint JFK "A Life of Service" medal	40 mm	Silver-plated copper	Reverse: life and legacy
K-2008-7A	American Mint JFK "A Life of Service" medal	40 mm	Bronze, Proof	Reverse: life and legacy
K-2008-8	American Mint JFK commemorative gold coin	11 mm	.585 fine gold	Reverse: eagle
K-2008-9	J.D. Tippit memorial medal, type 1	38 mm	Enameled nickel silver	400 struck; rare; reverse: Dallas police badge, Officer Tippit
K-2008-10	JFK micro coin	9⁹/₁₀ mm	.585 fine gold	Reverse: eagle
K-2008-11	Cradle Rockers Playschool Fund JFK encasement	46 mm	Aluminum encasement	Reverse: 2008 Kennedy half dollar
K-2008-12	"Ich Bin Ein Berliner" 5-dollar coin, Republic of Liberia	40 mm	Cupronickel	2,000 struck; reverse: Republic of Liberia coat of arms
K-2008-13	JFK-White House motion-image medal	40 mm	Cupronickel	Reverse: stylized U.S. Seal
K-2008-14	JFK tribute medal	13 mm	.585 fine gold	Reverse: treasure chest
K-2008-15	JFK "Berlin Wall Speech" medal, Germany	40 mm	Silver-plated copper with stone inlay	Reverse: eagle and stars
K-2008-16	American Mint "JFK Naval Service" medal	40 mm	Silver-plated copper	Reverse: life and legacy
K-2008-17	Grabener Coin Press medal over 1991 Kennedy half dollar	31 mm	Clad	Reverse: Moonlight Mint, Daniel Carr
K-2008-18	American Mint JFK Cuban Missile Crisis medal	40 mm	Silver-plated copper	Reverse: life and legacy
K-2008-19	American Mint JFK "Nuclear Test Ban Treaty Signing" medal	40 mm	Silver-plated copper	Reverse: life and legacy
K-2009-1	J. Leavelle tribute medal	44 mm	Enameled pewter	800 struck; very rare; Dallas police
K-2009-2	JFK trial dollar	50 mm	24K gold overlay	Reverse: Statue of Liberty
K-2009-3	American Mint "JFK Acceptance Speech" medal	40 mm	Silver-plated copper	Reverse: life and legacy
K-2009-4	Wellington Mint bar-medal set, medal only	33½ mm	Gold-colored base metal	Reverse: "Let the Word go Forth" quote
K-2009-6	American Mint "Profiles in Courage" medal	40 mm	Silver-plated copper	Reverse: life and legacy
K-2009-7	American Mint "Civil Rights Speech" medal	40 mm	Silver-plated copper	Reverse: life and legacy
K-2009-8	American Mint JFK portrait medal	40 mm	.999 fine silver	Reverse: eagle
K-2009-9	JFK Berlin visit commemorative medal	36 mm	24K gold with silver	Reverse: German eagle
K-2009-10	American Mint JFK photo medal	33 mm	Silver-plated copper	Reverse: eagle
K-2009-11	American Mint JFK commmemorative gold coin	11 mm	.585 fine gold	Reverse: eagle
K-2009-12	JFK-K. Adenauer memorial medal	40 mm	Cupronickel	Reverse: "Binig Vaterland"
K-2009-13	JFK-White House memorial medal, China	40 mm	Gold over bronze, Proof	Obverse: JFK facing left; reverse: White House
K-2009-13A	JFK-White House memorial medal, China	40 mm	Silver over bronze, Proof	Obverse: JFK facing left; reverse: White House
K-2009-14	"America's Royal Family Father Joseph P. Kennedy" medal	40 mm	Silver-plated copper, Proof	Reverse: family tree
K-2009-14A	"America's Royal Family Mother Rose F. Kennedy" medal	40 mm	Silver-plated copper, Proof	Reverse: family tree
K-2009-14B	"America's Royal Family Son Joseph P. Kennedy Jr." medal	40 mm	Silver-plated copper, Proof	Reverse: family tree
K-2009-14C	"America's Royal Family Son John F. Kennedy" medal	40 mm	Silver-plated copper, Proof	Reverse: family tree
K-2009-14D	"America's Royal Family Son Robert F. Kennedy" medal	40 mm	Silver-plated copper, Proof	Reverse: family tree
K-2009-14E	"America's Royal Family Son Edward M. Kennedy" medal	40 mm	Silver-plated copper, Proof	Reverse: family tree
K-2009-14F	"America's Royal Family Daughter Rosemary Kennedy" medal	40 mm	Silver-plated copper, Proof	Reverse: family tree
K-2009-14G	"America's Royal Family Daughter Kathleen A. Kennedy" medal	40 mm	Silver-plated copper, Proof	Reverse: family tree
K-2009-14H	"America's Royal Family Daughter Eunice M. Kennedy" medal	40 mm	Silver-plated copper, Proof	Reverse: family tree
K-2009-14I	"America's Royal Family Daughter Patricia Kennedy" medal	40 mm	Silver-plated copper, Proof	Reverse: family tree
K-2009-14J	"America's Royal Family Daughter Jean Ann Kennedy, 2010" medal	40 mm	Silver-plated copper, Proof	Reverse: family tree
K-2009-14K	"America's Royal Family Wife Jacqueline B. Kennedy" medal	40 mm	Silver-plated copper, Proof	Reverse: family tree
K-2009-14L	"America's Royal Family Son John F. Kennedy Jr." medal	40 mm	Silver-plated copper, Proof	Reverse: family tree
K-2009-14M	"America's Royal Family Daughter Caroline B. Kennedy" medal	40 mm	Silver-plated copper, Proof	Reverse: family tree
K-2009-15	Paolo Scognamiglio Jacqueline Kennedy cameo, Italy	40 x 32 mm	Sarodonyx shell from the Bahamas	Unique; cost: $750
K-2009-16	American Mint JFK 50-dollar U.S. banknote tribute trial medal	50 mm	.99 fine silver-plated copper	
K-2010-1	"Ich Bin Ein Berliner" medal, Germany	40 mm	.999 fine silver	Reverse: Berlin shield
K-2010-2	Presidents of the USA medal, Germany	40 mm	Gold on silver	Reverse: Statue of Liberty
K-2010-3	Presidential Seal limited-edition coin	37 mm	Multi-colored enamel	500 struck; reverse: White House
K-2010-4	"Atlantis 104-STS 122" Kennedy Space Center, Florida medal	39 mm	.999 fine silver	Reverse: space design
K-2010-5	"The Kennedys An American Legacy" medal set	44 mm (each)	Bronze	Reverse: individual quotes

ID	Description	Size	Material	Notes
K-2010-5A	"The Kennedys" JFK medal (from set K-2010-5)	44 mm	Bronze	Reverse: "Ask Not" credo
K-2010-5B	"The Kennedys" RFK medal (from set K-2010-5)	44 mm	Bronze	Reverse: "Hope" quote
K-2010-5C	"The Kennedys" Edward M. Kennedy medal (from set K-2010-5)	44 mm	Bronze	Reverse: "Endures" quote
K-2010-6	"50th Anniversary of JFK's Election to President" medal, Nauru	38$\frac{3}{5}$ mm	.999 fine silver	2,000 struck; reverse: Nauru coat of arms
K-2010-7	Edward M. Kennedy memorial medal	19$\frac{1}{2}$ mm	Bronze	Uniface
K-2010-7A	Edward M. Kennedy memorial medal	28$\frac{7}{10}$ mm	Bronze	Uniface; no loop
K-2010-7B	Edward M. Kennedy memorial medal	28$\frac{7}{10}$ mm	Bronze	Uniface; looped
K-2010-8	JFK-White House memorial medal, China	40 mm	Gold over bronze, Proof	Obverse: JFK facing front; reverse: White House, Washington, D.C.
K-2010-8A	JFK-White House memorial medal, China	40 mm	Silver over bronze, Proof	Obverse: JFK facing front; reverse: White House, Washington, D.C.
K-2010-9	JPK Jr.-JFK-RFK "Fallen Heroes" medal, China	38$\frac{7}{10}$ mm	Gold over bronze, Proof	Reverse: large presidential eagle with qt.
K-2010-10	JFK photo and signature medal	40 mm	Polished goldine, Proof	Reverse: great U.S Seal
K-2010-11	JFK silver memorial portrait	39 mm	.999 fine silver, 28$\frac{2}{5}$ g., Proof	Reverse: 6 over M mint mark
K-2010-12	JFK large tribute medal with signed bust, Portugal	120 mm	Bronze, gold finish	Uniface; reverse for engraving
K-2010-13	American Mint "A Life of Service and Bravery" 50th-anniversary coin set	165 x 108 mm	24K gold-plated copper	40 mm medal; reverse: standard Kennedy half dollar, dated 2010
K-2011-1	JFK inauguration 50th-anniversary medal, JFK Library	44$\frac{3}{5}$ mm	Bronze	Plain edge; reverse: JFK 50
K-2011-2	JFK commemorative medal, Czech Republic	50 mm	.999 fine silver, Proof	1,000 struck; reverse: U.S. Capitol building
K-2011-3	American Mint JFK 50th-anniversary medal	40 mm	Silver plated	Reverse: "JFK 50th, 1917–1963"
K-2011-3A	American Mint JFK 50th-anniversary medal	40 mm	Electroplated 24K gold and cupronickel	Reverse: "JFK 50th, 35th President"
K-2011-4	USA "911 Official Freedom" medallion	39 mm	Silver	Reverse: JFK quote
K-2011-5	JFK color-photo insert medal, China	40 mm	Polished brass, Proof	Reverse: This We'll Defend" quote, eagle
K-2011-6	JFK "Fallen Hero" copper round	39 mm	Copper .999 fine	Reverse: Engraved shield
K-2011-6A	JFK "Fallen Hero" copper bar	51 x 85 mm	Copper .999 fine, 453$\frac{3}{5}$ g.	Rounded corner; obverse: dated; reverse: plain
K-2011-7	John F. Kennedy Memorial Hwy. medal, Delaware	51 mm	Bronze with blue center	Reverse: JFK Memorial Highway
K-2011-8	JFK Historic Auto Attractions medal, limited special-event edition	44 mm	Antique bronze	Reverse: car with the company's logo
K-2012-1	Kennedy half dollar tribute coin, copy	40 mm	Copper, one avoirdupois ounce	Reverse: U.S. flag, Air Force wings
K-2012-2	American Mint presidential leadership medal	40 mm	24K .999 fine gold over cupronickel	Reverse: Presidential Seal
K-2012-3	Kennedy half dollar–style silver bar, replica	29 x 50 mm	.999 fine silver, 10 g.	Reverse: cross pattern
K-2012-4	World Treasures Mint Denver Mint Kennedy half dollar silver bar	28 x 50 mm	.999 fine silver, 1 Troy oz.	Serial number; reverse: 2012, first strike, 1964 Kennedy half dollar reverse
K-2012-5	1964 Kennedy half dollar, copy	39 mm	.999 fine copper, one avoirdupois ounce, Proof	Reeded edge; reverse: U.S. eagle and breast shield below USA
K-2013-1	2-euro commemorative 50th-anniversary JFK coin (never made), San Marino			
K-2013-2	5-euro commemorative 50th-anniversary JFK coin, San Marino	32 mm	.925 fine silver, Proof	8,000 struck; reverse: San Marino coat of arms
K-2013-3	50th-anniversary "Ich Bin Ein Berliner Speech" 10-dollar coin, Samoa	38$\frac{3}{5}$ mm	.999 fine silver	Reverse: Samoa seal, dated 2013
K-2013-4	10-euro JFK "50th Anniversary of Visit to Ireland" medal, Ireland	38$\frac{3}{5}$ mm	.925 fine silver	15,000 struck; reverse: Irish harp
K-2013-4A	20-euro JFK "50th Anniversary of Visit to Ireland" medal, Ireland	13$\frac{9}{10}$ mm	.999 fine gold	10,000 struck; reverse: Irish harp
K-2013-5	Pobjoy Mint JFK "50th Anniversary of Death" coin, British Virgin Islands	38$\frac{1}{2}$ mm	.925 fine silver	10,000 struck; reverse: Queen Elizabeth
K-2013-6	"Famous Americans on U.S. Coinage" Kennedy half dollar tribute coin	50 mm	Silver-plated copper with gold half dollar	No serial number; plain edge; reverse: eagle and U.S. Treasury seal
K-2013-7	Atlantis Mint presidential series JFK medal	15 mm	.999 fine silver, 1 g.	Reverse: wreath
K-2013-7A	Atlantis Mint presidential series JFK medal	15 mm	Gold over .999 silver, 1 g.	Reverse: wreath
K-2013-7B	Atlantis Mint presidential series JFK medal	15 mm	.999 fine copper, 1 g.	Reverse: wreath
K-2013-8	Annual JFK 50-mile hike "Official Finishers" medal	68 mm	Nickel silver	Ribbon; uniface; looped
K-2013-9	Pedro Villarrubia hobo 1968-D Kennedy half dollar	30 mm	Cupronickel	Unique; reverse: standard Kennedy half dollar
K-2013-10	Pedro Villarrubia hobo 1967 Kennedy half dollar	30 mm	Cupronickel	Unique; reverse: standard Kennedy half dollar
K-2013-11	American Mint "Head of State" JFK medal, type 1	60 mm	Silver-plated copper with gold	Plain edge; reverse: JFK standing, portrait profile, Presidential Seal
K-2013-12	American Mint "Head of State" JFK medal, type 2	60 mm	Silver-plated copper with gold	Plain edge; reverse: JFK standing, facing front, Presidential Seal
K-2014-1	U.S. Mint "Civil Rights Act" silver dollar	38$\frac{1}{10}$ mm	90 percent silver and 10 percent copper, Proof	350,000 struck; reeded edge; reverse: eternal flame
K-2014-1A	U.S. Mint "Civil Rights Act" silver dollar	38$\frac{1}{10}$ mm	90 percent silver and 10 percent copper, Uncirculated	350,000 struck; reeded edge; reverse: eternal flame
K-2014-2	National Law Enforcement Memorial J.D.Tippit memorial medal	45 mm	Pewter and blue cloisonné	1,000 struck; reverse: American hero, car and memorial wall
RK-1-2006	Numint RFK Arlington memorial medal, Holland	30 mm	.900 fine silver	Reverse: eagle with wreath
RK-2-1967	Robert Fitzgerald Kennedy medal (middle name error), Mexico	40$\frac{1}{4}$ mm	Silver	Reverse: paix interieure, pre death, name

RK-2A-1968	Robert Fitzgerald Kennedy medal (middle name error), Mexico	40¼ mm	Silver	Reverse: wreath, 1926–1968, post-death, birth
RK-2B-1968	Robert Frances Kennedy (correct middle name), Mexico)	40¼ mm	Silver	Reverse: wreath, 1926–1968, post-death, birth
RK-3-1970	"10th Anniversary of Independence" RFK 100 francs, Chad	25½ mm	.925 fine silver, Proof	975 struck; minted in Brussels; reverse: map, RFK
RK-4	RFK memorial medal	47 mm	.999 fine silver	Looped; reverse: stippled, dated 1968
RK-5	Presidential Art Medals RFK memorial medal	38⅖ mm	.999 fine silver	Serial number; reverse: "Some Men See" quote
RK-5A	Presidential Art Medals RFK memorial medal	38⅖ mm	Bronze	Reverse: "Some Men See" quote
RK-6	RFK memorial medal, Germany	50 mm	.999 fine silver	Hallmark; reverse: six-bar cross, III
RK-6A-2005	RFK memorial medal, Germany	35 mm	.999 fine silver	Reverse: six-bar cross, I
RK-7	Bradshaw & Darlington RFK memorial medal, England	51¼ mm	.925 fine silver	Reverse: "I Dream of Things" quote
RK-8	RFK welcome to Berlin, Germany	40½ mm	.999 fine silver, Matte Finish	Reverse: Berlin bear shield
RK-9	RFK memorial medal, Germany	40 mm	.999 fine silver, Matte Finish	Reverse: dove with olive branch
RK-10	RFK memorial medal, Canada	39 mm	Nickel silver, Proof	Reverse: "He Saw Wrong" quote
RK-11-1969	RFK memorial medal	37⁷⁄₁₀ mm	Nickel silver, Matte Finish	Reverse: Senate Seal
RK-12	RFK memorial medal, Austria	34 mm	.999 fine silver	Hallmark; reverse: pro libertate
RK-13-2002	Metal Arts RFK memorial medal	38 mm	.999 fine silver	Hallmark; reverse: dedicated to honor
RK-14	RFK "United States Senator" medal	39⅖ mm	Cupronickel	Reeded edge; reverse: wreath and text
RK-15	RFK "Police Medal of Honor" medal	28¹⁄₂.₅ mm	Silvered bronze	Looped; reverse: memorial text
RK-16	RFK Stadium Black Expo medal	31³⁄₅ mm	Bronze	Reverse: world image
RK-17-2000	U.S. Mint RFK medal	33⁷⁄₁₀ mm	Bronze	Reverse: eagle on shield
RK-17A	U.S. Mint RFK medal, JFK Library	33⁷⁄₁₀ mm	Gold-plated bronze	Reverse: eagle on shield
RK-17B-2000	U.S. Mint RFK medal	76 mm	Bronze	Reverse: eagle on shield
RK-18	"In Honor of RFK" Waterville Valley World Cup pin	44 x 42 mm	Red, white, and blue with silver lettering	Clasp lock; uniface; reverse: stippled
RK-19	RFK "America Calls Another Kennedy" wooden nickel	37⁹⁄₁₀ mm	Wood	Reverse: Native American
RK-20	RFK key-chain medallett	32 mm	Base metal, cast	Reverse: "Some Men See" quote
RK-21-1974	RFK-Arthur Ashe tennis tournament medal	51¾ mm	Bronze	Uniface
RK-22	Senator RFK award medal	45 mm	Silvered bronze with a gold rim	Obverse: RFK facing right; reverse: P. Kramer Neuchatel
RK-23	U.S. Mint RFK commemorative dollar	40 mm	Silver, Uncirculated	Reverse: eagle and Senate Seal
RK-24	U.S. Mint RFK commemorative dollar	40 mm	Silver, Proof	Reverse: eagle and Senate Seal
RK-25-1970	RFK 100-franc coin, Chad	21 mm	.925 fine silver	975 struck; minted in Belgium; reverse: map of Africa
RK-26	Caesar Chavez-MLK token	27¼ mm	Brass	Reverse: MLK
RK-27	RFK elongated portrait on 1968 Kennedy half dollar		Clad	35 struck; reverse: "Victim of Violence"
RK-28	RFK flying eagle penny	20 mm	Copper	Reverse: flying eagle
RK-29	RFK tribute medal	20 mm	.900 fine gold	Reverse: crossed flags
RK-29A	RFK tribute medal	50 mm	Silver	Reverse: crossed flags
RK-30-2008	RFK tribute medal, Italy	26 mm	Gold	Reverse: liberty shield with rays
RK-31	RFK tribute medal, Italy	25¼ mm	.900 fine gold	Reverse: eagle and scales
RK-32	Huguenin Médailleurs RFK tribute medal	40 mm	Silver	Uniface
RK-33	RFK round pocket-knife charm	40 mm	Goldine	Pearl-colored plastic insert
K-S-1	Kennedy "Painted Red Cap and Cape" 1960 quarter	24 mm	Silver	Reverse: eagle
K-S-2	"Catholic States of America" joke medal, England	32 mm	Bronze	1,200 struck; reverse: "Good For One Confession"
K-S-2A	"Catholic States of America" joke medal, England	32 mm	Silver	75 struck; reverse: Good For One Confession"
K-S-2B	"Catholic States of America" joke medal, England	32 mm	Gold	3 struck; reverse: "Good For One Confession"
K-S-3	Kennedy "Dollar After Taxes" money clip with 1962 U.S. cent	25 x 54 mm	Steel with copper cent	Reverse: plain
K-S-4	1968 Dottie Dow elongated "Someone's Kid Brother" U.S. cent	34 x 19 mm	Bronze	Reverse: standard U.S. cent
K-S-4A	1968 Dottie Dow elongated "Someone's Kid Brother" U.S. cent	33 x 19 mm	Clad	Reverse: standard U.S. dime
K-S-5	1977 "Richard Nixon The Double Standard" medal		Bronze	Reverse: Chappaquidick
K-S-6	1965 "LBJ No Silver" satire coin	26 mm	Brass	Reverse: "No Gold, No Silver, Just Brass"
K-S-7	2009 Edward M. Kennedy U.S. cent	19 mm	Alloy	Reverse: Lincoln Memorial
K-S-8	2005 Edward M. Kennedy U.S. nickel	21 mm	Alloy	Reverse: buffalo nickel
K-S-9	2001 Edward M. Kennedy U.S. quarter	24 mm	Alloy	Reverse: New York state quarter
K-S-10	"Dodo Bird Symbol of Extinction" JFK satire coin	35 mm	Nickel silver	Plain edge; reverse: "Bird Was, Coin Wasn't"
CCC-01	JFK "Inauguration" elongated cent and Osborne medal commemorative cover, type 1	4-cent U.S. flag stamp		Cancelled: Washington, D.C., January 20, 1961
CCC-02	JFK "Inauguration" elongated cent and Osborne medal commemorative cover, type 2	4-cent U.S. flag stamp		Cancelled: Washington, D.C., January 20, 1961
CCC-03	JFK "Fighter for World Peace" elongated coin commemorative cover	5-cent eternal flame stamp		Cancelled: Boston, May 29, 1964
CCC-04	JFK "In Memoriam" horizontal elongated cent commemorative cover, type 1	5-cent eternal		Cancelled: Boston, May 29, 1964 flame stamp

CCC-05	JFK aerogramme vertical elongated cent commemorative cover	11-cent Airmail envelope		Cancelled: Boston, May 29, 1964
CCC-06	JFK aerogramme "Birthplace" horizontal elongated cent commemorative cover	11-cent Airmail envelope		Cancelled: Boston, May 29, 1964
CCC-07	JFK aerogramme PT-109 elongated and U.S. cents commemorative cover	13-cent Airmail envelope		Cancelled: Chicago, May 29, 1967
CCC-08	JFK aerogramme PT-109 horizontal elongated cen commemorative cover	13-cent Airmail envelope		Cancelled: Chicago, May 29, 1967
CCC-09	JFK "In Memoriam" elongated cent commemorative cover, type 2	5-cent eternal flame stamp		Square portrait; cancelled: Boston, May 29,1964
CCC-10	JFK "Birthplace" horizontal elongated cent commemorative cover	13-cent JFK stamp		Cancelled: Brookline, May 29, 1967
CCC-11	JFK "Prominent American" vertical elongated cent commemorative cover	Four 13-cent JFK stamps		Cancelled: Brookline, May 29, 1967
CCC-12	JFK German memorial elongated cent and medal commemorative cover	German tribute stamp		Cancelled: Berlin, Germany, November 21, 1964
CCC-13	JFK Airport-Rockwell portrait elongated cent commemorative cover	5-cent JFK Airport stamp		Cancelled: Jamaica, NY, April 2, 1964
CCC-14	JFK Italian memorial horizontal elongated cent commemorative cover	Italian standard postage		Cancelled: Rome quirinale, November 22, 1964
CCC-15	JFK memorial cachet vertical elongated coin commemorative cover	No postage		Not cancelled in the postal system
CCC-16	JFK 10th-anniversary insert card elongated cent commemorative cover	No postage		Insert card, November 22, 1973
CCC-17	JFK "Presidents of the United States, Birthplace" station	22-cent JFK stamp		Cancelled: Brookline, May 29, 1967
CCC-18	JFK "Great American" stamp series commemorative cover	7 stamps of various denominations		Tribute, Brookline, May 29, 1964
CCC-19	JFK "Prominent Americans" elongated cent and half dollar commemorative cover	13-cent JFK stamp		Cancelled: Brookline, May 29, 1967
CCC-20	JFK "In Memoriam" elongated cent and Osborne medal commemorative cover, type 3	5-cent eternal flame stamp		Cancelled: Boston, May 29, 1964
CCC-21	JFK Memorial-eternal flame-JFK Jr. elongated cents commemorative cover	41-cent U.S. flag stamp		Cancelled: Washington, D.C., August 15, 2007
CCC-22	JFK "Famous Americans" gold stamp replica commemorative cover	5-cent eternal flame stamp		Cancelled: date of 1st issue, May 29, 1964
CCC-23	RFK "Famous Americans" gold stamp replica commemorative cover	15-cent RFK stamp		Cancelled: date of 1st Issue, January 12, 1979
CCC-24	JFK "In Memoriam" Sarzin first-day coin cover	5-cent eternal flame stamp		Cancelled: Jamaica, NY, May 29, 1964
CCC-25	JFK Boston Philatelic Society first-day coin cover	5-cent eternal flame stamp		Cancelled: Boston, May 29, 1964
KCC-01	Presidential Art Medals JFK-CVA-67 emblem challenge coin	38 mm	Bronze	100 struck; reverse: ship emblem
KCC-02	JFK "Proud Naval Tradition" challenge coin	40 mm	Bronze	Obverse: JFK facing left; reverse: front view of CV-67
KCC-03	JFK "Proud Naval Tradition" challenge coin	40 mm	Bronze	Obverse: JFK facing left; reverse: red, white, and blue JFK with planes
KCC-04	Department of the Navy eagle and sail ship challenge coin	40 mm	Bronze, colored	Rope-like edge; reverse: multi-colored ship emblem
KCC-05	View of CV-67 USS JFK challenge coin	40 mm	Bronze	Reverse: multi-colored ship emblem
KCC-06	JFK Medical Department two crosses challenge coin	40 mm	Bronze, laquer finish	Reverse: multi-colored ship emblem
KCC-07	"Presented by the Chief Engineer Big John" challenge coin	40 mm	Bronze with red and blue	Reverse: multi-colored ship emblem
KCC-08	Two views of CV-67 challenge coin	41 mm	Bronze with a blue center and a white rim	Polished rim; reverse: multi-colored ship emblem
KCC-09	CV-67 with ship emblem and helicopter challenge coin	41 mm	Bronze, multi colored with a red rim	Spoke rim; reverse: Department of the Navy
KCC-10	CV-67 "Chief Petty Officer" challenge coin, type 1	40 mm	Bronze	Obverse: three chief insignia; reverse: CV-67, JFK, planes taking off
KCC-11	Physical Therapy Department with flying Navy goat challenge coin	41 mm	Bronze	Rope-like edge; reverse: ship under way
KCC-12	"Honor-Courage-Commitment" JFK profile challenge coin	41 mm	Bronze with a red, white, and blue flag	Reverse: naval mobile construction
KCC-13	"Desert Storm 1991" CV-67 jet and helicopter challenge coin	39 mm	Nickel silver	Reverse: "Hutt River Province, Five Dollars"
KCC-14	Carrier Wing One challenge coin	39 mm	Antiqued bronze	Reverse: cruise 2000
KCC-15	Carrier Group Six/Carrier Airwing Seven challenge coin	40 mm	Bronze, multi colored	Reverse: combat cruise 2002
KCC-16	"CV-67 1968–2007" ship under way challenge coin	41 mm	Bronze	Reverse: multi-colored ship emblem
KCC-17	Operation Iraqi Freedom map of Iraq challenge coin	45 mm	Nickel silver, multi colored	Rope-like edge; reverse: "Doing the Work of the Republic"
KCC-17A	Operation Iraqi Freedom map of Iraq challenge coin	45 mm	Bronze, multi colored	Rope-like edge; reverse: "Doing the Work of the Republic"
KCC-18	JFK profile facing left over ship "1968–2007" challenge coin	55$^{7/10}$ mm	Antiqued nickel silver	Reverse: U.S. Navy, Big John, JFK in color
KCC-19	JFK with flag behind 35th president challenge coin	41 mm	High-polished bronze	Reverse: holding JFK Jr.'s hand, rocket
KCC-20	Northwest Territorial Mint CVN-67 error challenge coin	45 mm	Bronze	Rope-like edge; reverse: ship emblem
KCC-21	Northwest Territorial Mint CVN-67 error challenge coin	40 mm	Gold-plated bronze	Reverse: ship emblem
KCC-22	Northwest Territorial Mint CV-67 corrected challenge coin	44$^{1/2}$ mm	Bronze	Rope-like edge; reverse: ship emblem

KCC-23	Northwest Territorial Mint "39 years CV-67 1968–2007" challenge coin	44½ mm	Bronze, blue cloisonné	Rope-like edge; reverse: ship emblem
KCC-24	JFK profile "U.S. Navy Recruiting Command" challenge coin	51 mm	Bronze	Reverse: eagle with anchor in tallons
KCC-25	JFK International Airport TSA Homeland Security challenge coin	45 mm	Antiqued nickel silver	Reverse: Homeland Security shield
KCC-26	USS Grasp ARS 51 challenge coin	41 mm	Brass	Recovered JFK Jr.'s plane; obverse: ship, section left blank for engraving
KCC-27	"Senior Medical Officer CV-67 Thomas Hatley" challenge coin	40 mm	Bronze, blue cloisonné	Reverse: medical insignia and AC wings
KCC-28	USS JFK "In Service of Our Nation Since 1968" challenge coin	40 mm	Bronze with red, white, and blue JFK	Rope-like edge; reverse: ship emblem
KCC-29	JFK planes taking off challenge coin	40 mm	Bronze	Concave; reverse: ship seal
KCC-30	CV-67 planes taking off challenge coin	40 mm	Bronze	Obverse: JFK forms bow of the ship; reverse: Judge Advocate General
KCC-31	Kennedy Space Center Cape Canaveral, Florida, challenge coin	40 mm	Bronze with red, white, and blue	Reverse: shuttle lifting off
KCC-32	JFK Special Warfare Museum, Fort Bragg, NC challenge coin	39 mm	Silver	Serial number on rim and edge; reverse: ten divisions, training
KCC-33	United States Army JFK Special Warfare Center and School challenge coin	40 mm	Antique pewter	Reverse: beret, scroll, "Truth and Liberty"
KCC-34	United States Army JFK Special Warfare Center challenge coin	39½ mm	Bronze	Reverse: beret, scroll, "Truth and Liberty"
KCC-35	JFK Special Warfare Center Special Ops Training Division challenge coin	40³⁄₁₀ mm	Brass	Reverse: beret, scroll, "De Oppresso"
KCC-36	JFK Special Warfare Center "Support Any Friend" JFK profile challenge coin	45³⁄₅ mm	Bronze, laquered	Reverse: Warfare Center colored emblem
KCC-37	JFK Special Warfare Center "Military Freefall Instructor" challenge coin	40 mm	Bronze, cloisonné	Reverse: silver wings and star
KCC-38	JFK Special Warfare Center and School "Airborne Commander" challenge coin	46 x 49½ mm	Bronze, cloisonné	Reverse: MG Kenneth R. Bowra
KCC-39	JFK Special Warfare Center "Military Freefall Instructor" challenge coin	44³⁄₁₀ mm	Bronze	Reverse: free-fall jumpers out
KCC-40	JFK Special Warfare Center Special Forces "Airborne Ranger" challenge coin	35 x 43 mm	Bronze, cloisonné	Obverse: "Presented by the Commanding General"; reverse: airborne
KCC-41	JFK Special Forces "Airborne Anywhere-Anytime" challenge coin	50½ mm	Bronze, cloisonné	Reverse: ten divisions
KCC-42	JFK profile CV-67 ship challenge coin	30 mm	Gold-colored metal	Reverse: CV-67 ship
KCC-43	Mayport, Florida, naval station CV-67 coin challenge coin	40 mm	Bronze, cloisonné	Rope-like edge; reverse: ship emblem
KCC-44	JFK Special Warfare Center "A Special Breed" challenge coin	44 mm	Bronze	Reverse: sword and scroll
KCC-45	JFK "We Dare Not Forget" challenge coin	45 mm	Bronze, cloisonné	Reverse: Liberty Bell
KCC-46	LTC Greg "Possum" Powell "Serve With Pride" challenge coin	45 mm	Nickel silver, cloisonné	Reverse: CV-67 JFK ship emblem
KCC-47	JFK Special Warfare Center "De Oppresso Liber" challenge coin	40 mm	High-polished nickel silver	Obverse: Special Forces U.S. Army; reverse: "De Oppresso"
KCC-48	"Courage-Country-Honor" CV-67 Navy challenge coin	40 mm	Silver plated	Reverse: CV-67 ship emblem
KCC-49	Kennedy Battle Group Comcargru Six challenge coin	40 mm	Bronze, cloisonné	Reverse: Operation Primacy
KCC-50	Ancient and Honorable Artillary Co. challenge coin	40 mm	Bronze	Reverse: Rome, Berlin
KCC-51	Operation Enduring Freedom "JFK Quote" challenge coin	45 mm	Bronze, cloisonné	Reverse: "Let Every Nation Know" quote
KCC-52	Northwest Territorial Mint USS JFK "39 Years of Defending America" challenge coin	44 mm	Bronze, cloisonné	Uniface
KCC-53	JFK CV-67 "Big John Keep the Spirit Commander" challenge coin	44 mm	Bronze, cloisonné	Reverse: "Any Man" quote
KCC-54	JFK U-2 Dragon Lady Cuban Missile Crisis challenge coin	40 mm	Bronze, gold cloisonné	Reverse: pilot in pressure suit, motto
KCC-55	Operation Iraqi Freedom "JFK Inaugural Quote" challenge coin	45 mm	Bronze	Reeded edge; reverse: JFK inaugural quote
KCC-56	JFK CV-67 First Class Association challenge coin	38 mm	Bronze with yellow and white	Reverse: ship image, "First Class Association"
KCC-57	CV-67 JFK looped charm cloisonné challenge coin	23 mm	Bronze with yellow and white	Uniface
KCC-58	U.S. Navy USS JFK challenge coin	40 mm	Golden bronze, cloisonné	Reeded edge; reverse: Department of the Navy, eagle
KCC-59	JFK CV-67 Carrier Strike Group challenge coin	38 mm	Bronze with red, white, and blue cloisonné	Reverse: Comcargru Six, trident
KCC-60	JFK CV-67 Judge Advocate General's Corps challenge coin	45 mm	Bronze, cloisonné	Reverse: oak leaves and bars
KCC-61	Special Forces Airborne School "All the Way" challenge coin	39 mm	Antique silvered bronze	Reverse: "All the Way", MCMXL
KCC-62	CV-67 "Commissioned 1968-Decommissioned 2007" challenge coin	41 mm	Golden bronze with red, white, and blue cloisonné	Obverse: CV-67 ship emblem; reverse: JFK
KCC-63	John Kennedy School of Government Harvard University challenge coin	50 mm	Bronze	Pentagonal; reverse: emblems of five service branches
KCC-64	CV-67 "Chief Petty Officer" challenge coin, type 2	40 mm	Bronze	Obverse: painted JFK; reverse: "Chief Petty Officers"
KCC-65	JFK CV-67 "In Service of Our Nation 1968 to 2007" challenge coin	40 mm	Bronze	Obverse: eagle, AIMD; reverse: 1968 to 2007
KCC-66	JFK Center Freefall Committee challenge coin, type 1	40 mm	Bronze	Reverse: aircraft without jumpers
KCC-66A	JFK Center Freefall Committee challenge coin, type 2	40 mm	Bronze	Reverse: aircraft with jumpers
KCC-67	Great Lakes Navy Training Command JFK challenge coin	45 mm	Silver-like nickel	Reverse: Great Lakes
KCC-68	JFK CV-67 "LDO CWO Mustang" challenge coin	45 mm	Bronze with red, white, blue, and black cloisonné	Reverse: black background; JFK aircraft
KCC-69	JFK CV-67 "VF-103 Jolly Roger Last Tomcat Cruise" challenge coin	40 mm	Bronze with a colored image	Reverse: F-14 Tomcat, "Last Time Baby"

KCC-70	JFK CV-67 "Mustangs LDO CWO" challenge coin	40 mm	Bronze	Reverse: from the deck plates
KCC-71	JFK Space Center 50th-anniversary challenge coin	44 mm	Bronze, cloisonné	Reverse: metal flown on Apollo
KCC-72	NY-NJ Port Authority Police JFK challenge coin	38 mm	Bronze, cloisonné	Reverse: colored NY-NJ coat of arms
KCC-73	JFK Special Warfare Psyops Deputy Commander challenge coin	40 mm	Golden bronze, cloisonné	Reverse: Patt Maney insignia
KCC-74	JFK Special Warfare Center and School award bar	27 x 55 mm	Bronze, cloisonné	Reverse: "Presented by the Deputy Commanding General"
KCC-75	JFK Special Warfare Center and School holed bar	31 x 55 mm	Bronze, cloisonné	Reverse: two airborne insignia sergeant patches
KCC-76	60th anniversary Special Forces Convention JFK challenge coin	51½ mm	Bronze and nickel, cloisonné	Reverse: "60 Years of Sacrifice & Success"
KCC-77	Green Beret Special Forces U.S. Army JFK School emblem challenge coin	45 mm	Bronze, cloisonné	Reverse: "To Liberate the Oppressed"
KCC-78	USS JFK Boston 2007 challenge coin	50 mm	Golden bronze, cloisonné	Reverse: "Morale, Welfare and Recreation"
KCC-79	"JFK In Memory 50th anniversary 11/22-70th anniversary 8/2" PT-109 challenge coin	51 mm	Antique bronze, cloisonné	Reverse: Presidential Seal
KCC-80	NASA Kennedy Space Center geodetic challenge coin	38 mm	Antique bronze, cloisonné	Reverse: "M205, 1963, Geodetic Survey"
KCC-81	Special Forces 25th anniversary "San Diego 1961–1986" challenge coin	40 mm	Antique bronze	Reverse: Green Beret, "With Honor"
KCC-82	"U.S. Navy Retired I Stood the Watch JFK Quote" challenge coin	43¼ mm	Bronze with blue cloisonné	Reverse: "I Served in the U.S. Navy" JFK quote
KCC-83	JFK Special Warfare Center Military Freefall School challenge coin	40 mm	Bronze with silver wings	Reverse: aircraft with jumpers, "Work Hard, Play Harder"
KCC-84	JFK Special Warfare Center "I Am a Museum Supporter" challenge coin	38 mm	Golden bronze with blue cloisonné insignia	Reverse: Warfare Museum, Fort Bragg, NC
KCC-85	JFK Taps Keith Clark 50th-anniversary challenge coin	45 mm	Dull nickel silver with blue cloisonné	Reverse: "Taps for Veterans", bugle
KCC-86	Master Chief Command Bravo Zulo "JFK Navy Quote" challenge coin	45 mm	Golden bronze with multi-colored cloisonné	Reverse: "I Served in the U.S. Navy" JFK quote
KCC-87	Combined Federal Campaign 50th-anniversary "1961–2011 JFK Quote" challenge coin	38 mm	Golden bronze, cloisonné	2,120 struck; reverse: "When the Dust Settles" quote
KCC-88	JFK Special Army Warfare School "Presented by Commanding General" challenge coin		Golden bronze, cloisonné	Reverse: flag and two stars; "For Excellence"
KCC-89	ICE JFK International Homeland Security challenge coin	40 mm	Golden bronze with a black background	Reverse: Homeland Security
KCC-90	JFK Special Warfare Museum	52⅖ mm	Pewter with green paint insignia	Reverse: four Association Presidents Award challenge coin group insignias, John F. Kennedy
KCC-91	U.S. Army Special Operations Command challenge coin	57 mm	Bronze, cloisonné	Obverse: eight airborne insignias; reverse: oath of enlistment
KCC-92	JFK CVN-79 Newport News Shipbuilding challenge coin	45 mm	Bronze	Roped edge; obverse: JFK ship and portrait; reverse: NN shipyard insignia

U.S. Currency Issued During the Kennedy Administration

Executive Order 11110

The Impact

Some assassination researchers believe that Executive Order 11110, signed by President Kennedy on June 4, 1963, was the reason behind the president's assassination five months later.

This order directed the U.S. Department of the Treasury to create and distribute silver certificates directly into circulation, bypassing the interest charged by private bankers to the American people for using their own money. Just prior to his own assassination, President Abraham Lincoln had ordered his secretary of the U.S. Treasury, Salmon P. Chase, to do the same. The interest-free currency issued by President Lincoln is now known as Lincoln Greenbacks.

The total amount of interest-free currency brought into circulation by President Kennedy totaled more than four billion dollars—without a single penny of debt accrued through interest. Within a few short years, the backlog of U.S. national debt would have been eliminated and the remaining yearly debt managed as outlined in article 2, section 4, part 5 of the U.S. Constitution. It is believed that, because of this order, there would be no further need for the Federal Reserve Act; private banking would again join the ranks of non-governmental commerce and compete like any other private business.

Five months later, under Johnson's administration, all silver certificates were no longer issued. The U.S. Treasury immediately returned to printing private-bank interest-bearing currency. Within months of John F. Kennedy's assassination, plans to remove silver from the coinage of the United States went into effect. The readjustment and control of the new American and world economy profit structure was set into motion.

Eva Adams, Director of the U.S. Mint, 1961–1969

K-61-32

K-62-5: By Gilroy Roberts.

U.S. Currency, 1961-1963

Coins

1961

1962

1963

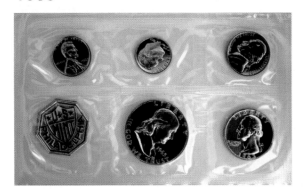

Paper Money

$1 Federal Reserve Note.
Series of 1963, Green Seal.

$5 Legal Tender Note.
Series of 1963, Red Seal.

$10 Federal Reserve Note.
Series of 1963, Green Seal.

$2 Legal Tender Note.
Series of 1963, Red Seal.

$10 Federal Reserve Note.
Series of 1963, Green Seal.

$20 Federal Reserve Note.
Series of 1963, Green Seal.

$1 Silver Certificate. Series of 1957A. With
C. Douglas Dillon signature.

$1 Silver Certificate. Series of 1957B.
With C. Douglas Dillon signature.

$5 Federal Reserve Note. Series of 1950C.
With C. Douglas Dillon signature.

The Kennedy Children

Four sons and five daughters were born to Joseph and Rose Kennedy between 1915 and 1932: Joseph Jr., John, Rose Marie, Kathleen, Eunice, Patricia, Robert, Jean, and Edward. Raised with an appreciation for history and politics, the Kennedy household fostered an environment of creativity, ambition, and public service.

Joseph Patrick Kennedy Jr.

Joseph Patrick Kennedy Jr., circa 1942.

The eldest child of Joseph and Rose Kennedy, Joseph Patrick Kennedy Jr. was born in 1915. Like his younger brother John, he attended the London School of Economics and Harvard University, from which he graduated in 1938. He volunteered as a Navy flier during World War II.

With more than 50 difficult missions under his belt, Joe was recruited from B-24 liberator submarine patrol at Dunkeswell, England, and sent to a secret airbase in Fersfield designated Special Attack Unit One. He volunteered to be a jump pilot and take a radio-controlled PB4Y drone loaded with 20,000 pounds of Torpex and 600 pounds of TNT across the English Channel, bail out, and send the aerial bomb into the German rocket-launch bases.

On Saturday, August 12, 1944, at 6:00 p.m., Lieutenant Kennedy, with his co-pilot Wilford John "Bud" Willy, lifted off the runway in PB4Y number 32271, code name Zootsuit Black, with a perfect takeoff—and disappeared into history.

A faulty arming panel caused the mission to fail and the death of the two pilots. The story surrounding this operation was classified for many years.

Commander James Smith recommended Lt. Kennedy for the congressional Medal of Honor, but that medal was disallowed by the Navy's board of medals and awards. Both Joseph Patrick Kennedy Jr. and Bud Willy received the Navy Cross posthumously.

The Kennedy family had a lifelong relationship with Bud's wife Edna Willy, her two sons, and her newborn daughter. The Kennedy family paid all expenses for the Willy sons to attend the college of their choice.

In *Johnny, We Hardly Knew Ye*, Kenneth P. O'Donnell and David F. Powers recall a later meeting between the Kennedys and the Willys. After three years as president, Kennedy invited the Willy family to have breakfast with him in Fort Worth, Texas. He embraced 18-year-old Karen Willy and said, "I want you to remember, your father was just as much a hero as my brother was, and there were no two finer people." That afternoon, John F. Kennedy was assassinated.

K-00-7

K-2009-14B

Rose Marie Kennedy

Rose Marie "Rosemary" Kennedy, circa April 1940.

Born Rose Marie Kennedy on September 13, 1918, the eldest Kennedy daughter was called Rosemary by her family and friends. As a teenager she attended dances and concerts, and, along with her brothers Joseph and John, she met President Roosevelt at the White House.

In 1938, Rosemary traveled to England with her family and was presented at court with her mother and sister Kathleen.

However, Rosemary was a slow learner and often suffered from bouts of erratic behavior of which her parents deeply disapproved. In 1941, her father authorized an experimental lobotomy in order to curb what he deemed her inappropriate tendencies. Unfortunately, the lobotomy was not a success; it left Rosemary essentially incapacitated and unable to care for herself. She was soon after placed at St. Coletta's School for Exceptional Children in Wisconsin. Rosemary

Kennedy would spend the rest of her life institutionalized. She passed away in 2005.

K-2007-10

Kathleen Kennedy Cavendish

Kathleen Kennedy in London, circa 1943.

Kathleen Kennedy, nicknamed "Kick" by her family, was the fourth child of Joseph and Rose Kennedy. In 1938, shortly after finishing school, she moved to England with her family (with the exception of Joe Jr. and John, who were both attending Harvard at the time) when her father was appointed ambassador to Great Britain by President Roosevelt. Kathleen Kennedy thrived in England, cultivating an extensive circle of friends from the upper echelons of British high society. However, when Great Britain declared war on Germany in 1939, she returned to the United States with her mother and siblings.

After working for the *Washington Times-Herald* as a columnist, Kennedy began working as a volunteer at the Red Cross, and in 1943 she returned to London in this capacity. She began a relationship with politician William Cavendish, the Marquess of Hartington; the two were married in 1944. Four months later, Cavendish was killed while serving honorably as a major with the Coldstream Guard's armored division in Belgium.

This beautiful pin, worn by Kathleen Kennedy Cavendish, bears the insignia of the Coldstream Guards, her husband's regiment of the British Army.

After her husband's death, Kathleen Kennedy Cavendish remained in London. In May 1948, she died in a plane crash in France.

K-2009-14G

Eunice Kennedy Shriver

Eunice Kennedy Shriver, circa 1952.

A meeting was held in January 1995 to voice opinions on the authorization of a proposed silver dollar commemorating the Special Olympics World Games to be struck by the U.S. Mint. In attendance were the Citizens Coinage Advisory Committee and representatives from the U.S. Treasury.

The stunning portrait of Eunice Kennedy Shriver, sister to John F. Kennedy, by world-renowned artist Jamie Wyeth, son of American artist Andrew Wyeth, had little impact on the committee. Their announced objection to the Shriver portrait was that they believed no living person could be allowed on a U.S. commemorative coin. However, in past years there had been four living people pictured on U.S. commemorative coins: a state governor, two senators, and a president.

Coin World published statements that the collecting public was unhappy with the selection of Eunice Shriver for the obverse of the coin. A few letters to the editor made claims that she did not deserve that honor, but that comedian Bob Hope did.

The anti-Kennedy minority was alive and well as it had been since Joseph P. Kennedy was the head of the Security and Exchange Commission, when he imposed strong regulations on banks and Wall Street moguls in the 1930s. However, Robert Edward Rubin, the secretary of the Treasury under President William Clinton, authorized Eunice Shriver's portrait on the coin.

Shriver's life was lived in service to others. Her list of humanitarian efforts and accomplishments is extensive. In 1962, she founded Camp Shriver at her Maryland farm, Timberlawn. In 1968, Camp Shriver became the Special Olympics. Her selfless devotion to those with disabilities for more than 60 years is astounding. If a desire to compete is inherent in the Kennedy blood, it was to manifest in Eunice Shriver as a drive to serve others. Her life was truly a profile in courage.

When a child with a disability looks at the lady on the silver coin, they will see a person who would trade all the medals and honors bestowed upon her for one child who could walk straight and smile at the world.

This special lady earned every downward drop of the die that stamped her image onto the U.S. silver coin.

K-95-10

K-2009-14H

Patricia Kennedy, circa 1948.

During the 1960 presidential campaign, she spoke on her brother's behalf at various events around the United States.

In later life, Patricia founded the National Committee for the Literary Arts and worked tirelessly with the Kennedy Library on its exhibits. She died on September 17, 2006, at the age of 82.

K-2009-14I

Patricia Kennedy Lawford

Patricia Kennedy was the sixth child of Joseph and Rose Kennedy. As a student, Patricia excelled in mathematics. She also enjoyed acting, appearing on the stage in various plays during her time at Rosemont College in Pennsylvania. She graduated in 1945.

Patricia pursued theater as a career. Her resume included time as an assistant in the production department at NBC and for multiple radio programs in Los Angeles. She married actor Peter Lawford in 1949 and began a family. However, the two divorced in 1965.

As a sister of the future president, Patricia was a co-host at many of the "Kennedy teas" held during her brother's various political campaigns.

Robert Francis Kennedy

John F. Kennedy speaking with his brother Robert F. Kennedy.

Born on November 20, 1925, Robert Francis Kennedy was the third son and seventh child of Rose and Joseph Kennedy.

Like his two older brothers, Robert attended Harvard University and served in the U.S. Navy during World War II. He later earned his law degree from the University of Virginia Law School.

Heavily involved in politics, Robert was the manager of John F. Kennedy's 1952 campaign for the U.S. Senate. He later worked as chief counsel for the Senate Rackets Committee, investigating trade-union corruption and, in the process, exposing union leaders Jimmy Hoffa and David Beck.

After his brother's successful presidential campaign, Robert Kennedy was appointed attorney general in the Kennedy cabinet. During this time, he pushed against organized crime and strongly supported the Civil Rights movement.

He also aided in negotiations with the Soviet Union concerning the Cuban Missile Crisis.

In 1964, after the assassination of John F. Kennedy, Robert was elected to the U.S. Senate from New York. In his capacity as senator, he sought to contain unemployment, improve the lives of those in poverty, and end the war in Vietnam.

He announced his candidacy for the presidency on March 18, 1968. On June 5, 1968, at only 42 years old, Robert Kennedy was assassinated at the Ambassador Hotel in Los Angeles, California. He had just won the California primary.

RK-1-2006: Holland.

RK-2-1967: Mexico.

RK-2A-1968: Error reverse.

RK-2B-1968: Correct reverse.

RK-25-1970: Chad. Very rare.

RK-5

RK-26: Robert F. Kennedy was a strong supporter of Cesar Chavez and Martin Luther King Jr., both leaders in the Civil Rights movement. In 1968, Kennedy joined Chavez in California in support of his hunger strike to protest violence against Spanish-speaking Americans.

RK-17B-2000

RK-29

RK-18

RK-31: Italy.

RK-34-1969

K-2009-14D

A fantasy note depicting Robert Kennedy.

Robert F. Kennedy
Commemorative Silver Dollar

This dollar coin, authorized by Public Law 103-328 and signed by President Bill Clinton, was minted in 1998 to commemorate the 30th anniversary of the assassination of Robert F. Kennedy. Thomas D. Rogers Sr. designed both the obverse and the reverse.

While Congress authorized 500,000 silver RFK dollars, the market was resistant; only 40 percent of the total minted were sold.

The original coin cost $32.00, with the Proof version sold for $37.00. Two coin sets were offered by the U.S. Mint. One included the Proof and Uncirculated versions of the silver dollar. The other included the Proof dollar and a special 1998-S Matte Finish silver Kennedy half dollar. A portion of the surcharge for each coin purchased went to the Robert F. Kennedy Memorial.

K-98-7

Jean Kennedy Smith

The youngest daughter of Joseph and Rose, Jean Kennedy was born in Boston in 1928. After attending Sacred Heart schools in England and the United States, she majored in English at Manhattanville College.

Jean married Stephen E. Smith and had four children: Stephen Jr., William, Amanda, and Kym. Shortly after her marriage, she joined her

Jean Kennedy, circa 1953.

Edward Moore Kennedy

John F. Kennedy applauds his brother Edward at a Democratic fundraiser on October 19, 1963.

siblings and traveled throughout the United States in order to speak on behalf of her brother John during his 1960 presidential campaign.

Jean served as the U.S. ambassador to Ireland from 1993 to 1998. She was appointed by President Bill Clinton. She is a member of the board of trustees for the Joseph P. Kennedy Jr. Foundation and served on the board for the John F. Kennedy Center for the Performing Arts.

Jean Kennedy continues her charitable and philanthropic works today. She has been honored with awards for her work with the mentally disabled since 1964.

Edward Moore Kennedy was born in 1932, the youngest of the nine Kennedy children. Following in the footsteps of his father and brothers, Kennedy served in the military and attended Harvard University. Like his brother Robert, he received his law degree from the University of Virginia Law School.

Elected to the U.S. Senate from Massachusetts nine times, Edward Kennedy is its third longest-serving member. His career as the "Lion of the Senate" was expansive, and he fought for improvements in a multitude of important areas, including education, racial and gender equality, immigration reform, and healthcare. Kennedy was admired by both Democrats and Republicans for his drive and his determination to improve the lives of the American people.

K-2009-14J

Ted Kennedy died of brain cancer in 2009. He was survived by his wife, three children, two stepchildren, and his sister Jean.

K-2009-14E

A fantasy note depicting Ted Kennedy.

Bibliography

Ballard, Robert D. *Collision with History: The Search for John F. Kennedy's PT 109.* Washington, D.C.: National Geographic Society, 2002.

Barnes, Clare Jr. *John F. Kennedy: Scrimshaw Collector.* Boston: Little, Brown, 1969.

Bunyan, John. *Pilgrim's Progress.* Girard, KS: Haldeman-Julius, 1924.

Cutler, R. B. *The Umbrella Man: Evidence of Conspiracy.* Beverly Farms, MA: R. B. Cutler, 1975.

Dorfles, Gillo. *Kitsch: The World of Bad Taste.* New York: Universe Books, 1969.

Garduno, Joseph A. *Museum for a President.* New York: Carlton Press, 1966.

Goldman, Alex J. *John Fitzgerald Kennedy: The World Remembers.* New York: Fleet Press, 1968.

Graves, Charles P. *John F. Kennedy: The New Frontiersman.* Champaign, IL: Garrard Publishing, 1965.

Hamilton, Charles. *The Robot that Helped Make a President: A Reconnaissance into the Mysteries of John F. Kennedy's Signature.* New York: C. Hamilton, 1965.

Hunt, Conover. *JFK for a New Generation.* Dallas: Southern Methodist University Press, 1996.

Jones, Penn Jr. *Forgive My Grief.* Midlothian, TX: Midlothian Mirror, 1966.

Kennedy, Caroline. *Poems to Learn by Heart.* New York: Disney/Hyperion Books, 2013.

Kennedy, John F. *Profiles in Courage.* New York: Harper & Row, 1956.

———. *Why England Slept.* New York: W. Funk, 1940.

Kennedy, Joseph P. *I'm for Roosevelt.* New York: Reynal & Hitchcock, 1936.

Kennedy, Rose Fitzgerald. *Times to Remember.* Garden City, NY: Doubleday, 1974.

Martin, Ralph G. *A Man For All People: A Pictorial Biography of Hubert H. Humphrey.* New York: Grosset & Dunlap, 1968.

Mayhew, Aubrey. *The World's Tribute to John F. Kennedy in Medallic Art.* New York: William Morrow and Company, 1966.

Miller, Tom. *The Assassination Please Almanac.* Chicago: Regnery, 1977.

O'Donnell, Kenneth P., and David F. Powers. *Johnny, We Hardly Knew Ye: Memories of John Fitzgerald Kennedy.* Boston: Little, Brown, 1972.

Oglesby, Carl. *The Yankee and the Cowboy War.* New York: Berkley Publishing, 1977.

Olsen, Jack. *Aphrodite: Desperate Mission.* New York: Putnam, 1970.

Rochette, Edward C. *The Medallic Portraits of John F. Kennedy.* Iola, WI: Krause Publications, 1966.

Rosato, Angelo. *Encyclopedia of the Modern Elongated.* New Milford, CT: Angros, 1990.

Thomas, Evan. *Robert Kennedy: His Life.* New York: Simon & Schuster, 2000.

Tomaska Rick. *A Guide Book of Franklin and Kennedy Half Dollars.* Atlanta: Whitman Publishing, 2010.

United States Office of the Federal Register. *Public Papers of the Presidents of the United States: John F. Kennedy.* Washington, D.C.: U.S. Government Printing Office, 1962–1964.

Illustration Credits

In **chapter 1**, the photograph of John F. Kennedy with his father and grandfather is courtesy of the John F. Kennedy Presidential Library and Museum in Boston. The image is by Hy Peskin and was taken for *Look* magazine in 1946. In **chapter 2**, the image of the flag of Troop Two is from the Bronxville Boy Scouts and the illustration of the saluting Boy Scout is from the front cover of *John F. Kennedy: The New Frontiersman* by Charles P. Graves. In **chapter 4**, the caricature of John F. Kennedy holding *Profiles in Courage* is courtesy of Perfect Learning. It was created by Steven Keay. In **chapter 5**, the photograph of John F. Kennedy receiving his inaugural medal was taken by Abbie Rowe and the image of K-61-60 was taken by Robert Knudsen. Both images are courtesy of the John F. Kennedy Presidential Library and Museum. In **chapter 7**, the image of the national park ranger plaque belongs to the Yosemite Archives. The photograph of John F. Kennedy admiring the Whiskeytown Dam was taken by Cecil Stoughton and is courtesy of the John F. Kennedy Presidential Library and Museum. The photographs of John F. Kennedy receiving a replica of the freedom bell, the Kennedy coat of arms, and the silver lanterns also belong to the John F. Kennedy Presidential Library and Museum and were taken by Abbie Rowe. In **chapter 8**, the image of the Bronze Star Medal is courtesy of the L. Tom Perry Special Collections at Brigham Young University. The photograph of Hubert Humphrey, Lyndon B. Johnson, and John F. Kennedy was taken by Abbie Rowe and belongs to the John F. Kennedy Presidential Library and Museum. In **chapter 9**, the images of the Colt pistols, JFK holding a gun, and the letters between President Kennedy and Franklin L. Orth are reprinted with permission of the National Rifle Association of America. The photograph of Alan Shepard was taken by Abbie Rowe and belongs to the John F. Kennedy Presidential Library and Museum. The photograph of Kennedy and Loretta Jaronik is courtesy of Corbis Images. In **chapter 10**, the photograph of the John F. Kennedy Memorial in Dallas is courtesy of Matthew Rutledge. In **chapter 11**, the photograph of the Red Room was taken by Robert Knudsen and belongs to the John F. Kennedy Presidential Library and Museum. K-94-4 was kindly provided by Jean Tatge, vice president of development for the Municipal Art Society. In **chapter 13**, the photograph of the John F. Kennedy Memorial in Hyannis is courtesy of T.S. Custadio. In **chapter 14**, the images of K-75-12 belong to Ken Potter. In **chapter 15**, K-64-48 was kindly provided by the Massachusetts Historical Society. In **chapter 17**, the picture of K-61-41 is courtesy of Dietrich Herfurth and can be found in his book, *Soviet Awards: A Catalog, 1918–1991*. The photograph of Golda Meir was taken by Cecil Stoughton and belongs to the John F. Kennedy Presidential Library and Museum. In **appendix C**, all images of the Kennedy children are courtesy of the John F. Kennedy Presidential Library and Museum.

About the Author

William Rice was born in New England just months before the start of World War II. A native of Maine, he was exposed to first-hand examples of U.S. history.

His first residence was Old Orchard Beach, Maine, where, incidentally, Joseph Kennedy met his future wife, Rose, when they were children. After the death of Rice's father in 1945, his mother remarried and they moved to Newport, Rhode Island, where, later, John F. Kennedy and Jacqueline Bouvier were married. In the summer of 1953, Rice's family moved to San Diego, California.

During the years that followed, Rice's interest in photography increased. He was hired at one of the major photofinishing firms in San Diego, delivering and picking up film from the Navy Locker Clubs and other businesses in the city. His ambition was rewarded when he was given an inside position and was trained to process film and learn photographic enlarging. Rice's break came when he accepted a position with the renowned Hollywood photographer Charles Schneider of La Jolla, California. He was assigned to photograph and prepare assignments for such famous personalities as Nat King Cole, Lloyd Bridges, Buster Keaton, Jayne Mansfield, Richard Crenna, and Agnes Moorehead. Rice's photographs were featured regularly in *San Diego Magazine*.

In 1960, Rice attended a Nixon For President rally at West Gate Park in San Diego. Much to his surprise, he was asked to take photographs for the vice president as Nixon's photographer had not arrived. A small group formed before Rice, including the actors Robert Young, Ginger Rogers, and John Payne; the chairman of the Republican Party; and Vice President and Mrs. Nixon.

Rice later joined the U.S. Air Force, and was awarded the Air Force Specialty Code of Still Photographer. His commander-in-chief was President John Fitzgerald Kennedy. Rice was assigned to the 552nd Airborne Early Warning Wing, served honorably during the Vietnam War, and received the Air Force Outstanding Unit Award. During his time in the service, Rice was on temporary assignment in Florida and was present for a Polaris missile launch at Cape Canaveral. President Kennedy was also in attendance. Rice and the world were not aware that only six days later, the commander-in-chief would be assassinated. After leaving the Air Force, Rice went to work for the Technicolor Corporation in Hollywood-Burbank, California.

In 1975, with the assistance of his wife, Rice released a privately printed and published book, *John and Robert Kennedy Assassination Bibliography*. This volume was one of the early works for serious researchers of the Kennedy brothers' assassinations, and it covered all public and privately printed books on the topic in the United States and Europe at that time.

Since 1975, Rice's research and photographs have appeared in such published works as *The Assassination Please Almanac* by Tom Miller, R.B. Cutler's *The Umbrella Man: Evidence of Conspiracy*, *Forgive My Grief Volume 4* by Penn Jones Jr., *The Los Angeles Technical Journal*, *Aviation Weekly* and scores of worldwide corporate publications.

Rice has lectured publicly and appeared on numerous radio and television programs. While several have claimed the title, he was the first researcher to show a complete copy of the famous Zapruder film of the assassination of President Kennedy on a network television station in the United States.

For the final years of his photographic career, Rice was a medical illustration photographer at the University of California Davis Medical Center in Sacramento. He also spent three years providing photographic support for university professors at the UC Davis campus in Davis, California.

William Rice now resides with his wife in the lakes region of western Maine, enjoying the nature and beauty of northeastern New England.

Index